Making Sense of the Arab State

EMERGING DEMOCRACIES

Series Editors

Dan Slater is James Orin Murfin Professor of Political Science
and Director, Center for Emerging Democracies
University of Michigan

Pauline Jones is Professor of Political Science
and Edie N. Goldenberg Endowed Director,
Michigan in Washington Program, University of Michigan

Struggles for Political Change in the Arab World: Regimes, Oppositions, and External Actors after the Spring
Lisa Blaydes, Amr Hamzawy, and Hesham Sallam, Editors

Autocrats Can't Always Get What They Want: State Institutions and Autonomy under Authoritarianism
Nathan J. Brown, Steven D. Schaaf, Samer Anabtawi, and Julian G. Waller

Seeds of Mobilization: The Authoritarian Roots of South Korea's Democracy
Joan E. Cho

None of the Above: Protest Voting in Latin American Democracies
Mollie J. Cohen

The Troubling State of India's Democracy
Šumit Ganguly, Dinsha Mistree, and Larry Diamond, Editors

Lobbying the Autocrat: The Dynamics of Policy Advocacy in Nondemocracies
Max Grömping and Jessica C. Teets, Editors

Ghosts in the Neighborhood: Why Japan Is Haunted by Its Past and Germany Is Not
Walter F. Hatch

Making Sense of the Arab State
Steven Heydemann and Marc Lynch, Editors

The Dictator's Dilemma at the Ballot Box: Electoral Manipulation, Economic Maneuvering, and Political Order in Autocracies
Masaaki Higashijima

State Institutions, Civic Associations, and Identity Demands: Regional Movements in Greater Southeast Asia
Amy H. Liu and Joel Sawat Selway, Editors

Opposing Power: Building Opposition Alliances in Electoral Autocracies
Elvin Ong

A complete list of titles in the series can be found at www.press.umich.edu

MAKING SENSE OF THE ARAB STATE

Steven Heydemann and Marc Lynch, Editors

University of Michigan Press
Ann Arbor

Copyright © 2024 by Steven Heydemann and Marc Lynch
Some rights reserved.

This work is licensed under a Creative Commons Attribution-NonCommercial 4.0 International License. *Note to users*: A Creative Commons license is only valid when it is applied by the person or entity that holds rights to the licensed work. Works may contain components (e.g., photographs, illustrations, or quotations) to which the rightsholder in the work cannot apply the license. It is ultimately your responsibility to independently evaluate the copyright status of any work or component part of a work you use, in light of your intended use. To view a copy of this license, visit http://creativecommons.org/licenses/by-nc/4.0/

For questions or permissions, please contact um.press.perms@umich.edu

Published in the United States of America by the
University of Michigan Press
Manufactured in the United States of America
Printed on acid-free paper
First published July 2024

A CIP catalog record for this book is available from the British Library.

Library of Congress Cataloging-in-Publication data has been applied for.

ISBN: 978-0-472-07698-7 (hardcover : alk. paper)
ISBN: 978-0-472-05698-9 (paper : alk. paper)
ISBN: 978-0-472-90461-7 (open access ebook)

Library of Congress Control Number: 2024935193

DOI: https://doi.org/10.3998/mpub.12839265

The University of Michigan Press's open access publishing program is made possible thanks to additional funding from the University of Michigan Office of the Provost and the generous support of contributing libraries.

Cover art by Ayman Baalbaki, "Untitled," 2016. Used with the generous permission of the Ramzi and Saeda Dalloul Art Foundation, Beirut, Lebanon

Contents

Tables	vii
Acknowledgments	ix
Introduction: Making Sense of the Arab State Steven Heydemann and Marc Lynch	1

SECTION 1: DIMENSIONS OF STATENESS

ONE Seeing the State or Why Arab States Look the Way They Do Steven Heydemann	25
TWO Understanding State Weakness in the Middle East and North Africa Raymond Hinnebusch	55
THREE Rethinking the Postcolonial State in the Middle East: Elite Competition and Negotiation within the Disaggregated Iraqi State Toby Dodge	85
FOUR Legibility, Digital Surveillance, and the State in the Middle East Marc Lynch	111

SECTION 2: DIMENSIONS OF REGIME-NESS

FIVE What We Talk about When We Talk about the State in Postwar Lebanon   141
Bassel F. Salloukh

SIX The "Business of Government": The State and Changing Patterns of Politics in the Arab World   169
Lisa Anderson

SEVEN Palace Politics as "Precarious" Rule: Weak Statehood in Afghanistan   198
Dipali Mukhopadhyay

SECTION 3: CONTESTING STATENESS: SOCIETY AND SITES OF RESISTANCE

EIGHT State Capacity and Contention: A View from Jordan   231
Jillian Schwedler

NINE Water, Stateness, and Tribalism in Jordan: The Case of the Disi Water Conveyance Project   247
Sean Yom

Conclusion: The Specter of the Spectrum: Escaping the Residual Category of Weak States   274
Dan Slater

Contributors   283

Index   285

Tables

5.1 Total Government Spending, 1993–2017   158
5.2 Structure of Government Spending on Salaries and Wages   159
5.3 Capital Outflows, 2010–18 ($ billion)   160
5.4 BDL FX Subsidies Bill   160

Acknowledgments

This book grew out of a workshop organized by the Project on Middle East Political Science (POMEPS), with the support of the Carnegie Corporation of New York. The original plan of developing the book at a workshop at the European University Institute (EUI) in the summer of 2020 did not survive contact with the COVID-19 pandemic. Despite being denied the pleasures of Florence, our group persevered through a series of online workshops, sharing a series of draft papers repeatedly in hopes of crafting a cohesive set of chapters despite the far-ranging theoretical and empirical perspectives of the participants. We would like to thank Luigi Narbone for his enthusiastic support of the original EUI workshop and the EUI-affiliated discussants and participants in the online workshop that followed. Prerna Balaeddy and Tessa Talebi of POMEPS cheerfully and tirelessly organized the logistics of our meetings and kept everyone on schedule and on task. The Doha Institute for Graduate Studies invited us to present the project in October 2022, a rare opportunity for systematic and rigorous exchange of views on the Arab state between Western and Arab scholars. We take full responsibility for any errors that survived this process.

Steven Heydemann, Northampton, MA
Marc Lynch, Washington, DC

Introduction

Making Sense of the Arab State

Steven Heydemann and Marc Lynch

For scholars of the Arab world, the state remains an elusive, unsettled, and unsettling presence. Since mandatory and then independent states emerged in the Arab world in the aftermath of World War I, theorizing the Arab state has been a central preoccupation for generations of regional specialists. The gravitational pull of the state is not surprising. As a product of war, imperial collapse, and colonial impositions—intertwined with local political struggles and crudely grafted onto an international order in which norms of state sovereignty favored some pathways while foreclosing others—Arab states have long challenged received wisdom about what states are and how they form, develop, and become organized. They complicate understandings of how states relate to regimes and to societies. Their formal borders often fractured the boundaries of existing communal identities, while their internal demarcation from society often remained ambiguous. These features are not necessarily unique to Arab states, yet arguably Arab states manifest particular characteristics—strengths and weaknesses, presences and absences, effects and affects—that set them apart from states in other postcolonial regions.

Thus, Arab states exhibit modes of governance, institutional formations, and processes of adaptation and change that are common attributes of stateness, a term we define as an indicator of state capacity—the effectiveness with which state institutions and actors deliver various forms of governance—as well as the symbolic, performative, and spatial attributes through which states manifest themselves in and through societies.[1] Seen in these terms, Arab states stand as examples of what Meyer et al. define as a "worldwide institution constructed by worldwide cultural and associational processes," displaying high levels of isomorphism.[2] Arab regimes certainly embrace such attributes as affirmations of their sovereignty and legitimacy. Yet Arab states often defy expectations of stateness that are widely held not only among social scientists but, as chapters in this volume show, among Arab societies as well. What is more, they do so in intriguing ways that differ from the patterns observed in other postcolonial regions and areas of the Global South.

Navigating the tensions between the peculiarities that mark Arab states and the criteria we routinely encounter as essential in defining stateness weighs heavily on scholars of the region. Its impact is especially evident, however, in the *vernaculars of comparison* that scholars of the Middle East deploy and in the idiosyncratic concerns that have animated successive waves of research on the Arab state. This often means theories built around accounting for differences and explaining variation from what are presumed to be the modal experiences of non-Arab states—in other words, theories that explain the Arab state through what it lacks in comparison either to Western ideal types or to states in other postcolonial regions. Such "deficit" approaches have framed a vast range of research programs. Their presence is visible in the postwar rise of modernization theory; engagement with questions about the relative autonomy of states and the structure of state-society relations; work on the effects of war on Arab state formation; research that explores the distinctive features of rentier political economies; explanations for why the Arab region has not given rise to developmental states comparable to those in East Asia; and in research on problems of state failure and fragility. In addressing these questions, the analytical focus typically revolves around the extent to which Arab states mimic or diverge from Weberian ideal types.

To suggest that such comparisons construct non-Arab trajectories of state development as normative and Arab trajectories as deviant is too simplistic. More often than not, research of this type is undertaken precisely to highlight the limits of claims that universalize non-Arab models of state formation, state-society relations, and political development. Chapters in

---

1. On the concept of stateness, see Beichelt, "Stateness." See also the approach to stateness in Haugbolle and LeVine, "The Remaking of the Political in the Arab World Since 2010."
2. Meyer et al., "World Society and the Nation-State," 144.

this volume offer ample evidence of how literatures that draw on the experiences of non-Arab cases can enrich and deepen our understanding of stateness in the Arab region. In doing so, moreover, they push back against forms of deficit research in which Arab cases are explored in light of their failure to produce outcomes that are present in non-Arab cases. In such research, as Toby Dodge and Jillian Schwedler emphasize in their chapters, the analytic emphasis is on attributes that Arab cases are missing, the specific features that explain their failure to produce developmental states, democracies, or Tocquevillian models of civil society. The deficit model routinely characterizes states in the Arab world as flawed, weak, fragile, and ineffective—even as they deploy fiercely effective repressive power over their own citizens.[3]

Chapters in this volume move beyond the deficit model to critically deploy foundational theoretical texts—such as Max Weber, Antonio Gramsci, Michael Mann, Charles Tilly, Pierre Bourdieu, J. P. Nettl, Timothy Mitchell, Joel Migdal, and James C. Scott—to develop empirically rich studies that, in the aggregate, reframe how we think about states in the Arab region.[4] By design, these encounters between theory and cases are notable for the breadth and diversity of their approaches. We did not begin, or emerge, with a single master theory of the Arab state. Not all Arab cases are represented here; one case, Jordan, is the subject of two chapters; and one chapter focuses on non-Arab Afghanistan. Our intent is not to provide comprehensive coverage but to showcase research that contributes to new comparative vernaculars in the study of the Arab state. Nonetheless, the chapters in this book convey shared perspectives in questioning what the Arab state is and is not. In their focus on trajectories of stateness in the post-2011 period, in particular, they provide crucial insight into fundamental questions about the interplay of states, regimes, and societies during one of the most tumultuous and politically formative periods in the modern history of the Middle East. They reflect crosscutting insights and elements of convergence that suggest important baselines for future research.

Four such elements stand out. First, authors highlight the centrality of regimes as crucial actors in analyses of the Arab state. As Dan Slater suggests in the volume's conclusion, scholars of the Arab region need to

---

3. Ayubi, *Over-stating the Arab State*.
4. Weber, *Economy and Society*; Gramsci, *Selections from the Prison Notebooks*; Mann, *Sources of Social Power*; Tilly, *Coercion, Capital, and European States*; Bourdieu, *On the State*; Nettl, "The State as a Conceptual Variable"; Mitchell, "The Limits of the State"; Migdal, *Strong Societies and Weak States*; Scott, *Seeing Like a State*.

consider "regime-ness" rather than stateness alone as a driving force in accounting for trajectories of state development. Of particular importance in this regard is the priority that Arab regimes attach to their own survival. While survival is the default preference of rulers in general, among Arab regimes, we argue, it takes on an intensity that sets them apart from their counterparts in other world regions. Thus, as used in this volume, regime-ness refers to definitions of the term "regime" as it is widely applied in the social sciences, meaning the rules, norms, and practices that structure politics and help us distinguish between regime types. However, we also apply the term more narrowly to refer to ruling coalitions: the principal power holders who exercise definitive authority in a polity. Regime-ness thus refers to the capacity of rulers to establish the rules, norms, and practices that both constitute a regime type in the larger sense and define its particular features, practices, and characteristics. Using this approach, the convergence among Arab regime types in the 1990s and 2000s draws attention: presidential regimes came to resemble monarchies in their preference for dynastic succession, while in the 2010s monarchies in the Gulf cultivated forms of nationalism traditionally associated with republican regimes.

For several contributors to this volume, it is regimes and the determined pursuit of regime survival that have produced particular configurations of state capacities, influenced the domains in which stateness is most developed, and enabled us to understand how state capacities—institutional, legal, regulatory, technological, coercive, or distributional—are allocated or withheld. For Bassel Salloukh, Sean Yom, Schwedler, Dodge, and Dipali Mukhopadhyay, regime preferences in the organization and management of stateness—whether in the form of large-scale construction projects, the design of urban spaces, the delegation of authority to local actors, or the allocation of collective goods—have been decisive in structuring the political, social, economic, and spatial contexts in which actors struggle to advance competing understandings of the appropriate role of the state and bring their own agency to bear in shaping the terms of their relationship with state authorities. As in Raymond Hinnebusch's chapter on the regime-state distinction, operationalizing regime-ness as a variable through Mann's work opens up possibilities for addressing enduring puzzles in research on the Arab state, including the presence of strong regimes in states that are weak in developmentalist terms. In turn, Steven Heydemann explains variation in configurations of stateness as a result of the priority regimes attach to survivalist over developmentalist criteria. He cites the transactional strategies of state development that regimes adopted as an expression of their survivalist preferences. Both Lisa Anderson and

Marc Lynch explore how regimes exploit attributes of stateness and instrumentalize state capacities—whether as instruments of their own economic interests or in the form of newly developed surveillance technologies—to further consolidate and deepen their hold on power.

A second element of convergence emerges from those authors who underscore the imperative to move beyond considerations of state autonomy to focus instead on states as expressions of specific social actors. This state *as* society conception, emphasizing how closely the two are intertwined, expands on Migdal's useful "state in society" approach.[5] For decades, research programs on the state wrestled with concerns about the autonomy of the state, whether relative, embedded, partial, or otherwise. Research programs on the Arab state have pursued similar questions, notably in work on the state bourgeoisie.[6] Mitchell's Foucauldian approach to "state effects"—one of the few theories inspired by the Middle East and North Africa (MENA) to inform the broader state literature—sought to sidestep the issue of autonomy by conceptualizing the uncertain boundary between state and society not as a problem for conceptual precision but rather as precisely the phenomenon to be explained.

Theories of state autonomy developed for the specific historical experiences of capitalist state formation in the Global North have less to offer in making sense of the Arab state or, as Mukhopadhyay's chapter indicates, of peripheral, late-developing states in other world regions. In the African context, studies of the legacies of the postcolonial state have often emphasized the reproduction of forms of colonial violence and isolation from society by new elites who captured the mechanisms of the state. What stands out in the cases we explore in this volume is the extent to which state development manifests itself in large measure as an ongoing domain of social contestation and conflict, such that trying to identify where the social ends and the state begins is generally counterproductive. Embracing a state *as* society approach does not mean that stateness is therefore irrelevant or an empty category. Rather, it leads us toward research strategies that question how the social expresses itself *in and through* the state and how states manifest themselves as expressions of the social. This approach draws our attention to the role of social actors in shaping trajectories of state development, configurations of state capacity, how state policies and practices become constituted, and how state-society relations and modes of resistance to the state become organized.

---

5. Migdal, *State in Society*.
6. Waterbury, "Twilight of the State Bourgeoisie?"; Haddad, "Syria's State Bourgeoisie."

The third element of convergence lies in how the authors give particular emphasis to the variability of the state's presence and the significance of its absence—both in defining everyday experiences of stateness and in understanding how regimes practice, manage, transcend, withhold, and even violate stateness in pursuit of regime interests. This variation in *presence* can be geographic, as with states opting to concentrate their capacity building in politically central areas such as cities while forgoing penetration of rural areas.[7] Rough terrain, distance from the capital, or organized societal resistance may frustrate efforts by states to extend their presence even if they attempt to do so. Or variation in presence can be cultural, ethnic, or religious, determined either by identity or by the opacity of existing societal structures. A Sunni-dominated regime such as Ba'thist Iraq may have difficulty gaining access to Shi'a networks, while Kurdish areas may prove incomprehensible and inaccessible to either Turkish or Arab state agents due to language differences and strong social organization against state intrusion.[8] Lynch's chapter in this volume reads the state's variable presence through the lens of uneven societal legibility, with important political and security implications.[9] The seeming absence of the state does not necessarily mean an absence of governance, however. This insight marks a key distinction from earlier state theory, which might have ended the analysis at the point of demonstrating the limits of state penetration into particular areas or social sectors. But, as Lisa Wedeen argues elsewhere in the context of Yemen and Mukhopadhyay in this volume in the context of Afghanistan, local political orders can substitute for the state quite effectively, and efforts to expand state presence can be destabilizing by disrupting those already existing local orders.

This attention to state absences as a key variable is especially evident in Salloukh's chapter on Lebanon, where the phrase "there is no state" (*ma fi dawla*) marks the failure of state institutions to provide the essential functions necessary for public order. Yet as Salloukh emphasizes, the limits of state capacity in Lebanon are constructed, the intentional outcome of a process of limited, selective state development overseen and maintained by a deeply consolidated coalition of predatory ruling elites. Even the disastrous explosion at the Beirut port in August 2020 and the equally disastrous collapse of the Lebanese economy have failed to produce meaningful changes in Lebanese politics. Heydemann's chapter provides a longer-term, cross-regional view of the role of Arab regimes in the con-

---

7. For a similar argument in the African context, see Boone, *Political Topographies*.
8. Blaydes, *States of Repression*.
9. Scott, *Seeing Like a State*.

struction of asymmetric forms of stateness in which the absence of state capacity can be mapped as an expression of regime priorities about how best to fend off potential rivals. Dodge and Mukhopadhyay explore the effects of elite contestation on configurations and limits of stateness in the cases of Iraq and Afghanistan, respectively. In contrast, as Yom's chapter shows, the Hashemite regime's attempts to expand the state's presence in ways that Jordanian tribes viewed as violating local prerogatives provoked a campaign of violence to restore a status quo the state had challenged. Anderson's chapter offers a regional perspective on the variability of stateness, highlighting how the transregional economic interests of rulers influence the form and content of state policies and elite practices. Increasingly, she argues, it is these economic interests that determine how state capacity is deployed, producing forms of stateness that are at times incommensurate with conventional notions of state sovereignty. In each case, unpacking the production of stateness, its absence, and its transformation is crucial for understanding political dynamics writ large.

Assessing stateness also means assessing citizenship, a crucial site of contestation around stateness. In Arab states, the bundles of rights, entitlements, obligations, and responsibilities that define formal citizenship are enshrined in constitutions and receive formal benediction from regimes that proclaim their adherence to the rule of law. Yet in practice, citizenship, like stateness, is highly variable, applied differentially or withheld arbitrarily. It is managed by regimes as a negotiated outcome dependent on a wide range of attributes, including sect, region, profession, ethnicity, or the perceived political or economic salience of a particular community for the security of a regime. Jose Ciro Martinez has shown how Jordan managed to create a remarkably effective state-run system for the provision of subsidized bread through licensed bakeries across every corner of the country.[10] This system, he argues, shows a pocket of strength in what is often seen as a weak state. It also generates citizen demands for more, not less, stateness: if the state can provide cheap, quality bread, then why can it not also provide decent education or health care?

As Lynch's chapter shows, the rights and the limits of citizenship are being transformed through processes of technological innovation as authoritarian regimes upgrade their repressive capabilities. The ability to render society legible is a key component of state power, in Scott's formulation, while citizens have good reason to remain illegible when confronted by a capricious or violent state. The growing use of innovative surveil-

---

10. Martinez, *State of Subsistence*.

lance and data mining software expands the capacity of states to render citizens legible to their scrutiny and thus to their control. Still, the fluidity of actual citizenship aligns uneasily with its formal standing, contributing to the intensity of social struggles over conflicting conceptions of citizenship and its entitlements. Such conflicts are evident in Schwedler's chapter on the uses of urban planning to thwart citizen mobilization, in Yom's chapter on the struggle of Jordanian tribes to reclaim what they viewed as prerogatives of citizenship, and in Heydemann's discussion of transactional citizenship as a core component of asymmetric state-building strategies by Arab regimes.

Finally, chapters in this volume pay less attention than might be expected to the elusive concept of legitimacy, which dominated the comparative politics literature on the Middle East and North Africa for a generation following the publication of Michael Hudson's *Arab Politics* in 1977. Legitimacy has always been difficult to define or to directly observe. Still, as Ayubi reminds us, stateness requires *legitimation*, if not legitimacy, to move beyond despotic power and direct domination. Wedeen's work offers one productive guide for exploring the political culture of stateness from the dual vantage points of citizens and regimes.[11] The ways in which states legitimate themselves through the performance of stateness, and how citizens evaluate and experience those performances, run through the chapters in this collection.

Why the "Arab" State?

The chapters presented in this volume develop new comparative approaches to the elusive Arab state. Yet they also raise important questions about the distinctiveness of Arab states and whether the Arab state can be, or should be, singled out as an object of study. Why would one assume there is something unique and distinctive about Arab states as opposed to a wider universe of postcolonial states? Why would one expect to see the same pathologies or innovations across nearly two dozen countries in very different geographic regions, with very different resource endowments and demographic profiles, and following different historical experiences of colonialism and transitions to independence? Why would those distinctive characteristics stop with the borders of the Arab League? An earlier generation of scholars would perhaps have viewed attempts to address these

---

11. Wedeen, "Conceptualizing Culture"; and Wedeen, *Peripheral Visions*.

questions as an exercise in Orientalism, seeking to pathologize an essentialized Arab state as ontologically Other. More recent scholarship has, for the most part, shed such prejudice. But to a remarkable degree, MENA scholarship tends to limit its view to the MENA region, often without feeling the need to justify limiting its datasets to Arab countries.

In this volume we actively resist reproducing the tunnel vision of insular comparison that has long afflicted the field of Middle East Studies. Indeed, recognizing the value of broader comparisons, we compare Arab states to other postcolonial regions throughout and include a chapter on Afghanistan. But what brings the Afghan case within the scope of this book? Its presence makes it all the more important for us to explain why the core of this volume focuses on Arab cases. In our view, potential similarities and differences are posed as questions, not as assumptions. Are there good reasons to compare Morocco to Jordan, as examples of Arab monarchies, as opposed to comparing Morocco with other West African former French colonies and comparing Jordan with other Levantine post-Ottoman constructs? What is gained by comparing the wealthy oil producers of the Arab Peninsula with other Arab countries rather than with other oil producers such as Nigeria or Venezuela—or, for that matter, Iran directly across the Gulf? On what grounds other than geography would it be fruitful to include Israel, an advanced industrial semi-democracy, in comparisons with Arab countries? There are strong reasons in particular to treat the Arab Gulf states differently, given their extreme wealth, small citizen populations, and monarchical political forms. Anderson's conception of Arab states as having evolved into little more than business enterprises of ruling family networks, for instance, may work better in the entrepreneurial hubs of Dubai and Riyadh than in the massive, lumbering state-dominated economies of Egypt or Algeria.

This volume takes the Arab state as its object of analysis while applying theories developed in other contexts and adopting different comparisons as appropriate. This approach does not mean smuggling in normative assumptions about modal state forms from the Global North. Instead, it means taking Arab states on their own terms to assess what objectives the regimes that control them intend to achieve, how effectively they do so, and what explains variations in outcomes. Whether there are systematic characteristics of Arab states that differ from those seen in non-Arab states becomes a question rather than an assumption as we cast our analysis of Arab states as a window into bigger questions of stateness in (especially) the Global South. The differences in how such questions are treated across varied regional contexts are themselves an indicator of potential difference.

Consider the extent to which the African literature on the state has been dominated by questions of postcoloniality and the perpetuation of colonial violence, while Arab literature on the state has been more dominated by questions of Arab nationalism and the failures of unification.[12] Historians of the Middle East have, of course, explored the legacies of colonialism in depth, but the political science of the Arab state has overall been much less deeply constituted by the dilemmas of postcolonial subjectivity.[13]

There are several reasons why we might expect to see such similarities, though few of them stand up to scrutiny. What is the case for overlooking these differences in search of some distinctive analytical category of the "Arab state"?

First, Arab states have experienced a broadly similar *historical trajectory*. In the popular imagination, this entails perhaps a passage from Ottoman rule to a relatively brief window of British or French colonialism following World War I and then independence.[14] Arab states tended to develop similar bureaucratic institutions, educational systems, and other instruments of stateness in part because of the role of colonial powers in establishing or adapting them. Postcolonial rulers thus inherited relatively isomorphic state forms. But this pattern really only applies to the Levant and, to some extent, Egypt. French colonialism came to North Africa a century earlier, and its settler colonialism had far deeper transformative effects on the state and society than anything observed in the Levant, even though France imported many of the same colonial bureaucrats from French Africa to administer the new mandates in Syria and Lebanon (just as the British colonial apparatus shared personnel and operating standards from India and its global empire). Italy practiced an exceptionally violent and incompetent form of colonial rule, which shattered state institutions in Libya and its other colonies. Meanwhile, the small Arab Gulf states remained largely self-governing British protectorates until 1971 before gaining independence on the eve of a fantastic wave of new oil wealth. Saudi Arabia looks more like a European state since its borders were established by military expansion to the point of being stopped by other powers, which explains why there is no longer a Kingdom of the Hejaz and why Saudi Arabia was unable to absorb the small littoral states of the Arabian coast. It is difficult to see why states with such different historical origins would obviously share institutional features.

A second reason for similarities across the Arab states is that the transi-

---

12. Mbembe, *On the Postcolony*; Mamdani, *Citizen and Subject*.
13. But see Neep, *Occupying Syria*.
14. Wyrtzen, *Worldmaking in the Long Great War*.

tion to independence came at a time when they faced a *shared set of competitive pressures* that differed from those faced by states in other regions of the world. There is some evidence to support this notion. As Anderson and Hinnebusch argue in this volume, the importance of oil and the geographic centrality of the Middle East to the Cold War meant an unusually high level of involvement by external powers and the impossibility of superpower indifference to changes in political regimes or state borders. At the same time, the transnational potency of Arab nationalist identity meant that Arab states—more than most non-Arab states and especially in the Levant—faced common challenges of asserting their authority over their territory and population in the absence of an accepted national identity.

Those challenges manifested most obviously in the 1950s and 1960s during the so-called Arab Cold War, but they arguably continued in later eras through the rise of a Palestinian national movement, the spread of pro-Iranian militias, or the distinctive engagements of regimes with transregional political Islam and jihadist movements. Such international and transnational intrusions on state sovereignty are not limited to the Middle East, of course, as Melissa Lee makes clear in the post-Soviet and African contexts, but they do take distinctive forms and perhaps have more consistent impacts.[15] These features are often seen as contributing to a distinctively permeable regional system, in which states were exceptionally vulnerable to external, especially transregional, flows of ideas, money, and weapons.

Third, Arab states may have some distinctive *resource endowments* that enable certain types of political economies. The rentier state literature looms heavily here, as one of the most important theoretical contributions to the post–World War II comparative politics literature that largely originated in the study of the Middle East. But here, again, the differences across Arab states are more obvious than the similarities, at least if the oil states of the Gulf are included in the comparison set. There are certainly complementarities between these economies, particularly in the 1970s and 1980s, when Arab states with large populations but few resources sent huge numbers of workers to the Gulf and survived on their remittances. At the same time, as David Waldner and Benjamin Smith suggest, the political effects of oil rents seem to be different in the Middle East than in other areas of the world, with the expected effects on suppressing democracy not seen in oil producers in Latin America and Africa.[16]

---

15. Lee, *Crippling Leviathan*.
16. Smith and Waldner, *Rethinking the Resource Curse*.

Fourth, there may be *similar international and regional effects* that influence patterns of state development. Arab regimes and states learned from each other. The bureaucracies of rapidly growing Gulf states were staffed with well-educated Egyptians, Jordanians, and Palestinians who brought their norms and practices along with their expertise. The disruptions of the competitive interventionism of the Arab Cold War, the rise of transnational terrorism, the increase in mass refugee flows, and the growth of transregional crime have forced leaders hoping to survive to "harden" their states against external intrusions. Border walls, tightening border controls, and an expanded military presence in border regions are all indicators of this trend. Similarly, such common characteristics as smothering control over the media, expansive and empowered security services, and coup proofing arguably reflect adaptations against threats rather than just baseline authoritarian impulses. Such instincts were reinforced by the Cold War, where the United States and the Soviet Union each sought to support the domestic survival of their clients and turned a blind eye toward human rights abuses. These instincts have been bolstered more recently by the uprisings of 2011, the growing prominence of social media, and Iran's post-2003 emergence as a regional disrupter. At the same time, Arab leaders tended to remain in power for decades, and they also observed and learned from each other. They adopted repressive best practices that worked for their counterparts and learned from their failures. This institutional isomorphism could be seen in the move toward hereditary succession among several of the key Arab presidential republics—most obviously, the Mubaraks in Egypt and the Assads in Syria—blurring the once sharp distinction between monarchies and republics. Such trends have perhaps been accelerated by the rapidly expanding role of wealthy Gulf states such as the United Arab Emirates and Saudi Arabia in financing other Arab regimes, distorting those political economies while pushing particular styles of governance and institutional practices in return.

Finally, there may be a shared *political culture* that enables certain types of state forms. Such analysis does not require an Orientalist condescension toward Arab societies that sometimes attends culturalist claims. For Hisham Sharabi and generations of Arab feminist theorists, patriarchy was that common feature, fostering autocracy and shaping patterns of authority from the household to the palace.[17] For others, monarchy—no matter how ahistorical its roots—offered a uniquely effective form of government in the Arab context, perhaps because of its resonance with more

---

17. Sharabi, *Neopatriarchy*; Mako and Moghadam, *After the Arab Uprisings*.

deeply rooted tribal structures. Still others looked to tribes and tribalism to ascribe a common set of cultural referents and expectations. A mountain of research has been published searching for patterns linking Islam or Arab culture to the absence of democracy, with inconclusive results.

This volume, in a sense, sidesteps rather than engages these five traditional avenues of inquiry. Rather than look for a grand theory of the Arab state, we seek to observe it in practice: to explore the relationship between regime behavior and state forms and to explain variations in state institutional capacity and other attributes of stateness. The authors in this volume approach these questions differently. Anderson and Hinnebusch each see the regimes and states of the region passing more or less together through a series of phases linked to developments in global politics and the international economy. Heydemann and Lynch, by contrast, each highlight specific dimensions of state capacity: Lynch focuses on its informational capacity, or what James Scott termed "legibility"; Heydemann focuses on asymmetric infrastructural capacity to explain patterns of state development that overinvested in survivalist capacities and underinvested in developmentalist capacities. Salloukh and Dodge each situate the state within broader social fields, challenging Weberian or Mannian assumptions about state autonomy or discrete borders. Yom, Schwedler, and Mukhopadhyay each recenter the state by viewing it through the eyes of citizens and non-state power centers, finding strength where others see weakness. For all these authors, the "Arab-ness" of the Arab state is less important than understanding stateness on its own terms in a shared Arab context.

As we noted above, however, we do observe one notable feature in the literature on the Arab state that sets it apart from the wider literature: the emphasis on regime security. Scholars of the Arab world homed in early on the overarching priority placed on regime survival by Arab leaders. While this is, of course, not unique to the Middle East—Steven David developed his original concept of "omnibalancing" primarily in the African context, and Achille Mbembe places the brutality of the insecure new rulers of postcolonial states at the center of his notion of postcoloniality—it is something profoundly central to the operation of the Arab state.[18] The turbulence of the 1950s and 1960s, with repeated military coups and surges of popular mobilization in many countries, left Arab leaders obsessed with protecting themselves against the same fate. It is nothing short of remarkable that every single Arab regime in power in 1970 was still in power in 2010, with the sole exception of President Saddam Hussein's Ba'thist

---

18. David, "Explaining Third World Alignment."

regime in Iraq, which was toppled by a direct American invasion. This extreme regime resilience is not found in any other region of the Global South. Arab leaders pioneered forms of coup proofing, direct and indirect control over the public sphere, and co-optation through clientelism, subsidies, and public service employment—what Michael Albertus et al. refer to as coercive dependence.[19] Each of these regime security measures required the expansion of certain dimensions of state capacity while deprioritizing others, which could explain the otherwise odd similarities across subregions and regime types.

What renders the Arab state distinctive for our purposes, therefore, is not a set of shared historical or ascriptive attributes alone but how these have intersected and interacted with broader processes of state, social, and economic transformation over the course of the twentieth century. These interactions, varied across space and over time, produced and continue to shape particular forms of stateness and regime-ness. The states and regimes that result are distinctive in the extent to which they bear the imprint of— are captured by or otherwise harnessed to the ambitions of—specific social actors. This, in turn, centers stateness and regime-ness both in hierarchies of social power and in the social struggles through which such hierarchies are maintained and contested. Boundaries between the domestic, regional, and international are no less porous, meaning that relevant processes of transformation must also encompass factors like the post–Cold War globalization of neoliberalism (as in Hinnebusch's and Anderson's chapters), global processes of technological change (discussed by Lynch), shifts in the regional security landscape, and the effects of external intervention (a prominent theme in the chapters by Schwedler and Mukhopadhyay).

Questioning States

Chapters in this volume differ in approach and emphasis. However, they all situate their analyses precisely at the intersections that make visible the interplay between dimensions of stateness, regime-ness, and state-society relations. They reflect a shared commitment to treating empirical contexts as opportunities to pose questions about all three dimensions and, in the process, challenge conventional characterizations of Arab states as weak or strong, fierce or fragile. To organize chapters around one or another of these three dimensions is thus, in some sense, a contriv-

---

19. Albertus, Fenner, and Slater, *Coercive Distribution*.

ance. We do so nonetheless to highlight central lines of analysis that run throughout the volume.

Dimensions of stateness is a principal focus of one cluster of chapters, including those by Heydemann, Hinnebusch, Dodge, and Lynch. Each of these chapters engages with debates about state capacity, in particular questions about the relative weakness or strength of Arab states. Each one showcases the limits of approaches that overlook both variation in state capacity and the transformation of state capacity over time, while leaving unexplained how such variation came about. Rejecting claims that depict Arab states as either weak or strong, Heydemann traces trajectories of state development to explore the origins of asymmetric state capacities. He attributes configurations of state capacity to the survivalist preferences of postcolonial regimes in the Arab world, a product of the intense volatility and turmoil in which these regimes first rose to power. His analysis shows that these initial choices consolidated path-dependent processes that produced high levels of state capacity in security sectors and domains that ensured the economic dependence of citizens on the state, but less capacity in areas commonly associated with economic and social development. In such contexts, regime-society relations became fundamentally transactional, generating shallow, segmented forms of citizenship that rest on the exchange of benefits for loyalty or quiescence.

Hinnebusch draws on Mann's concepts of despotic and infrastructural power to account for the presence of resilient, persistent authoritarian regimes that rule over states that have become increasingly ineffective in delivering governance to citizens. In his view, regimes largely sustained their despotic power (their capacity to centralize authority in the hands of an elite) while their infrastructural power (their capacity to implement policy or to penetrate, mobilize, and control society) declined from a peak in the postcolonial period to lower levels today. Acknowledging variation in both forms of power within and across cases, he links their current configuration to the globalization of neoliberalism during a period when postcolonial, state-led strategies of economic development were under severe strain.

Focusing on the case of Iraq's "disaggregated state," Dodge's chapter develops an explicitly generalizable model of the state in which stateness is a dependent variable, the product of elite conflict across a set of distinct fields: economic, ideological, military, and political. Drawing on the work of Mann, Jessop, and Bourdieu, he emphasizes the fluidity of stateness and the apparent coherence of the state as outcomes contingent on shifts in the balance of power among competing elites. Tracing movement from periods of greater concentration of power, which reached their peak under Saddam, to periods of greater contestation following the US invasion of Iraq in 2003, Dodge maps patterns of elite competition to account for shifts in the form and content of stateness over time. In contrast to Lebanon, in today's Iraq an elite pact to manage the distribution of state resources—institutional, material, legal-regulatory, coercive—is thinly consolidated, at best, ensuring persistent instability as elite factions vie to improve their positions across various fields of competition.

Lynch focuses on one aspect of state capacity: the ability to render societies legible. In contrast to the trajectories of declining stateness that are discussed in other chapters, Lynch observes a dramatic increase in the ability of states to penetrate and order societies driven by new surveillance technologies. The ambition to gain full visibility into the actions, networks, and even thoughts of citizens is not unique to the Arab world, of course, but it resonates especially powerfully with the long-standing focus on regime survival of Arab regimes. From the mass collection of data exposing online behavior to the targeted surveillance of suspected dissidents, there has been a qualitative and quantitative expansion in the collection capacities of Arab states, with implications across a wide range of domains. Notably, however, access to data does not automatically translate into effective control. Many of the weaknesses of Arab states (areas where state capacity is less developed) spill over into the digital domain.

A second cluster of chapters offers insight into attributes that we associate with *dimensions of regime-ness*. They explore regime dynamics and their role in the formation and transformation of state capacities and practices, as well as their effects on state-society relations and forms of social conflict. Through examining wide-ranging contexts, including the non-Arab case of Afghanistan, these chapters provide strong empirical support for a "state *as* society" perspective in which dimensions of stateness are determined by struggles for power and resources among competing social actors.

This perspective takes on particular relevance in Salloukh's chapter on the Lebanese state. Critiquing characterizations of the missing or weak state, Salloukh views stateness in Lebanon as a direct result of social struggles over the control and allocation of material resources—"the condensation of the material and social relations"—that structured a distinctive configuration of state capacities, what he calls the "integral state." Selective in its capacities and notable for the putatively public functions allocated to non-state actors, stateness in Lebanon has been organized to serve the interests of sectarian power brokers and preserve understandings among them about the allocation of public budgets, public employment, and many other features of stateness that are managed as semiprivate, collective goods.

Anderson, like Hinnebusch, traces trajectories of state and regime development over time, but to very different analytic ends. In the early postcolonial era, she argues, states occupied positions of prominence as the focus of citizen loyalty. Over time, however, "regimes began to supersede states," relying on external rents to buy support if not legitimacy. With the Arab uprisings that began in 2011, she sees the region entering a new phase, reflecting the decline of regimes as the center of political gravity. Today, ruling elites are working to construct a post-political form of rule in which politics is being displaced as inimical to or a distraction from the economic interests of ruling elites. Regimes are rebranding themselves to emulate modern multinational corporations, disparaging politics as a divisive distraction from the demands of economic competition and success. In the small, wealthy Gulf states that have moved furthest in this direction, regime-ness and stateness are being instrumentalized to advance what is, in essence, a performance-based model of governance, tied to a conception of citizenship that no longer obscures its transactional underpinnings. Larger, less wealthy states may find this model difficult to emulate, yet Anderson sees elements of it taking hold even in such states, notably the larger Arab republics.

Afghanistan presents a fascinating comparative case for students of the Arab state. The volume is richer for its inclusion. Some of Afghanistan's features were similar to those found in its Arab counterparts, especially— for obvious reasons—in the case of post-US invasion Iraq. As in the Arab cases explored here, Mukhopadhyay presents Afghanistan as a case in which stateness, state forms, and state practices are dependent and unstable variables. They were contingent on bargaining and competition not only among fractious Afghan elites who viewed state resources as useful for their own survival strategies but also between these elites and US officials who sought to harness state capacity to their counterinsurgency agenda, often at the expense of their demands that Afghan presidents deliver good governance and effective state institutions. Here, as in Arab cases, the intersection of and interactions between regime-ness and stateness are crucial sites for the production of politics. Yet contrasts also loom large, notably in the extent to which Afghanistan's political field was marked by what Tilly called "high accumulation but low concentration of coercion" relative to Arab cases. In such a context, the principal challenges confronting a ruler, whether khan or president, are to navigate competing interests, build and maintain a winning coalition, and ensure the marginalization and disorganization of losers. As one of Mukhopadhyay's interview subjects noted, President Hamid Karzai was "extremely good at defeating possible and potential alliances against him," while his successor, Ashraf Ghani, proved singularly incapable of doing so. Amplified by the severe constraints imposed on him by the United States, Ghani's failures fueled the Taliban's resurgence and contributed to its eventual victory in August 2021.

The final set of chapters engages with a third dimension of stateness, *society as a site of resistance to the state* and to authorities who wield state capacities to regulate, control, and govern their populations. In these, as in other chapters, the relationships at issue cannot be narrowly framed in terms of neatly contained categories, whether state, society, or regime. Instead, these chapters examine complex landscapes in which the Jordanian state serves as a site of contestation and where resistance to state practices weighs heavily on how forms of stateness are exercised, challenged, and transformed. As Schwedler writes, these questions require us to address how we understand concepts such as state development and state capacity when viewed "through the lens of contentious politics and challengers to those who hold state power."

Schwedler's chapter provides important starting points for addressing such questions. In her account of Jordan, state development remains an active and ongoing field of contestation. Moreover, it is through challenges to state authority and how state actors respond that processes of state development are made visible. Resistance to state practices reveals where stateness is most vulnerable, and this, in turn, informs decisions by state actors about where to invest in strengthening state capacity—and where not to invest, as well. Over time, the built environment, urban landscapes in particular, become expressions of state capacity and state weakness that shape opportunities for contestation, mobilization, and resistance.

Yom's chapter reinforces understandings of state development and state capacity as fields of ongoing contestation. Shifting his empirical terrain to southern Jordan, where local tribes controlled the allocation of natural resources, Yom highlights what he characterizes as "uneven stateness" in a protracted dispute over the scope of state authority as well as state responsibility for the limits of its authority. When Jordanian officials acted to expand the state's presence and extend its control over local resources, undertaking a major infrastructure project to strengthen the state's capacity to deliver water, local tribes engaged in sustained and often successful efforts to sabotage the project. Defining the rights and entitlements of citizenship to include state recognition of their authority in such domains, tribal actors defended their actions as restoring a status quo that the government had violated. When foreign contractors sued the Jordanian government for failing to ensure their security, the court sided with Jordan, determining that the state had done what might reasonably be expected of it, thereby upholding the state's claims about the limits of its stateness.

Slater concludes by bringing a comparativist's eye to the questions motivating the volume. From his vantage point studying Southeast Asia, the variations in stateness in the Middle East look relatively limited, with commonalities more puzzling than divergences. But Slater goes further. The construction of scales of stateness, in his view, does little to elucidate politics as they actually happen within states weak or strong. In line with the spirit of this volume, he celebrates the heterogeneity both of analytical perspectives and of stateness itself. His invitation to comparison is a fitting conclusion to the volume.

Conclusion

This collection presents a variety of novel theorizations of the Arab state, united by a common focus on moving beyond both "deficit" models and Weberian ideal types. Authors adopt diverse perspectives to examine the ambiguous boundaries between society, regime, and state. They address variations in state capacity across different sectors, locations, and issues but do not fixate on capacity as the only element of concern in theorizing the state. They examine the performativity of stateness without losing sight of the materiality of power and juxtapose questions of regime-ness with the more familiar questions of stateness. Collectively, these chapters enable new conversations about the Arab state that should inform disciplinary approaches and enable cross-regional thinking that moves beyond conventional understandings and help us make sense of the Arab state.

BIBLIOGRAPHY

Albertus, Michael, Sofia Fenner, and Dan Slater. *Coercive Distribution*. New York: Cambridge University Press, 2018.

Ayubi, Nazih. *Over-stating the Arab State: Politics and Society in the Middle East*. London: I. B. Tauris, 1996.

Beichelt, Timm. "Stateness." In *The Handbook of Political, Social, and Economic Transformation*, edited by Wolfgang Merkel, Raj Kollmorgen, and Hans-Jürgen Wagener. New York: Oxford University Press, 2019.

Blaydes, Lisa. *States of Repression: Iraq under Saddam Hussein*. Princeton, NJ: Princeton University Press, 2018.

Boone, Catherine. *Political Topographies of the African State: Territorial Authority and Institutional Choice.* New York: Cambridge University Press, 2003.
Bourdieu, Pierre. *On the State: Lectures at the Collège de France, 1989–1992.* New York: Polity, 2020.
David, Steven R. "Explaining Third World Alignment." *World Politics* 43, no. 2 (January 1991): 233–56. https://doi.org/10.2307/2010472
Gramsci, Antonio. *Selections from the Prison Notebooks.* New York: International Publishers, 1989.
Haddad, Bassam. "Syria's State Bourgeoisie: An Organic Backbone for the Regime." *Middle East Critique* 21, no. 3 (Fall 2012): 231–57. https://doi.org/10.1080/19436149.2012.717798
Haugbolle, Sune, and Mark LeVine. "The Remaking of the Political in the Arab World since 2010." In *Altered States: The Remaking of the Political in the Arab World*, edited by Sune Haugbolle and Mark LeVine, 1–23. New York: Routledge, 2023.
Hudson, Michael C. *Arab Politics: The Search for Legitimacy.* New Haven, CT: Yale University Press, 1977.
Lee, Melissa M. *Crippling Leviathan: How Foreign Subversion Weakens the State.* Ithaca, NY: Cornell University Press, 2020.
Mako, Shamiran, and Valentine Moghadam. *After the Arab Uprisings: Progress and Stagnation in the Middle East and North Africa.* New York: Cambridge University Press, 2021.
Mamdani, Mahmoud. *Citizen and Subject: Contemporary Africa and the Legacy of Late Colonialism.* Princeton, NJ: Princeton University Press, 2018.
Mann, Michael. *The Sources of Social Power.* New York: Cambridge University Press, 1986.
Martinez, Jose Ciro. *State of Subsistence: The Politics of Bread in Contemporary Jordan.* Stanford: Stanford University Press, 2022.
Mbembe, Achille. *On the Postcolony.* Berkeley: University of California Press, 2001.
Meyer, John, John Boli, George Thomas, and Francesco Ramirez, "World Society and the Nation-State." *American Journal of Sociology* 103, no. 1 (July 1997): 144–81. https://doi.org/10.1086/231174
Migdal, Joel S. *State in Society: Studying How States and Societies Transform and Constitute One Another.* Princeton, NJ: Princeton University Press, 2012.
Migdal, Joel S. *Strong Societies and Weak States: State-Society Relations and State Capabilities in the Third World.* Princeton, NJ: Princeton University Press, 1988.
Mitchell, Timothy. "The Limits of the State: Beyond Statist Approaches and Their Critics." *American Political Science Review* 85, no. 1 (March 1991): 77–96. https://doi.org/10.2307/1962879
Neep, Daniel. *Occupying Syria under the French Mandate: Insurgency, Space, and State Formation.* New York: Cambridge University Press, 2012.
Nettl, J. P. "The State as a Conceptual Variable." *World Politics* 20, no. 4 (July 1968): 559–92. https://doi.org/10.2307/2009684
Scott, James C. *Seeing Like a State: How Certain Schemes to Improve the Human Condition Have Failed.* New Haven, CT: Yale University Press, 1999.
Sharabi, Hisham. *Neopatriarchy: A Theory of Distorted Change in Arab Society.* New York: Oxford University Press, 1988.

Smith, Benjamin, and David Waldner. *Rethinking the Resource Curse*. New York: Cambridge University Press, 2021.

Tilly, Charles. *Coercion, Capital, and European States, A.D. 990–1990*. Oxford: Blackwell, 1990.

Waterbury, John. "Twilight of the State Bourgeoisie?" *International Journal of Middle East Studies* 23, no. 1 (February 1991): 1–17. https://www.jstor.org/stable/16 3929

Weber, Max. *Economy and Society: An Outline of Interpretive Sociology*. Somerville, NJ: Bedminster Press, 1968.

Wedeen, Lisa. "Conceptualizing Culture: Possibilities for Political Science." *American Political Science Review* 96, no. 4 (December 2002): 713–28. https://doi.org/10.1017/S0003055402000400

Wedeen, Lisa. *Peripheral Visions: Publics, Power, and Performance in Yemen*. Chicago: University of Chicago Press, 2009.

Wyrtzen Jonathan. *Worldmaking in the Long Great War*. New York: Columbia University Press, 2022.

SECTION 1

Dimensions of Stateness

ONE

Seeing the State or Why Arab States Look the Way They Do

Steven Heydemann

More than ten years ago, a wave of mass protests across the Arab world reanimated research programs on the Arab state. While the causes of the Arab uprisings continue to be debated, state weakness, state dysfunctions, and failures of the state loom large in explaining the most significant episode of anti-regime mobilization in the modern history of the Middle East.[1] Although the specific forms of state failure that researchers link to the onset of the uprisings differ, with some accounts highlighting economic factors and others focusing on political or social conditions, some common themes are evident. Perhaps most prominent are failures of governance by self-interested ruling elites. In such accounts, feckless leaders privileged their parochial interests over the hard work of nation building and ruled in ways that excluded and marginalized large segments of their societies.[2] They oversaw failed development strategies, pursued predatory economic practices, captured and corrupted state institutions, and proved unable to provide citizens with economic security or social mobility.[3]

Instead, state elites exacerbated social cleavages, undermined prospects for inclusive and equitable development, and corroded crosscutting

---

1. For references to state weakness as a principal cause of the 2011 uprisings and their aftermath, see Salloukh, "Overlapping Contests," and Kamrava, ed., *Fragile Politics*.
2. Gause, "Beyond Sectarianism."
3. Achcar, *The People Want*.

bonds of citizenship.[4] These dysfunctions are on vivid display in this volume. They rendered states vulnerable to both the accumulation of domestic grievances and external pressure, notably demands to adopt neoliberal economic reforms that further weakened state capacity and exacerbated economic and social precarity.[5] For most Arab citizens, therefore, national identities are loosely held and easily discarded in response to states that appear incapable of meeting their needs. For rulers seeking legitimacy, state weakness has elevated the appeal of sectarian identity politics.[6] State elites exploit and instrumentalize sectarian identities to mobilize popular support, advance state interests, and undermine regional adversaries.

If the uprisings of 2011 are the proximate inspiration for these accounts, they have deep roots in earlier generations of research on the Arab state.[7] Claims of state weakness and failures of governance as causes of the uprisings resonate with broader comparative research programs on modernization, political development, and the conditions associated with the formation of developmental states, including work that explores why such states have not emerged in cases that exhibit the institutional dysfunctions seen as widespread in the Arab world.[8] Echoes of these accounts are evident as well in comparative literature on state failure and in practitioner literature on failed states and state fragility.[9] Post-uprising literatures thus fit neatly within a conceptual and theoretical landscape saturated with claims about conditions that contribute to weak and ineffective state institutions in general and to the weakness and fragility of the Arab state in particular.

To be sure, there are ample reasons to view Arab states as flawed and ineffective. Global indices routinely rank states in the Middle East poorly on control of corruption, rule of law, civic freedoms, education, service delivery, and any number of other indicators. Nonetheless, taking state failure as a starting point for research—establishing one or another deficiency as the outcome of interest—has come at a cost. To do so may bring some questions into sharper focus, such as accounting for poor economic performance, but obscures many others. In particular, state failure as a start-

---

4. Kamrava, *Inside the Arab State*.
5. Hinnebusch, "Change and Continuity."
6. Gause, "Beyond Sectarianism."
7. Ayubi, *Over-stating the Arab State*; Hudson, *Arab Politics*; Salame, ed., *The Foundations of the Arab State*.
8. Greif, *Institutions and the Path to the Modern Economy*; Kohli, *State-Directed Development*; North, *Institutions, Institutional Change and Economic Performance*; Waldner, *State Building and Late Development*.
9. Rotberg, ed., *When States Fail*; World Bank, *World Development Report 2011*; World Bank, *World Bank Group Strategy for Fragility, Conflict, and Violence*.

ing point falls short in accounting for the resilience of Arab regimes, in considering the variation in capacities across regimes and within regimes, or in explaining the transformations of authoritarian governance and the selective expansion of state capacity that regimes have engineered since the 2011 uprisings, issues that Lisa Anderson, Marc Lynch, and Raymond Hinnebusch all address in their chapters in this volume.

Questions of resilience and regime continuity, and the capacity of Arab regimes to effectively reconfigure elements of authoritarian governance as conditions change, are central for an understanding of the state of the Arab state. Simply put, if states are so weak, if state institutions are so ineffective, if governance is so poor, how did the majority of Arab regimes survive the largest wave of mass protests in the region's modern history? How can we explain the extraordinary continuity of regimes, which in Arab republics such as Algeria, Syria, and Egypt are now in their sixth or seventh decade of rule, even though they consistently produce suboptimal social and economic outcomes? Is it plausible to argue, as Hinnebusch does in this volume, that the Middle East and North Africa (MENA) region has strong regimes but weak states? If we begin by assuming state weakness or by assuming that what matters in assessing state capacity is whether states can promote social and economic development—what I term a developmentalist bias in literature on the state—how do we account for the puzzle of regime resilience in the context of weak states and ineffective institutions? Once we accept state weakness as a starting point we leave ourselves with few theoretical or conceptual tools for addressing such questions.

Perhaps not surprisingly, when we start from the assumption of state weakness, the explanatory focus in accounting for regime resilience turns toward coercion. Rather than asking how it is that purportedly weak states acquire the capacities needed to produce high levels of regime continuity, to sustain the loyalty of a social base, or to manage complex systems of social regulation, service provision, or a legal-juridical apparatus, scholars have often focused on narrower questions concerning coercive capacity.[10] Such work emphasizes the conditions under which regimes will resort to violence to contain the political effects of developmental weakness or social fragmentation and highlights the capacity of coercive institutions as a key determinant of regime resilience. It has less to tell us, however, about the noncoercive domains in which regimes have consolidated institutional mechanisms that provide for regime survival or how the presence of such

---

10. Bellin, "The Robustness of Authoritarianism"; Bellin, "Reconsidering the Robustness of Authoritarianism."

mechanisms might inform our understanding of trajectories of state building, patterns of state-society relations, or how political economies are organized.

However, if we move beyond approaches shaped by developmentalist biases, alternative questions and alternative research agendas come into sharper focus. We have an opportunity to see Arab states as they are rather than to define them by what they lack—the "deficit approaches" familiar to us from earlier research on failures of democratization and developmentalism. We open up possibilities for exploring how the Arab state got to be the way it is—to account for actual trajectories of state development and consolidation in the Arab Middle East—rather than treat such states as flawed versions of their developmentally more successful counterparts in Europe or East Asia.[11]

For example, what hypotheses might follow if we assume that regimes in the Arab Middle East prioritize their security and continuity over developmentalist outcomes? How might regimes' perceptions of threats from within and without influence their choices about the design of state institutions? What kind of economic and social policies and what sort of state-society relations would be consistent with regimes that viewed the primary purpose of the state as facilitating regime survival, even while recognizing the importance of economic and social development as crucial for their stability? How would such regimes organize political economies? How would they construct notions of citizenship? Would the assumption that regimes act on the basis of "survivalist" preferences as opposed to developmentalist preferences help us understand why governance functions are often allocated to non-state mechanisms?[12] How might survivalist biases shape how regimes manage external pressures of various forms, whether economic, political, or strategic, including the pressures of economic globalization?

To begin to address such questions, I start from the assumption that state weakness and the closely related concept of state fragility offer unproductive starting points. Rather than trying to account for state weakness—with weakness defined in developmentalist terms as the dependent variable—I view it as more productive to ask a simple, straightforward question: How can we explain the configurations of state and non-state institutions that deliver governance in the Arab Middle East today? Or, more simply, how did the Arab state get to be the way it is?

With this starting point, what becomes evident is that states exhibit

---

11. Waldner, *Late Development*.
12. Hibou, ed., *Privatizing the State*.

asymmetric institutional capacities, varying from higher in some domains, such as the capacity to surveil, coerce, and contain the populations they govern, and lower in others, including innovation, rule of law, or the capacity to foster inclusive economic and social development. In yet others, including service delivery, education, or health care, capacities vary but are often measured as comparable to, if not greater than, those of other regions in similar World Bank income categories.[13] As we emphasize in the introduction to the volume, however, state capacity is only one dimension of regime capacity, or regime-ness. In addition, it becomes evident that large domains of governance in the Arab world fall outside the state and operate through regime-controlled but non-state mechanisms that work in tandem with state institutions. Understanding the organization of asymmetric state capacity, therefore, requires expanding the scope of our research to encompass domains in which regimes have intentionally allocated state functions to non-state mechanisms and domains in which regimes have intentionally withheld the development of state capacity. *The key questions, then, focus on understanding the organization of asymmetric state capacity and accounting for patterns in the co-construction of state and non-state modes of governance.*

For those who see the state in the Middle East as weak, such patterns are often explained as the unintended outcome of failed state-building projects by regimes that embraced developmentalist logics. In this view, moreover, informal governance is often seen as a cause of developmentalist failures. Challenging this explanation, I treat institutional configurations—combinations of state and non-state modes of governance—as the expression of regime preferences about how best to ensure their stability and survival. The state institutional configurations we see in the Arab Middle East today reflect how regimes view the purposes of the state and how the region's autocrats thought—and still think—about the problems they need the state to solve. Among these purposes is the imperative of resolving what Milan Svolik identifies as the two principal challenges confronting any autocrat: mitigating challenges from within and preventing challenges from below.[14]

Challenges of both types were acute in absolute terms during the early phases of MENA's postcolonial state building and institutional development, perhaps even in relative, cross-regional terms. They were amplified for Arab regimes by the distinctive permeability of the Arab state system:

---

13. The Worldwide Governance Indicators database of the World Bank shows the Middle East as performing at lower levels on government effectiveness measures than Latin America and at higher levels than South Asia and Africa. https://info.worldbank.org/governance/wgi/

14. Svolik, *The Politics of Authoritarian Rule*.

the extent to which Arab societies and politics were subject to intense, transregional flows of ideas and political movements that rejected the legitimacy of both states and regimes—such as Arab nationalism or pan-Islamism—and to external interventions driven by regional competition and the Cold War.

In such an environment, the core dilemmas confronting Arab autocrats go beyond the two that Svolik highlights to include challenges from without. How to address these challenges provided the principal impetus that shaped the state-building strategies of ruling elites, giving a rationality and intentionality to configurations of stateness in the Middle East that are rooted in survivalist rather than developmentalist logics. This does not imply that today's Arab states emerged seamlessly, full blown, from blueprints in the heads of state builders. The weight I attach to survivalist logics is consistent with ad hoc, reactive, and even flawed decision-making. It simply emphasizes that such decisions are most heavily influenced by survivalist criteria.

Specifically, I argue that trajectories of state development can be understood as the result of three linked conditions.

First, postcolonial rulers in the Arab Middle East viewed state development as a means to strengthen regime-ness above all: to consolidate regime power, mitigate threats, control the extraction and allocation of resources, and provide for the continuity of their rule. Developmentalist outcomes were seen as a means to these ends.

Second, these rulers—the immediate predecessors of those who hold power today in most Arab countries—deployed the allocation and development of state capacity instrumentally to advance regime interests. Stateness was extended or withheld based on criteria reflecting the survivalist preferences of rulers rather than those associated with "good governance" or economic and social development.

Third, rulers viewed citizenship as transactional and segmented and treated legitimacy as a contingent outcome of transactional relationships that defined and organized state-society relations. State development was used to ensure the quiescence and loyalty of citizens. It provided mechanisms to manage and contain possibilities for social mobilization from below while structuring and restructuring the boundaries of political and economic inclusion to favor privileged categories of citizens and marginalize others.

Embracing this transactional-instrumental view of stateness, ruling elites pursued flexible, adaptive, and plural strategies of state development. As Arab political economies took shape, these strategies led to what Steffen Hertog calls segmented market economies, with distinctively rigid "insider-outsider" divides that are deeper in the Arab world than in any other region.[15] At times, rulers asserted the exclusive authority of the state in Weberian terms, both internally and externally. At other times, they cultivated non-state frameworks of rulemaking and governance, often exploiting formal institutions as sites within which non-state, personalistic, and clientelist practices were grafted onto and interwoven with formal bureaucratic rules and procedures. Consistent with postcolonial experiences of state building in other regions, Arab ruling elites adopted developmentalist ideologies that expressed inclusionary conceptions of economic and social rights yet managed access to such rights on a contingent, transactional basis. The result—my own dependent variable—is the distinctive configurations of asymmetric stateness we see in the region today.

Trajectories of Stateness in the Arab Middle East

To unpack configurations of asymmetric state capacity, this chapter first assesses historical patterns in the development of stateness as a variable that expressed the survivalist priorities of regimes. I then assess the informal mechanisms of non-state governance that stabilize and sustain asymmetric stateness, which can also be seen as forms of limited statehood.[16] In a closing section, I show how Arab regimes have responded to rising mass mobilization since 2011 by amplifying existing patterns of asymmetric stateness and redefining state-society relations to manage and contain the threat of newly mobilized publics. By tracing what I refer to as *trajectories of stateness* in the MENA region, it will be possible to examine the development of limited and asymmetric statehood along key dimensions—territorial, sectoral, temporal, and social.

My focus on the MENA region does not imply that the interactions of interest are unique to the Arab Middle East. The odds are high that comparable interactions are present in different forms across the Global South. Yet the specific arrangements that define political, social, and economic orders in the MENA region nonetheless exhibit distinctive attributes. Not least, these include the persistence and resilience of authoritarian regimes—a factor that matters more than is understood in the literature on governance in areas of limited statehood—to a degree that is unique

---

15. Hertog, "Segmented Market Economies in the Arab World."
16. Börzel and Risse, *Effective Governance under Anarchy*.

among world regions.[17] They also include distinctive patterns in the interactions between regimes, states, and societies that are central to understanding modes of contestation and why these have produced crises of governance, cases of violent conflict and state collapse, and the subsequent restructuring of asymmetric state capacities by Arab regimes since the 2011 uprisings—for example, in the expansion of state capacity to surveil societies, as highlighted by Lynch in this volume.

The states we see today in the Arab Middle East thus reflect the path-dependent outcomes of the preferences and strategic choices of rulers in the period following decolonization. Initially, the nationalist elites who governed in the immediate aftermath of independence, typically representatives of landed and business interests, worked with and adapted institutions they inherited as legacies of colonial rule. As new cohorts of autocrats seized power and pushed established elites aside, they modified these formal institutions, weaving them into and making them more permeable to informal mechanisms for exercising authority, allocating resources, and privileging some social groups while excluding others. They melded ascriptive and other forms of social identity linked to combinations of family, sect, class, clan, region, and profession—each with their own distinctive norms, practices, and hierarchies—to state-based, formal rules, norms, and practices. Whether we call the resulting frameworks social pacts, political settlements, or rent-seeking coalitions in closed access orders, they gave Arab rulers a widely varied, flexible, if sometimes unwieldy, set of tools they could deploy to overcome the problem of power sharing among potential rivals, manage the effects of external pressure, and build institutional frameworks of social control to suppress potential threats from below.[18]

All three sets of challenges abounded in the postcolonial Middle East. Across the region, decolonization, however it was achieved, ushered in extended periods of political turmoil, social conflict, and struggles for power and legitimacy.[19] Coups and countercoups; assassinations of rulers both attempted and successful; "years of lead," as the period under King

---

17. Research programs on limited statehood and contested orders note that limited forms of statehood and multilayered governance are present in many types of regimes and thus discount the relevance of regime type (Börzel and Risse, *Effective Governance under Anarchy*). I hope to show that there is a correlation between regime type and forms of limited statehood, with meaningful implications for governance and contestation. I argue that it is not possible to understand "interactions between order contestations and areas of limited statehood," a central focus of research on governance in areas of limited statehood, without taking regime type into account. See Börzel and Risse, "Background Paper Elaborating the State of the Art."
18. Khan, "Political Settlements"; North et al., eds., *In the Shadow of Violence*.
19. Hudson, *Arab Politics*; Kerr, *The Arab Cold War*.

Hassan II is referred to in Morocco; external interventions; bitter ideological struggles among competing political factions in Algeria, Egypt, Syria, and Iraq; the nationalization by newly empowered reformist regimes of land and other assets held by notables, landlords, and major capitalists; experiments in unification; and episodes of armed popular resistance were prominent features of the region's political landscape for several decades. So were the episodes of popular resistance to the intrusion of state authority by local communities, as detailed by Jillian Schwedler, Sean Yom, and Dipali Mukhopadhyay in their chapters. Layered onto and interacting with these conditions were the pressures of Arab nationalist ideas and movements, a deeply destabilizing "Arab Cold War," and the effects of global Cold War rivalries on regional dynamics.[20] These struggles took place in the context of ambitious attempts to transform societies and economies, using states as instruments to overturn and remake the political and social orders of the colonial and immediate postcolonial eras.

To do this, Arab regimes built states and political economies that rested on transactional models of governance, reflecting what I define as dual logics in the provision of collective goods. The first of these logics is clientelist and neopatrimonial. It is organized around the allocation of selective benefits to key constituencies. The second consists of authoritarian bargains—modes of "coercive distribution" that define broader patterns in state-society relations across the Arab Middle East (and beyond).[21]

In both respects, the organization of asymmetric stateness can be traced through the distribution of social provision and of state institutional capacity. Further, the resulting forms of asymmetric governance have given rise to distinctive modes of contestation. Across MENA, these most often take the form of bargaining between regimes and citizens over access to collective goods and the benefits of social provision, over the distribution of selective benefits, and, as we see in the chapters by Sean Yom and Bassel Salloukh, over the distribution of state capacity itself. Counterintuitively, in some cases, notably Yemen, Lebanon, and Libya, this bargaining was characterized by regimes *withholding* state development and limiting state capacity while social actors demanded state expansion.[22]

The states that have resulted from these processes are not fragile but fierce.[23] They are states in which ruling elites elevate survival above devel-

---

20. Kerr, *The Arab Cold War*.
21. Albertus, Fenner, and Slater, *Coercive Distribution*.
22. Alley, "The Rules of the Game."
23. Heydemann, "Beyond Fragility." I define fierce states differently than Ayubi in *Overstating the Arab State*. To Ayubi, the hard or fierce states of the Arab world relied heavily on

opment and design institutions to support this aim. In fierce states, the consolidation of such institutions and the effectiveness with which they contribute to regime survival are often in tension with the attributes that developmentalist and fragility-based models associate with state capacity and good governance, including accountability, voice, equity, transparency, and inclusion. Instead, ruling elites in fierce states construct stateness as an expression of a zero-sum existential struggle in which conflict reinforces their determination to defend existing institutional arrangements, including by force if necessary.

Privileging regime security, however, does not imply that fierce states are indifferent to development. Across the region, postcolonial regimes confronted a vast array of social and developmental needs neglected by colonial powers. In every Arab republic, newly empowered ruling elites were deeply committed to ideologies of social and economic transformation and viewed the state as an indispensable instrument for achieving developmental goals. Even conservative, pro-Western monarchies adopted state-centric development strategies following independence. Moreover, regimes understood the threat that disaffected populations could pose. They well understood the benefits they derived from authoritarian bargains that offered social provision in exchange for political quiescence. They were attentive to the value of popular legitimacy, despite their reliance on repression. Regimes in fierce states also valued the international benefits they secured by adopting developmentalist discourses and engaging instrumentally with international financial institutions and Western governments as partners.[24]

In addition, authoritarian regimes in fierce states have constituencies. They rest on a social base. Through the widespread use of constituency clientelism, regimes construct alliances and coalitions based on transactional loyalty that generates, at best, contingent legitimacy. They also benefit from the loyalty of social groups cultivated on the basis of ascriptive ties, whether ethnic, sectarian, or both, creating bonds that link transactional benefits and dependencies to deeper forms of legitimacy and loyalty.

Both strategies contribute to the construction of asymmetric stateness and non-state forms of governance, with mixed effects. They weaken national, citizenship-based identities and dilute the rulemaking and rule-enforcing role of the state. They push significant aspects of governance

---

coercion and repression to remain in power but were nonetheless vulnerable, brittle, and unable to adapt to changing environments. He argues that their reliance on coercion masked an underlying weakness, a view I challenge in this chapter.

24. Randeria, "Cunning States."

into informal, non-state channels. Yet they can strengthen *regime* legitimacy by tightening the transactional ties that bind regimes to privileged social groups. Thus, when challenged by mass protests or insurgencies, fierce states may prove more resilient than fragility-based models of state weakness and vulnerability assume. Not all fierce states survive when challenged from below. Those that do, however, like President Bashar al-Assad's regime in Syria and King Hamad bin Isa al-Khalifa's regime in Bahrain, credit their survival to the very institutions, norms, and practices that fragility-based models treat as causes of poor governance and symptoms of institutional weakness.

Transactional Stateness and the Construction of Asymmetric State Capacity

Postcolonial forms of asymmetric stateness in the MENA region have emerged through what can best be described as transactional processes of state building. Notwithstanding the commitment of virtually all postcolonial regimes in the Middle East to state-led development strategies, the expansion and strengthening of state institutions, inclusive and redistributive social policies, and egalitarian conceptions of citizenship, such processes were (and in most cases continue to be) managed by authoritarian regimes that have used state mechanisms to extend, consolidate, and secure their own political and economic power at the expense, in developmentalist terms, of the societies over which they rule.[25]

This conception of states as subordinate to, and the instrument of, regimes that were typically dominated by elites associated with specific regional, sectarian, ethnic, and professional (typically military) identities led to transactional and asymmetric processes of state development that were widespread not only in MENA but across the Global South. In the wake of decolonization, Arab regimes claimed the prerogatives and privileges of both international and domestic sovereignty, asserted their monopoly over the legitimate use of force, demanded the exclusive right to make and enforce collectively binding rules, and embraced developmentalist aspirations.[26] Yet the state-building strategies pursued by these regimes reflected an alternative set of priorities, flowing from their determination to consolidate their grip on power, defeat potential rivals, and strengthen

---
25. I include Saudi Arabia here though it was neither colonized nor governed under a League of Nations mandate during the interwar period.
26. Krasner, *Sovereignty*.

their hold over societies viewed as fractious if not rebellious. They invested most heavily in state capacity in areas they saw as essential for achieving these aims, especially security sectors, expansive state corporatist systems of social control, redistributive frameworks that served as instruments of coercive distribution, and educational systems that became platforms for the construction of compliant citizens.[27] At the same time, rulers built parallel constellations of informal, clientelist mechanisms to bolster their legitimacy and authority among key constituencies, empowering alternative, non-state modes of rulemaking and resource allocation that were both exclusionary and selective.[28]

How these parallel processes unfolded determined patterns of asymmetric state capacity and non-state governance. In Egypt, for example, the small cohort of officers who led the 1952 coup that brought Gamal Abdel Nasser to power dominated these parallel processes for six decades. The armed forces became their principal beneficiary, consolidating durable patterns of military-bureaucratic privilege that continue to structure Egypt's political economy.[29] Algeria's military has occupied a similarly dominant position since it achieved independence from France in 1962.[30] In Syria after 1963 and Iraq after 1968, secretive cliques of officers within the leadership of the Ba'th Party seized power, engineered the capture and transformation of state institutions, and developed elaborate non-state governance networks based on ties of sect, region, and family. In other cases, from republican Tunisia to the monarchies of Jordan, Morocco, and the Gulf, we see similar processes at work. Ruling elites oversaw asymmetric processes of state building that produced uneven state capacity, while consolidating extensive informal networks that served as alternative sources of rulemaking, legitimacy, coercion, and resource allocation.

One effect of these processes was a dramatic expansion in the size of states in the postcolonial Middle East. State capacity increased significantly across the MENA region as the scale of public expenditure and the scope of state activity grew. Reversing decades of low public spending by colonial regimes, MENA states spent a higher percentage of GDP by the mid-1960s than their counterparts in any other world region. They would continue to do so for the next two decades. The positive effects of expanding stateness were experienced by tens of millions of people in the form of tangible, visible improvements in their everyday lives. Moreover, the impact

---

27. Ismail, *The Rule of Violence*.
28. Ruiz de Elvira, Schwarz, and Weipert-Fenner, *Clientelism and Patronage*.
29. Sayigh, *Owners of the Republic*.
30. Werenfels, "Obstacles to Privatisation of State-Owned Industries in Algeria."

of these developmental gains in the 1960s–1980s was formative in shaping popular expectations about the levels of governance that citizens looked to regimes to provide—and for which they mobilized to hold regimes accountable in 2011. Populist and redistributive social policies may have embedded citizens in systems of coercive dependence on regimes, but they also created deeply held norms of state social provision and citizen entitlement that regimes found it near impossible to discard even as their costs became unsustainable.

Parallel Trajectories, Asymmetric Stateness, and Segmented Citizenship

Even as states expanded, however, the distribution of stateness—the extent to which regimes built their capacity to make and enforce binding rules across a national territory, the presence of state institutions such as schools or hospitals, the opportunities for participation in state-owned and -controlled sectors of the economy, as well as access to the benefits of social policy—developed along two distinct and parallel paths. On the one hand, regimes invested in the capacity of states to enforce binding rules and deliver nominally public goods, establishing entitlements to education, housing, employment, subsidized energy and basic subsistence goods, and health care. These investments increased literacy, life expectancy, and incomes; reduced poverty and inequality; and produced large increases in GDP.

On the other hand, access to the benefits of state expansion and social provision was unevenly and selectively allocated, based on the specific political and economic calculus of regimes intent on ensuring their own survival. Annika Rabo and Sulayman Khalaf both note, for instance, the extension of state-managed peasant unions created by the ruling Ba'th Party into the Syrian city of Raqaa during the 1960s.[31] These organizations empowered small-scale farmers but also served to integrate them into transactional, clientelist relations with the state that included access to selective benefits. With the appearance of corporatist peasant unions—regime-controlled "popular organizations"—the authority of established notables and large landowners over local politics and economies diminished. Targeted as adversaries by the Ba'th Party, these "Cotton Sheikhs" of the pre-Ba'th period were marginalized through processes of state building that nationalized the property of the largest landowners and appropriated

---

31. Rabo, "Anthropological Methods"; Khalaf, *Social Change in Syria*.

larger shares of the surpluses that landowners had previously extracted from peasants and smaller landholders.[32] With the arrival of the state, these surpluses were now redistributed through mechanisms that discriminated against former elites, who were also excluded from the selective benefits provided to members of peasant unions and the Ba'th Party. In exchange for these benefits, however, newly empowered peasants and small landholders, public sector employees, state functionaries, and members of the ruling party were required to demonstrate loyalty to the regime and to act on its behalf as needed.

Regime-led processes of state expansion thus restructured local governance, producing new configurations of winners and losers, new patterns of inclusion and exclusion, and a politicized, transactional conception of entitlement to collective goods. The net effect was to institutionalize segmented citizenship in the organization of state-society relations and segmented economies with exceptionally rigid insider-outsider divides. Moreover, while regimes justify these state-building strategies through nominally inclusive developmentalist, populist, and anti-colonial/anti-Western narratives, they have exploited economic governance as an instrument of coercive distribution. They deploy redistributive social policies to render citizens dependent on the state for their economic and social well-being, while access to channels of social and economic mobility was filtered through regime-controlled patronage networks.[33]

These parallel paths also shaped the organization of stateness, governance, and state-society relations. Across the MENA region, in both republics and monarchies, postcolonial regimes imposed top-down, hierarchical state-corporatist frameworks to regulate and manage relations between the state and an array of politically relevant interest groups, ranging from workers and peasants to journalists, lawyers, doctors, women, and students.[34] Corporatist institutions, which were most highly developed in the presidential republics of Algeria, Egypt, Iraq, Syria, and Tunisia significantly expanded the capacity of regimes to manage and discipline societies—serving as mechanisms of infrastructural power in Michael Mann's terms.[35] Formally, they established channels for the mobilization

32. Hinnebusch, *Peasant and Bureaucracy*; Hinnebusch, *Authoritarian Power and State Formation*.
33. Albertus, Fenner, and Slater, *Coercive Distribution*.
34. Ayubi, *Over-stating the Arab State*.
35. Michael Mann, *States, War, and Capitalism*. Hinnebusch argues in this volume that the infrastructural power of Arab regimes, defined in terms of the formal, state-based mechanisms through which regimes can shape political norms and practices, has declined dramatically in recent decades. In contrast, I define infrastructural power as a product of both formal,

and representation of important collective actors. In fact, however, state corporatist structures have everywhere functioned to regulate, control, and contain potential challenges "emanating from the social distress that accompanies development."[36] They provided the means to consolidate social bases and frameworks of legitimation for regimes that rose to power through anti-colonial nationalist movements, as in Tunisia and Algeria; through extralegal means such as coups d'état, as in Egypt, Syria, Libya, Iraq, and Yemen; or through colonial dispensations, as in Jordan. In addition, like other state institutions, they have served as mechanisms for allocating privileged access to the state and to collective goods.

As a result, diverse postcolonial patterns in the development of assymetric statehood across the MENA region reflected dual logics. One involved the politically motivated provision of collective goods and redistributive social policies—in the form of state-led, redistributive development strategies widely characterized as populist authoritarianism. The other rested on the use of politically determined criteria guiding where state capacity would be concentrated and how selective benefits and access to collective goods were to be allocated, including through informal clientelist mechanisms.[37] The tensions inherent in this dual strategy of regime-led state building have been well captured by Stein Sundstol Erikson, who points out that the resulting forms

> of state-society linkages driven by domestic socio-political conditions, led to a type of state-society relations that undermined both state power and the project of national development that the state sought to promote. At the same time, the idea of the state was reinforced through this process since the struggle for political survival and the politics of patronage took place within a framework in which the state idea was taken for granted and used to justify state policies.[38]

In short, selective processes of state development and the selective provision of governance became the means through which authoritarian

---

state-based and informal, non-state mechanisms and argue that regimes continue to exercise significant infrastructural power.

36. Ayubi, *Over-stating the Arab State*, 177. Structuring state-society relations on the basis of corporate interests was also intended to suppress class-based forms of social mobilization that might benefit regime rivals, notably communist parties in Egypt, Syria, and Iraq.

37. On the adaptability of these frameworks, see Heydemann, "Social Pacts and the Persistence of Authoritarianism."

38. Erikson, "'State Failure' in Theory and Practice," 243.

regimes in the MENA region constructed asymmetric stateness and segmented citizenship—notwithstanding their insistent affirmations of the state's hegemony with respect to its domestic sovereignty and its commitment to inclusive citizenship. Regime elites in MENA have thus behaved precisely as rationalist accounts of limited statehood predict: they have focused their state-building efforts on "areas and functional activities that would help them to stay in power."[39] Moreover, despite regime rhetoric about the centrality of the state as an agent of social transformation and social welfare, the criteria on which ruling elites made decisions about the allocation of institutional and governance capacity were fundamentally transactional, reflecting their strategic choices about the most effective ways to exploit stateness and governance to bolster regime capacity, preserve their hold on power, maintain social stability, and sustain the loyalty of privileged social groups.[40]

By far the most common and widespread manifestation of transactional state building—in MENA as in other world regions—has been the use of patronage to provide selective benefits and privileged access to collective goods to key regime constituencies.[41] Similar patterns of clientelism emerged across the region based on the exchange of material benefits for loyalty to ruling elites. However, while every Arab regime engaged in similar clientelist and transactional strategies of state building, there are consequential differences in how regimes structured patronage that reflect the context-specific calculus of rulers. The sect, ethnicity, regional origin, and professional identity of rulers were always crucial factors in the organization of clientelism, the allocation of state capacity, and the provision of governance. In Syria, constituency clientelism disadvantaged most Sunnis. In Iraq until 2003 and in Bahrain, it favored them. In Yemen, neopatrimonialism reflected the complex tribal and regional calculus of President Ali Abdallah Saleh, who managed powerful tribes through ongoing cycles of bargaining, accommodation, and coercion. The supply of state capacity was a principal source of regime leverage for Saleh. He allocated it selectively depending on which tribes he viewed as useful allies at any given

---

39. Krasner, "Theories of Development and Areas of Limited Statehood," 29.
40. In asserting the transactional nature of state development in MENA, I differ with analysts who have argued that transactional forms of state-society relations and governance are recent, post-2011 developments. See Khatib and Sinjab, "Syria's Transactional State."
41. This phenomenon is too familiar to require further elaboration. For examples from specific cases, see Van Dam, *The Struggle for Power in Syria*; Batatu, *The Old Social Classes*; Gengler, *Group Conflict and Political Mobilization in Bahrain and the Arab Gulf*; Corstange, *The Price of a Vote*; and Ruiz de Elvira, Schwarz, and Weipert-Fenner, *Clientelism and Patronage*.

moment.[42] Tribal affinities played a prominent role in determining access to stateness and its benefits in Libya and Oman, as well.

The side payments that rulers extended to different categories of regime loyalists, clients, and constituents also varied widely. They include a laundry list of direct and indirect material benefits such as preferential access to employment and accelerated career advancement; preferential educational opportunities; impunity to engage in formally illicit activities such as smuggling or access to highly regulated foreign exchange markets; privileged access to licenses needed to import, export, or establish firms; exemption from legal obligations (e.g., military conscription or taxation); small-scale, direct financial support through mechanisms such as vote buying; or participation in predatory and criminal networks tolerated, sponsored, or controlled by regimes.[43]

The organization of clientelism within states also varied across sectors and over time. In Yemen, for example, labor migration and the remittances it generated weakened patronage ties between migrant workers and the Saleh regime during periods when oil prices in neighboring Saudi Arabia were high. Increased remittance flows moved through private channels that diminished citizens' dependence on the state and altered the balance of power between regime and society. As oil prices fell and remittances declined, the regime again gained leverage over these components of Yemeni society.[44] In Syria, Egypt, Jordan, Morocco, and Tunisia, selective processes of neoliberal economic reforms reconfigured patronage networks. Politically connected private sector actors consolidated their privileged positions within frameworks of crony capitalism, while public sector employees saw the relative value of their access to selective benefits decline.[45]

Clientelism, in other words, not only established boundaries between insiders and outsiders but also constructed hierarchies of inclusion and exclusion that are important for understanding the interactions between asymmetric stateness, transactional governance, and segmented citizenship. In Arab republics and in Jordan, for example, membership in state-corporatist organizations, including state-controlled trade unions,

---

42. Alley, "Rules of the Game"; Dresch, *A History of Modern Yemen*.
43. Corstange, *Price of a Vote*; Gallien, "Informal Institutions and the Regulation of Smuggling"; Gallien and Weigand, "Channelling Contraband."
44. Challand and Rogers, "The Political Economy of Local Governance in Yemen."
45. Heydemann, ed., *Networks of Privilege*; Donati, "The Economics of Authoritarian Upgrading in Syria"; Cammett et al., *A Political Economy of the Middle East*; El-Haddad and Gadallah, "The Informalization of the Egyptian Economy."

brought a measure of preferential treatment. Those who belonged to a ruling party, such as the Democratic Constitutional Rally in President Zine al-Abidine Ben Ali's Tunisia, the National Liberation Front in Algeria, Egypt's National Democratic Party, Yemen's General People's Congress, or the Ba'th Party in Syria and Iraq, also received favorable treatment in the allocation of collective goods; access to employment, health care, and education; and, within limits, deferential treatment from state bureaucrats. Those well positioned within the armed forces or one of the region's vast internal security agencies fared better yet.

In other cases, including the Gulf monarchies and Libya, family and tribal identities produced similar hierarchies of privilege and inclusion. In the Libyan case, President Muammar Qaddafi's efforts to radically restructure and deinstitutionalize governance after he seized power in 1969 eventually gave way to a tribally based, transactional mode of clientelism. Reflecting the survivalist criteria that guided Qaddafi's decision-making, A. H. al-Shadeedi and Nancy Ezzedine characterize the Libyan state as a straightforward example of an authoritarian bargain or model of coercive dependence.[46] It was, they claim, "a reasonably simple patronage system: the regime's survival and support were derived from the tribes. In return, the regime provided economic and government positions for loyal tribesmen."[47]

This reliance on loyalist tribes featured prominently in the design of asymmetric statehood in other cases in which tribal considerations loomed large, including Yemen, Qatar, Saudi Arabia, and Oman.[48] Even where tribal identities played a less significant role, every Arab regime used similar transactional practices to strengthen ties of loyalty and dependence between rulers and select constituencies. These practices led everywhere to varieties of asymmetric statehood, which developed uneven forms of stateness and institutional profiles along several dimensions: territorial-spatial, sectoral, and social.

Asymmetric processes of state development may well be universal. The organization of limited statehood routinely reflects the different starting points that existed across territories that were integrated into states as national boundaries came to define the landscape of global modernity. It

---

46. Al-Shadeedi and Ezzeddine, "Libyan Tribes in the Shadows."
47. Al-Shadeedi and Ezzeddine, "Libyan Tribes in the Shadows," 4. For two different but useful perspectives on limited statehood in Libya, see Anderson, *The State and Social Transformation in Tunisia and Libya*; and Ahmida, *Forgotten Voices*.
48. Burrows, "State-Building and Political Construction"; Weir, *A Tribal Order*; Crystal, "Tribes and Patronage Networks in Qatar"; Gengler, *Group Conflict*.

also reflects the path-dependent effects of the institutions that state builders in postcolonial countries inherited from former rulers. Yet in MENA, the irregular presence of state institutions and the uneven development of state capacity and social provision are also products of the strategic choices of regime elites. These rulers used their power to extend or withhold the development of stateness and state capacity—in functional, spatial, or social domains—as a potent bargaining chip in their interactions with allies and adversaries alike.[49]

Asymmetric Stateness and Non-State Governance

MENA's experience in this regard highlights an important but overlooked facet of state building as it occurred in the postcolonial Arab world: under certain conditions, rulers prefer limited statehood to its more expansive alternative. This point is worth emphasizing. Literatures on state formation treat the steady growth of state institutions over time as processes that move ineluctably from lower to higher levels of efficacy, capacity, and control, including their increased ability to extend their reach more deeply into society—to expand "legibility," to use the term that Lynch borrows from Scott—and the consolidation of centralized authority. Greater state capacity is routinely assumed to be in the interest of rulers. Even in literatures that sharply critique theories that assume the coherence of states and the uniformity of stateness, limited statehood is cast as a second-best outcome that occurs when constraints prevent rulers from pursuing more ambitious, encompassing state-building schemes. "Limited" in this lexicon becomes a synonym for incomplete. It is often used to advance pejorative comparisons to purportedly more complete forms of statehood.

Trajectories of state building in MENA challenge such perspectives. The possibility that state builders might exploit the development of state capacity strategically, withholding it when doing so is to their political advantage, is rarely given consideration. Also overlooked is the extent to which the development of centralized institutions—for the provision of public services, health care, or education, to cite just a few examples—goes hand in hand with the selective and asymmetric distribution of these services, in terms of both where they are most widely available and who can access them. Examples of both phenomena abound in the MENA region.

---

49. Ultimately, withholding state capacity as a mode of bargaining between regimes and non-state actors may well have been self-destructive, contributing to regime and state collapse in Yemen and Libya.

These regime practices have had an outsized influence on trajectories of state development in MENA. In the Arab Middle East, asymmetric and limited forms of statehood result from the strategic choices of rulers about how most effectively to marshal and target state capacity to defend against threats from within, below, or without and to manage potential challengers, maintain the support of loyalists, exploit the benefits of sovereignty, and enhance their own legitimacy. The resulting forms of limited and asymmetric stateness are about exclusion as much as inclusion. Governance is focused as much on the withholding of collective goods as on their provision. Politics and contestation over access to governance are a matter of not only who gets what, when, and how, as Harold Lasswell famously noted, but also who does not get, why they do not get, and what they do about not getting.[50]

A close corollary of such forms of state building has been the persistence of abundant varieties of non-state governance even as stateness expands and rulers deploy state institutions to consolidate their grip over societies. In spatial terms, in areas where stateness is less extensive—especially in peripheries, both urban and rural, that are viewed by ruling elites as socially and politically marginal or in areas where the local population lacks ascriptive ties to regime elites—non-state, local modes of rulemaking, hierarchies of authority, and customary justice coexist alongside of and often supersede state-based rules, laws, and regulations.[51]

For example, locally recognized non-state authorities retain significant influence in many domains of life and are often seen as crucial brokers mediating relations between local populations and state institutions.[52] In areas where stateness is more fully developed, such as urban centers and coastal zones, non-state forms of governance are no less prominent but take on different forms. In these spaces, rulers construct neopatrimonial and clientelist hierarchies to filter and control access to nominally public institutions and services. State institutions become arenas within which non-state forms of rulemaking and hierarchies of authority are inscribed. When the two come into conflict, for example, in the enforcement of for-

---

50. Lasswell, *Politics*.
51. "Periphery" is not necessarily a spatial designation. Peripheries are defined not by their physical distance from a capital city but by their economic, social, and political distance from a regime and their exclusion from flows of public revenues. The rise of ruling parties like the Ba'th in Syria, the National Liberation Front in Algeria, and the Yemeni Socialist Party in South Yemen led to a significant expansion of state intervention in rural areas, reshaping local social and economic structures while preserving neopatrimonial and clientelist modes of governance.
52. Hertog, "Defying the Resource Curse"; Khaddour, "The Assad Regime's Hold."

mal rules and regulations, it is typically non-state, clientelist hierarchies of authority that prevail.

Similarly, it is common in the MENA region to find spatial asymmetries in the allocation of stateness: regions designated as loyalist benefit from higher levels of stateness than others—better roads and utility services; more schools, hospitals, and public services; more regular supplies of electricity.[53] In some cases, these uneven patterns of state development reflect the priority that regimes attach to more densely populated urban centers over rural peripheries or to coastal over inland regions—a pattern of "resource regionalism" that is a standard component of the MENA dictator's toolkit.[54] In yet other cases, uneven state building may result from transactional ties linking regime elites and local notables of one form or another. Although the allocation of stateness is often negotiated, as Yom's chapter shows, with local actors mobilizing to retain their authority in select domains, regimes typically hold the upper hand in how state capacity is distributed. Toby Dodge's chapter illustrates how variations in stateness can also develop in the wake of conflict, such as the violence that accompanied the US invasion of Iraq in 2003. The subsequent dismantling of the Iraqi state by the United States gave new impetus to the role of tribes as "state-like entities" in the provision of local governance.[55]

No less common, MENA's rulers routinely withhold state capacity to weaken and penalize groups or regions viewed as disloyal or politically suspect. Ba'thist regimes in both Iraq and Syria adopted economically punitive policies toward areas heavily populated by Kurds. Morocco's King Hassan II was widely believed to have deprived the greater Tangier region of public spending for decades following an assassination attempt in 1972 led by air force pilots from the Kenitra air base south of the city. Urban Palestinian refugee communities in Lebanon, Jordan, and Syria have historically been subjected to the underdevelopment of state capacity and disadvantaged in the provision of collective goods. Residents of southern Yemen long complained of discrimination in state development and governance by a Saleh regime that favored the north over the south—though Saleh used state building as a bargaining chip in managing tribal coalitions in the north as well. Shi'a citizens in Saudi Arabia's eastern provinces have suffered from a lack of state infrastructural capacity in service provision. In Libya, stateness took on distinctive forms under Qaddafi's "state of the masses," or *Jama-*

---

53. De Juan and Bank, "The Ba'athist Blackout?"; Mazur, "Networks, Informal Governance, and Ethnic Violence"; Mazur, *Revolution in Syria*.
54. Mills and Alhashemi, "Resource Regionalism."
55. Strakes, "Arab and Non-Arab Tribes as State-Like Entities."

hiriyya, but the regime also provided more services and dispensed larger amounts of state revenue in areas where loyalist tribes resided, including the Qadhadhfa, Megharha, Warfalla, and Tarhouna, while reducing public services and spending in areas controlled by tribes viewed as disloyal.[56]

Through these transactional strategies of state building, regimes in MENA constructed limited and asymmetric stateness through ad hoc, piecemeal processes of bargaining and accommodation with a wide range of local power holders. Regimes established higher levels of state capacity in domains—whether territorial, functional, or social—deemed essential for their security and stability. Some of the domains that have been privileged with respect to institutional capacity building include security sectors, institutions to oversee the exploitation of natural resources, and surveillance infrastructure, as discussed in Lynch's chapter. Others focus on the management of state-society relations, such as corporatist structures to regulate and control defined interest groups. Yet others are established in functional domains linked to the production of compliant citizens such as education or the governance of religious affairs. All are areas in which MENA states generally exhibit greater capacity. Thomas Pierret traces this process in the Assad regime in Syria, which developed the institutional capacity to promote authorized forms of Islamic practice as a way to counter oppositional Islamist movements like the Muslim Brotherhood, gradually bringing religious institutions and the training of clerics under the authority of the state.[57]

Alternately, regimes invested less in building state capacity in domains— again, both functional and spatial—deemed less threatening or less relevant to their survival and stability. They selectively delegated authority to nonstate actors, at times doing so in otherwise "reserved domains," including aspects of social provision, local-level conflict resolution, and control over local access to public services. Such conditions are reflected in Yom's discussion of limited stateness in tribal regions of Jordan. Regimes even delegate limited authority to select groups of loyal non-state actors in the maintenance of internal security.[58] Regimes in Syria, Yemen, Iraq, Libya,

---

56. Some notable caveats apply when speaking of tribes. Tribes are not monolithic, their loyalties are not mechanically extended to a regime simply on the basis of ascriptive identities, and they are not static. Their interactions with regimes are often quite fluid. In Jordan, processes of neoliberal reform have been linked to the erosion of transactional loyalties between East Bank tribes—long seen as a key pillar of the monarchy's social base—and the Hashemite regime. See Yom, "Tribal Politics in Contemporary Jordan"; Watkins, "Tribes and Tribalism in a Neoliberal Jordan"; and Schwedler, *Protesting Jordan*.
57. Pierret, *Religion and State in Syria*.
58. Ahram, *Proxy Warriors*; Cheng, "Private and Public Interests"; Ungor, *Paramilitaries*.

and Egypt have made use of paramilitaries or non-state loyalist militias, or both, as elements of hybrid security sectors. The emergence of Popular Mobilization Forces in Iraq and of non-state armed groups in Syria (drawn from state-sponsored loyalist networks such as the Shabiha and the National Defense Forces) are among the most significant instances of this phenomenon.[59]

The forms of asymmetric stateness and modes of non-state governance described here are the product of strategies deployed by authoritarian state builders who set out to construct states and political economies able to withstand challenges, whether from within a regime or from below. Their efforts resulted in the consolidation of states built around segmented citizenship and transactional models of governance that combined the dual logics of constituency clientelism for the privileged few and authoritarian bargains for the many. Trajectories of state building in MENA thus produced states that are neither weak nor fragile but fierce and asymmetric, where stateness and governance reflected imperatives of regime survival.

In keeping with Douglass North et al., these are not developmental states that sought but have been ineffective in achieving inclusive development. Nor are they the atavistic, premodern creatures that populate Atul Kohli's work on lineages of the developmental state.[60] They are eminently modern state forms in which regime elites viewed stateness and the provision of collective goods as the means for resolving the twin problems of authoritarian power sharing and authoritarian control. The instruments they used to achieve these aims included transactional bargains over the distribution of rents to select constituencies; the dispersal of state power to informal, multilevel, non-state mechanisms of local governance; and frameworks of coercive distribution that demanded citizens concede rights and participation in exchange for personal security and access to the benefits of social provision.

For Robert Bates, this model of limited statehood represents state failure. In his view, state failure is defined by two main features: the "transformation of the state into an instrument of predation" and "a loss of monopoly over the means of coercion." This definition may hold for developmental states that, in Bates's term, "implode." Yet these two characteristics have emerged as the intended outcomes of state-building processes by authoritarian elites who subordinate their interest in development to their interest in regime survival and stability. Bates, "State Failure."

59. Mansour, "Networks of Power"; Leenders and Giustozzi, "Outsourcing State Violence"; Ungur, *Paramilitarism*.

60. Kohli, *State-Directed Development*.

Conclusion: Revisiting Trajectories of State Development in the MENA Region

The masses of Arab protesters who swept into the streets in 2011 and again in 2019 focused their anger on the developmental failures of regimes that excluded and marginalized large segments of the populations they ruled. From Morocco to Bahrain, protesters railed against autocrats who had failed to uphold their commitments to distributive justice, economic security, and social mobility. Demanding the fall of regimes, protesters hoped to remake political and social orders and reform state institutions to advance developmentalist commitments to economic inclusion, participation, accountability, and fairness. In short, they sought what developmentalist scholars and practitioners characterize as good governance. Without in any sense diminishing the uprisings' achievements or their lasting effects on the region's politics, they largely failed to achieve their aims.

In the wake of mass protests, regimes that pursued asymmetric strategies of state building have been effective in deploying the extensive coercive capacity of states to suppress mobilization. They have used their authority over legal and regulatory institutions to enhance the state's effectiveness in areas where protests had exposed vulnerabilities, such as control over social media. In keeping with the ad hoc and often reactive approach to governance that has defined postcolonial state development in MENA, autocrats worked to shore up frameworks of asymmetric stateness by reorganizing transactional modes of governance. Rather than address the underlying grievances that drove protesters into the streets in 2011, regimes expanded their capacity to prevent a second wave of uprisings and foreclose possibilities for citizens to mobilize around demands for redistributive justice and economic security.

With the exhaustion of postcolonial systems of coercive dependence, regimes have erected new coercive and legal-regulatory mechanisms to contain urban middle classes that are no longer as tightly bound to state systems of social provision. In the process, constituency clientelism and the capacity of regimes to control and manage the boundaries of political and economic inclusion through informal, non-state forms of governance have become increasingly important. Reflecting the priority that regimes attach to survivalist over developmentalist aims, autocrats continue to exploit asymmetric stateness and their capacity to allocate or withhold stateness as crucial resources in their efforts to navigate the challenges of authoritarian power sharing and authoritarian control.

Post-uprising shifts in governance and state-society relations underscore the failure of developmentalist accounts to explain patterns of state development in the Arab Middle East. The assumptions that shape such accounts offer a poor starting point for understanding why Arab states look the way they do. They fall short in explaining the strategic choices of the autocrats who have dominated regimes across the region since the 1950s and approached the challenges of state building with preferences and priorities that developmentalist accounts treat as secondary. They are not. In the sharply contested political environments of postcolonial states, Arab rulers prioritized the consolidation of their power and the need to ensure their capacity to address threats from within, without, and below. They adapted and expanded state institutions and managed state-society relations to advance these aims.

Prioritizing political survival does not imply that Arab rulers disregarded economic development. Without exception, the autocrats who ruled postcolonial republics styled themselves as socialists, embraced state-centered, populist strategies of economic development, and used state institutions and social provision to achieve significant improvements in social indicators. Broadly similar strategies, absent the socialist rhetoric, were followed by virtually all Arab monarchies. Postcolonial state expansion made state institutions essential in shaping the life chances of tens of millions of people. Yet these achievements moved hand in hand with, and were shaped by, parallel processes that strengthened and expanded the capacities needed to ensure regime survival.

Throughout MENA, with important variations, "dual-use" state institutional frameworks responded to the neglect of social development by colonial authorities and underpinned authoritarian bargains. They produced systems of coercive dependence and provided platforms for the development of dense clientelist networks and the proliferation of informal, non-state mechanisms of governance that were crucial in the maintenance of regime security. Even as states expanded, regimes deployed stateness—the allocation of state capacity—strategically to cultivate transactional ties of loyalty and legitimacy, on the one hand, and to marginalize and disempower social groups viewed as potential threats, on the other hand.

Over the course of more than fifty years, Arab regimes' reliance on combinations of asymmetric stateness and forms of non-state governance along with transactional strategies of social control have served them well even as they imposed significant long-term costs on societies. The uprisings of 2011 were a dramatic response to the price that Arab societies have paid for the choices of their leaders. They caution us against the presumption that existing regimes will persist indefinitely. Nonetheless, the resilience and adaptability of both regimes and the states they have constructed cannot be reconciled with characterizations of such states as weak or fragile.

As I have shown, state capacities in MENA vary widely and are certainly less well developed in domains that scholars and practitioners have established as necessary to achieve sustainable social and economic development. Yet an emphasis on the ineffectiveness of state institutions measured by their lack of developmental capacity offers little help in understanding or explaining how state capacities have become organized or in accounting for how regimes have instrumentalized stateness in the Arab Middle East. Nor can we respond to such questions by labeling states in the Arab world as dysfunctional cases of developmentalist states in waiting. To understand trajectories of state development in the Middle East requires, instead, that we take seriously how Arab state builders themselves viewed the role and purposes of state institutions. We need to unpack their preferences and choices as products of the contexts in which they struggled to achieve and maintain their hold on power. Ultimately, this will only be possible once the study of state building in the Arab world steps out of the shadow of developmentalism, sets aside its teleological biases, and looks at Arab states as they are, not as how we might wish them to be.

BIBLIOGRAPHY

Achcar, Gilbert. *The People Want: A Radical Exploration of the Arab Uprising*. 2nd ed. Berkeley: University of California Press, 2022.

Ahmida, Ali Abdullatif. *Forgotten Voices: Power and Agency in Colonial and Postcolonial Libya*. London: Routledge, 2005.

Ahram, Ariel. *Proxy Warriors: The Rise and Fall of State Sponsored Militias*. Stanford: Stanford University Press, 2011.

Albertus, Michael, Sofia Fenner, and Dan Slater. *Coercive Distribution*. New York: Cambridge University Press, 2018.

Ally, April. "The Rules of the Game: Unpacking Patronage Politics in Yemen." *Middle East Journal* 64, no. 3 (Summer 2010): 385–409.

Al-Shadeedi, A. H., and Nancy Ezzeddine. "Libyan Tribes in the Shadows of War and Peace." Clingendael: Netherlands Institute of International Relations, 2019.

Anderson, Lisa. *The State and Social Transformation in Tunisia and Libya, 1830–1980*. Princeton, NJ: Princeton University Press, 1986.

Ayubi, Nazih. *Over-stating the Arab State: Politics and Society in the Middle East*. London: I. B. Tauris, 1995.

Batatu, Hanna. *The Old Social Classes and the Revolutionary Movement in Iraq*. London: Saqi Books, 2004.

Bates, Robert H. "State Failure." *Annual Review of Political Science* 11 (June 2008): 2–12.

Bellin, Eva. "Reconsidering the Robustness of Authoritarianism in the Middle East: Lessons from the Arab Spring." *Comparative Politics* 44, no. 2 (January 2012): 127–49.

Bellin, Eva. "The Robustness of Authoritarianism in the Middle East: Exceptionalism in Comparative Perspective." *Comparative Politics* 36, no. 2 (January 2004): 139–57.

Börzel, Tanja A., and Thomas Risse. "Background Paper Elaborating the State of the Art—EU-LISTCO's Conceptual Framework." EU-LISTCO Working Paper no. 1 (September 2018).

Börzel, Tanja A., and Thomas Risse. *Effective Governance under Anarchy: Institutions, Legitimacy, and Social Trust in Areas of Limited Statehood.* New York: Cambridge University Press, 2021.

Burrows, Robert. "State-Building and Political Construction in the Yemen Arab Republic, 1962–1977." In *Ideology and Power in the Middle East*, edited by Peter J. Chelkowski and Robert J. Pranger, 210–38. Durham, NC: Duke University Press, 1988.

Cammett, Melani, Ishac Diwan, Alan Richards, and John Waterbury. *A Political Economy of the Middle East.* 4th ed. New York: Routledge, 2015.

Challand, Benoit, and Joshua Rogers. "The Political Economy of Local Governance in Yemen: Past and Present." *Contemporary Arab Affairs* 13, no. 4 (December 2020): 45–69.

Cheng, Christine. "Private and Public Interests: Informal Actors, Informal Influence, and Economic Order after War." In *Political Economy of Statebuilding: Power after Peace*, edited by Mats Berdal and Dominik Zaum, 63–78. Abingdon, UK: Routledge, 2012.

Corstange, Daniel. *The Price of a Vote in the Middle East: Clientelism and Communal Politics in Lebanon and Yemen.* New York: Cambridge University Press, 2017.

Crystal, Jill. "Tribes and Patronage Networks in Qatar." In *Tribes and States in a Changing Middle East*, edited by Uzi Rabi. New York: Oxford University Press, 2016.

De Juan, Alexander, and André Bank. "The Ba'athist Blackout? Selective Goods Provision and Political Violence in the Syrian Civil War." *Journal of Peace Research* 52, no. 1 (January 2015): 91–104.

Donati, Caroline. "The Economics of Authoritarian Upgrading in Syria: Liberalization and the Reconfiguration of Economic Networks." In *Middle East Authoritarianisms: Governance, Contestation, and Regime Resilience in Syria and Iran*, edited by Steven Heydemann and Reinoud Leenders, 35–60. Stanford: Stanford University Press, 2013.

Dresch, Paul. *A History of Modern Yemen.* New York: Cambridge University Press, 2000.

El-Haddad, Amirah, and May Mokhtar Gadallah. "The Informalization of the Egyptian Economy (1998–2012): A Driver of Growing Wage Inequality." *Applied Economics* 53, no. 1 (2020): 115–44.

Erikson, Stein Sundstol. "'State Failure' in Theory and Practice: The Idea of the State and the Contradictions of State Formation." *Review of International Studies* 37 (January 2011): 229–47.

Gallien, Max. "Informal Institutions and the Regulation of Smuggling in North Africa." *Perspectives on Politics* 18, no. 2 (June 2020): 492–508.

Gallien, Max, and Florien Weigand. "Channeling Contraband: How States Shape International Smuggling Routes." *Security Studies* 30, no. 1 (2021): 79–106.

Gause, Gregory F. "Beyond Sectarianism: The New Middle East Cold War." Brookings Doha Center Analysis Paper 11. Doha, Qatar: Brookings Institution Doha Center, 2014.

Gengler, Justin. *Group Conflict and Political Mobilization in Bahrain and the Arab Gulf*. Bloomington: Indiana University Press, 2015.

Grief, Avner. *Institutions and the Path to the Modern Economy: Lessons from Medieval Trade*. New York: Cambridge University Press, 2006.

Hertog, Steffen. "Defying the Resource Curse: Explaining Successful State-Owned Enterprises in Rentier States." *World Politics* 62, no. 2 (April 2010): 261–301.

Hertog, Steffen. "Segmented Market Economies in the Arab World: The Political Economy of Insider–Outsider Divisions." *Socio-Economic Review* (July 2020): 1211–47.

Heydemann, Steven. "Beyond Fragility: Syria and the Challenges of Reconstruction in Fierce States." Washington, DC: Brookings Institution, 2018.

Heydemann, Steven, ed. *Networks of Privilege in the Middle East: The Politics of Economic Reform Revisited*. New York: Palgrave, 2004.

Heydemann, Steven. "Social Pacts and the Persistence of Authoritarianism in the Middle East." In *Debating Arab Authoritarianism: Dynamics and Durability in Non-Democratic Regimes*, edited by Oliver Schlumberger, 21–38. Stanford: Stanford University Press, 2007.

Hibou, Beatrice, ed. *Privatizing the State*. New York: Columbia University Press, 2004.

Hinnebusch, Raymond A. *Authoritarian Power and State Formation in Ba`thist Syria: Army, Party, and Peasant*. Boulder, CO: Westview Press, 1990.

Hinnebusch, Raymond A. "Change and Continuity after the Arab Uprising: The Consequences of State Formation in Arab North African States." *British Journal of Middle Eastern Studies* 42, no. 1 (January 2015): 12–30.

Hinnebusch, Raymond A. *Peasant and Bureaucracy in Ba`thist Syria: The Political Economy of Development*. Boulder, CO: Westview Press, 1989.

Hudson, Michael. *Arab Politics: The Search for Legitimacy*. New Haven, CT: Yale University Press, 1977.

Ismail, Salwa. *The Rule of Violence: Subjectivity, Memory and Government in Syria*. New York: Cambridge University Press, 2018.

Kamrava, Mehran, ed. *Fragile Politics: Weak States in the Greater Middle East*. New York: Oxford University Press, 2016.

Kamrava, Mehran. *Inside the Arab State*. New York: Oxford University Press, 2018.

Kerr, Malcolm H. *The Arab Cold War: Gamal `Abd Al-Nasir and His Rivals, 1958–1970*. 3rd edition. New York: Oxford University Press, 2004.

Khaddour, Kheder. "The Assad Regime's Hold on the Syrian State." Washington, DC: Carnegie Endowment for International Peace, 2017.

Khalaf, Sulayman N. *Social Change in Syria: Family, Village and Political Party*. New York: Routledge, 2021.

Khan, Mushtaq. "Political Settlements and the Governance of Growth-Enhancing

Institutions." Unpublished paper. London: School of Oriental and African Studies, 2010.
Khatib, Lina, and Lina Sinjab. "Syria's Transactional State: How the Conflict Changed the Syrian State's Exercise of Power." London: Chatham House, 2018.
Kohli, Atul. *State-Directed Development: Political Power and Industrialization in the Global Periphery*. Princeton, NJ: Princeton University Press, 2004.
Krasner, Stephen D. *Sovereignty: Organized Hypocrisy*. Princeton, NJ: Princeton University Press, 1999.
Krasner, Stephen D. "Theories of Development and Areas of Limited Statehood." In *The Oxford Handbook of Governance and Limited Statehood*, edited by Thomas Risse, Tanja A. Börzel, and Anke Draude, 29–47. Oxford: Oxford University Press, 2018.
Lasswell, Harold. *Politics: Who Gets What, When, How*. New York: McGraw-Hill, 1936.
Leenders, Reinoud, and Antonio Giustozzi. "Outsourcing State Violence: The National Defence Force, 'Stateness' and Regime Resilience in the Syrian War." *Mediterranean Politics* 24, no. 2 (October 2019): 157–80.
Mann, Michael. *States, War, and Capitalism*. Oxford: Blackwell, 1988.
Mansour, Renad. "Networks of Power: The Popular Mobilization Forces and the State in Iraq." London: Chatham House, 2021.
Mazur, Kevin. "Networks, Informal Governance, and Ethnic Violence in a Syrian City." *World Politics* 72, no. 3 (July 2020): 481–524.
Mazur, Kevin. *Revolution in Syria: Identity, Networks, and Repression*. New York: Cambridge University Press, 2021.
Mills, Robin, and Fatema Alhashemi. "Resource Regionalism in the Middle East and North Africa: Rich Lands, Neglected People." Brookings Doha Center Analysis Paper No. 20. Doha, Qatar: Brookings Institution, 2018.
North, Douglass C. *Institutions, Institutional Change and Economic Performance*. New York: Cambridge University Press, 1990.
North, Douglass C., John Joseph Wallis, Steven B. Webb, and Barry Weingast, eds. *In the Shadow of Violence: Politics, Economics, and the Problems of Development*. New York: Cambridge University Press, 2013.
Pierret, Thomas. *Religion and State in Syria: The Sunni Ulama from Coup to Revolution*. New York: Cambridge University Press, 2013.
Rabo, Annika. "Anthropological Methods and an Analysis of Memory: Migration, Past and Present in Raqqa Province, Syria." *Middle East Journal of Refugee Studies* 2, no. 1 (2017): 51–72.
Randeria, Shalina. "Cunning States and Unaccountable International Institutions: Legal Plurality, Social Movements and Rights of Local Communities to Common Property Resources." *European Journal of Sociology* 44, no. 1 (April 2003): 27–60.
Rotberg, Robert I., ed. *When States Fail: Causes and Consequences*. Princeton, NJ: Princeton University Press, 2003.
Ruiz de Elvira, Laura, Christoph H. Schwarz, and Irene Weipert-Fenner. *Clientelism and Patronage in the Middle East and North Africa: Networks of Dependency*. London: Routledge, 2018.

Salame, Ghassan, ed. *The Foundations of the Arab State*. Vol. 1. New York: Taylor and Francis, 1987.

Salloukh, Bassel F. "Overlapping Contests and Middle East International Relations: The Return of the Weak Arab State." *PS: Political Science and Politics* 50, no. 3 (July 2017): 660–63.

Sayigh, Yezid. *Owners of the Republic: An Anatomy of Egypt's Military Economy*. Washington, DC: Carnegie Endowment for International Peace, 2019.

Schwedler, Jillian. *Protesting Jordan: Geographies of Power and Dissent*. Stanford: Stanford University Press, 2022.

Strakes, Jason E. "Arab and Non-Arab Tribes as State-Like Entities: Informal Alliances and Conflict Patterns in the Historic and Contemporary Middle East." *Journal of the Middle East and Africa* 2, no. 2 (2011): 235–53.

Svolik, Milan W. *The Politics of Authoritarian Rule*. New York: Cambridge University Press, 2012.

Ugur, Umit Ungor. *Paramilitaries: Mass Violence in the Shadow of the State*. New York: Oxford University Press, 2020.

Van Dam, Nikolaos. *The Struggle for Power in Syria: Politics and Society under Asad and the Ba`th Party*. 4th ed. London: I. B. Tauris, 2011.

Waldner, David. *State Building and Late Development*. Ithaca, NY: Cornell University Press, 1999.

Watkins, Jessica. "Tribes and Tribalism in a Neoliberal Jordan." *LSE Middle East Centre Blog*, August 2018.

Weir, Shelagh. *A Tribal Order: Politics and Law in the Mountains of Yemen*. Austin: University of Texas Press, 2007.

Werenfels, Isabelle. "Obstacles to Privatisation of State-Owned Industries in Algeria: The Political Economy of a Distributive Conflict." *Journal of North African Studies* 7, no. 1 (March 2002): 1–28.

World Bank. *World Bank Group Strategy for Fragility, Conflict, and Violence 2020–2025*. Washington, DC: World Bank, 2020.

World Bank. *World Development Report 2011: Conflict, Security, and Development*. Washington, DC: World Bank, 2011.

Yom, Sean L. "Tribal Politics in Contemporary Jordan: The Case of the Hirak Movement." *Middle East Journal* 68, no. 2 (Spring 2014): 229–47.

TWO

Understanding State Weakness in the Middle East and North Africa

Raymond Hinnebusch

The Problematique: The State Weakness–Regime Resilience Paradox

The paradox of the Middle East is the way seemingly "weak" *states*, which are chronically unstable (vulnerable to coups, revolution, and rebellion) and lack the infrastructural power needed to carry out policy, are combined with the exceptional resilience of authoritarian *regimes*.[1] Yet even though these "fierce" regimes also often enjoy high repressive capacities, they see themselves as insecure and are preoccupied with survival.[2]

Explanations of this weakness-resilience paradox in the Middle East and North Africa (MENA) tend to stress either agency or structure. The former attributes the paradox to ruthless leaders who prioritized preserving the regime over all else—hence overdeveloping security agencies and stunting inclusion of social forces needed to strengthen statehood. Focusing only on regime elites is, however, problematic. If the origin of the problem of governance in MENA is bad leaders, then regime change—getting rid of the "bad" leaders, for example, President Saddam Hussein in Iraq and President Muammar Qaddafi in Libya—ought to have improved rather than worsened the situation. Instead, successor leaders replicated

1. Kamrava, *Fragile Politics*.
2. Ayubi, *Over-stating the Arab State*.

the power-building strategies of their predecessors, which points to the inherited structural situation: the external imposition and continual reinforcement of the deeply flawed state system that came out of what David Fromkin called the "peace to end all peace" after World War I.[3] Yet overstressing this point denies the agency of MENA actors who have clearly affected outcomes.

Indeed, only by exposing the historic *interaction* of structure and agency, the approach of Weberian historical sociology, can we adequately explain outcomes. First, the inherited structure shapes what is possible for agency, foreclosing on some possibilities and making others more likely. Second, agency can nevertheless alter structure, and indeed state builders have a menu of authority-building strategies (as identified by Max Weber) from which to choose. While legal rational authority is expected to deliver superior *state* capacity, charismatic and patrimonial authority has been very effectively deployed in premodern and transitional societies to concentrate *regime* power.[4] Third, the states system (structure) and state (agency) co-constitute each other: even as the global states system constituted the regional states, so these states in their interactions reshaped the regional system over time. Put differently, the historical legacy—both inherited political culture and the external imposition of the states system—constituted the cards dealt; while most MENA state builders were dealt poor hands, how they played their hands made a difference and further set up the hands dealt to their successors.[5] This chapter takes this approach in its historical overview of state trajectories, where first the export of the flawed states system is discussed, followed by an account of the agency of state builders as they interacted with internal and external forces.

Conceptual Approaches to State Formation

Conceptualizing Degrees of Statehood

To study the paradox of durable regimes but weak states, one needs notions of stateness—criteria for judging differences among regional states and change over time. First, the notion of state weakness must be interrogated, qualified, and refined. Christopher Clapham usefully speaks of "degrees of

---

3. Fromkin, *A Peace to End All Peace*.
4. Hobden and Hobson, *Historical Sociology of International Relations*; Mahoney, "Path Dependence in Historical Sociology"; Sørensen, *Changes in Statehood*.
5. Hinnebusch, "Toward a Historical Sociology of State Formation in the Middle East."

statehood," suggesting a continuum. Fully functioning Weberian Westphalian statehood, enjoying both authoritative and autonomous centralized institutions, infrastructural power to implement policy, and recognized sovereignty over its territory, lies at one pole, with failed states at the opposite pole.[6] Most MENA states would be located in the in-between zones of what Thomas Risse terms "limited statehood."[7] Moreover, state capacity has to be disaggregated into its multiple dimensions since states can be "overdeveloped" in some dimensions, such as coercion, and "underdeveloped" in others, such as fostering economic development—what Steven Heydemann refers to as "asymmetric statehood."

Further, typical of middle cases would be "hybrid governance" in which rational-legal Weberian bureaucracy overlaps with traditional informal authority, as in *neopatrimonialism*. This hybrid system may facilitate despotic (regime) power concentration, at least in the short term, but may leave a deficit of statehood, "infrastructural power" in Michael Mann's terminology, such that states have precarious control over their peripheries and cannot deliver much development or services or defend their security without sovereignty-compromising dependence on a great power patron.[8] In this scenario, state institutions typically have limited autonomy, being "colonized" to some degree by the ruling family, powerful indigenous social forces (e.g., crony capitalists), or even foreign states.

At the *failed* states end of the spectrum, this problem goes much further. The collapse of infrastructural power and the state's monopoly of legitimate violence leave "un-governed spaces" filled by rebel governance characterized by heterarchy—overlapping jurisdictions between the withered regime, non-state actors, and external powers.[9] In extreme cases, the regime center dissolves, possibly leaving a near-total anarchy (as may be the case in Libya).

Historical Sociology Approaches to Understanding State Building

We cannot explain degrees of statehood without a theory of how states (and regimes) get constructed—and deconstructed. A starting point is Mann's identification of the two dimensions of state power: despotic power

---

6. Clapham, "Degrees of Statehood."
7. Risse, ed., *Governance without a State?* See also Polese and Santini, "Limited Statehood and Its Security Implications."
8. Mann, "Infrastructural Power Revisited."
9. Arjona, *Rebel Governance in Civil War*; Santini, "A New Regional Cold War in the Middle East."

denotes the concentration of power in a centralized ruling elite, a *regime*, while infrastructural power is the ability to penetrate society, control territory, mobilize support, and carry out policy.[10] The *concentration of despotic power equates with regime building and infrastructural power with state building*. Despotic power requires the autonomy of the state's center and its institutions of societal or external interests since colonization by them deprives the state of the capacity to act in some notion of the public interest. Samuel Huntington adds a crucial dimension to infrastructural power: it depends on mass political inclusion and hence entails not just bureaucratic output capacity but also political infrastructure (parties, elections) to input, or incorporate, mass participation.[11] Degrees of despotic and infrastructural power constitute continuums, with actual cases more often located at midpoints, while very high and very low power are present only in extreme cases. As such, the power profile of each state will have quite different and complex combinations of the power dimensions.

A key issue is whether there is a trade-off between despotic power (regime building) and infrastructural power (state building), since power concentration is needed to build countrywide penetrative institutions yet may stunt the mass inclusion in political institutions required by state building. In practice, the dilemma has, Huntington suggests, been overcome by the prioritization of different dimensions in different phases.[12] For him, the first phase is the *concentration* of (despotic) power in a ruling elite—by defeating rival elites. The second phase is the *expansion* of power as central elites mobilize and organize support via political institutions (e.g., a single ruling party), while in the final phase the state is sufficiently established and society sufficiently differentiated that *diffusing power*, through a multiparty system, for example, becomes desirable. Huntington argued that modernization widens political mobilization from the upper class to the middle and finally the lower classes, with regimes faced at each such watershed with the choice of either incorporating the new participants, hence increasing state power, or increasing the repression of opposition, at the possible cost of its mobilization against the regime. While Huntington's first phase equates to regime building and the last to state building, in the second, middle phase, despotic and infrastructural power expand and reinforce each other. The widening of participation is compatible with the centralization of power as, for example, middle classes are mobilized by

---

10. Mann, "The Autonomous Power of the State."
11. Huntington, *Political Order in Changing Societies*.
12. Huntington, *Political Order in Changing Societies*; Saouli, following Elias, in "States and State-Building in the Middle East."

populist regimes against the resistance of traditional oligarchs. But if in the third phase power diffusion is aborted, the contraction of infrastructural power—or at least the inclusionary dimension of it—is likely to follow. Thus, just as power can expand, so also can it contract: intra-elite infighting can fracture despotic power, infrastructural power can wither away, and inclusion can turn into exclusion.

Weber provides an alternative model, drawing on Ibn Khaldun's cycle of authority creation in North Africa, that may be more appropriate for the MENA region, The trajectory begins with the rise of an inclusive movement built on egalitarian ideology under a charismatic leader.[13] After the movement establishes or seizes the state center and concentrates power, charismatic leadership historically followed a cyclical trajectory of "decline" into patrimonial forms. Time-tested patrimonial power-building techniques—clientelism, divide and rule—have historically proven robust and appeared to regime builders as "natural" ways of creating support and constraining opposition in premodern societies, at least in the short term but over the longer term they risk precipitating resistance by the excluded. This cycle of decline can be arrested to the extent that rational bureaucratic infrastructure capable of penetrating the periphery and co-opting social forces is developed. In modernizing societies, this often results not in pure rational-legal statehood but rather in hybrids such as *neopatrimonialism* wherein the bureaucratic dimension serves the aims of the patrimonial leader yet, if developed enough, can constrain the arbitrariness of the ruler's "despotic" power. Yet this pathway may obstruct, even close off, Huntington's third stage of power diffusion.

A glimpse at MENA's historical record reveals that in actually existing states despotic and infrastructural power dimensions have varied together in complex ways. Thus, low despotic power (high intra-elite contestation) and low mass inclusion were typical of the early independence landed oligarchies—combining weak regimes with weak states. Under the authoritarian populist republics that dominated the sixties increasing despotic power was paralleled by an expansion of mass inclusion—resulting (temporarily) in strong regimes that increased state strength. But the two dimensions could also be separated, as in "post-populist" republics that emerged after the 1980s where the maintenance, even increase, of despotic power coexisted with different degrees of infrastructural power in different functional domains. Thus bureaucratic capacity, especially secu-

---

13. Weber, *The Theory of Social and Economic Organization*; Lindholm, *The Islamic Middle East*.

rity services, remained robust even as political inclusion and service delivery shrank; thus, states could be "strong" in certain dimensions in certain time periods and not others.[14] This gave regimes impressive authoritarian resilience through the 1990s and beyond but it also signified the abortion of power expansion through inclusion and popular participation, which, as Huntington predicts, did indeed lead in MENA uprisings to mobilization outside and against state institutions. Regimes proved vulnerable in the uprisings to both the fracturing of despotic power as the ruling elites fell out and, in parallel, the withering of the state center's monopoly of legitimate violence, leaving ungoverned spaces where rebel governance arose. Making the transition to Huntington's last power-building stage, in which legal rational authority is combined with power-diffusing, inclusive political institutions, is a challenge MENA regimes have not yet met, with Turkey perhaps a partial exception.

To understand the reasons why different choices and trajectories prevail in different times and places requires, however, that we go beyond theory and more thoroughly examine the historic record of state-building projects and stateness deficits in MENA. The next section does this by first examining the *structure* that framed the context for regional state builders and then by examining the *agency* of state builders in both periods of state strengthening and of state weakening, thus showing how the interaction of structure and agency shaped state-formation trajectories.

The Structural Origins of MENA's Weak States

The Export of the Westphalian States System and Late Development

State weakness in MENA originates in its historically "late" imposition from without. In the English School narrative, the Westphalian states system was "exported" from the Western core to the periphery in the age of imperialism.[15] The multiethnic Ottoman Empire was destroyed, and the Western imperial powers arbitrarily divided it up as it suited their geopolitical interests, imposing new states—initially territorial "shells" and bureaucratic command posts—and co-opting oligarchic ruling classes. Thereafter, nationalist movements fought for independence, and after decolonization indigenous state builders tried to fill these territorial "shells" with political

---

14. Risse, *Governance without a State*.
15. Bull and Watson, *The Expansion of International Society*.

institutions and national identities. They sought to forge a national identity among their populations since claiming to represent the nation was the key to legitimacy, hence the ability to mobilize populations to fight and pay taxes that were essential to survive in international power struggles.[16] The greater the congruence of national identity with statehood, the more robust the latter was thought likely to be; the less congruence, the greater the levels of internal conflict and irredentism. Thus, the nation-state model, affording legitimacy inside and enhanced power capacity vis-à-vis the outside, could alone defend their newly won sovereignty. National sovereignty required a drive to "catch up" with the core, beginning with Ottoman "defensive modernization" and later exemplified in Mustafa Kemal Ataturk's forging of a Turkish nation-state out of Ottoman ruins. Arab leaders who inherited states in the former Ottoman domains faced the greater obstacle of Western-imposed arbitrary borders but, similarly, sought to forge the nation from above accompanied by Weberian state centralization of power.

However, it was by no means inevitable that Westphalia would effectively take hold outside the West, and indeed the gaps between the ideal and the reality of both Weberian statehood and sovereignty were acknowledged to be wide and particularly marked in MENA for several reasons traceable to its late timing and the arbitrary manner of external imposition.

Identity-Territory Incongruence

Several factors obstructed the importation of the nation-state model in MENA. First, in this arid region of trading cities and nomadic tribes, the strongest identifications attached to substate units—cities, tribe, religious sects—or the larger Islamic *umma*. Islamic empires were built by instrumentalizing both supra- and substate identities while their boundaries fluctuated greatly as they rose and fell, such that identifications with these territorial states (*dawla*) were often tepid.[17]

But equally important, the post–World War I Western imposition of often arbitrary boundaries erected major additional obstacles to the nation-state model by cutting across preexisting identities and frustrating an emergent Arab identity through the fragmentation of the region into multiple ministates. The new state sovereignties coexisted with and contradicted supra-state Arabism and Islam, diminishing loyalty to the indi-

---

16. Smith, "States and Homelands."
17. Weulersse, *Paysans de Syrie et du Proche-Orient*.

vidual states.[18] This incongruence between the new territorial states and preexisting identities was especially marked in the Arab Mashreq where, following the infamous World War I Sykes-Picot Agreement, the dismantling of historic Syria and the invention of Iraq, Jordan, and Lebanon led to a continuing contestation of state legitimacy by competing supra- and substate identities. This identity heterogeneity made it harder to generate consensus around an inclusive national identity within states and kept them vulnerable to insurgency, irredentism, and trans-state interference. Yet it also enabled political agents—regime builders and their opponents—to instrumentalize multiple identities in their power struggles, including *both* nationalism and substate identities such as tribalism and sectarianism, inadvertently keeping alive identities that competed with loyalty to the nation-state.

Core-Periphery Hierarchy and Weak Statehood

European expansion also incorporated MENA into the periphery of the world capitalist system. Local industries and trade routes that provided the economic base of the Ottoman state were undermined or captured, a process deepened under direct colonial rule during which regional economic relations were shattered and reoriented to the core economies. The peripheralization of the MENA economy meant its incorporation into a global division of labor as primary product (agricultural and mineral raw materials) producer and exporter to the core (often of a single product, such as cotton or oil) and dependent on imports of technology and manufactured goods from the core capitalist states. Because raw material terms of trade are poor or take a boom-bust character leading to debt, dependency was continually reproduced. The development of an industrial bourgeoisie was retarded while compradors (large import-export merchants), great landlords, and oil monarchs exported their profits to the core. This kept the area economically underdeveloped, hence politically and militarily weak.[19] Even today, in no region is the absence of NICs (newly industrialized countries) more striking than in MENA.

The arbitrary external imposition of territorial boundaries made for big variations in the resource endowments available to state builders. States with a sufficient territorial mass and population, together with resources such as land, water, and hydrocarbons, were better positioned for sustain-

---

18. Buzan and Gonzales-Palaez, eds., *International Society and the Middle East.*
19. Amin, *The Arab Nation.*

able development: lopsided endowments made for lopsided dependent development. Thus, the concentration in the Gulf of huge hydrocarbon resources in small-population microstates unable to defend themselves against larger neighbors inevitably made for high dependence on the core. Large populations without resource endowments, such as Egypt, faced enduring economic vulnerabilities.

This political economy shaped the kinds of ruling-class coalitions on which regimes were erected and whether their development policies required inclusion or exclusion of social forces (Gramsci's historical bloc), thereby impacting state strength.[20] Thus, as Barrington Moore argued, varying strategies of agricultural modernization shaped regimes: while the move of the landed oligarchies toward capitalist agriculture alienated peasants—making them available for anti-regime mobilization that destabilized the early liberal oligarchies—the inclusion of peasants was crucial to stabilization of the subsequent populist republics.[21] In parallel, reacting against retarded industrialization, interventionist regimes arose and attempted to overcome dependent development via statist "revolution from above."[22] This leveling of the class terrain, together with oil rent, enabled the rise of Bonapartist regimes that, in balancing above and autonomous from any one social class, developed considerable despotic power. These regimes fostered state capitalism, which under neoliberalism morphed into crony capitalist regimes that inflicted austerity on the middle and lower classes, shrinking the regimes' ruling coalitions and withering their infrastructural inclusion. The peripheral political economy, whether reacting against or succumbing to core constraints, shaped the ups and downs of state formation in the region.

Constraints on War as a Road to State Building

Charles Tilly famously showed how war created stronger and more inclusive states in the Western early developers. War making required the development of bureaucracy to collect taxes, which drove demands for representation. Mobilizing populations for war on the basis of nationalism empowered their demands for democratic and social rights.[23] In MENA, the region's fragmentation into multiple states with often-contested borders did lead to regional insecurity. However, many state builders from

---

20. Ayubi, *Over-stating the Arab State*; Bromley, *Rethinking Middle East Politics*.
21. Moore, *The Social Origins of Dictatorship and Democracy*.
22. Trimberger, *Revolution from Above*.
23. Tilly, *Coercion, Capital, and European States, AD 990–1990*.

the beginning enjoyed protection by international patrons that was institutionalized through treaties and military bases to the point that some states, notably in the Arab Gulf, could therefore dispense with reliance on citizen-soldiers. Later, arms transfers substituted for treaty mechanisms. Given high regional conflict, arms access was critical to the security of states, allowing suppliers to use arms as instruments of influence over regional states. As foreign aid to facilitate arms sales and oil revenues increased in MENA in the 1970s, states also had less need for taxation and hence for robust bureaucracy.[24]

While in the West survival of the fittest anarchy allowed the multitude of small political units to be absorbed in the construction of larger stronger states, in the periphery, the Western core powers' periodic interventions in MENA were aimed at preventing an "organization of the region" against them by a dominant regional power.[25] Thus, at the beginning of Western penetration, Muhammed Ali's attempt to create an Egyptian empire was checked by a Western concert of powers; the Western intervention against Iraq replicated 150 years later the unwillingness of the global great powers to permit any local power to challenge their control of the region. In sustaining the multitude of weak states in the region by international guarantees of their borders against absorption by stronger regional powers, the global order deterred wars of expansion in which less viable political units would be absorbed by stronger states.

States therefore remained weak because many were small, populations did not initially strongly identify with them, and ruling elites put in power by Western imperialism or buttressed by Western support lacked legitimacy. This made regimes even more dependent for survival at home on support and resources from core patrons. Indeed, after Iraq's 1991 defeat, Western treaties and bases in Arab Gulf states that had been rolled back in the period of Arab nationalism were restored, amounting to near protectorates typical of the pre-independence period. Thus, what Robert Jackson called quasi-states survived despite lacking robust Weberian statehood within, through support from without.[26] None of this was by accident: the imperial West, far from seeking to export fully sovereign states, aimed to establish a hierarchy in which MENA states inhabited the bottom rungs. They did this by dismantling the existing Ottoman great power and fragmenting the Middle East into a multitude of weak states, which enjoyed merely a semi-sovereignty that would be compatible with

---

24. Chaudhry, *The Price of Wealth*.
25. Lustik, "The Absence of Middle East Great Powers."
26. Jackson, *Quasi States*.

the survival, even after independence, of informal Western empires and hegemonies over the region.

Telescoped Developmental Challenges

Late developers face a telescoping of the challenges of development. For Leonard Binder and Joseph LaPalombara, conditions for political development were optimal when its distinct challenges were solved sequentially, with state building and nation building, for example, preceding the expansion of participation and social distribution.[27] By contrast, in developing countries, the telescoping of these challenges greatly increased stress on the state. This problem was greatly exacerbated by the way the MENA states system was exported—resulting notably in identity-territorial incongruence and economic underdevelopment.

Thus, in early developers, the prior development of a sense of shared nationhood diluted the conflict inherent in the expansion of political participation, but in later developers, participation that was expanded in the absence of hegemonic national identities increased the risks of communal conflict.[28] MENA's multiple identities, both supra- and substate, made the region particularly susceptible to this dynamic. Additionally, in the early developers, the prior development of the economy enabled expanded welfare distribution, but in developing states, regimes were under popular pressure to redistribute at a time when economic modernization had been retarded by the core-periphery system. Hence, a "premature Keynesianism" manifested in the region's "populist social contract," diluted capital accumulation and made the region dependent on rents and aid, and, at a later point, left them highly vulnerable to the global surge of neoliberalism.[29]

Intra-Regional Variations in State Formation

The significant degree to which all MENA states were shaped by the interaction of the above structural factors helps us understand their *similarities*—notably their shared vulnerabilities, such as identity-state incongruence and external dependency. However, differences of *degree* in the common vulnerabilities allow us to pinpoint key variations across the region in state strength (and their causes). In particular, external territorial demarcation

---

27. Binder and LaPalombara, *Crises and Sequences in Political Development*.
28. Rustow, "Transitions to Democracy."
29. Waldner, *State Building and Late Development*.

created sharp variations in both identity congruity and resource endowments, which are the primary shapers of variations in state-building trajectories, indicative of how far the structure inherited from imperialism has outweighed local agency in shaping variations in such trajectories.

First, stronger states emerged where their foundations and boundaries resulted from indigenous agency. States that originated in military expansion, especially over many centuries—as was true of the cores of Middle East empires in Turkey and Iran—had a head start in state formation over those that were part of imperial peripheries, like the Arab states. Particularly in the exceptional case where the state escaped Western imperial takeover, as in Ataturk's successful repulsion of imperial occupation of Anatolia after Ottoman collapse, the state had more agency to defend boundaries that satisfied identity and incorporated the balanced power resources (sufficient land, population, and natural resources) to minimize dependency on the core and allow the state to defend its territorial sovereignty. To a lesser extent, Saudi Arabia also partly fits this scenario, being able to expand despite imperialism rather than being diminished by it. And, even where imperialism does occupy a long-existing state, if it ratifies inherited indigenously forged boundaries , it is less likely to permanently debilitate state strength—hence, Morocco's and Egypt's relative state strength compared to the Levant.

On the other hand, the most *externally weak* states are those with unbalanced resources, notably small territories that make self-defense impossible and huge hydrocarbon resources that make them natural targets of expansive neighboring powers, as in the Arab Gulf. These states are the product of external global powers (Britain) obstructing expansion by larger indigenous state builders—the Ottoman Empire, Saudi Arabia, Iraq, Iran—to protect dependent client regimes that would otherwise have been absorbed, thus eliminating the weaker states and leading to stronger regional powers. These weak states remain dependent on external great powers for survival; hence, they lack much nationalist legitimacy but substitute for it by traditional legitimacy and rentier social contracts that co-opt tribal societies.

States are more likely to be weak *internally* when they are directly the products of imperial engineering, with arbitrary boundaries that frustrate more than satisfy identity, as, to an extent, in Syria. Among the weakest states are those where identity cleavages are institutionalized at the expense of national identity in so-called consociational regimes (Lebanon, post-invasion Iraq). These are the states with the lowest capacity to deliver public goods (relative to their resources); the least able to monopolize violence over their territory; the most penetrated—they are often battlegrounds of rival states; and the most vulnerable to civil war. In spite of this, since they give all communal elites a stake in the status quo, they have proven very durable despite their governance dysfunctionality. Of all the Levant states, Jordan is the most extreme case, lacking sufficient economic capacity within its arbitrarily imperial-assigned boundaries to support itself. Jordan is thus permanently dependent on subsidies and protection from without, which is provided to enable its service to the West as a buffer state between Israel and the Palestinians and the wider Arab world.

State Formation over Time

Agency I: Regime Construction and State Strengthening (1960–90)

The "original sins" of a flawed state system were major incentives for the state building that peaked in the 1970s and 1980s. State builders were not without agency and, indeed, had certain advantages: as late state builders they could imitate not only early Western state-building strategies but also the practices designed to promote a speedy catch-up by other late developers, such as the communist model of industrialization pioneered by the USSR that was widely imitated in the populist republics. Late developers can also take advantage of technology transfers (political and economic) from the core to compensate for telescoping developmental challenges. These allowed regimes and states to seemingly strengthen over time. But these solutions turned out to have their own negative side effects that made them unsustainable and paved the way for a return to weaker statehood after 1990, and particularly after 2010. As such, state formation in MENA has followed a bell-shaped curve.

Early formal independence (1945–56) was inevitably a period of state weakness and semi-sovereignty, in terms of both external dependence and internal territorial control. Internally, semi-feudal landed classes or tribal formations created or reinforced under imperialism—ruling as liberal oligarchies or monarchies and reproducing peasant impoverishment and global dependency—were, in most cases, too narrowly based to survive the politicization of the middle and subordinate classes. Their regimes were also highly permeable to trans-state and international penetration, with external interference in their politics the norm and irredentist projects to reconstitute state boundaries in the name of supra-state identities (Pan-Arabism, Pan-Syrianism, Pan-Islam) widespread. Thus, in the era of Pan-

Arab revolution in the 1950s and 1960s, many oligarchic and monarchic regimes were overthrown, initially replaced by equally unstable military regimes subject to "praetorianism"—coups and riots, for example. In time, however, two kinds of regime proved able to advance state formation: the populist authoritarian republics (PA) and the traditional rentier monarchies. This narrative mostly applies to the Arab states, with non-Arab Turkey, in particular, on a different trajectory, as noted above.

Populist Authoritarian Republics (PAs): These regimes tended to come to power in settled class societies with large cities and peasantries that experienced considerable nationalist mobilization and struggle, owing either to a particularly damaging impact of imperialism (Syria, Iraq, Algeria) or to longer length and intensity of imperial colonization (Algeria, Egypt, Tunisia). In the anomalies (Yemen, Libya) where republics came to power in tribal societies, the regimes would prove more fragile and have to make greater use of traditional practices such as tribal *asabiyya*.

The emergence of the PAs was, in the first place, an outcome of revolutions against the oligarchic order that brought to power broader-based movements recruited from the middle class and peasantry. Under the new regimes, revolution from above involved land reform, nationalizations of the heights of the economy, and state-led import substitution industrialization (ISI) that was meant to break foreign dependency and the power of the old oligarchies, put the levers of the economy in the hands of the new elite, and mobilize popular constituencies.[30] This leveling of threats and constraints from regimes' domestic societal and international environments prepared the way for their stabilization.

However, stabilization also took the deployment of the region's historically proven Khaldunian practices that, fused with imported Weberian political technology, produced durable neopatrimonial hybrid regimes.[31] Thus, typically charismatic, military or ruling party leaders concentrated "despotic power" in "presidential monarchies," relying on appointment to the command posts of the security bureaucracies of "trusted men" (owing to shared tribal, sectarian, or local *asabiyya*). This was combined with co-optation via clientelism of independent or opposition elites. At the same time, the bureaucratic side of neopatrimonialism was expanded such that ministerial bureaucracies, ruling parties, and corporatist institutions penetrated society and co-opted broader social forces, widening the support bases of regimes and producing a measure of infrastructural power that

---

30. Trimberger, *Revolution from Above*.
31. Bacik, *Hybrid Sovereignty in the Arab Middle East*.

enabled PA states to propel economic modernization and more equitable distribution of its benefits. The Leninist-like single party proved particularly effective at both concentrating despotic power and expanding a kind of participation.[32] Thus, the populist version of authoritarianism excluded the old oligarchy while incorporating (through corporatist institutions and populist social contracts that traded political loyalty for welfare entitlements) salaried middle-class, worker, and peasant constituencies.

The prototype of the consolidated PA state was President Gamal Abdel Nasser's Egypt, where a combination of charismatic leadership, bureaucratic expansion, and populist revolution became a widely imitated model for establishing authority in other Arab republics.[33] Egypt had, however, long enjoyed a degree of stateness lacking elsewhere in the Arab world. What was remarkable was that even in notoriously fragmented Syria and Iraq, which had no such tradition, quite similar Ba'thist leader-army-party regimes were consolidated by incorporating, via bureaucratic and party organization, coalitions of broader social forces. Malik Mufti showed how growing stateness was reflected in the extension of infrastructural power, in terms of command over the economy, delivery of state education and increased literacy, investment in physical infrastructure, and creation of large bureaucracies and military forces, measurable by the growing proportion of GDP in state hands.[34] Indeed, it was widely believed in the 1980s that Arab states' durability was down to factors "beyond coercion," such as the development of institutions.[35]

War and war preparation had a role in propelling state bureaucratic expansion, citizen inclusion through conscription, and national identification with the state. Indeed, Arab populist authoritarian regimes legitimated themselves largely through nationalism, which was regularly inflamed by periodic conflicts with external enemies, notably Israel. Wars also propelled the exceptional role for the military in defending the state, particularly in countries bordering non-Arab states. The buildup of military capabilities was manifest in the unprecedented ability of Syria and Iraq to wage war with huge conscript armies prepared to fight for the state against its enemies (most striking was the willingness of Shi'a Iraqi Arabs to fight for Iraq against Shi'a Iranians in the Iran-Iraq War). Yet the nationalist mobilization of citizen-soldiers was diluted in many other MENA states where access to rent and external protection relieved pressure on regimes to trade

---

32. Huntington and Moore, eds., *Authoritarian Politics in Modern Society*.
33. Dekmejian, *Egypt under Nasir*.
34. Mufti, *Sovereign Creations*.
35. Dawisha and Zartman, *Beyond Coercion*.

political rights for urgently needed taxes and conscription, thus diluting war's inclusionary dynamic. And conscription in Syria and Iraq propelled corporatist rather than democratic inclusion.

Traditional Rentier Monarchies: In certain situations, the traditional monarchy also proved an effective road to state formation.[36] The monarchies were, until the mid-1970s, seen as more fragile than the republics, suffering from what Huntington called the "King's Dilemma."[37] These regimes were traditionally based on landed and tribal elites. To survive they had to modernize, but doing so strengthened the forces that could undermine them, notably a new middle class that seemed to reject traditional authority and, with the rise of nationalism, sought to reverse the monarchies' Western alignments. This vulnerability was manifest in the military coups that toppled several monarchies across the region in the 1950s and 1960s—albeit mostly in the settled societies while they survived on the tribal peripheries of the region.

Indeed, monarchies tended to survive only if some of the following conditions held: they were most congruent with small-population tribal societies or ones divided between settled and tribal populations, wherein the monarchy was based on support from tribal elites and the urban middle class was small or was later co-opted via large oil rents accruing to the regime. Their establishment also required external agency and protection, either from a British protectorate established over what was previously a fluid tribal entity (Gulf emirates) or, in the case of Jordan, through the literal carving out of a state in southern Syria for a British client king. Or else the monarchy had indigenous roots but nevertheless acquired Western protection or patronage (Saudi Arabia and Morocco). Finally, it was no accident that of the monarchies that fell, nearly all did so before the height of the oil boom. Once the monarchies were awash with oil, they became nearly immune to overthrow, at least in the many cases where small populations enabled the co-optation of the whole citizenry, while noncitizens were imported to do the manual labor and were easily expelled if they demanded political or socioeconomic rights.

Monarchies also had a certain advantage in generating despotic power where, as in tribal societies, traditional legitimacy remained viable. One monarchy that seemed robust, that of Saudi Arabia, survived owing to the tribal nature of society, its religious legitimacy from the Wahhabi movement, and as the guardian of the Islamic holy cities and the selective strategies of modernization that preserved traditional values, hence authority.

---

36. Anderson, "Absolutism and the Resilience of Monarchy in the Middle East"; Gause, *Oil Monarchies*.

37. Huntington, *Political Order in Changing Societies*.

The regime kept the military small so that it could be significantly staffed by members of the royal family or by loyal tribes such that conscription and middle-class recruitment to the officer corps were minimized. The large ruling family functioned not only as a "ready-made" regime core but also as a kind of surrogate "single party" stretched throughout society. Crucial, however, was the growing oil wealth that, particularly after the 1970s oil boom, allowed groups that had hitherto seemed susceptible to Arab nationalism—the new middle class and oil industry workers—to be co-opted by jobs and material entitlements. Western alignment also turned out to be a plus for monarchies that were perceived to enjoy British or US protection against revolutionary forces.

It is worth comparing Saudi durability to that of the Shah's monarchy in Iran, where amassing oil wealth, rather than immunizing the monarchy, increased its vulnerability. Indeed, Iran was a classic case of the King's Dilemma, where royal modernization helped create the forces and conditions that brought the monarchy down. In Iran, oil led to massive social mobilization—urbanization, expansion of education—and raised expectations that could not be met because of Iran's very large population and the disproportionate allocation of the benefits of oil rent to regime crony capitalists. The political system provided no effective channel of political inclusion for the mobilizing middle and lower classes. Further, the monarchy enjoyed little legitimacy: Having alienated the clergy via its Westernizing form of modernization that marginalized religion, the Shah lacked the religious legitimacy claimed by the rest of the region's monarchies. He also lacked the main regional alternative, nationalist legitimacy, because, having been put into power by a Western-backed coup against the popular prime minister, Muhammed Mossadeq, who had nationalized Iran's oil, the Shah was seen as a Western puppet by many Iranians. Indeed, the Shah spent large amounts of oil income on expensive Western arms and positioned Iran to act as a Western "gendarme" in the Gulf. The Iranian experience exemplified how many of the same factors that led to increased regime resilience in the Saudi case—big oil revenues, Western alignment—could, where there was a legitimacy deficit and a large, mobilized population, produce increased vulnerability.

Even where monarchic *regimes* showed resilience, monarchy was, unlike in the republics, accompanied by continuing *state* weakness. Indeed, rent (whether from oil or aid) debilitated the tax collection capacity, thus the bureaucratic muscle, of the state.[38] And, in enabling the co-optation of populations via material benefits, rent retarded their incorporation through

---

38. Chaudry, *The Price of Wealth*.

political institutions, except to a degree in Morocco, Jordan (which had less rent), and Kuwait. Many economies were highly tertiary and reliant on expatriate labor, thus debilitating the work ethic among citizens and exporting much of their capital to the West rather than investing it in their tiny domestic markets or in the region. Thus, the economic basis of national power (industry, skilled labor forces) was undeveloped. Not being able to defend themselves—because many states were deliberately created too small by the British and most distrusted their own populations too much to establish conscripted standing armies—they could not dispense with Western protection; hence, their sovereignty was limited outside as well as inside.

Enabling Structural Conditions of State Formation

In addition to the agency of state builders, the stabilization of the Arab state in the 1970s was, according to Oliver Schlumberger, due to an emerging relative congruence with its environment.[39] First, the global context of bipolarity was favorable. There was a certain diffusion of power to the periphery as nationalist movements took power across the Middle East and took advantage of great power rivalries to gain, for a period, greater sovereignty. The countervailing powers of the two superpowers made Western military intervention more difficult and created survival space for anti-imperialist nationalist regimes. Three decades of rising state formation in MENA coincided with the rivalry of the two Cold War blocs that empowered the state building of their respective clients—the West backing the monarchies, the USSR the populist republics. The Soviet Union encouraged the spread of new political technologies, notably the single mass political party, that enabled authoritarian regime builders to narrow contestation at the elite level while widening mass inclusion.[40] As the superpowers competed for clients in the Third World, Eastern Bloc technology, aid, and markets were made available at concessionary terms to the republics. Despite East-West rivalries, there was a certain global convergence in governance formulas between communism in the East and social democracy, or Keynesian "mixed economies," in the West that legitimized the developmental state as the solution to Third World modernization. This encouraged statist populist forms of state building in MENA republics, although it put the monarchies at an initial disadvantage.

---

39. Schlumberger, "Political Regimes of the Middle East and North Africa."
40. Huntington and Moore, *Authoritarian Politics in Modern Society*.

A second stabilizing factor was an increasing convergence, in both republics and monarchies, toward similar neopatrimonial practices that were congruent with the region's transitional societies and rentier economies. On the one hand, personalism and clientelism were congruent with the traditional patriarchal family, especially strong in tribal societies. At the same time, the region's explosion of hydrocarbon rents from the 1970s not only enabled populist distribution strategies and bureaucratic expansion that incorporated social forces into state institutions but also filled the treasuries of regimes with enormous patronage resources that across the region lubricated co-optation of local elites and businessmen via clientelist networks, thereby giving extra shelf life to premodern Khaldunian practices. Rentier economies made states independent of societal support, in varying degrees, and by clientelizing and demobilizing publics they diluted class conflicts. Paradoxically, however, while rent helped enable *regime* consolidation where it absolved states of the need to extract taxation or enforce conscription, it reduced the incentive to develop the infrastructural power that made for strong *states*.

Built-in Flaws: Sources of State Weakening

Several vulnerabilities were built into these state-building projects that would, unless overcome, enervate state strength and potentially limit regime durability.[41] First, reliance on "insider" elite *asabiyya* (based on tribalism and sectarianism) to concentrate "despotic" power tended to alienate "outsiders"—other identity groups. The extent to which outsiders could be co-opted depended on the availability of rents, which proved quite variable. In the populist regimes, revolution was partly institutionalized in single-party systems, but when ideology declined, leaders substituted elite *asabiyya* and clientelism to control state institutions, narrowing participation to cronies and clients. Thus, neopatrimonial practices, while initially strengthening *regimes*, deterred sufficient institutional development to sustain the strengthening of *states*. Such was the power of substate and supra-state identities that state builders could not avoid instrumentalizing them—as *asabiyya* or clientele networks—but this had the effect of sustaining identities that competed with identification with the state. Patrimonalized states were "fierce," as Nazih Ayubi put it, in their intolerance of opposition and high repressive capabilities but had much less of the infrastructural power needed to implement effective policies, especially to

---

41. Saouli, "States and State-Building in the Middle East."

foster economic development.[42] Over the long term, the more mobilized societies that accompany socioeconomic modernization could not be effectively governed without corresponding political modernization.[43] Specifically, patrimonial tendencies had to be counteracted by the development of the mass-incorporating institutional side of the state, which, however, tended to lag behind the former, in part because socioeconomic substitutes for participation were for a time exceptionally available, especially in the oil monarchies.

Second, state-led modernization in time exhausted itself, particularly in the oil-poor republics due to insufficient capital accumulation and investment. While attacks on private property (nationalizations) alienated private capital, the public sector did not become a substitute engine of capital accumulation. Populist regimes sought to maximize their support by distributing the benefits widely, compatible with political inclusion, but this "precocious Keynesianism" sacrificed savings and investment to consumption, while population growth exceeded employment opportunities.[44] Only if the PA regime was able to foster a "national capitalist" class as a partner with the state and extract an investment surplus from society (as in Turkey) was it able to make a breakthrough from early ISI toward the next stage of capital deepening and industrial exports. While these vulnerabilities could be temporarily managed, notably when oil rents were high, in periods of declining oil prices, regimes in large-population states encountered fiscal crises. The oil-rich monarchies (with small citizen populations) did not face the same dilemma between capital accumulation and distribution or co-optation.

Third, the republics, specifically, suffered from the fact that their main bases of legitimacy—nationalism, anti-imperialism, and anti-Zionism—embroiled them in protracted and economically costly regional conflicts. While successful wars consolidate legitimacy, allowing moves toward the democratic diffusion of power, the region's history of lost wars tended to delegitimize regimes and disincentivize power diffusion; the exception was where states emerged victorious from wars of national liberation (Turkey under Ataturk and, to a lesser extent, Algeria). Such wars of independence aside, the region's many lost wars are almost entirely accounted for by the presence of Israel, a state with "strategic depth" outside the region that no Arab state can match. Thus, a key basis of state strength in the core—nationalist mobilization forged in war—was much more tenuous

---

42. Bill and Springborg, *Politics in the Middle East*.
43. Bank and Richter, "Neo-Patrimonialism in the Middle East."
44. Waterbury, *The Egypt of Nasser and Sadat*.

in MENA. Not only that, but nationalist regimes' hostility to Israel and imperialism attracted the animosity of the US hegemon; while Soviet protection sheltered them to some degree, they were left exposed after the end of bipolarity.

Agency II: From State Weakening to Deconstruction (1990–2020)

Just as state building was an outcome of agency within certain enabling structural conditions, so also was state weakening an outcome of agency—attempts by state leaders to adapt to a much more hostile global environment.

Global Drivers of State Weakening: While under bipolarity global dynamics had been favorable to state formation in MENA, the fall of communism and the rise of US hegemony, combined with the globalization of Anglo-American finance capital and the neoliberal revolution, made for largely unfavorable conditions, albeit unevenly between the republics and monarchies.

At the global level, the Westphalian sovereignty that MENA regimes had struggled to actualize was becoming obsolete. Globalization fostered structures of governance "above" states, notably international financial institutions, to which they ceded parts of their sovereignty, with a disproportionate impact on periphery states.[45] Thus, Ian Clark argues that in this period the core sought to *reverse* the diffusion of power to the periphery resulting from decolonization and the Cold War and to reconstitute periphery states as merely semi-sovereign.[46] For neo-Gramscians, such as Richard Cox and Stephen Gill, this process aimed to turn periphery states into transmission belts of neoliberalism that enforced global capitalist discipline on periphery societies.[47] This provoked resistance among the victims of globalization, thereby catching states in a pincer movement from above and below—in Barber's words, between "McWorld" and "Jihad"—simultaneously weakening their sovereignty without and within.[48]

The Internal Reconstitution of States: Toward Post-Populist Authoritarianism (1990–2010): While the global order under bipolarity had enabled more inclusionary forms of authoritarianism, it now incentivized exclusionary authoritarianism needed to make regional states transmis-

---

45. Friedrichs, "The Meaning of New Medievalism."
46. Clark, "Another Double Movement."
47. Cox, "Social Forces, State and World Orders"; Gill, "Globalization, Marketization and Disciplinary Neoliberalism."
48. Barber, *Jihad vs. McWorld*.

sion belts of neoliberalism. A number of factors made MENA states vulnerable to this process. The failure of capital accumulation in the public sectors of the populist republics demonstrated the exhaustion of populist statism, forcing most MENA states to enter a post-populist phase of reintegration into the world capitalist economy (*infitah*). While the oil price boom had provided extra resources to enable significant infrastructural penetration and service delivery, and an "overdevelopment" of state apparatuses relative to their economic bases, with the oil price bust (around 1986), regimes—unable to rapidly increase domestic extraction—sought to sustain themselves via foreign debt and investment. Debt empowered International Monetary Fund–promoted structural adjustment—austerity for the masses in order to pay off debt—while reliance on foreign and private capital required a capital-friendly investment climate and export competitiveness, hence driving down wages and labor rights. This development strategy required the inclusion of emerging crony capitalists and the exclusion of the old populist constituency in a *post-populist* version of authoritarianism.

This reconstitution of the republican regimes planted the seeds that would provoke the Arab uprisings. Gilbert Aschar sees their weakness in the contradiction between the imported capitalist mode of production and the blockage of growth by crony capitalist rent-seeking patrimonial regimes that failed to invest in productive enterprise, resulting in massive numbers of educated unemployed.[49] R. J. Heyderian argues that a premature economic opening to global competition pushed by international financial institutions and the funneling of speculative foreign direct investment inflows into trade, real estate, services, and short-term ventures led to deindustrialization, thereby retarding the main pathway for increasing the technology and skilled labor needed for upward mobility in the global production chain.[50] In generating mass grievances against inequality, corruption, and the end to social protections, the neoliberal wave cost republican regimes their initial cross-class social bases. This was especially destabilizing when combined in the Arab authoritarian republics with regimes' abandonment of the nationalist stances on which they had initially been legitimized. The victims of neoliberalism withdrew their loyalty from the state and attached it to trans- and substate movements and identities—Islamism, sectarianism, and ethnicity.[51]

Nevertheless, authoritarian states developed survival strategies,

---

49. Aschar, *The People Want*.
50. Heydarian, *How Capitalism Failed the Arab World*.
51. Guazzone and Pioppi, *The Arab State and Neo-Liberal Globalization*.

as exposed in Heydemann's discussion of "authoritarian upgrading" and "networks of privilege" and in Stephen King's discussion of "new authoritarianism."[52] These included fostering of new crony capitalist bases of support and off-loading of state welfare functions to charities that diluted the damaging impact of structural adjustment on populations. Limited political liberalization—allowing opposition parties to compete on an unlevel playing field for parliamentary seats—enhanced regimes' ability to co-opt and to divide and rule the opposition. This was combined with the retooling of corporatist institutions, initially created as instruments of populist inclusion, into enforcers of the mass demobilization needed to impose austerity and labor discipline. Temporarily, *regimes* acquired enhanced resilience even as *states'* public functions and capacities contracted and refocused on protecting rather than diluting socioeconomic inequality. While the grievances thus fostered provided the conditions for periodic protest, which after 2010 acquired the momentum to put regimes under exceptional pressure from below, it arguably took simultaneous pressures from the international level to tip a slew of MENA countries into *state* failure.

The International Level II: War, Resistance, and Competitive Intervention: State deconstruction was further enabled by the global, post–Cold War emergence of the United States as a global hegemon, opening the door to the new phenomenon of US-engineered "*regime* change" as it targeted states it saw as resistant to this hegemony. The two decades (1990–2010) of US hegemony over MENA was enabled by the end of the bipolar check on US power projection in MENA and initiated by the 1990 US-Iraq War, which led to Iraq's defeat, a massively increased US military presence in the Gulf, and a decade of sanctions that debilitated the Iraqi state, culminating in the 2003 US invasion. Yet, ultimately, the consequence of two US wars against Iraq was not just *regime* change but also a failed *state*, a power vacuum in which jihadist, armed, non-state movements and sectarian discourses flourished and spilled out across the region. The invasion also unleashed a destabilizing regional power struggle between two axes. On the one hand, the "Resistance Front" grouped Iran with Syria, Lebanese Hezbollah, and Palestinian Hamas, which mobilized to defend the region against the unprecedented US penetration. On the other hand, the post-Saddam shift of Iraq into Iran's orbit alarmed Sunni powers, especially Saudi Arabia and Egypt (together with Jordan and Israel), who looked to the United States for protection and conducted a campaign to stir up trans-

---

52. Heydemann, *Networks of Privilege in the Middle East*; Heydemann, "Upgrading Authoritarianism in the Arab World"; King, *The New Authoritarianism in the Middle East and North Africa*.

state Sunni animosity against what they called a "Shi'a Crescent." Then, as Washington's failure to stabilize Iraq debilitated the declining hegemon's capacity to control events in MENA and led it to retreat to "offshore balancing," the bids of regional powers Turkey, Iran, and Saudi Arabia to fill the power vacuum intensified the regional power struggle, especially after 2010 in the string of failing states following the Arab uprisings. The power vacuum, both regional and within failing states, also drew in other global powers: thus, the Western intervention to overthrow the Qaddafi regime in Libya provoked Russian moves to prevent a similar scenario in Syria, adding an additional layer of global rivalry to the regional power struggle.

The Arab Uprisings: Regime Change and (Degrees of) State Failure (2010–2020): The Arab uprisings starting in 2010 led to *regime* change in Egypt and Tunisia, but it was in Libya, Yemen, and Syria where its consequences for *state deconstruction* were most strongly felt. In Libya, overt Western intervention on the side of insurgents led to the collapse of the state, which a decade later remained splintered. In Yemen, Saudi and Iranian intervention intersected with civil war, leading to near state collapse and still on-going civil war. In Syria, an initially peaceful uprising morphed into violent civil war and a failing state, reversing decades of state formation and making the country the site of a proxy war.

While these civil wars were partly a result of the regimes' violent survival strategies, they would, at least in Libya and Syria, likely have successfully repressed the uprisings were it not for the intervention of hostile global and regional powers funding, arming, and providing safe haven to anti-regime fighters, even bringing their own air power to bear. In each of these states, the intervention of one power provoked competitive interference by others, driving proxy wars that heightened levels of violence and sectarianization parallel to their descent into civil war. Rival regional states, notably Iran, Turkey, and Saudi Arabia, financed the most sectarian actors, while their sectarian media discourses fostered trans-state jihadi culture, which drove much higher and more intractable levels of violent conflict, driving not just regime debilitation but also state deconstruction.

Iconic of states' failure was loss of their monopoly of violence as Weberian hierarchy gave way to an "oligopoly of violence." However, state failure did not mean a lack of all governance or the replacement of formal hierarchy by total anarchy but rather *heterarchy*, in which authority was fragmented among several contending actors, as is well illustrated by the Syrian case. In Syria, as the state's administrative reach contracted from areas lost to opposition forces; as the state failed to provide security, the vacuum was filled by "rebel governance," which established enough local "order" to mute violent anarchy. Sometimes, traditional (tribal or religious) leadership was activated, while in other places elected local councils were run by opposition activists.[53] The localized fighting groups that rose to defend their own areas were often built around trans- and substate ethnic and sectarian identities and generated a security dilemma rendering all less secure, as the distinction between combatants and noncombatants was eroded.[54] Both rebel and surviving regime governance frequently evolved into protection rackets by local warlords and criminal cartels, involving rent seeking and the redistribution of resources upward from the poor to enriched predators. Further reinforcing fragmentation was the fact that rival external funders financed their own clients, frequently against each other. In parallel, the shrinking of the normal economy as the national market disintegrated and internal trade barriers sprang up led to checkpoints controlled by fighters levying taxes on the flow of goods. The government lost control of many of its external borders—allowing the flow of external resources and fighters to and from neighboring countries—which all the fighting sides competed to control.[55]

Even as fragmentation generated a power vacuum, a countervailing tendency was stimulated, also notable in Syria: what might be called *competitive state remaking* in which the stronger actors competing to reestablish state-like order over the country's territory tended to absorb weaker, more localistic actors. In Syria, two exclusivist, militarized, would-be states dominated the competition—the regime rump and the jihadists—that is, those best able to play the Khaldunian cards that succeed in intensive power struggles. President Bashar al-Assad's regime adapted to civil war by adopting a more violent, exclusivist, and decentralized form of neopatrimonialism. The most effective counters to it were the Islamist movements whose charismatic authoritarian leaderships were effective in mobilizing armed activist followers yet exclusionary of all those who did not accept their visions of Islam, the most successful of which was initially the Islamic State.

But undermining these Syrian state–remaking drives were the regular violations of the state's nominal sovereignty by rival outside powers, exemplified in the carving up of Syria into sometimes overlapping spheres of influence among Russia, Iran, Turkey, and the United States, all with their armed client militias and exploiting the identity cleavages between Kurds and Arabs, Sunnis, and Shi'a. The United States, in particular, effectively

---

53. Khalaf, "Governance without Government in Syria."
54. Abboud, *Syria*; Zartman, *Collapsed States*; Kaldor, "Old Wars, Cold Wars, New Wars and the War on Terror"; Posen, "The Security Dilemma and Ethnic Conflict."
55. DelSarto, "Contentious Borders in the Middle East and North Africa."

obstructed both of the main state-remaking contenders, the Assad regime and the Islamic State. Similarly, Libya was caught between rival Turkey/Qatar and Egypt/UAE coalitions backing its two rival governments. Yemen also fell apart into rival centers of power backed by external patrons. In short, the governance vacuum in failing MENA states was filled by a struggle between state remnants, trans- and substate armed movements, and external interference, producing a particularly Hobbesian version of "neomedievalism" in which state sovereignty was contested by violent actors at the international and substate levels.

Nonlinear Trajectories: The Bell-Shaped Curve of MENA State Formation

There has been no progressive approximation of Weberian statehood in MENA. Rather, state building has resembled a bell-shaped curve, advancing from a low point after independence, reaching a high point in the 1980s, and then declining into weaker states and, after 2010, a high incidence of failing statehood. This trajectory comes closer to Ibn Khaldun's cycle than Huntington's phased political development.

The export of the states system from the core constituted a first step in state formation, creating territorial "quasi-states" but also numerous obstacles to the full reproduction of Weberian statehood, including identity incongruence, economic dependency, constraints on expansion through war, and telescoping developmental crises.[56] With independence, state builders saw defensive modernization, the adoption of the Weberian nation-state model, as best able to defend their independence. Postcolonial revolutionary republics sought to include mass constituencies to survive the enmity of old classes and imperialism: the redistribution of property under revolutions from above broke old class dominations, fostered the growth of sizable middle classes and the advancement of Human Development Index indicators, and generated broader bases of support for regimes. Traditional monarchies had to imitate some of the republics' inclusive practices to survive the revolutionary wave, and many possessed the highly favorable resource to population balance to enable this. Yet regimes were only stabilized as state builders effectively mixed Khaldunian power practices (elite *asabiyya*, personalistic charisma, clientelism) that concentrated power in regimes with Weberian bureaucratic practices that advanced

---

56. Jackson, *Quasi States*.

states' infrastructural power. The replication of such neopatrimonial states across the region in both republics and monarchies indicates a shared perception among ruling elites that they had stumbled on an effective state-building model.

Yet these regimes proved vulnerable to decline owing to built-in vulnerabilities—the resentment caused by patrimonial practices, legitimacy deficits from lost wars, and the exhaustion of state-led modernization amid high population growth. All of these vulnerabilities made inclusiveness dependent on resources deriving from favorable structural conditions of the 1960s and 1970s, notably bipolarity and high oil prices. When these conditions gave way during the 1990s and 2000s to global neoliberalism, the resulting declining autonomy of the state—captured by private interests from crony capitalists to ruling families—ushered in post-populist versions of neopatrimonial authoritarianism with narrowing social bases. Thus, overall state formation reached a peak in the mid-1980s and then declined for most MENA states.

However, this state decline was neither uniform nor precipitous. Some of the structural conditions that had enabled state building persisted, albeit in truncated and uneven form, such as periods of high oil prices that continued to enrich some states. The decline of the state was selective: what was mostly lost was inclusiveness, but various control capacities, such as surveillance and the divide and rule techniques of authoritarian upgrading, actually advanced, thus tempering the overall tendency toward decline in infrastructural power. However, the shrinking of inclusion, fostering rising disaffection and opposition, precipitated the Arab uprisings that marked an unprecedented new low in state formation as multiple Arab states suffered regime collapse or partial state failure after 2010. The latter was accompanied by intensified violence, loss of territorial control to insurgents, fragmentation of governance, and penetration by foreign spheres of influence: the very antithesis of Westphalian statehood.

State failure was, of course, not uniform across states and varied considerably. Arab states that inherited historic traditions of statehood congruent with their borders (Egypt, Tunisia) suffered regime change but not state failure. Where, as in Syria, some of the protections from bipolarity were restored by the retreat of US hegemony and the return of Russia to the region, the outcome was partial state failure but not regime change: remarkably, even amid unprecedented near *state* collapse, some authoritarian *regimes* persisted or were reconstituted. Finally, some states avoided both regime collapse and state failure. The non-Arab states, Turkey and Iran, benefited from their head start in state formation as imperial centers. The Gulf Arab oil monarchies enjoyed a combination of enormous oil revenues relative to population, persisting traditional legitimacy, and foreign protection. It was these states that became, after the Arab uprisings, the last standing competitors for regional leadership, intervening to shape outcomes in the now much weakened or failing Arab republics.

BIBLIOGRAPHY

Abboud, Samer. *Syria*. Cambridge, UK: Polity, 2016.
Amin, Samir. *The Arab Nation: Nationalism and Class Struggles*. London: Zed Press, 1978.
Anderson, Lisa. "Absolutism and the Resilience of Monarchy in the Middle East." *Political Science Quarterly* 106, no. 1 (1991): 1–15.
Arjona, Ana. *Rebel Governance in Civil War*. Cambridge: Cambridge University Press, 2015.
Aschar, Gilbert. *The People Want: A Radical Exploration of the Arab Uprising*. London: Saqi Books, 2013.
Ayubi, Nazih. *Over-stating the Arab State: Politics and Society in the Middle East*. London: I. B. Taurus, 1995.
Bacik, Gokhan. *Hybrid Sovereignty in the Arab Middle East: The Cases of Kuwait, Jordan and Iraq*. New York: Palgrave-Macmillan, 2008.
Bank, Andre, and Thomas Richter. "Neo-Patrimonialism in the Middle East: Overview, Critique and Alternative Conceptualization." Paper given at the German Institute of Global and Area Studies, Hamburg, August 23, 2010.
Barber, Benjamin R. *Jihad vs. McWorld*. New York: Times Books, 1995.
Bill, James, and Robert Springborg. *Politics in the Middle East*. New York: HarperCollins, 1994.
Binder, Leonard, and Joseph LaPalombara. *Crises and Sequences in Political Development*. Princeton, NJ: Princeton University Press, 1971.
Bromley, Simon. *Rethinking Middle East Politics*. Oxford: Polity Press, 1994.
Bull, Hedley, and Adam Watson. *The Expansion of International Society*. Oxford: Clarendon Press, 1984.
Buzan, Barry, and Ana Gonzales-Palaez, eds. *International Society and the Middle East: English School Theory at the Regional Level*. New York: Palgrave-Macmillan, 2009.
Chaudhry, Kiren Aziz. *The Price of Wealth*. Ithaca, NY: Cornell University Press, 1997.
Clapham, Christopher. "Degrees of Statehood." *Review of International Studies* 24 (1998): 143–57.
Clark, Ian. "Another Double Movement: The Great Transformation after the Cold War." In *Empires, Systems and States*, edited by M. Cox, T. Dunne, and K. Booth, 237–55. Cambridge: Cambridge University Press, 2001.
Cox, Richard. "Social Forces, State and World Orders." In *Approaches to World Order*, Richard Cox with Timothy Sinclair, 85–123. Cambridge: Cambridge University Press, 1996.
Dawisha, Adeed, and I. William Zartman. *Beyond Coercion: The Durability of the Arab State*. London: Croom-Helm, 1988.

Dekmejian, R. Hrair. *Egypt under Nasir: A Study in Political Dynamics.* Albany: State University of New York Press, 1971.
DelSarto, Raffaella. "Contentious Borders in the Middle East and North Africa: Concepts and Complexities." *International Affairs* 93, no. 4 (2017): 767–87.
Friedrichs, Jörg. "The Meaning of New Medievalism." *European Journal of International Affairs* 7, no. 4 (2001): 475–501.
Fromkin, David. *A Peace to End All Peace: The Fall of the Ottoman Empire and the Creation of the Modern Middle East.* New York: Avon Books, 1989.
Gause, F. Gregory, III. *Oil Monarchies: Domestic and Security Challenges in the Arab Gulf States.* New York: Council on Foreign Relations Press, 1994.
Gill, Stephen. "Globalization, Marketization and Disciplinary Neoliberalism." *Millennium: Journal of International Studies* 24, no. 3 (1995): 399–423.
Guazzone, Laura., and Daniela Pioppi. *The Arab State and Neo-Liberal Globalization: The Restructuring of the State in the Middle East.* Reading, UK: Ithaca Press, 2009.
Heydarian, Richard. J. *How Capitalism Failed the Arab World: The Economic Roots and Precarious Future of the Middle East Uprisings.* London: Zed, 2014.
Heydemann, Steven. *Networks of Privilege in the Middle East: The Politics of Economic Reform Revisited.* New York: Palgrave-Macmillan, 2004.
Heydemann, Steven. "Upgrading Authoritarianism in the Arab World." Analysis Paper No. 13. Washington, DC: Saban Center for Middle East Policy at the Brookings Institution, 2007.
Hobden, Stephen, and John Hobson. *Historical Sociology of International Relations.* Cambridge: Cambridge University Press, 2002.
Hinnebusch, Raymond. "Toward a Historical Sociology of State formation in the Middle East." *Middle East Critique* 19, no. 3 (2010): 201–16.
Huntington, Samuel P. *Political Order in Changing Societies.* New Haven, CT: Yale University Press, 1968.
Huntington, Samuel P., and Clement H. Moore, eds. *Authoritarian Politics in Modern Society: The Dynamics of Established One-Party Systems.* New York: Basic Books, 1970.
Jackson, Robert H. *Quasi States: Sovereignty, International Relations and the Third World.* Cambridge: Cambridge University Press, 1993.
Kaldor, Mary. "Old Wars, Cold Wars, New Wars and the War on Terror." *International Politics* 42 (2005): 491–508.
Kamrava, Mehran. *Fragile Politics, Weak States in the Greater Middle East.* Center for International and Regional Studies, Georgetown School of Foreign Service in Qatar, 2014.
Khalaf, Rana. "Governance without Government in Syria: Civil Society and State Building During Conflict." *Syria Studies* 7, no. 3 (2015): 37–72.
King, Stephen. *The New Authoritarianism in the Middle East and North Africa.* Bloomington: Indiana University Press, 2009.
Lindholm, Charles. *The Islamic Middle East: Tradition and Change.* London: Blackwell, 2002.
Lustik, Ian. "The Absence of Middle East Great Powers: Political 'Backwardness' in Historical Perspective." *International Organization* 51, no. 4 (Autumn 1997): 653–83.
Mahoney, James. "Path Dependence in Historical Sociology." *Theory and Society* 29, no. 4 (2000): 507–48.

Mann, Michael. "The Autonomous Power of the State: Its Origins, Mechanisms and Results." *European Journal of Sociology* 25 (1984): 185–213.
Mann, Michael. "Infrastructural Power Revisited." *Comparative International Development* 43 (2008): 355–65.
Moore, Barrington. *The Social Origins of Dictatorship and Democracy: Lord and Peasant in the Making of the Modern World.* Boston: Beacon, 1966.
Mufti, Malik. *Sovereign Creations: Pan-Arabism and Political Order in Syria and Iraq.* Ithaca, NY: Cornell University Press, 1996.
Polese, Abel, and Ruth Hanau Santini. "Limited Statehood and Its Security Implications on the Fragmentation of Political Order in the Middle East and North Africa." *Small Wars and Insurgencies* 29, no. 3 (2018): 379–90.
Posen, Barry. "The Security Dilemma and Ethnic Conflict." *Survival* 35, no. 1 (Spring 1993).
Risse, Thomas, ed. *Governance without a State? Policies and Politics in Areas of Limited Statehood.* New York: Columbia University Press, 2013.
Rustow, Dankwart. "Transitions to Democracy: Toward a Dynamic Model." *Comparative Politics* 2, no. 3 (1970): 337–63.
Saouli, Adham. "States and State-Building in the Middle East." In *Routledge Handbook of the Middle East States and States System*, edited by Raymond Hinnebusch and Jasmine Gani, 41–45. Abingdon, UK: Routledge, 2020.
Schlumberger, Oliver. "Political Regimes of the Middle East and North Africa." In *Routledge Handbook of the Middle East States and States System*, edited by Raymond Hinnebusch and Jasmine Gani, 51–66. Abingdon, UK: Routledge, 2020.
Smith, Anthony. "States and Homelands: The Social and Geopolitical Implications of National Territory." *Millennium* 10 (Autumn 1981).
Tilly, Charles. *Coercion, Capital, and European States, AD 990–1990.* Cambridge, MA: Blackwell, 1990.
Trimberger, Ellen Kay. *Revolution from Above: Military Bureaucrats and Development in Japan, Turkey, Egypt, and Peru.* New Brunswick, NJ: Transaction, 1978.
Waldner David. *State Building and Late Development.* Ithaca, NY: Cornell University Press, 1999.
Waterbury, John. *The Egypt of Nasser and Sadat: The Political Economy of Two Regimes.* Princeton, NJ: Princeton University Press, 1983.
Weber, Max. *The Theory of Social and Economic Organization.* Englewood Cliffs, NJ: Free Press, 1968.
Weulersse, Jacques. *Paysans de Syrie et du Proche-Orient.* Paris: Gallimard, 1946.
Zartman, I. William, ed. *Collapsed States: The Disintegration and Reconstruction of Legitimate Authority.* Boulder, CO: Lynne Rienner, 1995.

THREE

Rethinking the Postcolonial State in the Middle East

Elite Competition and Negotiation within the Disaggregated Iraqi State

Toby Dodge

In both popular and academic discussions of the politics of the Middle East, the state—its absence, profound weakness, or "capture"—has long been a central topic among the long-suffering populations of the region, among the ruling elite, and between analysts attempting to impose some form of ideational and analytical meaning. However, what is less certain, in the study of the region and in comparative political science more generally, is what this key unit of analysis actually encompasses, the empirical reality it seeks to comprehend.

As long ago as 1968, J. P. Nettl bemoaned the conceptual underdevelopment of state theory, arguing that we should treat the state not as a given but as a variable. However, a decade later, Alfred Stepan was not sure whether the state, under this rubric, would be an independent or dependent variable. It is this debate—whether the state has independent and coherent agency beyond the society it claims to regulate—that still dominates discussions in comparative politics today.[1]

---

1. Nettl, "The State as a Conceptual Variable"; Stepan, *Arguing Comparative Politics*; Brooke, Strauss, and Anderson, "Introduction: Approaches to State Formations."

In addition, the ongoing postcolonial turn in the social sciences has highlighted the negative role that dominant models of comparison, abstracted from ahistorical European examples, play in comparative politics and international relations. Here, the politics of the Global South are negatively juxtaposed against European case studies. The conclusions drawn from such comparisons focus on the barriers and failures that have supposedly stopped states in the Global South from obtaining European levels of coherence and prosperity.[2]

Using the dominant neo-Weberian concept of the state as a point of critical departure, this chapter seeks to develop an understanding of the state that treats it as a dependent variable. It also recognizes the postcolonial critique of Eurocentrism and seeks to avoid it by building a comparative model of the state that is not based upon the negative comparison of the state in the Middle East or wider Global South to an allegedly more coherent or developed European model. The chapter sets out instead to build a universal model of the state that can be applied to the Middle East, to Europe, and across the whole of the Global South. To do this, the chapter disaggregates the different institutions of the state, problematizing what neo-Weberian analysis identifies as barriers between state institutions and personnel and wider society. It also develops a critique of the hybrid state form, arguing that this approach has also failed to escape the negative juxtaposition of the Global South to Europe.

The alternative model of the state, placed at the center of this chapter, is developed by deploying insights from the work of Michael Mann, Bob Jessop, and Pierre Bourdieu. It conceives of the state as composed of a series of competitive fields—bureaucratic, political, coercive, and economic—that have been ideologically reified to give the impression of a coherent, agential whole. The actual coherence that exists between and within these competitive fields is gained through shifting balances of power between competing elites. For Mann, any state coherence is understood to result from the "higher-level crystallization" of elite struggles within its institutions.

In order to examine the explanatory veracity of this approach to both theorizing the Middle Eastern state and explaining its place within society, the chapter takes as a case study Iraq since the seizure of power by the Ba'th Party in 1968. The choice of Iraq allows the chapter to examine a state that has been profoundly transformed three times since 1968: first, when the Ba'th Party seized power; second, in 1990, when the invasion of Kuwait placed Iraq under some of the harshest international sanctions ever

---

2. Chakrabarty, *Provincializing Europe*; Bhambra, *Rethinking Modernity*.

applied; and, finally, after 2003, when a US-led invasion set out to impose a new ruling elite upon the reconstructed institutions of the state. Each of these transformations directly impacted the way the power of the competing elites crystallized in the higher levels of the state's institutions. They also directly influenced the capacity, reach, and coherence of actors within that state and their ability to shape society.

Neo-Weberian Points of Departure

The negative juxtaposition, identified in postcolonial studies, between a European model and the Global South, can easily be detected in the study of the state. Within comparative political science, it is Max Weber's ideal typical definition of the state that remains the most influential. Its influence comes not only from its frequent overt deployment but, more importantly, through the role it plays in providing an often implicit point of comparative departure for categorizing and then judging states that do not possess the cascading institutional hierarchies of administration and control that Weber outlined.[3]

At the core of Weber's understanding are the "servants of the state," who are the "decisive protagonists" of state action and who impose the concept of order, so central to his model.[4] The central leitmotif of those neo-Weberians who deploy his template in comparative politics is the autonomy that a coherent and agential state has gained from society, the state as an independent variable. For Theda Skocpol, as for Weber, this autonomy and agency is vested in its cadre of senior civil servants.[5]

Using this neo-Weberian model, states in the Middle East and the wider Global South are then negatively juxtaposed against this ideal type, to identify what has gone wrong, what they are lacking, or what they have failed to achieve.[6] This search for absence shapes the analytical approach to the Middle Eastern state, irrespective of the political leanings of the analysts involved. Nazih Ayubi, for example, was certainly one of the most insightful Marxist political scientists who worked on the politics of the Middle East. However, for Ayubi, the state in the region was "fierce" but could not be strong because, unlike in Europe, it was not "a natural growth of its own

---

3. Weber, "Politics as a Vocation"; Weber, *Economy and Society*.
4. Weber, "Politics as a Vocation," 79; Anter, *Max Weber's Theory of the Modern State*, 162.
5. Skocpol, "Bringing the State Back In."
6. See Migdal, *State in Society*.

socio-economic history or its own cultural and intellectual tradition."[7] This diagnosis, based on what the Middle East lacked in comparison to Europe, shaped Ayubi's argument that ruling classes in the Middle East could never achieve hegemony and had, instead, to base their rule primarily on violence. Writing more recently, Adham Saouli develops a comparably Eurocentric argument. Saouli negatively compares "late" state formation in the Middle East with the building of earlier European states. European state institutions, in contrast to their Middle Eastern counterparts, could, he argues, "incorporate different social powers."[8] This inability to incorporate social actors in the Middle East, Saouli argues, especially in Iraq, has been because of the lack of social homogeneity.[9]

Whether it is the absence of bourgeois hegemony for Ayubi or the absence of social homogeneity for Saouli, the Middle Eastern state, in both cases, is understood by crucial absences that set it apart from the definitive and positive European model. It is not understood on its own terms or through its own development, history, or capacity.

The empirical distance between Iraq (and so many other states) and the neo-Weberian ideal type has led some analysts to deploy the notion of "hybridity" in seeking to explain states in post-conflict or post-intervention situations.[10] In Iraq, a number of scholars have deployed the notion of hybridity to identify and attempt to transcend the analytical gap between Iraqi realities and neo-Weberian comparative abstractions.[11] However, the notion of hybridity, far from allowing its users to escape a neo-Weberian framework, actually accentuates it by juxtaposing the state in the Middle East against a Western ideal type, once again forcing analysts to look for absences or road blocks that have prevented the teleological development of the states they study toward a Weberian and European ideal.

Disaggregating the State

By deploying the work of Mann, Bourdieu, and Jessop, we can move away from neo-Weberian, Eurocentric, and hybrid understandings of the state in the Middle East. However, in doing this an analytical balance must be

---

7. Ayubi, *Over-stating the Arab State*, 3.
8. Saouli, *The Arab State*, 14.
9. Saouli, *The Arab State*, 108.
10. See, more generally, Jarstad and Belloni, "Introducing Hybrid Peace Governance."
11. See Doyle and Dunning, "Recognizing Fragmented Authority"; Cambanis et al., *Hybrid Actors, Armed Groups and State Fragmentation in the Middle East*.

struck between disaggregating the state, problematizing the autonomy of its civil service, and simply arguing that the state itself does not exist as a valid unit of analysis. At different times and from different theoretical perspectives, both Philip Abrams and Timothy Mitchell have argued that the state is little more than a reification of a set of disparate organizations. Abrams argues from a Marxist perspective that the state is an "essentially imaginative construction," an ideological construct, which "fail[s] to display a unity of practice" or "to function as a more general factor of cohesion."[12] Instead, he encourages social scientists to study the idea of the state. In a similar fashion, Mitchell, from a broadly Foucauldian perspective, rightly disputes the line drawn between state and society. He then argues that we should instead focus on micro-disciplinary practices that work not at a societal level but at a level of "detail," which, he argues, do not constrain individual actions as much as produce them. He concludes that the state should be studied as an "effect of mundane processes."[13]

Even in a state as historically contested as Iraq's, whose institutional position within contemporary society is weak, there is little doubt that it still has a major material presence, with the population heavily dependent upon its service delivery, however weak and inconsistent. To dismiss this mass dependence, and, more importantly, demands from across society for a greater state presence, as an "enormous, mass illusion" opens both Mitchell and, to a lesser extent, Abrams to the charge of idealism.[14] Their conception of the state lacks the historical and sociological grounding that could explain how and when the state became such a central part of the Iraqi people's everyday lives and why, because of this, the expansion and regulation of its activities have become long-running demands in popular political discourse.

The work of Mann may be of help here. Mann understands power to reside in both state and society. Actors in and across both spheres use their power on each other. To capture this dynamic, Mann develops the concept of the polymorphous state, with its shape and form resulting from a continuous, ongoing competition between rivals inside and outside the state. This struggle gives the state its form, with the balance of power between competing groups crystallizing its institutions but leaving it with no unity.[15]

Jessop further develops this approach, arguing that it cannot be the state that pursues development goals or implements policy but sets of state

---

12. Abrams, "Notes on the Difficulty of Studying the State," 76, 79.
13. Mitchell, "Society, Economy and the State Effect," 83, 86, 95.
14. Kalyvas, "The Stateless Theory," 115.
15. Mann, *The Sources of Social Power*, vol. II.

officials, often in competition and working against each other, in different state institutions. For Jessop, echoing Bourdieu's language, the state should be understood as a "strategic field," a competitive set of arenas where elites struggle to obtain dominance over a fractured set of state institutions.[16]

Mann's, Jessop's, and Bourdieu's understanding of the state eliminates the neo-Weberian focus on the autonomy of the state. It then draws attention to the role and agency of senior civil servants, along with other competitors for power, who are understood to be engaged in an intra-elite struggle that ranges across the state-society divide. Instead of autonomous rule enforcers, civil servants become another set of players in the ongoing struggle for power. The state is understood to be continually shaped by struggles across the whole of society.[17] Within this analytical framework, the state's coherence and form come from the balance of power between competing groups within society.[18] Different states are shaped by the different groups competing against each other at any given moment.[19] However, as one group obtains dominion over others, albeit temporarily, the outcome is institutionalized within the state, delivering some degree of coherence and stability.[20]

It is Bourdieu's field theory that adds analytical precision to the conception of the disaggregated state. For Bourdieu, competition within any society takes place in comparatively autonomous fields. Each field is united by the shared logic of the players active in it, the rules of the game.[21] As Bourdieu states: "Each field has its 'fundamental law,' its *nomos*: principle of vision and division."[22] These "principles of vision and division" dictate the terms under which competition takes place in each field and what is being fought over. The players within the fields are trying to amass different forms of capital to use in their struggle for dominance—economic, coercive, and social capital comes from the ability to organize and benefit from networks or group action.[23] People and groups also compete over symbolic capital, the power to determine the analytical units used within any field to construct shared meaning.[24]

---

16. Jessop, *State Power*, 37, 101; Mann, "The Autonomous Power of the State"; Bourdieu and Wacquant, *An Invitation to Reflexive Sociology*.
17. Morton, *Unravelling Gramsci*.
18. Jessop, *State Theory*.
19. Cox, *Production, Power and World Order*.
20. Mann, *The Sources of Social Power*, vol. II.
21. Bourdieu and Wacquant, *An Invitation to Reflexive Sociology*.
22. Bourdieu, *Pascalian Meditations*, 96.
23. Bourdieu, "The Forms of Capital."
24. Bourdieu, *Language and Symbolic Power*.

Following on from his field theory, Bourdieu's conceptualization of the modern state is especially useful for understanding Iraq. In a broadly similar approach to Jessop and Mann, Bourdieu agrees that the state cannot be a coherent actor in and of itself. Instead, the state comprises a number of different fields where actors compete against each other to dominate the state's institutions and to utilize its capital.[25]

The most important fields within the state where competition takes place are identified by Bourdieu as the bureaucratic and the political. Mann, comparably, identifies the ideological, economic, military, and political as the four sources of social power. Bourdieu's bureaucratic field would be the institutionalization of Mann's political power. It is the location of the neo-Weberian "servants of the state." However, for Bourdieu, this field, like all other fields, is created and continues to be shaped by competition over who can enter, claim authority, and control the resources in it.[26]

Bourdieu's political field is where Mann would locate ideological power. It is within the political field that politicians compete to impose their different "principles of vision and division." These may start as "speculative ideas" but gain coherence and influence as they successfully mobilize the population.[27] It is hence within the political field that ideological domination is won and lost.

Mann's two remaining sources of social power, economic and military, are, for Bourdieu, also competed for in separate economic and coercive fields. Coercive capital can be won or lost by those competing in the military field but is not exclusively controlled by those within the state: it is competed over by both those operating within the formal institutions of the state and those outside it in society.[28]

Given that Mann, Jessop, and Bourdieu all understand the state not as a coherent whole but as a disaggregated arena or set of competitive fields, where does any level of coherence or stability come from? For Mann, the state is "polymorphous" because different issue areas and institutions of the state attract different groups and constituencies from across wider society. The balance of power between these different competing groups "crystallizes" in the higher levels of the state's institutions. This crystallization is

---

25. Bourdieu, *On the State Lectures at the College de France, 1989–1992*; Bourdieu and Wacquant, *An Invitation to Reflexive Sociology*.
26. Bourdieu and Wacquant, *An Invitation to Reflexive Sociology*; Bourdieu, "From the King's House to the Reason of State."
27. Bourdieu, "Rethinking the State," 13; Bourdieu, "The Political Field, the Social Science Field and the Journalistic Field," 39.
28. Mann, *Sources of Social Power*, vol. I.

systemic and constraining and must be institutionalized to become stable.[29] It is these crystallizations across the various institutions of a given state that give it its form.

Finally, Bourdieu develops the notion of the field of power to explain elite competition and coordination within the state. The field of power denotes where those players who have become dominant in different fields come together to compete for and negotiate over which forms of capital are to be dominant overall.[30]

The Different Forms of a Disaggregated State: Iraq, 1968–2003

As a case study, this chapter examines the Iraqi state from when the Ba'th Party seized power in 1968 until the aftermath of regime change in 2003. When seeking to understand the state in the Middle East, Iraq offers an empirically diverse example. In a comparable way to states across the region, the Iraqi state greatly expanded its institutional capacity, both bureaucratic and coercive, from 1968 until the mid-1980s. However, like other regional states, this expansion stopped in the mid-1980s, due, in Iraq's case, to the spiraling costs of the Iran-Iraq War (1980–88). Capacity within the state's various fields went into steep decline from 1990 onward, after Saddam Hussein's decision to invade Kuwait placed Iraq under some of the harshest sanctions in diplomatic history. International isolation ended in 2003, with the US-led invasion and then the restructuring of the state. However, the contemporary Iraqi state has been left institutionally weak and plagued by corruption and low levels of popular legitimacy by the political settlement that restructuring was based upon and the waves of violence that swept the country after regime change.

The Creation of a Specifically Ba'thist State: 1968 to the 1980s

The Ba'th Party seized power in a coup d'état in July 1968. The party's economic capital, which then drove its increasing power across all the fields of the state, was dramatically expanded by the nationalization of the Iraq Petroleum Company in 1972 and the OPEC-driven, rapid increases in oil prices in 1973–74. Oil revenue jumped from ID 214 million in 1970 to ID 8.9 billion in 1980.[31] This newfound wealth drove an ambitious land

---

29. Mann, *Sources of Social Power*, vol. II.
30. Bourdieu, *The State Nobility*; Kandil, *The Power Triangle*.
31. Alnasrawi, *The Economy of Iraq*, 10–11, 74, 87.

reform policy that aimed to break any residual power of the old, landed elite in the economic field. It also drove the expansion of a state-dependent private sector, creating a contracting elite, profitably enmeshed in Ba'thist networks of patronage.[32]

With ambition and the resources to fund it, there was a rapid and extended expansion of Iraq's bureaucratic field, with the numbers employed in the civil service increasing from 276,605 in 1968 to 662,856 (20 percent of the population) by 1978. Government spending as a percentage of total GDP also rapidly expanded from 24.2 percent in 1958 to 59.2 percent by 1980.[33] At the same time, Iraq expanded the amount of oil it could export, leaving the government with a foreign exchange surplus of $40 billion by the end of the 1970s.[34]

As the Ba'thist regime set about building a complex and powerful bureaucratic field, they also set out to ensure it was subordinate to the party, with the aspiration of creating a party-state.[35] Senior security and educational posts within state institutions tended to be occupied by party members, while the rest of the civil service, both at a national and at a provincial level, were overseen by a myriad of party committees that monitored the behavior of civil servants and state institutions in an attempt to identify actions that could constrain the party's ability to exercise power.[36]

At the same time that the state was expanding and the Ba'th were seeking to dominate the bureaucratic field, there was a concentration of power within the highest echelons of the party. In the first decade after the seizure of power, the party ceased to become an arena for policy or political discussion.[37] It was during this time that the Revolutionary Command Council (RCC), created after the 1968 coup, became the dominant ruling body.[38] It was the RCC that gave orders to cabinet ministers and senior civil servants. After Saddam Hussein took power in 1979, he made it clear that a cabinet minister's role was limited to making sure that RCC policy was implemented by the civil servants they controlled.[39]

The final stage in this centralization of power was the increasing dominance of the political field by a cult of personality surrounding Saddam Hussein. As Saddam became the "final decision maker on almost every

32. Tripp, *A History of Iraq*.
33. Mufti, *Sovereign Creations*, 201–2.
34. Alnasrawi, *The Economy of Iraq*, 87.
35. Faust, *The Ba'thification of Iraq*.
36. Faust, *The Ba'thification of Iraq*; Sassoon, *Saddam Hussein's Ba'th Party*.
37. Farouk-Sluglett and Sluglett, *Iraq since 1958*.
38. Aburish, *Saddam Hussein*.
39. Sassoon, *Saddam Hussein's Ba'th Party*.

important issue," the Presidential Diwan became the hub for all supporting information.[40] Aaron Faust estimates that by 1986 forty memoranda a day were sent directly to Saddam for his personal decisions, with subject-area advisers employed by the Diwan mirroring the ministerial structure of the state.[41]

However, as the work of Mann, Jessop, and Bourdieu would suggest, as the state's bureaucratic power expanded, there was an ongoing struggle for domination within both the ruling elite and the wider political field. Within the political field, the Ba'th's seizure of power in 1968 triggered a brutal crackdown. However, in 1973, the continued insecurity of the new ruling Ba'thist elite in the political field drove the group around President Hassan al-Bakr and Vice President Saddam Hussein to forge a short-lived, instrumental alliance with the Iraqi Communist Party. The aim was both to outflank rivals for power within the senior ranks of the party and to marginalize those who opposed their nationalization of the Iraq Petroleum Company and ambitious land reform measures.[42]

As the ruling group's capacity grew, the greatest threat to Hassan al-Bakr and later Saddam Hussein came from inside the senior ranks of the party itself, which had been, pre-1968, notoriously fractious. In the first years after the coup, al-Bakr consolidated his own position by outmaneuvering other senior Ba'thists who had rival power bases within the coercive field. Then, once Saddam Hussein seized power from al-Bakr in July 1979, he suppressed a range of other Ba'thist rivals for power.[43] When Saddam took over the pinnacle of power, he set about drastically reducing the size of the ruling elite. After an infamously brutal putsch and then ongoing purges, those who retained their positions were under no illusions that they did so because of their loyalty to one person.[44]

By 1980, Iraq's small ruling elite was more homogeneous than at any time in Iraq's history. However, although it was more powerful than any other Iraqi regime, its domination of the political field was continually challenged. Despite repeated purges, reorganization, and indoctrination, there remained recurrent threats from the coercive field, as opponents unsuccessfully attempted to launch coups from within the officer corps of the Iraqi army.

---

40. Sassoon, *Saddam Hussein's Ba'th Party*.
41. Faust, *The Ba'thification of Iraq*, 78; Sassoon, *Saddam Hussein's Ba'th Party*.
42. Farouk-Sluglett and Sluglett, *Iraq since 1958*.
43. Aburish, *Saddam Hussein: The Politics of Revenge*.
44. Tripp, *A History of Iraq*.

Transformation of the Iraqi State

If the period from 1968 until 1980 marked both the narrowing of the country's ruling elite and its increasing domination over the political, economic, coercive, and bureaucratic fields, the period from the mid-1980s onward saw a dramatic decline in the various forms of capital that the ruling elite had amassed and the transformation of their coercive, political, and institutional domination.

Saddam Hussein's decision to invade Iran in 1980, while it was in the midst of revolutionary turmoil, indicated both the ideological challenge he thought the revolution posed to his rule but also his hope for a quick victory against a divided and incoherent adversary.[45] However, the eight-year conflict transformed the Iraqi state and its relations with society. First, it greatly expanded the coercive field, with an estimated three million men, 25 percent of the population, serving at one time or another during the conflict.[46] The ruling elite hoped to control this hugely expanded force by turning it into *al-jaish al-'aqu'idi* (an ideological army).[47] Since 1968, the senior ranks of the military had been repeatedly purged, with loyal Ba'thists replacing career soldiers. Party cells, led by political commissars, were placed within each army unit.[48] The outcome was to break the officer corps' collective identity as guardians of the nation and remove their capacity for collective action.[49] However, competition within the coercive field still repeatedly produced challenges to Saddam Hussein's rule.

After two years of the costly conflict with Iran, the regime could no longer shield the economic field from the consequences of war.[50] At the end of 1982, the regime announced an austerity program cutting government expenditure across all areas that did not directly impact the war effort.[51] Although attempts at privatization started in 1983, it was not until 1987 that the regime embarked on a major attempt to sell off profitable sectors of the economy previously owned by the state.[52] The regime attempted to fracture areas of potential threat by deliberately pluralizing actors within the economic field, reversing its previous land reform policies and sell-

---

45. Dodge, "Bourdieu Goes to Baghdad."
46. Walter, "The Ba'th Party in Baghdad," 99.
47. Abbas, "The Iraqi Armed Forces, Past and Present."
48. Baram, "The Future of Ba'thist Iraq"; Faust, *The Ba'thification of Iraq*.
49. Makiya, *Republic of Fear*; Dodge, "Cake Walk, Coup or Urban Warfare."
50. Alnasrawi, *The Economy of Iraq*.
51. Walter, "The Ba'th Party in Baghdad."
52. Farouk-Sluglett and Sluglett, *Iraq since 1958*.

ing off land and agribusiness to the private sector.[53] This policy has been criticized for simply selling off state-owned businesses to those close to the ruling elite.[54] However, after twenty years in power, the ruling elite—when faced with the economic constraints of an ongoing conflict—reduced the size and power of the bureaucratic field, while also (through privatization) pluralizing and expanding the actors who were empowered to compete in the economic field in a search for other, nonthreatening sources of economic capital. This trend, the fracturing and weakening of the bureaucratic field, combined with an expansion in the number of competitors in the economic field, quickly accelerated in 1990 to become a dominant feature of Iraq until regime change.

The Consequences of the Invasion of Kuwait and Sanctions

The regime's decision to invade Kuwait in August 1990 was driven by an increasing sense of the threats it faced, both domestically and internationally.[55] However, the UN Security Council's collective response to this flagrant breach of international law was to place Iraq under the most comprehensive sanctions regime in modern diplomatic history. The country was then subject to an extended and devastating campaign of aerial bombardment, and its troops were quickly expelled from Kuwait.[56] In the aftermath of the formal military conflict, the regime faced an extended rebellion, driven in the south by Iraqi soldiers returning from Kuwait and in the north by the opposition forces of the Kurdistan Democratic Party and the Patriotic Union of Kurdistan. At the height of these twin uprisings, the state lost control of the majority of its own territory.

The immediate impact of war and the violent suppression of the uprisings, combined with an economic embargo of thirteen years, triggered a macroeconomic shock of devastating proportions. Iraqi imports dropped from $10.3 billion in 1988 to just $400 million 1991. This was accompanied by a precipitous and sustained fall in wages, dropping by 90 percent in 1990–91 and then by a further 40 percent between 1991 and 1996. The Iraqi dinar fell from 8 to the US dollar in 1991 to 2,950 at the end of 1995. Iraqi analysts in 1996 linked the levels of crime and violence in Baghdad to the fall and rise in the exchange rate of the dinar to the dollar.[57]

---

53. Chaudhry, "Economic Liberalization and the Lineages of the Rentier State."
54. Chaudhry, "On the Way to Market."
55. Gause, "Iraq's Decision to Go to War."
56. Graham-Brown, *Sanctioning Saddam*.
57. Dodge, "The Failure of Sanctions and the Evolution of International Policy Towards

The regime's response to the multifaceted defeat and the ongoing economic embargo accelerated the transformation of the state that began during the eight-year war with Iran. In each of the state's major fields (economic, bureaucratic, coercive, and political) the ruling elite strategically reduced its commitments, empowering other societal players to take over roles it had spent much of the last two decades attempting to dominate.

In the bureaucratic field, the ongoing concentration of power in Saddam Hussein's hands accelerated. Saddam was renowned within Iraq's Ba'thist elite as "an able administrator" within the formal structures of the state, but one with a profound distrust of constitutional structures.[58] After 1990, he further narrowed membership of the ruling elite to only include his closest comrades, the *Ahl al-Thiaqa*, the people of trust—his family, clan members, and long-term associates.[59] As the 1990s went on, the balance of power within the *Ahl al-Thiaqa* further contracted, with Saddam investing much greater power in members of his close family.

The consequences for the bureaucratic field of this switch from formal to informal strategies of rule were far reaching. Both Peter Harling and, especially, Achim Rohde argue that this change in strategy "rendered dysfunctional" the formal and visible institutions of state power, so carefully constructed since 1968.[60] This was exemplified by the government's abolition of the Ministry of Planning in 1994, with its functions taken over by a committee established in the Presidential Diwan.[61]

Civil servants saw their previously generous wages rendered insignificant by the devaluation of the dinar and inflation. This, in turn, led to widespread absenteeism as state workers supplemented wages by working in the informal sector.[62] Finally, petty corruption became commonplace across the civil service and health-care system, as the government encouraged state institutions to engage in various forms of "self-financing."[63]

A similar dramatic transformation occurred in the economic field. As sanctions bit and the government's ability to raise money through oil sales precipitously declined, the role of state institutions in the formal economy

---

Iraq"; Graham-Brown, *Sanctioning Saddam*, 164; Boone, Gazdar, and Hussain, "Sanctions against Iraq," 9, 40; MacFarquhar, "After War and Blockade."

58. Duelfer, *Comprehensive Report of the Special Adviser*, 13, 70.

59. Tripp, *A History of Iraq*; Baran, "Saddam Hussein's armourers."

60. Rohde, *State-Society Relations in Ba'thist Iraq*, 56, 66, 70; Harling, "Beyond Political Ruptures."

61. Rohde, *State-Society Relations in Ba'thist Iraq*.

62. Walter, "The Ba'th Party in Baghdad."

63. Dodge, "The Failure of Sanctions and the Evolution of International Policy towards Iraq," 88.

rapidly shrank. Into this vacuum stepped an array of businesspeople, specializing in imports, currency trading, construction, and the domestic production of food.[64]

The ruling elite's response to the dramatic decline in its ability to shape the economic field went through three stages. In the immediate aftermath of the invasion of Kuwait and the expulsion of Iraqi troops from the country, the regime took to reactive crisis management. Reconstruction was combined with a deliberate policy to encourage an expansion of private actors in the economic field, to replace the role that the state had played, by removing or not enforcing previously draconian regulations.[65] Domestic farmers were encouraged to increase their production through price deregulation. Those involved in the import trade and currency dealers were encouraged to increase their activity.[66] However, by 1994, the regime became more confident about its own survival. The informality that dominated the economic field remained, but key figures within the ruling elite, members of Saddam's family (notably his son and son-in-law, Uday Hussein and Hussein Kamal), started to use coercive power to dominate the most profitable sectors of the field: the sanctions-busting export of oil and import of consumer goods and currency exchange.[67] The final stage was the partial re-empowerment of some state institutions after the regime signed the Oil-for-Food agreement in May 1996, which allowed it to start limited imports and exports under heavy United Nations supervision.

The ramifications of this transformation in the economic field were far reaching: 7 to 9 percent of the population, integrated into the new economic circuits that developed to circumvent sanctions, greatly benefited.[68] Their newfound wealth visibly transformed Baghdad's traditional upper-middle-class neighborhoods, areas like Mansour and Jadriyah, as the new members of the economic elite invested in building ostentatious houses. With the encouragement of the regime, these "fat cats" or "embargo cats" became a focus of much resentment and social tension. However, of greater importance to regime survival was the removal of state-delivered economic support from the regime's previous core constituencies in the western provinces of Anbar, Salahuddin, and Nineveh. Those who made up the bulk of

---

64. Graham-Brown, *Sanctioning Saddam*.
65. Graham-Brown, *Sanctioning Saddam*.
66. Author interview with Sadoun Hammadi, former prime minister of Iraq and speaker of the Majlis al Watani, Baghdad, September 7, 2002.
67. Jones, *Societies under Siege*.
68. Jones, *Societies under Siege*.

the army's officer corps found themselves newly impoverished, thus contributing to a number of unsuccessful coup attempts through the 1990s.[69]

Overall, the regime's response to the massive and extended socioeconomic shock delivered by sanctions can be seen clearly in two of its most visible policy initiatives—the establishment of the rationing system and what was labeled the rise of "neo-tribalism." As the retreat of the state from the economic field began to trigger widespread economic suffering, the regime quickly set up a very successful rationing system that allocated a ration card to every household. Against a background of the deinstitutionalization of the bureaucratic field, the rationing system became one of the most coherent institutions of state power. It allowed the regime to mediate some of the worst social suffering while gathering data on every household and restricting population movement.[70]

Beyond the rationing system, in the face of a rapid and steep reduction in state revenues, the elite also heavily invested in the informal patronage networks that became known as neo-tribalism.[71] In the face of this crisis, they used their resources to fund a society-wide patronage network of between half a million and one million people in a population of over twenty million.[72] They gave this network unfair access to what had previously been state resources and delegated some local coercive enforcement roles to them. In doing so, the regime created a loyal social base that spread across the coercive and economic fields, justified with the reinvented primordial language of tribalism.

Overall, the Ba'thist regime, dominated by Saddam Hussein and his *Ahl al-Thiaqa*, managed to survive the cataclysmic defeat of 1991 and more than a decade of draconian sanctions—in spite of all predications to the contrary. They certainly depended on what Mann labels the "political lag," the partial survival of the institutionalization of previous struggles that they had won in the coercive, economic, and bureaucratic fields of the state between 1968 and the 1980s. However, the thrust of their survival strategy focused on empowering a series of societal actors in different fields. Economically, farmers, traders, and those who controlled transnational transport thrived in a haphazardly deregulated field. Coercively, local notables, designated as "tribal sheikhs," benefited from the decentering of the provi-

---

69. Blaydes, *State of Repression*.
70. Dodge, "The Failure of Sanctions and the Evolution of International Policy towards Iraq." The prime minister in 1991, Sadoun Hammadi, listed the rationing system as one of the regime's greatest achievements of this era. Author interview with Sadoun Hammadi.
71. Baram, "Neo-Tribalism in Iraq."
72. Tripp, *A History of Iraq*, 264; Baram, "Between Impediment and Advantage," 13.

sion of order. Above all else, the continual purging of the elite and its allies, from 1968 onward, in all the fields of the state meant that these elites could only engage in comparatively limited and fragmented competition. The multiplication of actors in the economic and coercive fields was carried out from a point of comparative competitive strength. The mixture of informal networks and institutional power by a narrow and fairly coherent elite meant they retained the competitive advantage in all fields. As the regime's confidence and resources began to grow from the mid-1990s onward, the newly empowered social elites were subjected to increasing levels of violence and state sanction to ensure that the autonomy they gained did not threaten the dominance of Saddam Hussein and his closest allies. The lasting legacy of this strategy was social impoverishment, the deinstitutionalization of the state's education and welfare systems, and, most importantly, the creation of a socioeconomic network tied directly to Saddam Hussein and his family.

The Iraqi State after Regime Change

It was this state that the United States inherited when its invasion forces seized Baghdad in April 2003. The bureaucratic field had been subject to a sustained and strategic deinstitutionalization under the last decade and a half of Ba'thist rule. In the aftermath of the invasion, the occupation authorities—the Coalition Provisional Authority (CPA) under the leadership of Paul Bremer III—sought to transform the state that they had seized. However, along with being largely ignorant about the state and society they were interacting with, CPA policymaking was beset by a series of competing aims and objectives. On the one hand, the CPA was determined to replace what it perceived as an overbearing totalitarian state with a minimal neoliberal one, reconstructed along neo-Weberian lines with autonomous institutions and an independent civil service. On the other hand, the CPA became increasingly dependent on a small group of formerly exiled political parties that wanted to use an informal consociational system to divide the state up between themselves in the name of ethno-sectarian "balance." Finally, as levels of politically motivated violence rose, the imposition of some form of sustainable order in the coercive field to facilitate the exit of US troops became the dominant goal.

These different objectives, especially the tension between US diplomats and the formerly exiled heads of the major parties, were largely mediated through a series of extended negotiations that stretched from 2003 to 2006. These established the new political system and shaped the institutions of the state. The negotiations encompassed the formation of the Governing Council in July 2003, the first post-regime-change cabinet that September, and the drafting of a new constitution in 2005. This period included the formation of two national governments after the first and second national elections of January and December 2005. It was in the first three years after regime change, dominated by these five events, that Iraq's new political system was built. In the language of Mann, it was through these ongoing negotiations (with their conflicts and concessions) that a new polymorphous state was built and a post-invasion balance of forces was institutionalized within the bureaucratic, coercive, and political fields, crystallizing the agreements reached within the higher levels of the state.

Bremer, as head of the CPA from May 2003 to June 2004, was initially dismissive of the leadership of the seven political parties that had become the dominant voice of the Iraqi exiles.[73] However, from the formation of the Governing Council onward, it was these parties that became Iraq's new governing elite, and it was the intense competition between them, in each of the state's fields, that shaped the form of governance after 2003.

In Iraq, the political system dictates that the most intense intra-elite negotiations take place after every national election, which happened twice in 2005, in 2010, 2014, 2018, and 2021. Within the political field, at least until 2014, most of the political parties were united around what Bourdieu would label a *nomos*, a "principle of vision and division." This was formed by a common ideological commitment to *Muhasasa Ta'ifia*, the rough system of informal consociationalism, which uses a sectarian understanding of Iraqi society to justify the division of state power and resources among the ruling elite.[74] This ideological and instrumental agreement facilitated the newly elected parties' dominance over the various fields of the post-2003 state.

On average, this process of painstaking negotiation that results in the formation of governments of national unity takes 203 days, or five months. During this time, the state and, more importantly, its resources are redivided among the parties every four years. The outcome of these negotiations means that the state in and of itself has little or no coherence, with the cabinet functioning as the only formal arena for mediating disputes and attempting to work toward some form of common approach. The major agreements that continue to shape this process were reached in the after-

---

73. The seven key parties were the Kurdistan Democratic Party, the Patriotic Union of Kurdistan, the Iraqi National Congress, Iraqi National Accord, the Supreme Council for the Islamic Revolution in Iraq, the Islamic Dawa Party, and the Iraqi Islamic Party.
74. See Dodge, "Iraq's Informal Consociationalism and Its Problems."

math of the January 2005 elections. The first was to divide the three most senior offices of state—the presidency, the premiership, and the speaker of parliament—between parties that claimed to represent Iraq's three major ethno-sectarian communities. The Islamist Shi'a parties claimed the office of prime minister on the basis that they claimed to represent Iraq's largest ethno-sectarian community. The two parties that claimed to speak for the Kurds—the Kurdistan Democratic Party and the Patriotic Union of Kurdistan—took the presidency, with the disparate forces rallying the Sunni vote being allocated the office of parliamentary speaker.

Of far greater importance was the second agreement reached after the 2005 elections: to divide all government ministries among the numerous parties that competed for and won substantial numbers of seats in national elections, again in the name of ethno-sectarian "balance." This informal consociationalism allows these parties to utilize the budgets and payrolls of the ministries they are awarded, through contract and employment fraud, to fund their political activities.[75]

It is these largely informal agreements, among Iraq's newly empowered governing elite, that mediated their competition and collaboration. They have had a profound impact on the state's bureaucratic field. This process started with the US-led coalition's implementation of aggressive de-Ba'thification in May 2003. This removed anyone who had been in the top four levels of the party from government service as well as forbade anyone who had been a party member from occupying the three most senior levels of the civil service. The implementation of the policy removed 41,324 civil servants, out of a total of between 850,000 and one million, in the first month of its operation. This created the space for the new ruling elite to place their members in the senior ranks of every state institution.[76]

From 2006, in the aftermath of the second set of national elections, the appointment of senior civil servants was brought into the *Muhasasa* system, thus delivering control of the bureaucratic field to the dominant party leaders while also regulating their competition. The number of these politically negotiated senior civil service appointments across the Iraqi state grew from 2,962 in 2006 to 5,308 in 2019. It is estimated that while in office, from 2006 to 2014, Prime Minister Nuri al-Maliki was responsible for the appointment of 35 percent of the total.[77]

---

75. Dodge and Mansour, "Politically Sanctioned Corruption and Barriers to Reform in Iraq."
76. Dodge, "Beyond Structure and Agency," 108–22; Sissons and Al-Saiedi, "A Bitter Legacy."
77. Khalifa, "Opening the Windows."

Maliki, when prime minister, attempted to use his power over civil service appointments to circumvent the *Muhasasa Ta'ifia* system and the divided cabinet it created.[78] In an attempt to increase his own power, bolster the coherence of the government, and reduce his reliance on the other political parties, Maliki appointed a number of powerful proxies or "*wakils*" in the senior ranks of the civil service across a number of ministries.[79] This creation of a network of loyal functionaries at the top of ministries centralized a degree of power in his own hands.[80]

Far from being comparable to a neo-Weberian ideal type, the bureaucratic field of the Iraqi state, post-2003, more accurately resembles the model of a competitive field described in Bourdieu's work. The distinction between state and society and the autonomy of state institutions and personnel, so central to Weberian definitions, is nonexistent in post-regime-change Iraq. Instead, the dominant political parties divide not only the appointment of government ministers between themselves during post-election government negotiations but also the appointment of senior civil servants. This disaggregates the institutions and resources of the state, reflecting the balance of power at the moment of each postelection set of negotiations. This system also deliberately removes any room for independent action or agential coherence for most senior civil servants. They gain their positions at the top of state institutions because of their loyalty to a specific party and then work to deliver state resources to that party.[81]

A similar but less regulated competition can be detected in the coercive field. The struggle to dominate Iraq's coercive field was accelerated in the aftermath of regime change by Bremer's decision to disband the Iraqi army in May 2003, making 400,000 soldiers unemployed.[82] By February 2004, in the face of a growing insurgency, the US occupation sought to rectify its own initial mistake in two ways. First, and conventionally, it sought to accelerate and expand its program for rebuilding the Iraqi armed forces, investing $5.7 billion in a plan to train 270,000 Iraqi troops and paramilitary police units.[83] As Iraq's armed forces were rapidly rebuilt, the dominant political parties competed to insert so-called *dimaj* officers into the senior

---

78. Dodge and Mansour, "Politically Sanctioned Corruption and Barriers to Reform in Iraq."
79. Confidential author interview with senior Dawa Party official, Baghdad, February 4, 2020.
80. Dodge, *Iraq*.
81. Dodge and Mansour, "Politically Sanctioned Corruption and Barriers to Reform in Iraq."
82. Dodge, *Iraq*, 37–38.
83. Dodge, *Iraq*, 117.

ranks of the military.[84] These political appointments were senior personnel from party-affiliated militias. As such, in a comparable way to the senior civil servants inserted into government ministries, the *dimaj* officers owed their allegiance to the dominant political parties that positioned them within the chain of military command.[85] Such placements undermined the barriers between the army and societal actors or any independence within the chain of command.

The second way the United States sought to rapidly reestablish the capacity of Iraqi security forces was through the wholesale integration of members of the Badr Brigades—the Shiʻa Islamist militia that had recently returned to the country from Iran—into the armed forces it was busy reconstructing.[86] This covert US policy, designed to give its allies among Iraq's new ruling elite resources in their struggle to dominate the coercive field, led directly to the much more widespread politicization and fracturing of Iraq's new armed forces.

The collapse of Iraq's armed forces in 2014, in the face of the Islamic State's advance on Mosul, gave a clear indication of how the ongoing struggle for control of the coercive field had fractured any remaining coherence in its command, control, and esprit de corps. Maliki during his two terms as prime minister had set out to individually tie senior military commanders to him personally through favoritism and promotion.[87] By early 2014, in the face of the Islamic State's military campaign, Maliki acknowledged the lack of coercive capital possessed by the formal institutions of the Iraqi state.[88] However, instead of reversing his previous policies and embarking on security sector reform, he set about re-empowering and then utilizing the more informal coercive capital possessed by the Shiʻa Islamist militias, including Badr, Kata'ib Hezbollah, and Asaib Ahl al-Haq, allied with him in the National Alliance coalition.[89]

Once Mosul fell to the Islamic State, Maliki accelerated this process, announcing on national television plans to "provide weapons and equipment to citizens who volunteer to fight against militants."[90] Maliki set up a formal organization, the Commission for the Popular Mobilization Forces (Hay'at al-Hashd al-Shaabi), to give financial and symbolic capital to the

---

84. Knights, "The Iraqi Security Forces."
85. Dodge, *Iraq*.
86. Confidential author interview with a Coalition Provisional Authority official involved in the policy.
87. Dodge, *Iraq*.
88. Author interview with Nuri al-Maliki, Baghdad, September 29, 2019.
89. Mansour and Jabar, "The Popular Mobilization Force and Iraq's Future."
90. "Iraq Government to Arm Citizens to Fight Militants."

militias.[91] In the months and years that followed the fall of Mosul, these militias used the economic, social, symbolic, and coercive capital given to them by their role in the fight against the Islamic State to increase their size but also their dominant role in Iraq's political and bureaucratic fields.

In Iraq today, government expenditure now funds the militia members' wages, their organizational capacity, and their arms purchases. Under Maliki's successor, Haider al-Abadi, the institutionalization of the role of Hash'd within the state increased with the passing of Executive Order 61 in February 2016 and the Law of the Popular Mobilization Authority in November 2016. Far from recognizing the separate status of these militia groups outside the state, the order and law unambiguously placed them within the state, giving them generous access to government funding through the annual budget process.[92] Any attempts to constrain the power of key groups working within the Hash'd have proven impossible, as these forces benefit from the state's financial and symbolic capital, can move around Baghdad at will, and have the power to challenge other government forces they are in competition with—most notably, the Counter Terrorism Service.

A close examination of the major militias currently operating in Iraq will highlight the permeability of any analytical division between state and non-state actors in the coercive field. The three dominant militias, Badr, Kata'ib Hezbollah, and Asaib Ahl al-Haq, for example, do not sit in opposition to the Iraqi state or pose a direct threat to it. Instead, they are major competitors within the state's coercive field, along with other members of the ruling elite. They have access to the financial capital of the state and benefit from any symbolic capital that accrues to the state. Like the rest of Iraq's political elite, they are competing to maximize the resources and power they can extract from the state.

Asaib Ahl al-Haq, one of the most feared of the Shi'a Islamist militias, was given the help it needed to become a major political, economic, and coercive player through the partnership the group formed with Maliki, during his second term in office (2010–14). This alliance gave the militia the legal cover it needed to thrive politically and economically. Its current political and economic power in Iraq today has its origins in this alliance with a previous prime minister. In the aftermath of the 2018 elections, as part of the political settlement agreed to among the national elite, the group took this a step further in the bureaucratic field by taking over a government ministry, with all the financial resources and prestige that brought

---

91. Mansour and Jabar, "The Popular Mobilization Force and Iraq's Future."
92. Mansour and Jabar, "The Popular Mobilization Forces and Iraq's Future"; Crisis Group, "Iraq's Paramilitary Groups."

it. Asaib Ahl al-Haq is now a key member of the ruling elite and a powerful player within the many fields of the state.

Conclusion

At no stage in its history since 1968 did the Iraqi state resemble a neo-Weberian model, with a clear distinction between its institutions and civil service and the wider society it was attempting to rule over. Instead, the state, like most states, is better understood as a series of competitive arenas or fields. Within each of these fields, various members of a fluid ruling elite compete with each other to gain domination. This competition is ongoing and shapes the state's individual institutions and their interaction with Iraq's population. The coherence of the state as a whole depends on two things: first, the balance of power among these competing elites, and second, the degree of consensus they manage to achieve. The Ba'thist regime that ruled from 1968 to 2003 certainly achieved a higher degree of elite coherence than any other ruling elite in Iraq's history. It did this through constant violent purges that narrowed the size of the ruling elite and suppressed opposition to it within the political, bureaucratic, and coercive fields. However, even at the peak of its coherence, it would be easy to overstate the dominance of Saddam Hussein and his allies. Throughout their time in office, they faced constant competition from within the elite itself and the political field and repeated challenges from the coercive field. After 2003, through the establishment of an informal consociational system, the new governing elite (empowered by US force of arms) deliberately recognized the fractured nature of the state and sought to institutionalize this within the country's new political system. The result was a fractured and largely enfeebled set of state institutions, with limited ability to control society, let alone deliver sustainable development. The Iraqi state, both at its peak of coherence under Saddam and at its weakest and most incoherent after regime change, could be seen as an aberration, an extreme case. However, in extremis, both under the Ba'th and today, it allows us to uncover and highlight the dynamics of competition that exist within the institutions of all states.

BIBLIOGRAPHY

Abbas, A. "The Iraqi Armed Forces, Past and Present." In *Saddam's Iraq: Revolution or Reaction?* edited by Committee Against Repression and For Democratic Rights in Iraq. London: Zed Books, 1989.

Abrams, Philip. "Notes on the Difficulty of Studying the State." *Journal of Historical Sociology* 1, no. 1 (1988): 58–89.
Aburish, Said K. *Saddam Hussein: The Politics of Revenge*. London: Bloomsbury, 2000.
Alnasrawi, Abbas. *The Economy of Iraq Oil, Wars, Destruction of Development and Prospects, 1950–2010*. Westport, CT: Greenwood Press, 1994.
Anter, Andreas. *Max Weber's Theory of the Modern State: Origins, Structure and Significance*. London: Palgrave Macmillan, 2014.
Ayubi, Nazih N. *Over-stating the Arab State: Politics and Society in the Middle East*. London: I. B. Tauris, 1995.
Baram, Amatzia. "Between Impediment and Advantage: Saddam's Iraq." United States Institute of Peace Special Report. Washington, DC: USIP, 1998. https://www.usip.org/publications/1998/06/between-impediment-and-advantage-saddams-iraq
Baram, Amatzia. "The Future of Ba'thist Iraq: Power Structure, Challenges and Prospects." In *The Politics of Change in the Middle East*, edited by Robert B. Satloff. Boulder, CO: Westview Press, 1993.
Baram, Amatzia. "Neo-Tribalism in Iraq: Saddam Hussein's Tribal Policies, 1991–1999." *International Journal of Middle Eastern Studies* 29 (1997): 1–31.
Bhambra, Gurminder K. *Rethinking Modernity: Postcolonialism and the Sociological Imagination*. London: Palgrave MacMillan, 2007.
Blaydes, Lisa. *State of Repression: Iraq under Saddam Hussein*. Princeton, NJ: Princeton University Press, 2018.
Boone, Peter, Haris Gazdar, and Athar Hussain. "Sanctions against Iraq Costs of Failure." Paper delivered at "Frustrated Development: The Iraqi Economy in War and in Peace," conference at University of Exeter, July 9–11, 1997.
Bourdieu, Pierre. "The Forms of Capital." In *Handbook of Theory and Research for the Sociology of Education*, edited by J. Richardson. New York: Greenwood, 1986.
Bourdieu, Pierre. "From the King's House to the Reason of State: A Model of the Genesis of the Bureaucratic Field." In *Pierre Bourdieu and Democratic Politics: The Mystery of Ministry*, edited by Loïc Wacquant. Cambridge, UK: Polity Press, 2005.
Bourdieu, Pierre. *Language and Symbolic Power*. Cambridge, UK: Polity, 1991.
Bourdieu, Pierre. *On the State: Lectures at the College de France, 1989–1992*. Cambridge, UK: Polity Press, 2014.
Bourdieu, Pierre. *Pascalian Meditations*. Cambridge, UK: Polity Press, 2000.
Bourdieu, Pierre. "The Political Field, the Social Science Field and the Journalistic Field." In *Bourdieu and the Journalistic Field*, edited by Rodney Benson and Erik Neveu. Cambridge, UK: Polity Press, 2005.
Bourdieu, Pierre. "Rethinking the State: Genesis and Structure of the Bureaucratic Field." *Sociological Theory* 12, no. 1 (1994).
Bourdieu, Pierre. *The State Nobility: Elite Schools in the Field of Power*. Cambridge, UK: Polity Press, 1996.
Bourdieu, Pierre, and Loic Wacquant. *An Invitation to Reflexive Sociology*. Chicago: University of Chicago Press, 1992.
Brooke, John L., Julia C. Strauss, and Greg Anderson, eds. *State Formations: Global Histories and Cultures of Statehood*. Cambridge: Cambridge University Press, 2018.

Cambanis, Thanassis, Dina Esfandiary, Sima Ghaddar, Michael Wahid Hanna, Aron Lund, and Renad Mansour, eds. *Hybrid Actors, Armed Groups, and State Fragmentation in the Middle East*. New York: Century Foundation Press, 2019.

Chakrabarty, Dipesh. *Provincializing Europe: Postcolonial Thought and Historical Difference*. Princeton, NJ: Princeton University Press, 2000.

Chaudhry, Kiren Aziz. "Economic Liberalization and the Lineages of the Rentier State." *Comparative Politics* 27, no. 1 (1994).

Chaudhry, Kiren Aziz. "On the Way to Market Economic Liberalization and Iraq's Invasion of Kuwait." *Middle East Report* 170 (1991).

Cox, Robert W. *Production, Power, and World Order: Social Forces in the Making of History*. New York: Columbia University Press, 1987.

Crisis Group. "Iraq's Paramilitary Groups: The Challenge of Rebuilding a Functioning State." Report no. 188, July 30, 2018.

Dodge, Toby. "Beyond Structure and Agency: Rethinking Political Identities in Iraq after 2003." *Nations and Nationalism* 26, no. 1 (2020).

Dodge, Toby. "Bourdieu Goes to Baghdad: Explaining Hybrid Political Identities in Iraq." *Historical Sociology* 31, no. 1 (2018).

Dodge, Toby. "Cake Walk, Coup or Urban Warfare: The Battle for Iraq." In *Iraq at the Crossroads: State and Society in the Shadow of Regime Change*, edited by Toby Dodge and Steven Simon. London: IISS and Oxford University Press, 2003.

Dodge, Toby. "The Failure of Sanctions and the Evolution of International Policy towards Iraq, 1990–2003." *Contemporary Arab Affairs* 3, no. 1 (2010).

Dodge, Toby. *Iraq from War to a New Authoritarianism*. Abingdon, UK: Routledge, 2012.

Dodge, Toby. "Iraq's Informal Consociationalism and Its Problems." *Studies in Ethnicity and Nationalism* 20, no. 2 (2020).

Dodge, Toby, and Renad Mansour. "Politically Sanctioned Corruption and Barriers to Reform in Iraq." Research Paper, Middle East and North Africa Programme, Chatham House, June 2021. https://www.chathamhouse.org/2021/06/politically-sanctioned-corruption-and-barriers-reform-iraq/04-expansion-special-grades

Doyle, Damian, and Tristan Dunning. "Recognizing Fragmented Authority: Towards a Post-Westphalian Security Order in Iraq." *Small Wars & Insurgencies* 29, no. 3 (2018): 537–59.

Duelfer, Charles. *Comprehensive Report of the Special Adviser to the DCI on Iraq's WMD*. Vol. I (2004). https://www.cia.gov/readingroom/docs/DOC_0001156395.pdf

Evans, Peter E., Dietrich Rueschemeyer, and Theda Skocpol, eds. *Bringing the State Back In*. Cambridge: Cambridge University Press, 1985.

Farouk-Sluglett, Marion, and Peter Sluglett. *Iraq since 1958: From Revolution to Dictatorship*. London: I. B. Tauris, 2001.

Faust, Aaron M. *The Ba'thification of Iraq: Saddam Hussein's Totalitarianism*. Austin: University of Texas Press, 2015.

Gause, F. Gregory. "Iraq's Decision to Go to War, 1980 and 1990." *Middle East Journal* 56, no. 1 (2002).

Graham-Brown, Sarah. *Sanctioning Saddam: The Politics of Intervention in Iraq*. London: I. B. Tauris, 1999.

Harling, Peter. "Beyond Political Ruptures: Towards a Historiography of Social Continuity in Iraq." In *Writing the Modern History of Iraq: Historiographical and Political Challenges*, edited by Jordi Tejel, Riccardo Bocco, Peter Sluglett, and Hamit Bozarslan. Hackensack, NJ: World Scientific Publishing, 2012.

"Iraq Government to Arm Citizens to Fight Militants." *Agence France-Presse*, June 10, 2014.

Jarstad, Anna K., and Roberto Belloni. "Introducing Hybrid Peace Governance: Impact and Prospects of Liberal Peacebuilding." *Global Governance* 18 (2012).

Jessop, Bob. *State Power: A Strategic-Relational Approach*. Cambridge, UK: Polity Press, 2008.

Jessop, Bob. *State Theory: Putting the Capitalist State in Its Place*. Cambridge, UK: Polity Press, 1996.

Jones, Lee. *Societies under Siege: Exploring How International Sanctions (Do Not) Work*. Oxford: Oxford University Press, 2015.

Kalyvas, Andreas. "The Stateless Theory: Poulantzas's Challenge to Postmodernism." In *Paradigm Lost: State Theory Reconsidered*, edited by Stanley Aronowitz and Peter Bratsis. Minneapolis: University of Minnesota Press, 2002.

Kandil, Hazem. *The Power Triangle: Military, Security, and Politics in Regime Change*. Oxford: Oxford University Press, 2016.

Khalifa, Hussein Allawi. "Opening the Windows . . . Private Grades in the Government Employment Ladder in Iraq." Akkad Center for Strategic Affairs and Future Studies, June 2019.

Knights, Michael. "The Iraqi Security Forces: Local Context and US Assistance." *Policy Notes* 4. Washington, DC: Washington Institute for Near East Policy, June 2011.

MacFarquhar, Neil. "After War and Blockade, Crime Frays Life in Iraq." *New York Times*, October 18, 1996.

Makiya, Kanan. *Republic of Fear: The Politics of Modern Iraq*. Berkeley: University of California Press, 1988.

Mann, Michael. *The Sources of Social Power: A History of Power from the Beginning to A.D. 1760*. Volume I. Cambridge: Cambridge University Press 1986.

Mann, Michael. *The Sources of Social Power: The Rise of Classes and Nation-States, 1760–1914*. Volume II. Cambridge: Cambridge University Press 1993.

Mann, Michael. *States, War and Capitalism Studies in Political Sociology*. Oxford: Blackwell, 1988.

Mansour, Renad, and Faleh A. Jabar. "The Popular Mobilization Forces and Iraq's Future." Carnegie Middle East Center, April 28, 2017. https://carnegie-mec.org/2017/04/28/popular-mobilization-forces-and-iraq-s-future-pub-68810

Migdal, Joel S. *State in Society: Studying How States and Societies Transform and Constitute One Another*. Cambridge: Cambridge University Press, 2001.

Mitchell, Timothy. "Society, Economy and the State Effect." In *State/Culture: State-Formation after the Cultural Turn*, edited by George Steinmetz. Ithaca, NY: Cornell University Press, 1999.

Morton, Adam David. *Unravelling Gramsci: Hegemony and Passive Revolution in the Global Political Economy*. London: Pluto Press, 2007.

Mufti, Malik. *Sovereign Creations: Pan-Arabism and Political Order in Syria and Iraq*. Ithaca, NY: Cornell University Press, 1996.

Nettl, J. P. "The State as a Conceptual Variable." *World Politics* 20, no. 4 (1968): 561–62.

Rohde, Achim. *State-Society Relations in Ba'thist Iraq: Facing Dictatorship*. Abingdon, UK: Routledge, 2010.

Saouli, Adham. *The Arab State Dilemmas of Late Formation*. Abingdon, UK: Routledge, 2012.

Sassoon, Joseph. *Saddam Hussein's Ba'th Party: Inside an Authoritarian Regime*. Cambridge: Cambridge University Press, 2012.

Schroeder, Ralph. "Introduction: The IEMP Model and Its Critics." In *An Anatomy of Power: The Social Theory of Michael Mann*, edited by John A. Hall and Ralph Schroeder. Cambridge: Cambridge University Press, 2005.

Sissons, Miranda, and Abdulrazzaq Al-Saiedi. "A Bitter Legacy: Lessons of De-Baathification in Iraq." New York: International Center for Transitional Justice, 2013. https://www.ictj.org/sites/default/files/ICTJ-Report-Iraq-De-Baathification-2013-ENG.pdf

Stepan, Alfred. *Arguing Comparative Politics*. Oxford: Oxford University Press, 2001.

Tripp, Charles. *A History of Iraq*. Cambridge: Cambridge University Press, 2007.

Walter, Alissa. "The Ba'th Party in Baghdad: State-Society Relations through Wars, Sanctions, and Authoritarian Rule, 1950–2003." PhD diss., Georgetown University, 2018.

Weber, Max. *Economy and Society*. Volume I. Berkeley: University of California Press, 1978.

Weber, Max. "Politics as a Vocation." In *From Max Weber: Essays in Sociology*, edited by H. H. Gerth and C. Wright Mills. London: Routledge, 1991.

FOUR

Legibility, Digital Surveillance, and the MENA State

Marc Lynch

The chapters in this volume paint a sweeping overview of how to think about the strengths and weaknesses of states in the Middle East and North Africa (MENA) region, moving beyond conventional assumptions about state capacity through novel theoretical framings and empirical observations. Their assessments of the nature of the MENA state draw on a wide range of theoretical inspirations, from Michael Mann's influential disaggregation of the dimensions of state capacity to Pierre Bourdieu's placing of the state within societal fields. This chapter follows recent trends in the broader comparative literature on the state to focus more narrowly on a single dimension of state capacity: legibility. It argues that MENA states have varied widely in their informational capacity, with observable implications for their extractive capacity, political stability, economic development, and regime security. Finally, it focuses on the novel ways in which new digital technologies have both challenged and dramatically increased state strength. It argues that the dramatic shifts in the nature and degree of a state's informational capacity—rendering the identities, beliefs, and behaviors of citizens visible in unprecedented ways—have underappreciated implications for our understanding of state strength and weakness. States have gained unprecedented visibility into every aspect of the lives and thoughts of their citizens—but may still be unable to act effectively based on this legibility.

What is legibility, and how does it relate to stateness? I follow Melissa Lee and Nan Zhang's definition of the informational component of state capacity as the "breadth and depth of the state's knowledge about its citizens and their activities."[1] Informational capacity is only one dimension of state strength, but it is an important one, underlying much of the state's extractive and infrastructural capacity as well as its ability to generate and enforce ideological hegemony. Like Heydemann (chap. 1, this volume), I am less interested in explaining state fragility than I am in explaining the changes and the asymmetries in the capacity of MENA states to render their societies both visible and legible and how this matters concretely for a wide range of political outcomes. And, in line with the other dimensions of state capacity discussed in Heydemann's chapter, the informational capacity of MENA states varies asymmetrically and at times independently of trends in other dimensions of state capacity.

State visibility into society has ebbed and flowed since the emergence of postcolonial states and their evolution into autocratic regimes. This is particularly apparent in the post-2011 period, where I argue that new digital technologies have tipped the balance toward informational visibility even as other dimensions of state capacity have waxed and waned. Even traditionally weak—or even fragile—states can now exploit relatively inexpensive surveillance technology to monitor not only online behavior but interpersonal communications in unprecedented ways. As Thomas Hegghammer has recently argued, the routine mass visibility of states into societies enabled by digital infrastructure has profound global implications for the prospects for sustained uprising and insurgency, as well as profound implications for democratic struggles.[2] Digital surveillance does not necessarily improve the governance performance, or even the coercive power, of the state: for example, consider the relatively ineffective response to COVID-19 by states such as Egypt that have invested quite heavily in repressive capacity.[3] But it can at least partially compensate for other deficiencies by rendering societies more legible, facilitating control, and allowing targeted deployment of limited repressive or co-optive resources.

The aspirational nature of the MENA state today might be seen where the societal panopticon of the United Arab Emirates (UAE) meets the aspiring *mukhabarat* state, with a detour through the ostensibly stateless

---

1. Lee and Zhang, "Legibility and the Informational Foundations of State Capacity," 118–32.
2. Hegghammer, "Resistance Is Futile," 44–53.
3. Lynch, ed., "COVID-19 in the Middle East and North Africa."

dystopian surveillance archipelago that is the Israeli-occupied West Bank.[4] Most MENA states will fall short of that ideal due to limited resources, deficient capacity in other state sectors, or societal ability to resist and conceal. The sheer volume of information may overwhelm the ability of states to render information legible or create an inaccurate sense of total information that distorts policy responses.

Legibility and State Capacity

States have always sought to penetrate their societies in order to render them legible. Indeed, this is a core element of their stateness. As James Scott famously observed, seeing like a state required detailed knowledge of the human geography from which taxes might be extracted, soldiers conscripted, nationalism mobilized, and dissent suppressed.[5] Failures to achieve such legibility invited unexpected challenges—peaceful or violent—and the growth of countermovements and counter-publics.[6] High legibility translates not only into efficient taxation and conscription but also into co-optation of potential elite challengers, the channeling of patronage through clientelistic networks, and the surveillance and repression of potential regime challengers. Lee and Zhang argue that high informational capacity enables taxation and the provision of public goods because it "allows the state to effectively monitor private behavior and enforce rules and regulations."[7] Effective state action requires the ability to collect accurate information about the beliefs and behaviors of those it rules and to assemble that information in a coherent, standardized form for analysis and policy action.

This focus on informational capacity fits comfortably with the theoretical approaches of the other chapters in this volume, while adding a particular point of emphasis. Michael Mann incorporates legibility into his concept of infrastructural power, on which many of the chapters in this volume draw.[8] Legibility can be understood as one facet of infrastructural power, but one that in my view sits in an apex relationship to its other three major dimensions. As Dan Slater and Sofia Fenner put it:

---

4. On Palestine, see Al-Shabaka, "Focus On."
5. Scott, *Seeing Like a State*.
6. Lee, *Crippling Leviathan*; Nathan, *The Scarce State*.
7. Lee and Zhang, "Legibility and the Informational Foundations of State Capacity," 118.
8. Bertwick and Christia, "State Capacity Redux."

When an authoritarian regime commands a state that exhibits the infrastructural capacity to register its population, it can render society more "legible" and enhance its social control. As the omnipresent *mukhabarat* (intelligence services) of MENA states have long understood, legibility is the foundation of effective surveillance, which is in turn the foundation not only of effectively targeted coercion, but of co-optation and negotiation . . . [which] makes threats of coercion more credible.[9]

To effectively carry out clientelistic patronage, the state needs to know who its clients are, where to find them, and precisely what benefits will keep them happy. High informational capacity allows states to cut out the traditional middlemen and brokers, the local elites or tribal figures or religious authorities who otherwise could represent poles of independent power within society. Surveillance, as we shall see, sits comfortably within the primary ambition of most MENA states: the political survival of the regimes that sit atop them.

Nazih Ayubi's influential articulation of the Arab state has been that it is a "fierce" state that has to "resort to raw coercion" because it lacks what Mann calls infrastructural power that "enables states to penetrate society effectively."[10] The super-developed national security state is, in essence, an overcompensation for the lack of ideological hegemony and the ability to decode the true preferences and capabilities of the society it governs. Even as regimes upgraded their techniques of authoritarianism, the states became no less fierce. As Heydemann argues in this volume, there is no reason to believe that regimes will use the legibility capacity available to their states in the interests of development, taxation, or the provision of public goods. To the contrary, all experience with MENA regimes suggests that they will primarily use that capacity to keep themselves in power by any means necessary. As Eva Bellin reminds us, they have been remarkably successful in that goal, at least up until the 2011 Arab uprisings.[11]

These contributions to regime survival are not guaranteed, of course, and could prove quite illusory. For Scott, legibility represents the first step in the causal chain not toward absolute state domination but rather toward the disastrous failures of state projects. In his influential account, the state first must render its population and territory legible before carrying out its most basic functions, such as taxation, conscription, and the provision

---

9. Slater and Fenner, "State Power and Staying Power," 22.
10. Ayubi, *Over-stating the Arab State*, 3.
11. Bellin, "Reconsidering the Robustness of Authoritarianism in the Middle East."

of social welfare. The creation of legibility lies at the heart of state capacity: equally a necessary condition, in Scott's perspective, for democratic accountability and social welfare as much as for mass killing and rapid state-led industrialization.[12] This insight informs this chapter's skepticism about the effects of the digitalization of modern life: increasing societal legibility strengthens states, which have more interest in domination than in development, but it also carries the seeds of other forms of power mobilization.[13] Saudi crown prince Mohammed bin Salman's modernization of the Saudi state has, for instance, expanded some social freedoms while even more ruthlessly suppressing any political freedoms. The "knowledge economy" his Vision 2030 aims to produce would, if enacted, likely dramatically expand the opportunities for digital surveillance and societal control discussed in this chapter's final section and seen vividly in repressive acts such as the imprisonment for thirty-four years of Selma Shehab, a London-based Saudi student, for tweets critical of the regime.[14]

The Weberian focus on the institutional forms of the state does not exhaust the ways in which the state structures society and establishes order. Several chapters in this volume, in line with a broader literature within MENA studies and comparative politics, focus on the state within society and the "state effects," which constitute the lived experience of its citizens. This too has an informational component. For Timothy Mitchell, the state's "structural effect" includes the ability to enact "social surveillance" through a range of institutions.[15] While drawing on Foucault, this concept of social surveillance mirrors Scott's concept of legibility and again directs our attention to "informational capacity" as a measure of state power.[16] The categories through which the state orders society, such as personal status laws, both constitute the identity and practices of citizens and facilitate the state's rendering and ordering of their place within a legible society.[17]

Arab states placed a particular, if not exceptional, emphasis on the security aspects of surveillance and thus on legibility. Rather than achieving it through efficient tax and property registries or detailed censuses, they typically did so through highly intrusive surveillance. The omnipresent *mukhabarat*, not rational state bureaucracy, was the agent of legibility. In some smaller countries, such as Jordan and Morocco, the state was able to

---

12. Scott, *Seeing Like a State*.
13. Zuboff, *The Age of Surveillance Capitalism*.
14. Kirchgaessner, "Saudi Woman Given 34-year Prison Sentence for Using Twitter."
15. Mitchell, "The Limits of the State."
16. Brambor et al., "The Lay of the Land."
17. Mikdashi, *Sectarianism*.

penetrate and monitor virtually every social network and achieve almost total visibility.[18]

But, as Lisa Blaydes demonstrates in her groundbreaking analysis of the captured *mukhabarat* files of Saddam Hussein's Iraq, even the most penetrative surveillance had its limits.[19] Saddam's intelligence services could penetrate some sectors of society more completely than others, allowing finer-grained means of coercion and control over Sunni Arab areas than over Shiʻa or Kurdish communities. Large but ramshackle states like Egypt and Algeria might aspire to full visibility, but they lacked the manpower or the reach to monitor tens of millions of citizens packed into dense, impersonal urban areas and often working in the informal economy. They could appoint the imams of mosques and dictate scripts for the Friday *khutba* but could not observe all the social dynamics and political organizing taking place inside of the mosques. Large and ostensibly stronger states might then achieve far less visibility into parts of their societies—for example, Egypt's peri-urban informal communities and rural areas or Algeria's Kabyle—than do smaller, ostensibly weaker states.

How should we understand the disjuncture between the vast expenditures made by Arab states on intelligence services and societal surveillance, on the one hand, and the relative weakness of its infrastructural power in terms of taxation or development, on the other? Perhaps because Arab states generally do not agree with what Jonathan Hanson views as the purpose of legibility: "The ability to raise revenues (extractive power) . . . serves as a marker for the capabilities that underlie state power. These include the legibility of the population, the capacity to gather and maintain information."[20] Most MENA states are as famously weak in their ability to extract tax revenues from their populations as they are overinvested in surveillance and repression of potential opponents. The holes in state capacity, as Heydemann argues in this volume, directly mirror the priorities of the regimes that sit atop them. The dominance of a regime security lens led to the stunting of extractive capacity or developmental success, which high informational capacity might otherwise have generated. Where states viewed societies primarily as potential sources of threat, many in those societies preferred to remain at least partially invisible: dissembling about their true opinions or identities, hiding their informal economic activity, and taking their oppositional political behavior underground. At other times, some states may prefer not to see, when seeing might be politically

18. Schwedler, *Protesting Jordan*.
19. Blaydes, *State of Repression*.
20. Hanson, "State Capacity and the Resilience of Electoral Authoritarianism."

dangerous: Lebanon's refusal to conduct a new census and Egypt's refusal to enumerate COVID deaths are good examples.

Arab states thus typically demonstrate high degrees of variation in the informational foundations of state power: more focused on potential security threats than on other areas and more penetration in some geographic or social sectors than in others.[21] This resembles the subnational variation in state capacity associated with territorial authority investigated by Juan Pablo Luna and Hillel Soifer in the Latin American context.[22] The ability of the central state to decode and thus control society clearly varies in the MENA context as well; as in other world regions, geography and terrain matter alongside size and social differences such as religion or ethnicity. Turkey's state has far greater visibility into its Turkish citizens than it does into the Kurdish areas; the Islamist-dominated neighborhood of Imbaba became illegible to Egypt's state in the early 1990s; Algeria's state long struggled to penetrate and impose its preferences on the Kabyle. Blaydes's investigation of the captured archives of Saddam Hussein's intelligence services revealed major blind spots plaguing these seemingly all-intrusive agencies, especially in Kurdish and Shi'a communities.[23] Ceren Belge shows how Kurdish kinship networks resisted Turkish efforts at imposing legibility and thus incorporation into a homogenous nation-state.[24] Kinship networks represented another center from which order emerged, one that could be neither understood nor replaced by the modern bureaucratic state's categories.

From another perspective, Kevin Koehler shows that limited state capacity complicates the management of elections by autocratic regimes such as in Egypt. They have the intention of managing and controlling but lack the detailed insights into society (legibility) that would allow them to do so smoothly. He notes that the weakness of the ruling National Democratic Party (NDP) was particularly acute in rural areas, precisely where the state had penetrated society the least: "This rural-urban divide in terms of the hegemonic party's institutional strength was exacerbated, rather than contained, by state administrative penetration."[25] The Muslim Brotherhood, by contrast, was far more present in society, with detailed local knowledge of individuals, families, and neighborhoods that allowed

---

21. Lee and Zhang, "Legibility and the Informational Foundations of State Capacity."
22. Luna and Soifer, "Capturing Sub-National Variation in State Capacity."
23. Blaydes, *State of Repression*.
24. Belge, "State Building and the Limits of Legibility."
25. Koehler, "State and Regime Capacity in Authoritarian Elections," 98.

them to effectively microtarget potential voters.[26] The ruling NDP might seek to compensate for that weakness by subcontracting to local elites or middlemen, but that leaves them vulnerable to the private agendas and local issues that those independent clients bring to the table. That contrasts with Jordan, where the state has been able to micromanage electoral results through electoral maps, deep familiarity with tribal networks' political machinations, co-optation, and targeted repression. While Jordan is a much weaker state in some ways than Egypt, Jordanian society is far more legible to the state: small in landmass and population, ordered through tribal networks, and pervasively surveilled by the intelligence services (see Yom, this volume).

Variation in legibility has direct implications for core state functions such as taxation. It also has profound implications for precisely the security outcomes of most concern to regimes. Consider three widely cited recent articles. Carl Müller-Crepon, Philipp Hunziker, and Lars-Erik Cederman find that conflict risk in Africa goes up where state relational capacity goes down. Their measure, road connectivity and time to travel from the center to the region, is plausibly a proxy for legibility. As they put it, "Individuals who believe that the state scrutinizes their behavior are less likely to join and more likely to denounce organizations that challenge state rule."[27] Cullen Hendrix finds that rough terrain (mountains, for instance) reduces the capacity of states to extract taxes—another measure of legibility—with implications for the likelihood of civil war onset.[28] Finally, James Fearon and David Laitin, in their influential 2003 account of insurgency, argue that features associated with legibility better explain insurgency than do grievances or ethnic divides: "Insurgency is favored by rough terrain, rebels with local knowledge of the population superior to the government's, and a large population."[29] All three of those indicators align with the degree to which the potentially rebellious society is legible to the state.

The Syrian civil war offers a good case for illustrating these dynamics. As Kevin Mazur has argued, the Assad regime faced a profound legibility problem in early 2011.[30] As the rebellion began, despite all its prowess at surveillance, torture, and control over the public sphere, the regime could not be certain of the loyalties of citizens or even members of the military. Falling back on the Alawi community for irregular militia support and hav-

---

26. Vannetzel, *The Muslim Brothers in Society*.
27. Müller-Crepon, Hunziker, and Cederman, "Roads to Rule, Roads to Rebel," 566.
28. Hendrix, "Head for the Hills?"
29. Fearon and Laitin, "Ethnicity, Insurgency and Civil War," 75.
30. Mazur, *Revolution in Syria*.

ing Assad's family networks at the pinnacle of the state reflected areas of higher visibility. As the war ground on, however, Syrian society became more legible to Assad. Those who fled to rebel-controlled territories or abroad could be identified as disloyal; those who remained had proven their reliability. Members of the officer corps who were disloyal clarified matters by defecting to the opposition, leaving behind a more transparently loyal institution. Nils Hägerdal makes a similar point about civilian victimization in the early days of Lebanon's civil war.[31] Ethnic identity acted as a signaling device for potential opposition to militias. Where militias could draw on local knowledge and networks to differentiate friend from foe, civilian displacement could be avoided. Where such legibility was lacking, the mass removal of members of potentially hostile sectarian or ethnic groups became the best path toward local security. The logic is compatible with Blaydes's account of Saddam's genocidal approach to rebellious Iraqi Kurds in the late 1980s and its heavy-handed repression of the Shi'a clerical establishment in comparison to its more nuanced approach to Sunni institutions—into which its security services had greater visibility.[32]

Such legibility issues go beyond questions of insurgency and violent repression, of course. Michael Rodriguez-Muniz focuses on the role of societal leaders in overcoming obstacles to state visibility by cultivating consent, easing the obstacles to their communities being counted.[33] But many MENA citizens and their community leaders preferred to remain as unseen as possible by corrupt, brutal, and unsympathetic state actors. This is especially the case for marginalized communities (such as LGBTQ communities or religious minorities), those working in the informal sector, and political dissidents. In general, Arab citizens recognized a pervasive surveillance—"the walls have ears"—and adapted their social and political lives accordingly. But all things equal, they preferred to keep their secrets and to avoid the scrutiny of a state whose attention almost always meant trouble: tax collection, conscription, demands for bribes, and arbitrary detention. Where states showed little interest in promoting development or providing public goods, little good could come from being rendered visible to a security-minded state. Societal preferences from below, then, reinforce the regimes' top-down preference for prioritizing security over development in terms of legibility.

This focus on "consent" reminds us that there is more to legibility than just the state's collection of and ordering of information about society.

31. Hägerdal, *Friend or Foe*.
32. Blaydes, *State of Repression*.
33. Rodriguez-Muniz, "Cultivating Consent."

Wyrtzen links the concept of legibility to Bourdieu's concept of symbolic power, in line with several contributions to this volume, with the imposing of legibility being a key expression as it forces this symbolic order and creates new realities through practice.[34] When all citizens adopt the same narrative of legitimacy—such as accepting the monarchy as a natural form of government—then their political behavior becomes more predictable and, by implication, controllable. Ayubi found Arab states deficient in the production of such hegemony. But, as Lisa Wedeen reminds us, the use of personality cults at some level substitutes for such hegemony, as long as citizens act as if they accept it in public.[35] To the extent that this public conformity is coerced, however, it generates the problem of preference falsification (key to many accounts of unexpected revolutions) as the public performance of compliance creates a false sense of legibility that masks real underlying dissatisfaction, which can shock regimes by seemingly appearing out of nowhere.[36]

An Alternative Trajectory of State Capacity through the Lens of Legibility

Several chapters in this volume offer a chronology, a periodization, of the evolution of the varying types and degrees of state strength (see those by Hinnebusch and Anderson). In some ways, their periodizations track relatively well when reviewed through the lens of legibility and informational capacity. But they diverge in interesting ways, especially in the 1990s and 2000s and even more so in the current digital era, which is the subject of the next (and final) section of this chapter. This section reviews the historical evolution of the MENA state through the singular lens of legibility and informational capacity, contrasting this aperture with other ways of coding state capacity. In other contexts, collecting such information might be used for purposes other than repression, such as development, distribution, and electoral incentives. But in the MENA region, repression and control have always taken the upper hand.

---

34. Wyrtzen, "Colonial Legitimization-Legibility Linkages and the Politics of Identity in Algeria and Morocco."
35. Wedeen, *Ambiguities of Domination*.
36. Kuran, "Now Out of Never"; Lohmann, "The Dynamics of Informational Cascades"; Kurzman, *The Unthinkable Revolution in Iran*; Bayat, "The Arab Spring and Its Surprises"; Hale, "Regime Change Cascades."

The colonial era demanded specific forms of legibility and ordering.[37] Mitchell's study of colonial Egypt, for instance, powerfully shows how this imperative from colonial bureaucracies reshaped Egyptian society through education, infrastructure, architecture, and categorization. Britain's first order of business after occupying Egypt in 1882, he argues, was "to determine, for every square meter of the country's agricultural land, the owner, the cultivator, the quality of the soil, and the proper rate of tax . . . to produce something never achieved before, a 'great land map of Egypt.'"[38] There has been a tremendous amount of research on colonial administration in the MENA region since, showing the efforts of Orientalists and bureaucrats to survey, record, and impose order on the communities they came to govern in order to both extract taxation and prevent costly revolts.

It is not only the land that colonial administrators sought to render legible. As Wyrtzen observes, the high-modern tendency toward homogenization identified by Scott is not the only form of cultivated legibility. Empire involved the cultivation of difference, assigning colonial subjects to categories by which they could be governed: "Colonial legibility entails strenuous efforts to maintain or even invent social differences through state practices." The colonial ethnographic state took seriously the urgency of "legibility—seeing, naming, and counting tribes, ethnic groups, religious minorities, and castes."[39] Abdelmajid Hannoum's discussion of the invention of the Maghreb details, for instance, how French colonial practices created a racially defined Maghreb that imposed categories of Berber, Arab, and African to demarcate ontologically different societies.[40] Bassel Salloukh, in this volume, points to the ways in which the supposedly weak Lebanese state constituted sectarianism and imposed identity categories. As Maya Mikdashi demonstrates, the state's legal categories and institutional practice shaped sexual, gender, and sectarian identities at the most intimate level.[41]

Postcolonial states inherited these legibility capacities in varying degrees. The massive flight of the pied-noir community from Algeria left the state largely bereft of preexisting state capacity or bureaucratic expertise. In other countries, especially those colonized by Britain, the tran-

---

37. Mitchell, "The Limits of the State"; Wyrtzen, "Colonial Legitimization-Legibility Linkages and the Politics of Identity in Algeria and Morocco."
38. Mitchell, *Rule of Experts*, 9.
39. Wyrtzen, "Colonial Legitimization-Legibility Linkages and the Politics of Identity in Algeria and Morocco," 205.
40. Hannoum, *The Invention of the Maghreb*.
41. Mikdashi, *Sectarianism*.

sition was less dramatic, and a stronger cohort of "native" bureaucrats remained in place to staff the newly independent governments. For many of the chapters in this volume, the postcolonial era was one of relative state weakness, as newly created states struggled to impose their authority and a monopoly on legitimate violence over societies that had no necessary allegiance. For much of the Levant, as Hinnebusch notes in this volume, this was famously the period of the Arab Cold War, marked by the ability of strong states such as Egypt to intervene extensively in the domestic affairs of "weaker" states.

Viewing this period through the lens of legibility tells a similar story. Relatively new states had to learn about the societies they governed. Pan-Arab passions reduced the legibility of local populations. In states such as Jordan and Lebanon, the influx of Palestinian refugees placed new burdens on the state, introduced new populations to the security services, and devolved significant degrees of state functions (education, welfare, housing) to the United Nations Relief and Works Agency (UNRWA).[42] In the Gulf, urbanization and the rise of the oil industry rapidly changed societies, which relied extensively on international oil companies and expatriates to staff their newly created bureaucracies. Arguably, with Egyptian Muslim Brotherhood expatriates staffing their ministries, these Gulf states lacked visibility even into their own state—much less their societies.[43] The visceral fear and hatred expressed by leaders of the UAE for the Muslim Brotherhood might in part be explained by their recognition of the extent to which the Brotherhood had penetrated their own state apparatus, which allowed the Brotherhood a view into UAE society as well as the ability to obstruct the state's visibility. But in other countries, such as Egypt, this was a period of state-led development that saw a massive expansion of state bureaucracy and state capacity. The erosion of the informational capacity of the Egyptian state would come in the post-1970 era of neoliberalism—typically seen as an era of high state capacity.

The oil-fueled rise of state strength in the 1970s and 1980s focused on expanding legibility through intensive, crosscutting surveillance agencies. Regimes obsessed with avoiding the military coups and popular uprisings of the 1950s and 1960s prioritized building vast apparatuses of intelligence, repression, and clientelistic patronage, which became the distinctive markers of Arab autocracy. These states sought to render legible previously rebellious societies to better control, co-opt, or suppress them. The shock

---

42. Irfan, *Refuge and Resistance*.
43. On the Egyptian Brotherhood's role in Saudi state formation, see Lacróix, *Awakening Islam*.

of the Iranian Revolution and the Sunni Islamist seizure of the Grand Mosque of Mecca in 1979 led Gulf states, especially, to invest heavily in the surveillance and mobilization of religious networks. The neoliberal turn, however, anticipated a retreat of the state from the provision of key social welfare provisions widely across the region in the 1990s, particularly in Egypt. Again, the legibility perspective largely aligns with the narrative offered by Hinnebusch in this volume.

While the narrative trajectory of state capacity outlined above is generally accepted, in the 1990s assessments begin to diverge. Where Hinnebusch sees a bell-shaped curve, with state capacity declining after its peak around 1990, a legibility account sees strengthening state capacity after 1990 in key areas. On the one hand, to be sure, this is an era of neoliberalism—the shrinking of the state and its retreat from key areas of the economy and society—and of what Hinnebusch calls "post-populism," which prioritized crony capitalism over the traditional populist constituencies. But it is also the period of what Heydemann elsewhere calls "upgraded authoritarianism," which involved, in part, improved state capacity to manage emergent challenges and compensate for the revealed weaknesses in the state.[44] Examining these contradictory trends through the lens of legibility can help to resolve these contradictions.

First, more freely contested elections and a more tolerant approach toward civil society and moderate Islamist challengers gave regimes a better view into the real preferences of society, without threatening their actual hold on power. Bringing previously tightly repressed groups out into the open signaled lower, or at least restrained, coercive capacity and introduced a wider space for oppositional speech and organization. But it also clearly increased the informational capacity of those states, allowing them to learn about the size and reach of Islamist movements, the degree and nature of societal dissatisfaction, and the identities of potential elite challengers. This would not save many of them from the systemic shock of the 2011 uprisings, which clearly revealed extreme gaps in their informational capacity. But for several decades this aspect of upgraded authoritarianism did seem to enhance their resilience.

A second impact on state capacity in this period came from the rise of civil society in response to neoliberal policies of reducing the public sector. The provision of social services by Islamist movements or political parties eroded state-centered clientelistic patronage while also closing off state

---

44. Heydemann, *Upgrading Authoritarianism in the Arab World*.

visibility into those networks.[45] Whereas in the 1960s the Egyptian state may have had records on almost every student and every citizen who used a hospital, its retreat opened the door to the Muslim Brotherhood to step in with its own networks of clinics, schools, and other social services. This transferred some degree of clientelistic political benefits from the state to the Muslim Brotherhood, but it also shifted visibility and legibility: closing the eyes of the state to the needs of those citizens while opening the eyes of the Brotherhood as a potential challenger.

Third, new media such as satellite television and the internet reduced state monopolies over information and the public sphere, badly eroding that aspect of state capacity.[46] But at the same time, it enabled states to monitor expression to better understand their potential challengers. Early on, social media such as blogs were inscrutable to regimes—they did not understand the internet, did not know why it was important, and did not much care relative to the efforts they put into controlling broadcast media. The Arab uprisings forced them to care, however. And once they did, they had intrinsic advantages as states, as discussed in the next section.

Fourth, scientific public opinion survey research was relatively scarce in the Middle East compared to other regions of the world until this period, when it rapidly boomed. In the 1990s, some Middle Eastern governments and associated research centers began to survey their populations, systematically making their policy preferences and social perceptions legible. These surveys escalated dramatically in quantity and quality in the 2000s, as the global war on terror suddenly made Arab public opinion important and relevant to the Washington policy agenda. Academic and policy interest then facilitated the building of local capacity in the form of highly professional survey organizations capable of administering surveys for international partners or for their own needs. The result was the proliferation of surveys providing highly detailed snapshots of the views of Arab citizens—a dramatic increase in their legibility to states (and to academics and the US government).

The surveys of those years surfaced attitudes toward democracy, religion, and US foreign policy highly familiar to readers of James Scott. The questions asked and the terms used were often those of importance to the United States, shaping the answers given into a form comprehensible to a Western audience but perhaps orthogonal to the actual concerns and concepts of the respondents. Cross-national surveys asking about attitudes

---

45. Brooke, *Winning Hearts and Votes*; Cammett, *Compassionate Communalism*.
46. Lynch, *Voices of the New Arab Public*.

toward "democracy" impose an artificial sense of commonality and universal knowledge, facilitating comparison across time and space as well as responsiveness to policy interventions. It is important to note that attitudinal surveys do not themselves create a public opinion, in the sense of being linked to actual policy outcomes. Nor do surveys call into being attitudes, opinions, or beliefs that did not previously exist.

Overall, then, even as the MENA neoliberal state retreated from significant aspects of social welfare provision, public sector employment, and other traditional dimensions of state capacity, its informational capacity manifestly increased. States were able to gather, systematize and analyze vastly more information about their citizens, both attitudinal and behavioral, and to thus better target both repression and co-optation. This greater legibility is at the heart of the "upgrade" in authoritarian practice and resilience. The Arab uprisings disrupted this perceived stability but, in fact, as we shall see, actually introduced radical increases in the informational capacity of most Arab states as they discovered the opportunities for surveillance available to them in the digital realm.

Digital Liberation, Digital Authoritarianism

How does digital authoritarianism change all of this? The literature on the political effects of the internet polarized early on between enthusiasts for what seemed like a liberation technology and skeptics who warned of its potential abuses by powerful states.[47] In the early days following the Arab uprisings, that pendulum swung too rapidly toward the enthusiasts, who saw social media such as Facebook and Twitter as the keys to the sudden eruption of mass protest and the shattering of the walls of fear. Cautionary voices warned that technologies were value neutral, that their effects were mediated by political and social structures, and that the key mechanisms affecting politics were all potentially double-edged.[48]

The arguments for emancipatory effects lay in the revolutionary new forms of networked communication.[49] Social media lowered the transaction costs for collective action, bridging divisions caused by physical separation and distance. It helped to erode state control over the public sphere and political communication, a capacity that had been central to the opera-

---

47. Diamond and Plattner, *Liberation Technology*; Shirky, *Here Comes Everybody*; Morozov, *The Net Delusion*.
48. Lynch, "After Egypt."
49. Bennet and Seneberg, *The Logic of Connective Action*; Tufekci, *Twitter and Tear Gas*.

tion of Arab authoritarianism. There were variations, of course, from the near total state domination of the public sphere found in Ba'thist Iraq and Syria to the contentious but carefully monitored and policed print public in Egypt and Jordan. Even without protest mobilization, social media layered on to the earlier satellite television revolution to shatter state control over information and public communication.[50] That, in and of itself, represented a significant erosion in state capacity with wide-ranging implications.

Shutting down this new media revolution was beyond the capacity of most states: they battled back instead by working within the new digital environment. Some, such as China and Iran, created national internet systems that allowed for control over which apps could be used and were endowed with a master key for total surveillance. But most regimes adapted by using their superior wealth and power to insert themselves into these new public spaces, shaping public discourse through open and covert interventions while extensively monitoring online behavior and opinions.[51] States recruited people to monitor and to engage on social media, amplified by bots and other coordinated inauthentic behavior.[52] It is important not to take this surfeit of legibility at face value, however. The mass collection of data cannot itself produce insights without the analytical capacity to translate data into information; the digital world has produced a steady stream of companies promising far more than they can deliver either politically or commercially through the collection of mass data. Mass collection of data is rather inefficient compared to the targeted surveillance of known actors. The seeming omnipresence of the state in the media realm might be more performative than effective—though no less significant for the behavioral patterns it produces. The targeted repression of well-known activists, for instance, sends a message to lesser-known digital users about their vulnerability, which may not be warranted.

The debate has shifted in recent years as the extent and nature of digital repression have become more clear.[53] In an influential statistical analysis, Nils Weidman and Espen Rød found that more wired countries were less, not more, likely to experience disruptive political protest.[54] Digital technologies "can substitute traditional repressive tactics that autocratic governments have relied on in the past . . . [and have] given autocratic leaders

50. Lynch, *Voices of the New Arab Public.*
51. Jones, *Digital Authoritarianism in the Middle East.*
52. Abrahams and Leber, "Comparative Approaches to Mis/Disinformation."
53. Diamond, "Rebooting Democracy"; Diamond, "The Road to Digital Unfreedom"; Deibert, "The Road to Digital Unfreedom."
54. Weidmann and Rød, *The Internet and Political Participation in Democracies.*

new ways to manipulate and control the population, which has reduced the need for traditional and sometimes costly repressive tactics."[55] Social media, for Seva Gunitsky, has become a critical vehicle for regimes to "cheaply gather information about citizen preferences."[56] This has unleashed new forms of digital authoritarianism that have radically expanded the ability of states to monitor the communications of their citizens.[57] Similar dynamics of autocratic regime strengthening have been observed not only in the Middle East but in Southeast Asia, Eurasia, and beyond.[58]

As Xu Xu puts it, "Digital surveillance resolves dictators' information problem of not knowing individual citizens' true anti-regime sentiments."[59] Xu focuses not on internet penetration but rather specifically on the deployment of digital surveillance technology. This resolves what he calls the "vertical information problem": "increasing digital surveillance shapes the repression-co-optation trade-off in substantively important ways by mitigating this *vertical information problem*, thereby allowing authoritarian governments to substitute targeted, preventive repression for more costly universal co-optation."[60] The implication, for Xu, is that autocratic regimes should be able to repress much more selectively as digital surveillance expands, while also scaling back expensive social programs aimed at mass co-optation. Anita Gohdes makes the case perhaps the most bluntly: "Surveillance of digital information exchange can provide intelligence that enables the use of more targeted forms of repression."[61]

Simply observing content publicly posted to social media offers insights into the political views, personal connections, and likely behavior of individual citizens. This can be done at scale through techniques of big-data analysis: network analysis, automated text analysis, sentiment analysis, and artificial intelligence. The risks this poses can be seen graphically after the US Supreme Court overturned *Roe v. Wade* in the use of information from period tracking apps and online communications to prosecute women who seek abortions or of location tracking of phones to monitor their potential travel to states that still provide abortions. The risks can also be seen in how Lebanese and Egyptian security services use apps such as Grindr to

---

55. Weidmann and Rød, *The Internet and Political Participation in Democracies*, 6–7.
56. Gunitsky, "Corruption of the Cyber-Commons," 42–54.
57. Lynch, ed., "Digital Activism and Authoritarian Adaptation."
58. Simpeng, "Digital Media, Political Authoritarianism, and Internet Controls in Southeast Asia."
59. Xu, "To Repress or to Co-opt?" 310.
60. Xu, "To Repress or to Co-opt?" 310.
61. Ghodes, "Repression Technology," 488.

identify LGBTQ individuals.[62] Or surveillance can be done simply by following influential individuals, or by joining WhatsApp, Telegram, or Facebook groups under real or assumed identities. But nefarious technology has proliferated to go beyond such reading of publicly available social media information. The Israeli cyber-intelligence organization NSO Group and its Pegasus software have taken this even further with no-click exploits, by which governments can take control of devices and access all their information without their targets even clicking a link. Spies inside Facebook and Twitter can reveal the identities of political dissidents.[63]

The magnitude and degree of digital surveillance that has emerged and flourished over the last decade is truly astonishing.[64] In globally high-informational-capacity states such as China and Singapore (and in the MENA region, the UAE), virtually every aspect of life that is digitally mediated is potentially open to state scrutiny. For upgrading authoritarian regimes, the China model of full digital surveillance and control is a goal, not a dystopia.[65] In what Özgün Topak calls an "authoritarian surveillant assemblage," overlapping and reinforcing levels of surveillance allow regimes to penetrate deeply and control society.[66] And there is little privacy, even in ostensibly anonymized mass data, as users are tracked across multiple apps and platforms in ways that create unique digital footprints to reveal shockingly intimate information about everything from their medical concerns to their food preferences to their political commitments.

Consider the Israeli surveillance apparatus in the occupation of the West Bank and Gaza.[67] Israel always engaged in a wide range of human intelligence operations through the use of collaborators and blackmail alike.[68] This came to be supplemented by telecommunications intercepts. The rise of digital surveillance techniques has brought intelligence operations to an [69]entirely new level. It is no accident that many of the key digital surveillance companies, such as NSO Group, are inextricably connected to the Israeli military and test their operations on Palestinian populations. During the June 2021 protests at the Al-Aqsa Mosque complex in Jerusalem, for instance, Israel flexed its information dominance by sending text messages to protestors whose phone's digital footprint placed them at the

---

62. On pregnancy apps, see Tufekci, "We Need to Take Back Our Privacy."
63. Lynch, ed., *Digital Activism and Authoritarian Adaptation*.
64. Shires, *The Politics of Cybersecurity in the Middle East*.
65. For details on China's model, see Chin and Lin, *Surveillance State*.
66. Topak, "The Authoritarian Surveillant Assemblage."
67. Shtaya, "Nowhere to Hide."
68. Zureik, Lyon, and Abu-Laban, eds., *Surveillance and Control in Israel/Palestine*.
69. Heydemann, "Upgrading Authoritarianism in the Arab World."

protest. Surveillance is also enabled by closed-circuit television cameras across Jerusalem, face-scanning apps that facilitate facial recognition surveillance, and the collection of biometric information at checkpoints. The "Wolf Pack" database includes a massive trove of personal information, with the goal of profiling every Palestinian living in the West Bank and matching them with facial recognition software.[70] During the 2023 Gaza War, Israel used an Artificial Intelligence (AI) system with this database in its targeting decisions.[71] The upshot is that, through the lens of legibility, the Israeli occupation arguably has more "stateness" in the stateless West Bank than most actual states.

This Israeli panopticon is not unique to the occupation, of course. Israeli tech companies have used the occupation to develop, test, and refine surveillance apps, which can then be marketed abroad. The UAE has pioneered the use of digital technologies for mass surveillance and control, including widespread monitoring of public spaces.[72] A full-scale infrastructure of surveillance and monitoring of public space facilitates social control and the suppression of dissent.[73] The UAE's ability to enact such comprehensive digital surveillance is testimony to its high state capacity. Other Arab states that are larger and less wealthy may aspire to such a digital surveillance architecture but lack the state capacity to build, use, and maintain it. Critically, however, these digital tools lower the costs and barriers to such surveillance, thus promising to put the tools for imposing legibility on society in the hands of even relatively poor states and enhancing this critical dimension of state capacity.

Access to Israeli surveillance technology was reportedly one of the key motivations for the UAE in its normalization of relations with Israel. A wide array of other Arab regimes—including relatively poor as well as wealthy states—use the Israeli Pegasus surveillance technology, including Bahrain, Saudi Arabia, the UAE, Jordan, Morocco, and Algeria.[74] Those not mentioned have probably just not yet been caught. In this age of transnational authoritarian learning, the use of such digital surveillance tools will likely become ever more ubiquitous. As a result, these states grow stronger relative to society: more able to render their populations legible and thus able to demonstrate higher capacity.

---

70. Amnesty International, *Automated Apartheid*.
71. Abraham, "A Mass Assassination Factory."
72. Ziadeh, "Surveillance, Race and Social Sorting in the United Arab Emirates."
73. Shires, "The Implementation of Digital Surveillance Architecture in the Gulf."
74. For regularly updated research on the use of Pegasus by Arab states, see Citizen Lab's Targeted Threats Project, https://citizenlab.ca/category/research/targeted-threats/

Of course, what states are actually able to do with this information will continue to vary in line with other metrics of state capacity. Knowing more about a society's needs might not matter if the state has neither the resources nor the interest in meeting them. This higher capacity, however, is likely to continue to be used primarily in the service of regime security rather than development, taxation, or the provision of public goods. It may not, therefore, solve any of the problems identified by Heydemann and others in this volume. Egypt, for instance, may have gleaned tremendous amounts of information from its digital surveillance. But this has not translated into better refined or discriminating repression. Its security state continues to rely on its more traditional methods of mass arrests and extended incarceration, often catching non-activists or non–Muslim Brothers in its dragnets around protests. Its extended, extralegal imprisonment of tens of thousands of citizens could be taken as an indictment of its ability to translate greater societal legibility into more targeted repression. It could, of course, also be an intentional strategy, to impose fear and passivity among potential opponents for fear that any expression of dissent could meet a draconian response.

Conclusion

Viewing MENA state capacity through the lens of legibility reorients some of the arguments and themes that run through this volume. During the 1950s and 1960s, generally seen as the era of state weakness, some MENA states (notably Egypt) made significant advances in rendering their societies legible. During the 1970s and 1980s, the era generally seen as one of strong states, the overwhelming focus on regime security distorted both the means and the goals of legibility. During the 1990s and 2000s, when the neoliberal turn is often seen as weakening those overdeveloped security states, societies actually became more legible to states through civil society, elections, and public opinion surveys as well as the emergence of new media platforms that allowed citizens to publicly express their views. The ability of states to use this new informational capacity should be seen as a key part of what Heydemann termed "authoritarian upgrading."

One of the key contentions of this chapter is that the rise of digital surveillance may represent a disjuncture in our understanding of state capacity, which forces us to consider the possibility of fundamentally new dynamics rather than repetition of familiar patterns. Many MENA societies have literally *never* been more transparent and legible to their states. The ability to access, organize, and analyze massive amounts of online data gives states unprecedented capacity to understand behavioral and attitudinal dynamics. The ability to surveil electronic communications allows a degree of penetration of ostensibly private behavior and interaction of which the old-school *mukhabarat* could only dream. It recalls an old but telling joke where a security official is explaining Facebook to a skeptical Arab president. After explaining that Facebook led citizens to voluntarily share their identity, their network of personal relationships, their political attitudes, and even their sexual and social behaviors, the security official chuckles and tells the president that it was their finest invention. That old joke is dated, though. The current level of digital surveillance capacity far exceeds what those early Facebook years offered.

I do not mean to claim that legibility is the only dimension of state capacity that matters. It interacts with the range of other dimensions highlighted by theorists of the state. Informational capacity alone does not help if a state lacks the infrastructural capacity to act based on that information. Informational capacity will not facilitate economic development or public goods provision if the regime has no interest in those outcomes. Nor will informational capacity necessarily save a regime threatened by large-scale public dissent, if it is unable to respond effectively through either repression or co-optation. Being aware of a threat does not mean that the threat can be countered. President Hosni Mubarak, after all, was not really taken by surprise by the protests of January 25, 2011: his security forces were ready, but they were just overwhelmed by the unexpected size, creativity, and tenacity of the marching crowds.

From the perspective of state-failure discourse, declining legibility typically signals incipient state weakness and potential political instability. As a state struggles with visibility into particular geographic areas or political/ethnic/religious communities, the risks go up that it will be unable to anticipate or prevent insurgency, political rebellion, or other forms of disruption. The solution, then, would be to encourage mechanisms to reduce opacity in the name of stability. In the Middle East, at least, this prescription is worse than the disease. Higher legibility has in general been an invitation to greater repression, which in turn compounds the problems that actually breed political instability. Giving autocratic regimes in Syria, Egypt, or Saudi Arabia more powerful digital tools to monitor and surveil their populations is not likely to contribute to the greater good.

This issue is not only about political dissent, narrowly defined. Take, for instance, the use of digital surveillance to identify and prosecute LGBTQ and other marginalized communities.[75] LGBTQ citizens have traditionally survived in conservative systems by remaining nonvisible, tolerated only to the extent that their sexuality did not appear before the public eye. In countries such as Lebanon and Egypt, digital platforms have been used by security services to pierce the illegibility that protected those communities. From police officers using honey trap accounts on Grindr to physically seizing phones to scrutinize chat logs and contact lists, digital surveillance has enhanced state capacity very much at the expense of personal freedoms and human rights.

Do these changes then mean that the Middle East is doomed to suffer eternal autocracy under the crushing weight of the digital panopticon? The rise of digital surveillance certainly seems to have shifted the balance of power decisively toward the state, not just in MENA but globally. The so-called China model of 360-degree societal surveillance, with state visibility into lives conducted virtually entirely online, is highly attractive to most MENA regimes. New technologies put into place to combat COVID-19 have already turned some of these fears into realities. These new capabilities may allow Middle Eastern states, which had long scored higher on despotic than infrastructural power, to leapfrog their past deficiencies. That is certainly the hope in Abu Dhabi, Cairo, and the region's many palaces.

But it is worth recalling James Scott's original intention when introducing "legibility" into the canon of state capacity theory. The modern state's drive to impose legibility on the societies it seeks to control has led, in his telling, to a consistent pattern of grand failure. The legibility produced by modernizing states distorted reality. By reducing social and natural life to codifiable metrics, states lost their sense of the deeper web of cultural relations, local knowledge, and social history that gave texture and meaning to society. Their grand projects of social transformation based on the legibility they imposed on society repeatedly failed.

Nor did the obsessive ethnography of the colonial powers protect them from the drive for decolonization. The French drive to render Algerian society legible helped to consolidate an artificially rigid divide between Berbers and Arabs that served them poorly in the face of a national war of liberation. The British ethnographic cataloging of colonial possessions did not help them keep Egypt any more than it helped them keep India.

There is a lesson here. The new digital legibility that has turbocharged state power similarly comes with costs. More and more of modern life may

---

75. Nagle and Fakhoury, *Resisting Sectarianism*.

have moved online, but the online and the offline are still not the same. What people do online makes up only one part of the totality of their identity, beliefs, relationships, and practices. As states grow confident in their total penetration of society, they will likely lose sight of those offline realities and build strategies of repression based on what they see rather than on what they do not see. And when they attempt to act on this distorted map, they will still lack the administrative, fiscal, and human capacity to carry out their intended reforms.

As societies come to understand these lacunae in the state's vision, individuals and groups too will adapt by moving key aspects of their political activity offline, engaging in deception and misdirection, and turning the ruler's methods against it. They will adapt and find new ways to challenge, just as they have in every other era and domain. Those outside the gaze of the new state will likely reside disproportionately in the marginal neighborhoods and peripheral areas. Regimes may find that their increased scrutiny of what Asef Bayat calls the "middle class poor"—educated, online, but underemployed urbanites—comes at the cost of less understanding of other potentially revolutionary sectors.[76] As the Arab uprisings of 2011 demonstrated, MENA societies have a remarkable ability to organize and act outside the gaze of security-obsessed regimes—even if their legibility to states continues to increase.

BIBLIOGRAPHY

Abraham, Yuval. "'A Mass Assassination Factory': Inside Israel's Calculated Bombing of Gaza." *972 Magazine*, November 30, 2023. https://www.972mag.com/mass-assassination-factory-israel-calculated-bombing-gaza/

Abrahams, Alexei, and Andrew Leber. "Comparative Approaches to Mis/Disinformation: Electronic Armies or Cyber Knights?" *International Journal of Communication* 15 (2021).

Abdullah, Wassim F., Zena Agha, Nur Arafeh, Sam Bahour, Ahmad Barclay, Tariq Dana, Marwa Fatfata, et al. "Focus On: Palestinian Digital Rights." Al-Shabaka, August 17, 2022. https://al-shabaka.org/focuses/focus-on-palestinian-digital-rights/

Amnesty International. "Automated Apartheid: How Facial Recognition Fragments, Segregates and Controls Palestinians in the OPT." Amnesty International, May 2, 2023. http://www.amnesty.org/en/documents/mde15/6701/2023/en/

Ayubi, Nazih. *Over-stating the Arab State: Politics and Society in the Middle East*. London: I. B. Tauris, 1996.

---

76. Bayat, "The Arab Spring and Its Surprises."

Bayat, Asef. "The Arab Spring and Its Surprises." *Development and Change* 44, no. 3 (2013): 587–601.
Belge, Ceren. "State Building and the Limits of Legibility: Kinship Networks and Kurdish Resistance in Turkey." *International Journal of Middle Eastern Studies* 43 (2011): 95–114.
Bellin, Eva. "Reconsidering the Robustness of Authoritarianism in the Middle East: Lessons from the Arab Spring." *Comparative Politics* 44, no. 1 (2012): 127–49.
Bennet, Lance, and Alexandra Seneberg. *The Logic of Connective Action: Digital Media and the Personalization of Contentious Politics*. New York: Cambridge University Press, 2013.
Bertwick, Elissa, and Fotini Christia. "State Capacity Redux: Integrating Classical and Experimental Contributions to an Enduring Debate." *Annual Reviews of Political Science* 21 (2018): 71–91.
Blaydes, Lisa. *State of Repression: Iraq under Saddam Hussein*. Princeton, NJ: Princeton University Press, 2018.
Brambor, Thomas, Agustin Goenaga, Johannes Lindvall, and Jan Teorell. "The Lay of the Land: Information Capacity and the Modern State." *Comparative Political Studies* 53, no. 2 (2020): 175–213.
Brooke, Steven. *Winning Hearts and Votes: Social Services and the Islamist Political Advantage*. Ithaca, NY: Cornell University Press, 2019.
Cammett, Melani. *Compassionate Communalism: Welfare and Sectarianism in Lebanon*. New York: Cambridge University Press, 2009.
Chin, Josh, and Liza Lin. *Surveillance State: Inside China's Quest to Launch a New Era of Social Control*. New York: St. Martin's Press, 2022.
Deibert, Ronald. "The Road to Digital Unfreedom: Three Painful Truths about Social Media." *Journal of Democracy* 30, no. 1 (2019): 25–39.
Diamond, Larry. "Rebooting Democracy." *Journal of Democracy* 32, no. 2 (2021): 179–83.
Diamond, Larry. "The Road to Digital Unfreedom: The Threat of Postmodern Totalitarianism." *Journal of Democracy* 30, no. 1 (2019): 20–24.
Diamond, Larry, and Marc E. Plattner. *Liberation Technology: Social Media and the Struggle for Democracy*. Baltimore: Johns Hopkins University Press, 2012.
Fearon, James, and David Laitin. "Ethnicity, Insurgency and Civil War." *American Political Science Review* 97, no. 1 (2003): 75–90.
Ghodes, Anita R. "Repression Technology: Internet Accessibility and State Violence." *American Journal of Political Science* 64, no. 3 (2020): 488–503.
Gunitsky, Seva. "Corrupting the Cyber-Commons: Social Media as a Tool for Autocratic Stability." *Perspectives on Politics* 13, no. 1 (2015): 42–54.
Hägerdal, Nils. *Friend or Foe: Militia Intelligence and Ethnic Violence in the Lebanese Civil War*. New York: Columbia University Press, 2021.
Hale, Henry E. "Regime Change Cascades: What We Have Learned from the 1848 Revolutions to the 2011 Arab Uprisings." *Annual Review of Political Science* 16 (2013): 331–53.
Hannoum, Abdelmajid. *The Invention of the Maghreb: Between Africa and the Middle East*. New York: Cambridge University Press, 2021.
Hanson, Jonathan K. "State Capacity and the Resilience of Electoral Authoritarianism: Conceptualizing and Measuring the Institutional Underpinnings of Autocratic Power." *International Political Science Review* 39, no. 1 (2018): 17–32.

Hegghammer, Thomas. "Resistance Is Futile: The War on Terror Supercharged State Power." *Foreign Affairs* 100, no. 5 (September/October 2021): 44–53.
Hendrix, Cullen. "Head for the Hills? Rough Terrain, State Capacity, and Civil War Onset." *Civil Wars* 13, no. 3 (2011): 345–70.
Heydemann, Steven. "Upgrading Authoritarianism in the Arab World." Brookings Institution Analysis Paper 13, October 2007.
Irfan, Anne. *Refuge and Resistance: Palestinians and the International Refugee System*. New York: Columbia University Press, 2023.
Jones, Marc Owen. *Digital Authoritarianism in the Middle East: Deception, Disinformation and Social Media*. London: Hurst, 2022.
Kirchgaessner, Stephanie. "Saudi Woman Given 34-Year Prison Sentence for Using Twitter." *The Guardian*, August 16, 2022.
Koehler, Kevin. "State and Regime Capacity in Authoritarian Elections: Egypt before and after the Arab Spring." *International Political Science Review* 39, no. 1 (2018): 97–113.
Kuran, Timur. "Now Out of Never: The Element of Surprise in the East European Revolution of 1989." *World Politics* 44, no. 1 (October 1991): 7–48.
Kurzman, Charles. *The Unthinkable Revolution in Iran*. Cambridge, MA: Harvard University Press, 2004.
Lacróix, Stephane. *Awakening Islam: The Politics of Religious Dissent in Contemporary Saudi Arabia*. Cambridge, MA: Harvard University Press, 2015.
Lee, Melissa M. *Crippling Leviathan: How Foreign Subversion Weakens the State*. Ithaca, NY: Cornell University Press, 2020.
Lee, Melissa M., and Nan Zhang. "Legibility and the Informational Foundations of State Capacity." *Journal of Politics* 79, no. 1 (2016): 118–32.
Lohmann, Susanne. "The Dynamics of Informational Cascades: The Monday Demonstrations in Leipzig, East Germany, 1989–91." *World Politics* 47, no. 1 (October 1994): 42–101.
Luna, Juan Pablo, and Hillel David Soifer. "Capturing Sub-National Variation in State Capacity: A Survey Based Approach." *American Behavioral Scientist* 61, no. 8 (2017): 887–907.
Lynch, Marc. "After Egypt: The Promise and Limitations of the Online Challenge to the Authoritarian Arab State." *Perspectives on Politics* 9, no. 2 (2011): 301–18.
Lynch, Marc, ed. *COVID-19 in the Middle East and North Africa: Two Years On*. POMEPS Studies 47 (June 2022).
Lynch, Marc, ed. *Digital Activism and Authoritarian Adaptation*. POMEPS Studies 43 (August 2021).
Lynch, Marc. *Voices of the New Arab Public: Al-Jazeera, Iraq, and Middle East Politics Today*. New York: Columbia University Press, 2007.
Mazur, Kevin. *Revolution in Syria: Identity, Networks, and Repression*. New York: Cambridge University Press, 2021.
Mikdashi, Maya. *Sectarianism: Sovereignty, Secularism and the State in Lebanon*. Stanford: Stanford University Press, 2022.
Mitchell, Timothy. "The Limits of the State: Beyond Statist Approaches and Their Critics." *American Political Science Review* 85, no. 1 (1991): 77–96.
Mitchell, Timothy. *Rule of Experts: Egypt, Techno-Politics, Modernity*. Berkeley: University of California Press, 2002.

Morozov, Evgeny. *The Net Delusion: The Dark Side of Internet Freedom*. New York: Public Affairs, 2012.
Müller-Crepon, Carl, Philipp Hunziker, and Lars-Erik Cederman. "Roads to Rule, Roads to Rebel: Relational State Capacity and Conflict in Africa." *Journal of Conflict Resolution* 65, no. 2–3 (2021): 563–90.
Nagle, John, and Tamirace Fakhoury. *Resisting Sectarianism: Queer Activism in Postwar Lebanon*. London: Bloombury Zed Books, 2021.
Nathan, Noah. *The Scarce State: Inequality and Political Power in the Hinterland*. New York: Cambridge University Press, 2023.
Rodriguez-Muniz, Michael. "Cultivating Consent: Nonstate Leaders and the Orchestration of State Legibility." *American Journal of Sociology* 123, no. 2 (2017): 385–425.
Schwedler, Jillian. *Protesting Jordan: Geographies of Power and Dissent*. Stanford: Stanford University Press, 2022.
Scott, James C. *Seeing Like a State: How Certain Schemes to Improve the Human Condition Have Failed*. New Haven, CT: Yale University Press, 1999.
Shires, James. "The Implementation of Digital Surveillance Architecture in the Gulf." *Digital Activism and Authoritarian Adaptation in the Middle East*, edited by Marc Lynch, 16–21. POMEPS Studies 43 (August 2021).
Shires, James. *The Politics of Cybersecurity in the Middle East*. London: Hurst Press, 2021.
Shirky, Clay. *Here Comes Everybody: The Power of Organizing without Organizations*. New York: Penguin Books, 2008.
Shtaya, Mona. "Nowhere to Hide: The Impact of Israel's Digital Surveillance Regime on the Palestinians." Washington, DC: Middle East Institute, April 27, 2022. https://www.mei.edu/publications/nowhere-hide-impact-israels-digital-surveillance-regime-palestinians
Simpeng, Aim. "Digital Media, Political Authoritarianism, and Internet Controls in Southeast Asia." *Media, Culture and Society* 42, no. 1 (2020): 25–39.
Slater, Dan, and Sofia Fenner. "State Power and Staying Power: Infrastructural Mechanisms and Authoritarian Durability." *Journal of International Affairs* 65, no. 1 (2011): 15–29.
Topak, Özgün. "The Authoritarian Surveillant Assemblage: Authoritarian State Surveillance in Turkey." *Security Dialogue* 50, no. 5 (2019): 454–72.
Tufekci, Zeynep. *Twitter and Tear Gas: The Power and Fragility of Networked Protest*. New Haven, CT: Yale University Press, 2018.
Tufekci, Zeynep. "We Need to Take Back Our Privacy." *New York Times*, May 19, 2022.
Vannetzel, Marie. *The Muslim Brothers in Society: Everyday Politics, Social Action, and Islamism in Mubarak's Egypt*. Cairo: American University of Cairo Press, 2021.
Wedeen, Lisa. *Ambiguities of Domination: Politics, Rhetoric, and Symbols in Contemporary Syria*. Chicago: University of Chicago Press, 2002.
Weidmann, Nils B., and Espen Geelmuden Rød. *The Internet and Political Participation in Democracies*. New York: Oxford University Press, 2019.
Wyrtzen, Jonathan. "Colonial Legitimization-Legibility Linkages and the Politics of Identity in Algeria and Morocco." *European Journal of Sociology* 58, no. 2 (2017): 205–35.

Xu, Xu. "To Repress or to Co-opt? Authoritarian Control in the Age of Digital Surveillance." *American Journal of Political Science* 65, no. 2 (2021): 309–25.

Ziadeh, Rafeef. "Surveillance, Race and Social Sorting in the United Arab Emirates." *Politics* (2021). https://doi.org/10.1177/02633957211009719

Zuboff, Shoshana. *The Age of Surveillance Capitalism: The Fight for a Human Future at the New Frontier of Power*. New York: Public Affairs, 2019.

Zureik, Elia, David Lyon, and Yasmeen Abu-Laban, eds. *Surveillance and Control in Israel/Palestine: Population, Territory and Power*. New York: Routledge, 2011.

SECTION 2

Dimensions of Regime-ness

FIVE

What We Talk about When We Talk about the State in Postwar Lebanon

Bassel F. Salloukh

> A *picture* held us captive. And we could not get outside it, for it lay in our language and language seemed to repeat it to us inexorably.
> —Ludwig Wittgenstein, *Philosophical Investigations*, §115

When I walk the streets of Beirut and see cars parked on sidewalks or double-parked on street corners, bots driving in every possible direction, pedestrians crossing intersections as if they are running for their lives through a firing range with street crossings doubling as targets for speeding cars, sidewalks colonized by illegal cafes armed with the omnipresent espresso machine, and that informal militia labeled "valet parking" with a Roman emperor's ultimate power to decide if and where you can park your car no matter what the law says—I wonder, where is the Lebanese state? Everyday parlance is saturated with references to state absence, and *"wayn el-dawle?"* is the inescapable Lebanese complaint par excellence.[1] This kind of haphazard political ethnography is deceiving, however, because the state

---

Acknowledgments: I would like to thank Lisa Anderson, Toby Dodge, Ibrahim Halawi, Wadood Hamad, Steven Heydemann, Marc Lynch, and Sean Yom for their constructive comments on earlier drafts of this chapter. I also thank Viviane Akiki for compiling the data in tables 5.1 and 5.2.

1. Mouawad and Bauman, *"Wayna al-Dawla?"*

is at the heart of a range of political economic, biopolitical, discursive, and performative practices that serve to incentivize and reproduce a particular type of sectarian politics and consent while precluding the emergence of viable organizational and ideological alternatives.

But what are we talking about when we talk about the state in postwar Lebanon? How do we conceptualize the state and its relation to society and a range of social actors? What picture of the state do we subscribe to when we label the state in Lebanon weak or absent, or when we demarcate analytical boundaries between the state and non-state actors, between the state and society, the private and the public realm, the formal and informal sphere, or when we contest these labels? What are we talking about when we make claims about the centrality of the state apparatus in the production and reproduction of sectarian subjectivities and control of gender and sexual differences or when we consider the state a site for the production of political economic relations and their social, organizational, and ideological forms?

This chapter surveys three very different pictures of the state in Lebanon: first, the so-called weak state picture and its critics; second, the immaterial and its limits; and third, borrowing from Antonio Gramsci, the integral state, gathering the material, ideological, and organizational dimensions in the production of the postwar order on the road to the current socioeconomic, fiscal, monetary, and financial collapse. These three pictures make different claims about the state and adopt different conceptions of the relation between state and society. I argue that the weak state picture—with its emphasis on how much the state in Lebanon falls short of the neo-Weberian ideal—is caught up in a largely binary image of the relation between the state and society, one that cannot account for postwar political economic dynamics. Moreover, critiques of the weak state thesis, whether based on accounts of mediated statehood, hybrid security, or hybrid sovereignties and despite their welcome corrections, do not go far enough in theorizing the transformations in the postwar order that have produced the integral state. Consequently, either they abstract the state to a level that ends up ignoring the material underpinnings of political dynamics, and thus fail to explain the causes of and reactions to the country's political economic collapse after 2019, or they gloss over the violence and distortions that come with hybridity. The immaterial picture confirms just how much the state as dominant idea has become entrenched in the everyday practices and affections of the Lebanese, even though they may imagine it differently. But this approach is of little utility to the centrality of the postwar state as condensation of the material and social relations that went into the making of the postwar order and is so essential to an explanation of the causes and management of the post–October 2019 collapse. Instead, a picture of the integral state captured by the postwar political economic and financial elite—and producing its social, political, ideological, and organizational forms—helps us explain not only the causes of the current fiscal, financial, monetary, and socioeconomic collapse but also the dearth of viable political, organizational, and ideological alternatives in response to this collapse and the shape of the management of this collapse with its disastrous consequences.

In making this argument about the intersection of the material, organizational, and ideological in postwar Lebanon, I join a number of scholars who are "thinking in a Gramscian way about the present" without, however, "rigidly 'applying' Gramsci's concepts."[2] The "state," Gramsci writes expansively, "is the entire complex of practical and theoretical activities with which the ruling class not only justifies and maintains its dominance, but manages to win the active consent of those over whom it rules."[3] Gramsci's key concept of the integral state helps us gather the material, organizational, and ideological activities that went into producing and maintaining the postwar order. It is also a concept that allows us to see the postwar state free from the imposed binaries of civil society/political society, consent/coercion, weak/strong state, private/public sphere, state/non-state actors, and formal/informal sectors. This, in turn, liberates us "from the conceptual binaries produced through conventional understandings of state-society relations."[4] With the picture of the integral state "Gramsci attempted to analyze the mutual interpenetration and reinforcement of 'political society' and 'civil society' (to be distinguished from each other methodologically, not organically) within a unified (and indivisible) state form."[5] It is a picture that can travel beyond its original location not only to capture analytically how the postwar political economic elite placed the state's fiscal and monetary policies at the service of capital accumulation *but also* to integrate substantial social constituencies into the postwar order along strictly sectarian clientelist lines. This, in turn, disaggregated cross-sectarian class interests and provided the material conditions—or "lived

---

2. Morton, *Unravelling Gramsci*, 208 and 213, respectively. See also Salem, "Gramsci in the Postcolony."
3. Gramsci, *Selections from the Prison Notebooks*, 244. See also Thomas, *The Gramscian Moment*; and El-Mahdi, "The Failure of the Regime or the Demise of the State?"
4. Chomiak and Schwedler, "Introduction to Special Issue," 94. See also Bou Akar, *For the War Yet to Come*.
5. Thomas, *The Gramscian Moment*, 137.

experience" in Gramscian language—to secure a level of sectarian ideological consent that precluded the emergence of viable political alternatives in the postwar era.[6] This was also accomplished by controlling the agents of ideological diffusion and cultural production, namely, the media, and by obstructing the emergence of those organizational formations, whether trade unions, professional syndicates, or nonsectarian parties with substantial followings, that could contribute to the emergence of nonsectarian forms of collective solidarities and organization that allow for contesting the political economic elite's postwar project. Far from reifying, underrating, or abstracting the state, then, this Gramscian picture foregrounds the state as part of a complex web of "social relations and material interests that constitute a social . . . order."[7] On this view, then, the distortions of the postwar period, from systemic corruption, lack of accountability, everyday lawlessness, and "the habitualisation and internalisation of [sectarian] social practices"[8] to the "predatory pursuit, or rush for the spoils, of wealth and power," are all part of a mode of governance that has less to do with state weakness, absence, or failure and more with "a mechanism of social organisation . . . through which political power is disseminated and wealth redistributed," one that served to reproduce sectarian modes of political mobilization, organization, and consent at the expense of alternative types.[9]

This approach shares close affinities with Steven Heydemann's chapter in this volume surveying the trajectories of limited statehood in the Middle East and North Africa. It takes stateness as constructed by an overlapping political economic elite, one in which the state/society, private/public, and formal/informal binaries are intentionally dissolved in the production of the "social relations and material interests" undergirding the sectarian postwar order. However, whereas in Heydemann's account the boundaries between levels of governance become "fluid," governance is "layered," and state and non-state actors are "intertwined," in my account the technologies of postwar consociational power sharing produce a more integral state, in which state and non-state actors are one and the same.[10] This postwar integral state expresses a very different picture and vocabulary of the state than our existing theoretical arsenal makes available. It is a "state *as* society" picture, as Heydemann and Marc Lynch describe it in this volume's introduction, where the making of the postwar order is shaped by, but also

---

6. Przeworski, "What Have I Learned from Marx and What Still Stands?"
7. Bilgin and Morton, "Historicising Representations of 'Failed States,'" 69.
8. Morton, *Unravelling Gramsci*, 171.
9. Bilgin and Morton, "Historicising Representations of 'Failed States,'" 74.
10. See Steven Heydemann's chapter in this volume.

shapes, the state and its political economy. The analytic difference between Heydemann's chapter and this one is a product of variations in regime types and concomitant elite choices.

This chapter is organized diachronically around the aforementioned pictures of the state as they appeared in studies of Lebanese politics. I start with the neo-Weberian picture of the state in terms of its autonomy from society and its possession of a measure of institutional capacity. Its emphasis on the congenitally weak institutional capacity of the Lebanese state has justifiably come under critical scrutiny from a range of perspectives accusing it of uncritically exporting neo-Weberian assumptions to the Global South. But I also interrogate this critical literature on its own terms, exploring whether it has gone far enough in dissolving the binary image of the relation between the state and society and between the state and non-state actors and whether it can account for the materiality involved in the production of the postwar order. The chapter then moves to explore immaterial representations of the state in postwar Lebanon culled from postmodern and anthropological standpoints. This picture of the state is indispensable for an understanding of how entrenched the idea of the state has become in everyday experiences but cannot on its own explain the material underpinnings of the postwar order and its unmaking. The balance of the chapter theoretically and empirically explores the picture of the integral state in the making of the postwar order through the production of new social relations and material interests and its role in the management of the socioeconomic and financial collapse in the aftermath of the October 2019 protests. Studying the state in Lebanon thus requires us to free ourselves from any one aspectival perspective and to appreciate instead the explanatory value and limits of all three different pictures explored in this chapter.[11]

Neo-Statist and Immaterial Pictures of the Lebanese State

Much like its counterpart on the Arab state,[12] the literature on the state in Lebanon subscribes to multiple pictures of the state. The first and earliest picture of the state in the literature on Lebanese politics captures the state in terms of its presumed institutional capacities: its ability to pen-

---

11. For a discussion of aspectival perspectives in Wittgenstein's approach to philosophy, see Moore, "The Politics of Wittgenstein."
12. See the chapters by Hinnebusch and Anderson in this volume and the collection of papers in the roundtable "Reevaluating the Nation-State."

etrate society, extract resources, and restructure state-society relations. Here the strength or weakness of states depends on "how closely they approximated the ideal type of centralized and fully rationalized Weberian bureaucracy, supposedly able to work its will efficiently and without effective social opposition."[13] In this neo-statist view, the Lebanese state was born institutionally weak—bereft of autonomy and penetrative infrastructural capacities—vis-à-vis an alliance of religious, political, and economic elites. These elites were more often than not divided along factional and intra-sectarian rather than inter-sectarian rivalries, but nevertheless they were determined after 1926 to exploit sectarianism "to assure access to the new political institutions and wealth of the state."[14] The state was also weak in facing the segmental autonomy and prerogatives enjoyed by the sectarian communities by virtue of the logic of corporate consociational power sharing.[15] This autonomy is protected by the powers of Articles 9 and 10 of both the pre- and postwar constitutions that grant substantial non-territorial autonomy in administering personal and cultural matters to what religious and political elites have always falsely presented as "internally homogeneous, externally bounded" sectarian communities.[16]

Even the Shihabist etatist strong state-building interregnum (1958–70) failed to impose its will on society and the political elite. The Shihabist strategy was based on using the alliance with President Gamal Abdel Nasser's Egypt to insulate the state from external and domestic interference. This, in turn, would allow a professional cadre of state administrators to push through a series of administrative and socioeconomic reforms that could promote national integration and increase state institutional capacity and autonomy, especially vis-à-vis the traditional *za'im* elite.[17] Fuad Shihab subscribed to a precise and linear state-building strategy: administrative reforms would create the kind of coherent institutions (*mu'asasat*) that make up the anatomy of a state (*dawla*) that would then create a nation (*watan*) from the multitude of sects gathered in Lebanon.[18] However, the

---

13. Evans, Rueschemeyer, and Skocpol, "On the Road toward a More Adequate Understanding of the State," 351.

14. Zamir, *Lebanon's Quest*, x. See also Hudson, *The Precarious Republic*; El-Khazen, *The Breakdown of the State in Lebanon*; Farha, *Lebanon*; and the literature reviewed in Mouawad and Bauman, "*Wayna al-Dawla?*"

15. Hudson, "The Problem of Authoritative Power in Lebanese Politics."

16. Brubaker, "Ethnicity without Groups," 164; Salloukh, "The State of Consociationalism in Lebanon"; Weiss, *In the Shadow of Sectarianism*; Mikdashi, "Sex and Sectarianism."

17. Hudson, *The Precarious Republic*; Johnson, *Class and Client in Beirut*; Goria, *Sovereignty and Leadership in Lebanon, 1943–1976.*

18. Nassif, *Jumhuriyat Fuad Shihab.*

Shihabist state was always one among many other social organizations competing for social control of the population in an "existing environment of conflict," to cite the language of Joel Migdal's original state-society model developed against the neo-Weberian image of the state in the Global South.[19] Its efforts at social control through monopoly over the stipulation of rules governing people's social behavior were actively resisted by existing social organizations—namely, patron-client dyads in the form of social and political elites claiming to represent sectarian communities or "groups."[20] In this "weblike" society, the Shihabist state stood no chance against the "mélange of fairly autonomous social organizations" vying for social control.[21] Moreover, the failure of the Lebanese state to achieve anything resembling a "*monopoly of the legitimate use of physical force*" within its territory undermined its sovereignty and exposed it to overlapping domestic and external contests that turned the country into a site for grander geopolitical competition.[22] This was exacerbated in the prewar years by the presence of a bevy of Palestinian commando groups, and it doubled in the postwar period with Hezbollah's oversized military capabilities both at the local and transnational levels.[23] Both "used the weakness and failure of the Lebanese state to advance their own, transnational, agendas."[24] This Lebanese state, understood in terms of institutional capacities and the ability to control its territory and population, has been in permanent erosion and backsliding vis-à-vis a host of competitors, sectarian or otherwise—a destination many other Arab states have belatedly reached, as Lisa Anderson shows in this volume.[25]

The presumed weakness of the Lebanese state to achieve a measure of administrative coherence and institutional autonomy from overlapping religious, political, and economic elites, and to defend its territorial sovereignty, does not imply that the state in Lebanon is "irrelevant" or "absent," especially biopolitically and legally.[26] Maya Mikdashi has demonstrated the indispensable role of the state's legal and bureaucratic apparatus in the production and reproduction of sectarian and sexual differences. The insti-

---
19. Migdal, *Strong Societies and Weak States*, 30.
20. Brubaker, "Ethnicity without Groups."
21. Brubaker, "Ethnicity without Groups," 37.
22. Gerth and Mills, trans. and eds., *From Max Weber*, 78; Salloukh, "The Art of the Impossible"; Najem, *Lebanon*.
23. Brynen, *Sanctuary and Survival*; Sharara, *Dawlat Hizballah*; Blanford, *Warriors of God*; Mikaelian and Salloukh, "Strong Actor in a Weak State."
24. Atzili, "State Weakness and 'Vacuum of Power' in Lebanon," 759.
25. See also Anderson, "Bread, Dignity and Social Justice."
26. Mouawad and Bauman, "*Wayna al-Dawla?*" 66.

tutions of the Lebanese state deploy a range of biopolitical technologies—including census registries, citizenship laws, and criminal laws—to regulate, manage, and reproduce both gender and sectarian inequalities. This "sextarianism" is "a way of viewing the Lebanese state that does not separate or privilege sectarian difference from sexual difference."[27] The state's postwar legal architecture is instrumentalized by the political elite to shield themselves from any measure of accountability, whether for the country's fiscal and financial collapse or the criminal negligence that led to the port explosion of August 4, 2020. The state apparatus is also involved in selective sanctioning or punishment of LGBTQ identities. John Nagle and Tamirace Fakhoury have documented how "the state makes distinctions between expressions of sexuality that are implicitly tolerated"—namely, middle class, affluent, clean, and contained—"and those that are proscribed. Commercial Queerspaces are tacitly incorporated into the neoliberal and sectarian state, while at the same time spaces and people deemed transgressive to the moral order—are violently erased."[28] Similarly, and against claims that the Lebanese state did not historically interfere in the country's laissez-faire economy, Jamil Mouawad and Hannes Baumann argue that Banque du Liban (BDL), the state's preeminent monetary institution, has played a central, autonomous role in managing Lebanese capitalism but in a manner that handsomely rewards the country's commercial and financial elites. They find this to be the case in both the prewar and the postwar periods—an autonomy that fits more the period before the end of the war in 1990. During the Amin Gemayel presidency (1982–88), BDL still exercised a measure of monetary autonomy from what would later develop into an overlapping postwar political economic and financial elite.[29] Finally, the state can perform weakness and inaction as a deliberate governance strategy to manage both local and refugee populations. As Lama Mourad and Fakhoury suggest, in this case central state authorities decide not to act as managers of a neo-Weberian state intent on policing its territory or regulating refugee populations in a bid to avoid making divisive political choices.[30] Rather, "state *inaction* played a major role in structuring the responses that did emerge 'below' and 'above' the state, from local authorities and international agencies," as Mourad demonstrates. Moreover, "indirect measures taken by the central government

---

27. Mikdashi, "Sectarianism," 4.
28. Nagle and Fakhoury, *Resisting Sectarianism*, 58.
29. Mouawad and Bauman, "*Wayna al-Dawla?*"; Hourani, "Capitalists in Conflict."
30. Mourad, "'Standoffish' Policy-Making"; Fakhoury, "Refugee Return and Fragmented Governance in the Host State."

facilitated and encouraged greater local autonomy in governing the refugee presence. This, in turn, served to further decentralize and fragment the response to the Syrian refugee crisis in Lebanon and legitimized discretionary action by municipal authorities."[31] Consequently, central state authorities were able to simultaneously distance themselves from the most discriminatory of these subnational policies while using "their presence as leverage to shift greater international donor support towards Lebanese host communities and Lebanese state institutions."[32] Far from an expression of absence, then, this liminality of the Lebanese state on such sensitive policy choices "operationalized through repressive acts and violent neglect" produces "perceptions of enmity among citizens and refugees resettled within its boundaries."[33]

Be that as it may, the weak state thesis is challenged by a substantial body of critical scholarship that positions itself squarely against what it considers a normative bias embedded in the exportability of neo-Weberian assumptions about state institutional capacity to the Global South. For example, the "mediated state" approach seeks to dissolve the state-society binary and instead underscores the interdependency between state and non-state forms of governance across a range of spatial, demographic, and hierarchical components of governance.[34] Nora Stel contends that far from contributing to the weakness of the Lebanese state, the Palestine Liberation Organization and the Lebanese state are caught in a relation of mutual interdependence that serves their different yet mutual interests in governance coordination: "States manipulate non-state governance actors, but non-state actors also use states to govern."[35] Alternatively, Najib Hourani contends that the Lebanese political terrain is itself constituted by a certain type of "hybrid sovereignties."[36] The blurring of the imagined state/non-state boundary is a constant strategy deployed by political aspirants in Lebanon: from Amin Gemayel's Kataeb Party to Hezbollah and including Rafiq Hariri. Not only have these actors blurred the domestic state/non-state boundary, but they have also made "themselves useful for larger regional or global politicoeconomic projects," in the process blurring the inside-outside boundary as well.[37] A crucial part of this dynamic involves

---

31. Mourad, "'Standoffish' Policy-Making," 250.
32. Mourad, "'Standoffish' Policy-Making," 266.
33. Carpi, "Winking at Humanitarian Neutrality," 92 and 86, respectively.
34. Stel, "Mediated Stateness as a Continuum"; Meier, "Hizbullah's Shaping Lebanon Statehood"; and Mazzola, "Mediating Security."
35. Stel, "Mediated Stateness as a Continuum," 367.
36. Hourani, "Lebanon."
37. Hourani, "Lebanon," 40.

the incorporation of "states within the state" where "political movements develop and become anchored in non-state and parastatal institutions that provide economic, social and security services and even military capabilities . . . [and] the embedding of such networks and institutions within the state apparatus."[38] In a similar vein, Waleed Hazbun "turns the weak-state approach upside down" when he considers the weakness of postwar Lebanon's plural system of security governance to be an effective means to contain domestic and external security threats.[39] Arguing against advocates of centralizing and expanding the coercive capacities of the Lebanese state, he finds in the "assemblage of conflicting state and non-state actors that constantly negotiate among rival understandings of security" the best guarantee for stability and protection against the violence of a strong state.[40] Similarly, hybrid security sectors may challenge neo-Weberian assumptions anchored on the state's exclusive right to coercive monopoly but nevertheless demonstrate how non-state actors "do not always operate completely outside the realm of the state, but often in partnership with or with the consent of the state."[41] Nor is the contest between state and non-state actors over territorial sovereignty something that can be considered only in binary terms: as state led or absent. Rather, Sara Fregonese blurs the boundary between state and non-state armed actors in civil war Lebanon. She considers non-state actors "agents of sovereignty through their use and control of urban space."[42] The result is "hybrid political actors" that "exist between the state and the nonstate"; they are "new entities that are both state and nonstate, entities which enact a hybridized sovereignty born from this cross-contamination."[43] In this view, then, Lebanon is "not a 'weak' state where sovereignty is lacking in light of the civil war, but one where sovereignty has become increasingly *hybrid*."[44]

Hybridity claims are often criticized for their "conceptual vagueness" and for not always acknowledging that "the state is in fact the space in which elements of the elite cooperate and compete with each other using the tools of ideology, economics and violence."[45] In the Lebanese

---

38. Hourani, "Lebanon," 41.
39. Hazbun, "The Politics of Insecurity in the Arab World," 658; Hazbun, "Assembling Security in a 'Weak State.'"
40. Hazbun, "The Politics of Insecurity in the Arab World," 657.
41. Mazzola, "Mediating Security," 205.
42. Fergonese, *War and the City*, 135.
43. Fergonese, *War and the City*, 135.
44. Fergonese, *War and the City*, 9.
45. Santini and Tholens, "Security Assistance in a Post-Interventionist Era," 497; Mansour and Khatib, "Where Is the 'State' in Iraq and Lebanon?"

context, however, hybridity claims do not actually go far enough in tracing the transformations in the postwar state form, transformations that have led to almost complete state capture by overlapping political, economic, and financial elites, thus dissolving altogether the private/public, state/non-state, and formal/informal binaries. Hezbollah is instructive in this regard, amplifying a broader pattern in the postwar state: it can be claimed that it is "both more and less than a state," as Anderson suggests; embeds its "networks and institutions within the state apparatus," as Najib Hourani argues; acquires public authority "whether alongside the state, in competition with the state, or in collaboration with the state," as Lina Khatib contends; and is "intertwined" with the state along different layers of governance, as Heydemann theorizes in this volume for similar non-state actors.[46] Hezbollah is also, however, both inside and outside the state (the state understood not just in terms of sovereignty and layered levels of governance but also as a political economy that transcends the private/public or formal/informal binary) no matter how much the discourse of the party's leaders blames the state for Lebanon's problems.[47] Moreover, and although it warns us about the limits of the weak state image and its origins outside the Global South, the hybridity literature's abstraction of the state and its sovereignty to capture those moments of blurriness underrates the materiality that goes into the production and reproduction of sectarian politics over a range of other political choices. It also invites us to celebrate the impact of non-state actors—armed or otherwise—on people's everyday security and encounters even if many citizens do not want to, thus glossing over the violence (especially cultural and social) imposed by these non-state actors on the very societies they claim to represent and protect. Celebrating plural security structures ends up reintroducing another normative bias in the name of debunking neo-Weberian assumptions.

Others celebrate the partial but never total absence of the state in Lebanon as antidote to the alienation and abstraction experienced in other national contexts with much higher levels of regulation of social life as a result of more state legal capacity. Ghassan Hage traces the experiences of middle-class expatriates in Lebanon as they navigate their ways through Beirut's lawlessness, traffic, and dilapidated infrastructure.[48] He contends that what these expats experience is an existence outside the law that "is not

---

46. Anderson, "'Creative Destruction,'" 377; Khatib, "How Hezbollah Holds Sway over the Lebanese State," 4.
47. Bou Akar, *For the War Yet to Come*; Khatib, "How Hezbollah Holds Sway over the Lebanese State," despite the latter's preference to describe the party in hybridity terms.
48. Hage, "Inside and Outside the Law."

just a negative attitude vis-à-vis the law and others." Far from it, because "it can become the space of a different sociality—a skill and an affirmation of a desire to co-exist with others differently."[49] Hage is careful lest his argument is interpreted as a celebration of the country's lawlessness and "perennial problems." Nevertheless, he argues that "the partial absence of the state and of any serious centralized planning does foster more than just lack and negativity. It offers a space for the flourishing of . . . [a] negotiated being." It follows then that any attempt to increase "the capacity of the laws of the state to saturate and regulate society, and as desirable as it might be," it inevitably "involves certain losses."[50] And so instead of seeing the experience of crossing the road as an event laden with dangerous possibilities, Hage considers it akin to "a festival of interpersonal interaction in which one has to actively engage with others, look drivers in the eye, and squeeze an ethical moment out of them by appealing to their better side and making them stop for you."[51] Of course, the rules of this sociality by which we relate to others outside the boundaries of the law are so fluid that any mistake or miscalculation can turn this festival into a violent act, a certainty confirmed by the high ratio of car accidents and flying bots on Lebanon's streets.[52] It also elides the dehumanizing effects this lawlessness has on those who live under it but do not want to live by its rules.

An altogether different picture of the state in postwar Lebanon defines it immaterially, as *imaginaire*, discourse, fantasy, or ideological construct.[53] Mouawad examines how marginalized Lebanese use sports "to 'imagine' a unified Lebanon, which is not only powerful and defiant but can also compete" with those countries that intervene in its domestic politics.[54] Here the state is imagined or articulated in everyday practices as the "other" of the weak, penetrated polity lacking national unity because of sectarian affiliations. Approaching national unity as a performative act reveals "a 'Lebanon' that differs from its dominant descriptions as disintegrated or a 'jigsaw of communities.'"[55] Alternatively, constructing a discourse of resilience around a weak Lebanese state is nothing more than a sectarian elite trope to consolidate the domination of the sectarian system and "undermine the

---

49. Hage, "Inside and Outside the Law," 104.
50. Hage, "Inside and Outside the Law," 105.
51. Hage, "Inside and Outside the Law," 101.
52. Leading to some five thousand accidents per year that cause around five hundred fatalities and an average of six thousand injuries, one-third of which are considered serious. Al-Zayn, "Istidamat al-Naqel fi Lubnan?"
53. See Mouawad and Bauman, "In Search of the Lebanese State."
54. Mouawad, "Lebanese Football," 290.
55. Mouawad, "Lebanese Football," 291.

state's public institutions, rendering the society dependent on a system of aid and clientelism rather than on state-driven development projects."[56] The state may also be conceived as fantasy through experiences of everyday cynicism. As Sami Hermez suggests, "People's fantasies of what should be the state strengthen the state's power and existence."[57] This happens because the mere act of everyday cynicism consolidates "the hegemonic sectarian structures of power making up the state."[58] Even those living on the margins of the state can actively experience the state "as a construct that has manifestations and effects."[59] Michelle Obeid shows how residents of Arsal invoke a different kind of state than the one responsible for their marginality, and in so doing, the state's history of neglect can be countered by citizens searching for a state that incorporates them and develops their rural towns.[60] Similarly, Mouawad and Bauman use a postmodern approach to demonstrate how Timothy Mitchell's state effect can "unfold from below" and thus produce the state as an ideological construct.[61] They show how the people of the marginalized region of Akkar "continue to defend the state, albeit indirectly, through their attachment to the army" and how this "speaks to the army's role in society. This is not a story of sectarian leaders mediating between a sectarian society and a weak state. It is a story that depicts the production of a diffuse state effect."[62]

This immaterial picture of the state captures what Charles Tripp describes as the everyday practices and effects "that produce and reproduce the state as dominant idea and as ultimate institutional frame in a particular time and place."[63] The problem in Lebanon, as Albert Hourani long observed, is that this dominant idea may be imagined differently by different—for him—sectarian groups.[64] To be sure, sectarianism in Lebanon does not "hinder popular aspirations for a 'strong' state and unified nationalism."[65] However, this nationalism is polyphonic, imagined differently not just by historically constructed sectarian groups, but also inside

56. Mouawad, "Unpacking Lebanon's Resilience," 4–5.
57. Hermez, "When the State Is (N)ever Present," 512.
58. Hermez, "When the State Is (N)ever Present," 519.
59. Obeid, "Searching for the 'Ideal Face of the State' in a Lebanese Border Town," 343.
60. Obeid, "Searching for the 'Ideal Face of the State' in a Lebanese Border Town."
61. Mitchell, "Society, Economy, and the State Effect"; Mouawad and Bauman, "*Wayna al-Dawla?*" 79.
62. Mouawad and Bauman, "*Wayna al-Dawla?*" 81.
63. Tripp, "The State as an Always-Unfinished Performance," 337.
64. Hourani, "Visions of Lebanon." See also Salibi, *A House of Many Mansions*; Beydoun, *Identité confessionnelle et temps social chez les historiens libanais contemporains*; Kaufman, *Reviving Phoenicia*.
65. Mouawad, "Lebanese Football," 291.

them, and by all those groups who position themselves against sectarian imaginings of the nation.[66] Sectarianism and nationalism in Lebanon are thus not incommensurate.[67] Consequently, immaterial approaches that underscore the making of the state effect in everyday practices confirm that some one hundred years after the country's creation in 1920 the Lebanese continue to imagine their state differently, and there is nothing wrong with that. But these approaches tell us little about political economic elite capture of the state on behalf of capital accumulation and redistribution in the making of the postwar order and how this shaped social relations and material interests in a manner that served to reproduce a sectarian type of politics.

Critics of the weak state thesis rightly reject neo-Weberian claims about state coherence and capacity. Yet their hybridity argument falls short of describing the extent to which the postwar state was captured by an overlapping political, economic, and financial elite in the production of an altogether new state form. Nor, paradoxically, can Migdal's refined "state in society" image of a state caught in struggles over domination with other social forces capture the postwar Lebanese state.[68] After all, this image is one where "a clash of social forces, including the state, ... mediated through the struggles and accommodations in society's numerous arenas" takes place at "the junctures of states and societies."[69] But what if this picture of a "recursive and mutually transforming as well as potentially empowering" relation between different social forces at the junctures of state and society is not the right one for postwar Lebanon or fails to explain postwar political economic dynamics?[70] What if what's at work is state capture by a complex, though not always coherent, alliance of political, economic, and financial elites inside and outside the state to preclude the very state domination assumed by Migdal? Can either the neo-Weberian or immaterial images of the state, and the languages of state weakness, strength, or hybridity, account for this alternative picture of the postwar state? The next section creatively deploys Gramsci's concept of the integral state to describe the production of the postwar order and its state form and explain its disastrous consequences after October 17, 2019.

---

66. Weiss, *In the Shadow of Sectarianism*; Bassel F. Salloukh, "War Memory, Confessional Imaginaries, and Political Contestation in Postwar Lebanon."
67. Weiss, *In the Shadow of Sectarianism*; Shaery-Eisenlohr, *Shi'ite Lebanon*.
68. Migdal, "The State in Society."
69. Migdal, "The State in Society," 23.
70. Grzymala-Busse and Luong, "Reconceptualizing the State," 533.

Capturing the Postwar State

Theorizing Lebanon's postwar state entails moving beyond Migdal's "state in society" approach. For whereas the latter underscores "the social embeddedness of state actors and the extent to which state elites and social actors engaged in contestation over the boundaries and limits of state power," in Lebanon the postwar alliance between former warlords-cum-political elites and neoliberal businessmen succeeded in fully capturing the state and deploying its fiscal and monetary policies in the interest of a mongrel process of capital accumulation and a range of redistributive mechanisms that eviscerated state institutions and turned the public sector into an archipelago of clientelist networks.[71] This alliance captured not just the strategic managerial, bureaucratic, judicial, and coercive sinews of the state but also middle- and lower-range positions across the public sector. Of course, this does not mean that the postwar public sector was bereft of merit and talent. Rather, the intersection of overwhelming constitutional-ministerial postwar powers with clientelist employment throughout the public sector across all grade levels and along a predetermined sectarian quota substantially neutralized the effects of this talent on public policymaking.[72] Consequently, and far from the picture of an embedded "state in society," the result was an even more extreme version of Najib Hourani's "states within the state" image where non-state and parastatal institutions embed themselves within the state apparatus. In fact, more than blurring the boundaries between the state and non-state actors, they *became* the postwar state. This was an unprecedented and incomparable development in the postwar years. The clientelism of the prewar *za'im* elite was mainly about securing access for partisans or regions to state appointments—usually but not always along meritocratic lines—and to resources without destroying the institutions and political economy of the state.[73] Michel Chiha, the theoretician of Lebanese identity and the postcolonial state, loathed a large public sector.[74] By contrast, the postwar political elite assumed a predatory approach to the political economy of the state, always in the name of

---

71. Heydemann, "Explaining the Arab Uprisings," 197; Traboulsi, *Al-Tabaqat al-Ijtima'iya fi Lubnan*; Baumann, *Citizen Hariri*; Salloukh, "Taif and the Lebanese State"; and Mouawad, "Unpacking Lebanon's Resilience."
72. Unless, of course, the minister empowered the public sector's professional cadre, as was the case with Elias Saba (2004–5) and George Corm (1998–2000) in the Ministry of Finance. See Jad Ghosn's interview with Alain Bifani, general director of the Ministry of Finance (2000–2020), July 8, 2021, https://www.youtube.com/watch?v=IAGOQ90sSVM
73. Johnson, *Class and Client in Beirut*.
74. Traboulsi, *Silat Bila Wasel*.

representing what are falsely presented as monolithic and closed sectarian societies. Their clientelist networks straddled the private/public and formal/informal sectors. For example, in their detailed study of the political economy of the van line number 4 transportation system in Beirut, Petra Samaha and Amer Mohtar use the example of one informal private initiative, transport vans, to expose how such initiatives straddle the private/public and formal/informal sectors and "are part of the clientelist system that forms what is the state today in Lebanon," or what is, more precisely, the integral state in postwar Lebanon. Samaha and Mohtar's argument equally applies to a range of other activities, from power generators, internet or fiber-optic providers, and power barges to cement, gas, oil, medical, and flour cartels.[75]

On this reading, then, the postwar Lebanese state is not a site of contestation between rival political economic coalitions aligned with different elements of the state and vying for the state's resources.[76] It is not "an arena where intersecting societal power networks fight with each other for dominance," as Toby Dodge accurately describes the contest over the "decentered" and "contradictory" post-2003 Iraqi state.[77] Nor is this the case of an authoritarian regime exploiting limited statehood or withholding stateness "to navigate the challenges of authoritarian power sharing and authoritarian control."[78] Rather, it is a case of complete state capture by overlapping and inter-sectarian political, economic, and financial elites operating in unison and camouflaged as representatives of sects and protected from accountability by the technologies of consociational power sharing. Gramsci's toolkit of the integral state helps us capture this complex picture of the postwar state as political economy located at the epicenter of a twin but mongrel process of capital accumulation *and* clientelist distribution by trans-sectarian political, economic, and financial elites with its derivative political, social, organizational, and ideological forms.

Capturing the postwar state was central to a process of capital accumulation and wealth concentration executed through the intersection of national and transnational "rentier capitalism."[79] It also served to finance a political economy of sectarianism inside and outside state institutions.[80] In

---

75. Samaha and Mohtar, "Decoding an Urban Myth," 8; Legal Agenda, "Ihtikarat al-Muhasasa al-Shamila," 68.
76. Migdal, "The State in Society," 19.
77. Dodge, "Gramsci Goes to Baghdad," 3.
78. Heydemann, "Seeing the State or Why Arab States Look the Way They Do," chap. 1, this volume.
79. Christophers, *Rentier Capitalism*; Assouad, "Lebanon's Political Economy."
80. Baumann, "Social Protest and the Political Economy of Sectarianism in Lebanon"; Salloukh, "Taif and the Lebanese State."

line with Gramsci's theorizing of the relation between the material, organizational, and ideological, this political economy of sectarianism provided the "material bases of consent" for substantial sectarian constituencies that were drawn into the postwar political elite's clientelist networks with profound sociological and organizational implications.[81] Moreover, alongside a larger ensemble of institutional, legal, and interpersonal practices, it distorted the very incentives structuring political action; disaggregated class loyalties; delivered a measure of ideological consent; reproduced sectarian modes of political identification and mobilization; and operated to preclude alternative oppositional organizational forms and political alternatives to sectarianism.[82] To appreciate the consequences of state capture on the economy, sociology, organizational forms, and hence politics of the postwar order, it is important to unpack in detail the political economy that undergirded its "social relations and material interests."

Part of the assemblage of "social relations and material interests" making up the postwar order unfolded at the level of fiscal and monetary policies. We have precise numbers for total government spending for the period from 1993 until 2017. Table 5.1 describes the political economy of a total of $192.5 billion in government expenditures during this period. The largest share of government spending, some $71.7 billion, financed rentier profits through interest payments, mainly to those Lebanese banks heavily exposed to the sovereign debt. A 2020 World Bank report notes that "interest cost has consumed about half of government revenues, averaging 9 percent of GDP over 2013–2018."[83] Consequently, net bank profits increased from $63 million in 1993 to $2.050 billion in 2018, with an accumulated total of $22.140 billion for 1993–2018.[84] The second largest share of government spending for the same period was on public sector salaries, pensions, and benefits, amounting to $63.4 billion, or some 32.9 percent of total spending. Transfers to the national power company, EDL ($22 billion, or 11.4 percent), constitute a regressive, indirect electricity subsidy, while operating expenses, transfers to public and private institutions ($19.6 billion, or 10.2 percent), and capital expenses ($15.2 billion, or 7.9 percent) are packed with payments that serve the political economy of clientelism and corruption.

If we zoom in on the makeup of government spending on salaries, wages, pensions, compensations, and social benefits for permanent and temporary

---
81. Przeworski, *Capitalism and Social Democracy*.
82. Salloukh et al., *The Politics of Sectarianism in Postwar Lebanon*; Deeb, "Beyond Sectarianism."
83. World Bank, "The Deliberate Depression," 8.
84. *The Monthly*, April 9, 2019. https://monthlymagazine.com/article/4846/221

TABLE 5.1. Total Government Spending, 1993–2017

Sector	$ Billion	Total (%)
Interest on debt & debt repayments	72.3 (71.7 interest payments)	37.6
Salaries, wages, pensions, compensations, & social benefits	63.4	32.9
EDL transfers	22	11.4
Operating expenses & transfers to public & private (CSO) institutions	19.6	10.2
Capital expenses	15.2	7.9
Total	**$192.5**	**100%**

Source: Privately compiled for the author by the economic analyst Viviane Akiki based on the ledgers of the Ministry of Finance, the only official numbers published by the Lebanese state, although their review by the Audit Bureau remains pending, Beirut, June 2021.

employees, we can appreciate the extent of postwar government spending on sectarian clientelist recruitment into the public sector as it emerged as a primary vehicle for the production of postwar social relations and material interests. Table 5.2 unpacks this process empirically: the salaries and wages of permanent and temporary public sector employees—excluding public officials and those in the Lebanese University and the municipalities—account for 90 percent of all salaries and wages, the equivalent of $31.3 billion. Whereas the salaries and wages of public sector employees do not exceed one-third of that sum, around $10.4 billion, the salaries of military and security personnel account for two-thirds, around $20 billion. More precisely, the Ministry of Finance estimates that of the $10.4 billion that constitute the salaries and wages of public sector employees, those in educational bodies account for 57 percent of that sum, or $6 billion, leaving the remaining $4.4 billion for permanent, temporary, and contractual public sector employees. This is not surprising, however, given that recruitment into the security services and the public educational system served as primary clientelist job-creating mechanisms for the political elite as they sought to create new social relations on which the postwar order was erected. Indeed, of a total of around 300,000 employees in the public sector in 2017, some 120,000 are security and military personnel and another 40,000 employees are spread across the public educational system.[85]

The postwar political economy also relied on a currency peg (LP 1,507.5 to the US dollar from 1997 until its collapse in 2019) as well as debt-creating capital flows and, commencing in 2016, unorthodox financial engineering schemes that were supposed to attract dollar depos-

---

85. Salloukh, "Taif and the Lebanese State," 46.

TABLE 5.2. Structure of Government Spending on Salaries and Wages

1993–2017	$ Billion	Total Spending on This Sector (%)	Total Government Spending (%)
Salaries & wages of permanent public sector & security services employees	28.4	44.8	14.8
Salaries & wages of temporary public sector employees & consultants	2.9	4.6	1.5
Salaries & wages of municipal employees	1.1	1.7	0.6
Salaries & wages of Lebanese University employees	2.5	4	1.3
Expenses & other benefits of public officials	0.197	0.3	0.1
Total value of salaries & wages	35.097	55.4	18.2
Compensation, offers & social benefits	11.4	18	5.9
Pensions	13.9	21.9	7.2
State contributions to mutual funds	3	4.7	1.6
Total	**63.4**	**100%**	**32.9%**

Source: Privately compiled for the author by Viviane Akiki.

its to finance the country's twin deficits but instead incurred huge losses on BDL's balance sheets and benefited only a handful of banks and large depositors.[86] The currency peg served as a camouflaged master subsidy that enabled living standards and consumption levels to be incommensurate with economic production levels and operated in a regressive manner that benefitted wealthier consumers. It also hampered industrialization and allowed the import of a range of commodities, from cars and luxury items to fuel products, medications, medical supplies, wheat, and other essential items at distorted prices. This fed an unequal consumerist lifestyle that can be gleaned from table 5.3. Of a total of $280 billion of cumulative capital inflows from January1993 until June 2018, $261 billion, or 93 percent, was squandered to finance the country's trade deficit—the consequence of an oversized import bill of $317 billion compared to exports of $55 billion, a mismatch rooted in a service-oriented, nonproductive, rentier postwar economy.[87]

---

86. Zbeeb, "Bil-Asma' wal-Arqam."
87. Zbeeb, "Ayna Dhahabat Kul Hadhihi al-Rasamil?"; Schellen, "We Could Have Built a Second Singapore."

TABLE 5.3. Capital Outflows, 2010–18 ($ billion)

Transfers & remittances	55
Petroleum products	45
Personal travel	40
Food imports	30
Vehicle imports	18
Total	**$188**

Source: "Lebanon's Financial Crisis."

TABLE 5.4. BDL FX Subsidies Bill

Item	$ Million
Fuel & fuel products	3,037
Medicines	1,105
Wheat	135
Food items	900
Public sector expenses	1,000
Total	**$6.2 billion**

The full impact of this political economy on everyday life became clear only after BDL started placing limits on import credits in 2019 and the banking sector limited dollar withdrawals starting in April 2019. When BDL started directly subsidizing fuel, wheat, pharmaceuticals, and medical supplies at the official exchange rate on September 30, 2019, while a basket of basic consumer goods was being subsidized at the platform rate of LP 3,900 to the dollar, the monthly cost was estimated at around $500 million.[88] Table 5.4 catalogs how BDL spent a total of $6.2 billion from March 2020 until March 2021 on subsidies for the import of fuel and other fuel products, medicines and medical supplies, wheat, a selection of industrial and agricultural food items, and payments on behalf of the Lebanese state.[89]

Capturing the postwar state allowed the political elite to deploy the political economy of sectarianism to organize the social relations that preclude the emergence of viable oppositional organizational forms that can otherwise contest the ideological hegemony of sectarianism. This worked through colonizing, and hence neutralizing, labor movements and professional associations as sites for oppositional organization to disaggregate the working and professional classes and ensure that they do not organize *as* classes and professional groups.[90] It also involved co-opting and intimidat-

---

88. Chehayeb, "The Weight of Lebanon's Unsustainable Subsidies Program."
89. "Masref Lubnan," 33.
90. Khater, "Public Sector Mobilisation Despite a Dormant Workers' Movement"; Bau-

ing anti-sectarian groups.[91] By contrast, those elements of civil society that served to reproduce sectarian hegemony at the ideological and organizational levels—sectarian parties, schools, scouts, media outlets, and social service providers—operated unhindered.[92]

Only when the structural crisis of the postwar political economy began manifesting itself as early as the 2015 You Stink protests, but more potently during the protests of October 17, 2019, did this result in what Gramsci labels "a crisis of authority," when "the social basis supporting the basic structure of the political system was undermined, resulting in a breakdown of social consensus."[93] This crisis was best expressed in syncretic, sporadic, periodic, unorganized, and leaderless protests targeting both the sectarian elite and what was euphemistically labeled the oligarchy—or the postwar alliance of political, economic, and financial elites.[94] The protests were doomed, however. They were forced to organize and mobilize as the political economic edifice was collapsing and in the context of a mushrooming of new opposition groups spanning the whole ideological spectrum. The structural crisis was also expressed in the sectarian elite's increasing recourse to coercion in defense of their material interests as the postwar political economy unraveled and jeopardized its concomitant ideological and organizational forms.[95] This violence came both from within the state's formal coercive agencies but also from outside, perpetrated by sectarian partisans. Faced with the prospect of difficult decisions to slow the financial, fiscal, and socioeconomic hemorrhaging, the alliance of political, economic, and financial elites decided to take the country to what the World Bank labeled a "deliberate depression," one that felt more like a deliberate destruction of society to save their own material interests.[96] This was the moment when the integral state—the entire network of social relations

---

mann, "Social Protest and the Political Economy of Sectarianism in Lebanon"; Salloukh et al., *The Politics of Sectarianism in Postwar Lebanon*.

91. Clark and Salloukh, "Elite Strategies, Civil Society, and Sectarian Identities in Postwar Lebanon"; Geha, "Co-optation, Counter-Narratives, and Repression."

92. Cammett, *Compassionate Communalism*; Shaery-Eisenlohr, *Shi'ite Lebanon*; Salloukh et al., *The Politics of Sectarianism in Postwar Lebanon*.

93. Morton, *Unravelling Gramsci*, 189.

94. Chalcraft, "Thinking Critically about Regional Uprisings"; Chalcraft, "Revolutionary Weakness in Gramscian Perspective"; Halawi, "Consociational Power-Sharing in the Arab World as Counter-Revolution"; Zbeeb interview with Jad Ghosn, September 2, 2021.

95. Przeworski makes a similar point about Gramsci's political theory: "Hegemony is 'protected by the armour of coercion,' and when consent breaks down coercion can still hold the system together"; Przeworski, *Capitalism and Social Democracy*, 164.

96. World Bank, "The Deliberate Depression." For a damning account of how this strategy unfolded, see Bifani, "The Origin of the Crisis in the Lebanese Banking Sector."

and "entire complex of practical and theoretical activities" "within a unified (and indivisible) state form"—was exposed in its fullness: in its political, economic, financial, monetary, ideological (media), coercive, and legal agencies and activities, at the political/civil society, formal/informal, and private/public levels.

Ma fi Dawle or Ma fi Sha'b?

There is a scene in Ziad Rahbani's 1993 dystopian play *Bikhsous el-Karame wel-Sha'b el-'Anid* when, after someone tries to exchange a defected new radio but is shot for no reason, citizens who otherwise casually ignore the law start voicing their outrage at the absence of the state: *"ma fi dawle,"* they start shouting, complaining about the state's inability to protect them. Then suddenly one of them shouts, *"ma fi sha'b,"* only to be informed by the reporter covering the scene that this game is scheduled for another day.[97] Rahbani's play was meant to be a warning of the dystopian future awaiting a postwar society wired on lies, lawlessness, consumption, contradictions, and superficiality. When Lebanon's socioeconomic and financial unraveling commenced in late 2019, this dystopian play proved hauntingly prophetic.

Originally set very early in the postwar years, but more prescient some two decades later, the above short scene in Rahbani's brilliant play reverses the blame game between *el-dawle* and *el-sha'b*: to escape accountability, the political economic elite abstracts the state and blames it for its absence and corruption while all along leveraging its fiscal and monetary policies for the purposes of accumulating capital and manufacturing the "social relations and material interests that constitute" the postwar order.[98] This abstraction effect is intensified through initiatives that straddle the private/public and formal/informal sectors.[99] In turn, most people—there is always the odd *muwaten 'adi*, or ordinary citizen, to use Rahbani's lingo—internalize this abstraction but accept to play by the incentive structures produced by the postwar state. Strategic social formations have thus gained—albeit in unequal proportions and disproportionally compared to the financial elite—from decades of clientelism; a currency peg that makes possible a life of *uber*-consumption; fuel, medical, and food subsidies; a bloated public sector; tax evasion; informal service providers; permeable borders for all kinds of smuggled products; uncollected custom duties; and a range of

---

97. See the scene at https://www.youtube.com/watch?v=8xvwSjfKh3Y at 15:50 minutes.
98. I owe this formulation to Ibrahim Halawi.
99. Mitchell, "Society, Economy, and the State Effect."

other direct or indirect benefits. Even the lawless scenes with which this chapter opens are a deliberate governance strategy deployed by those who have captured the postwar state but do not want it to act like a state because they want to perpetuate its abstraction and the foundational myth that only sects protect their members.[100] Corruption and impunity from everyday lawlessness at the base insulate those at the top from accountability. It camouflages the dense sinews of the integral state that straddle the private and the public, the formal and the informal. The integral state produces the political, organizational, and ideological forms that sustain it.

Not surprisingly, it was only after the socioeconomic and financial collapse that followed the October 2019 protests that some segments of the *sha'b* belatedly discovered the need to reclaim control of the state as a site for the production of new social relations and material interests. The objective of the most politicized and organized of these groups was to torpedo the postwar integral state from within, harness control of this state's political economy to produce new, fairer social and material relations, and hence create a new politics away from sectarianism.[101] That they have hitherto failed to do so despite the current financial collapse, the concomitant massive sociological and demographic transformations underway, and the criminality of the August 2020 port explosion speaks volumes to the ideological hegemony of the postwar order, despite the breakdown of its material and political bases of consent—as Gramsci long predicted.[102] That the overlapping political, economic, and financial elite have managed to sabotage all attempts by international actors and opposition political groups to wrest management of the collapse underscores the integral state's durability and ability to shield the perpetrators of this collapse from accountability and prosecution, even as they claim that the state is weak, absent, and corrupt.

BIBLIOGRAPHY

al-Zayn, Ali. "Istidamat al-Naqel fi Lubnan?" *Al-Akhbar*, November 8, 2021.
Anderson, Lisa. "'Creative Destruction': States, Identities and Legitimacy in the Arab World." *Philosophy and Social Criticism* 40, no. 4/5 (2014): 369–79.

---

100. Compared to Egypt, for example, where state violence is meant to restore the aura of the state. El-Mahdi, "The Failure of the Regime or the Demise of the State?"
101. The political party Mouwatinoun wa Mouwatinat fi Dawla, or Citizens in the State, anticipated the collapse well before the October 17, 2019, protests. See Nahas, *An Economy and a State for Lebanon*; Halawi and Salloukh, "Pessimism of the Intellect, Optimism of the Will."
102. Gramsci, *Selections from the Prison Notebooks*, 54–55; Przeworski, *Capitalism and Social Democracy*, 164.

Assouad, Lydia. "Lebanon's Political Economy: From Predatory to Self-Devouring." Carnegie Middle East Center, January 14, 2021. https://carnegie-mec.org/2021/01/14/lebanon-s-political-economy-from-predatory-to-self-devouring-pub-83631

Atzili, Boaz. "State Weakness and 'Vacuum of Power' in Lebanon." *Studies in Conflict and Terrorism* 33, no. 8 (2010): 757–82.

Baumann, Hannes. *Citizen Hariri: Lebanon's Neoliberal Reconstruction*. London: Hurst, 2016.

Baumann, Hannes. "Social Protest and the Political Economy of Sectarianism in Lebanon." *Global Discourse* 6, no. 4 (2016): 634–49.

Bifani, Alain. "The Origin of the Crisis in the Lebanese Banking Sector." Caravan Notebook, Hoover Institution, Stanford University, September 28, 2021. https://www.hoover.org/research/origin-crisis-lebanese-banking-sector

Bilgin, Pinar, and Adam David Morton. "Historicising Representations of 'Failed States': Beyond the Cold-War Annexation of the Social Sciences?" *Third World Quarterly* 23, no. 1 (2002): 55–80.

Blanford, Nicholas. *Warriors of God: Inside Hezbollah's Thirty-Year Struggle against Israel*. New York: Random House, 2011.

Bou Akar, Hiba. *For the War Yet to Come: Planning Beirut's Frontiers*. Stanford: Stanford University Press, 2018.

Bou Khater, Léa. "Public Sector Mobilisation Despite a Dormant Workers' Movement." *Confluences Méditerranée* 92, no. 1 (2015): 125–42.

Brubaker, Rogers. "Ethnicity without Groups." *Archives européennes de sociologie* 43, no. 2 (2002): 163–89.

Brynen, Rex. *Sanctuary and Survival: The PLO in Lebanon*. Boulder, CO: Westview Press, 1990.

Cammett, Melani. *Compassionate Communalism: Welfare and Sectarianism in Lebanon*. Ithaca, NY: Cornell University Press, 2014.

Carpi, Estella. "Winking at Humanitarian Neutrality: The Liminal Politics of the State in Lebanon." *Anthropologica* 61 (2019): 83–96.

Chalcraft, John. "Revolutionary Weakness in Gramscian Perspective: The Arab Middle East and North Africa since 2011." *Middle East Critique* (2021). https://doi.org/10.1080/19436149.2021.1872858

Chehayeb, Kareem. "The Weight of Lebanon's Unsustainable Subsidies Program." Tahrir Institute for Middle East Policy, April 30, 2021. https://timep.org/commentary/analysis/the-weight-of-lebanons-unsustainable-subsidies-program/

Chomiak, Laryssa, and Jillian Schwedler. "Introduction to Special Issue: Critical Interventions on the Spaces and Practices of State Power." *Middle East Law and Governance* 11 (2019): 91–102.

Christophers, Brett. *Rentier Capitalism: Who Owns the Economy, and Who Pays for It?* London: Verso Books, 2020.

Clark, Janine, and Bassel F. Salloukh. "Elite Strategies, Civil Society, and Sectarian Identities in Postwar Lebanon." *International Journal of Middle East Studies* 45, no. 4 (November 2013): 731–49.

Deeb, Lara. "Beyond Sectarianism: Intermarriage and Social Difference in Lebanon." *International Journal of Middle East Studies* 52, no. 2 (2020): 215–28.

Denning, Michael. "Everyone a Legislator." *New Left Review* 129 (May/June 2021): 29–44.

Dodge, Toby. "Gramsci Goes to Baghdad: Understanding the Iraqi State beyond Collapse, Failure or Hybridity." Paper delivered at "Rethinking Iraqi State and Society Eighteen Years after Regime Change" workshop, Middle East Centre, LSE, October 2, 2020.

El-Khazen, Farid. *The Breakdown of the State in Lebanon, 1967–1976.* London: I. B. Tauris, 2000.

El-Mahdi, Rabab. "The Failure of the Regime or the Demise of the State?" *International Journal of Middle East Studies* 50, no. 2 (2018): 328–32.

Evans, Peter B., Dietrich Rueschemeyer, and Theda Skocpol. "On the Road toward a More Adequate Understanding of the State." In *Bringing the State Back In*, edited by Peter B. Evans, Dietrich Rueschemeyer, and Theda Skocpol, 347–66. Cambridge: Cambridge University Press, 1985.

Fakhoury, Tamirace. "Refugee Return and Fragmented Governance in the Host State: Displaced Syrians in the Face of Lebanon's Divided Politics." *Third World Quarterly* 42, no. 1 (2021): 162–80.

Farha, Mark. *Lebanon: The Rise and Fall of a Secular State under Siege.* Cambridge: Cambridge University Press, 2019.

Fergonese, Sara. *War and the City: Urban Geopolitics in Lebanon.* London: I. B. Tauris, 2020.

Geha, Carmen. "Co-optation, Counter-Narratives, and Repression: Protesting Lebanon's Sectarian Power-Sharing Regime." *Middle East Journal* 73, no. 1 (2019): 9–28.

Gerth, H. H., and C. Wright Mills, trans. and eds. *From Max Weber: Essays in Sociology.* New York: Oxford University Press, 1958.

Goria, Wade R. *Sovereignty and Leadership in Lebanon, 1943–1976.* London: Ithaca Press, 1985.

Gramsci, Antonio. *Selections from the Prison Notebooks.* Edited and translated by Quintin Hoare and Goeffrey Nowell Smith. New York: International Publishers, 1971.

Grzymala-Busse, Anna, and Pauline Jones Luong. "Reconceptualizing the State: Lessons from Post-Communism." *Politics and Society* 30, no. 4 (December 2002): 529–54.

Hage, Ghassan. "Inside and Outside the Law: Negotiated Being and Urban *Jouissance* in the Streets of Beirut." *Social Analysis* 62, no. 3 (Autumn 2018): 88–108.

Halawi, Ibrahim. "Consociational Power-Sharing in the Arab World as Counter-Revolution." *Studies in Ethnicity and Nationalism* 20, no. 2 (2020): 128–36.

Halawi, Ibrahim, and Bassel F. Salloukh. "Pessimism of the Intellect, Optimism of the Will after the 17 October Protests in Lebanon." *Middle East Law and Governance* 12, no. 3 (2020): 322–34.

Hazbun, Waleed. "Assembling Security in a 'Weak State': The Contentious Politics of Plural Governance in Lebanon since 2005." *Third World Quarterly* 37, no. 6 (2016): 1053–70.

Hazbun, Waleed. "The Politics of Insecurity in the Arab World: A View from Beirut." *PS: Political Science and Politics* 50, no. 3 (July 2017): 656–59.

Hermez, Sami. "When the State Is (N)ever Present: On Cynicism and Political Mobilization in Lebanon." *Journal of the Royal Anthropological Institute* 21, no. 3 (2015): 507–23.

Heydemann, Steven. "Explaining the Arab Uprisings: Transformations in Comparative Perspective." *Mediterranean Politics* 21, no. 1 (2016): 192–204.
Hourani, Albert. "Visions of Lebanon." In *Toward a Viable Lebanon*, edited by Halim Barakat, 3–11. Washington, DC: Georgetown University Press, 1988.
Hourani, Najib. "Capitalists in Conflict: The Lebanese Civil War Reconsidered." *Middle East Critique* 24, no. 2 (2015): 137–60.
Hourani, Najib. "Lebanon: Hybrid Sovereignties and U.S. Foreign Policy." *Middle East Policy* 20, no. 1 (2013): 39–55.
Hudson, Michael C. *The Precarious Republic: Political Modernization in Lebanon*. Boulder, CO: Westview Press, [1968] 1985.
Hudson, Michael C. "The Problem of Authoritative Power in Lebanese Politics: Why Consociationalism Failed." In *Lebanon: A History of Conflict and Consensus*, edited by Nadim Shehadi and Dana Haffar Mills, 224–39. London: Centre for Lebanese Studies and I. B. Tauris, 1988.
Johnson, Michael. *Class and Client in Beirut: The Sunni Muslim Community and the Lebanese State, 1840–1985*. London: Ithaca Press, 1986.
Khatib, Lina. "How Hezbollah Holds Sway over the Lebanese State." Chatham House Research Paper, Middle East and North Africa Programme, June 2021. https://www.chathamhouse.org/2021/06/how-hezbollah-holds-sway-over-lebanese-state
"Lebanon's Financial Crisis: Where Did the Money Go?" An interview with Mike Azar, LCPS, 3 April 2020, at: https://www.lcps-lebanon.org/agendaArticle.php?id=158
Mansour, Renad, and Lina Khatib. "Where Is the 'State' in Iraq and Lebanon? Power Relations and Social Control." Chatham House Research Paper, Middle East and North Africa Programme, April 2021. https://www.chathamhouse.org/2021/04/where-state-iraq-and-lebanon
"Masref Lubnan: Bayn Da'm al-Sela' wa Iqrad al-Dawla." *The Monthly* 169 (July 2021).
Mazzola, Francisco. "Mediating Security: Hybridity and Clientelism in Lebanon's Hybrid Security Sector." In *Limited Statehood in the Middle East and Africa*, edited by Ruth Hanau Santini, Abel Polese, and Rob Kevlihan, 205–25. London: Routledge, 2020.
Meier, Daniel. "Hizbullah's Shaping Lebanon Statehood." *Small Wars and Insurgencies* 29, no. 3 (2018): 515–36.
Migdal, Joel S. "The State in Society: An Approach to Struggles for Domination." In *State Power and Social Forces: Domination and Transformation in the Third World*, edited by Joel S. Migdal, Atul Kohli, and Vivienne Shue, 7–34. Cambridge: Cambridge University Press, 1994.
Migdal, Joel S. *Strong Societies and Weak States: State-Society Relations and State Capabilities in the Third World*. Princeton, NJ: Princeton University Press, 1988.
Mikaelian, Shoghig, and Bassel F. Salloukh. "Strong Actor in a Weak State: The Geopolitics of Hezbollah." In *Fragile Politics: Weak States in the Greater Middle East*, edited by Mehran Kamrava, 119–43. New York: Oxford University Press, 2016.
Mikdashi, Maya. "Sectarianism: Notes on Studying the Lebanese State." In *The Oxford Handbook of Contemporary Middle Eastern and North African History*, edited by Amal Ghazal and Jens Hanssen. Oxford: Oxford University Press, 2015.

Mikdashi, Maya. "Sex and Sectarianism: The Legal Architecture of Lebanese Citizenship." *Comparative Studies of South Asia, Africa and the Middle East* 34, no. 2 (2014): 279–93.
Mitchell, Timothy. "Society, Economy, and the State Effect." In *The Anthropology of the State: A Reader*, edited by Aradhana Sharma and Akhil Gupta, 169–86. Malden, MA: Blackwell, 2006.
Morton, Adam David. *Unravelling Gramsci: Hegemony and Passive Revolution in the Global Political Economy*. London: Pluto Press, 2007.
Mouawad, Jamil. "Lebanese Football: Imagining a Defiant and United Lebanon?" *Middle East Critique* 27, no. 3 (2018): 289–302.
Mouawad, Jamil. "Unpacking Lebanon's Resilience: Undermining State Institutions and Consolidating the System?" IAI Working Papers 17, October 29, 2017. https://www.iai.it/sites/default/files/iaiwp1729.pdf
Mouawad, Jamil, and Hannes Bauman. "In Search of the Lebanese State." *Arab Studies Journal* 25, no. 1 (2017): 60–64.
Mouawad, Jamil, and Hannes Bauman. "*Wayna al-Dawla*? Locating the Lebanese State in Social Theory." *Arab Studies Journal* 25, no. 1 (2017): 66–90.
Mourad, Lama. "'Standoffish' Policy-Making: Inaction and Change in the Lebanese Response to the Syrian Displacement Crisis." *Middle East Law and Governance* 9 (2017): 249–66.
Nagle, John, and Tamirace Fakhoury. *Resisting Sectarianism: Queer Activism in Postwar Lebanon*. New York: Bloomsbury Publishing, 2021.
Nahas, Charbel. *An Economy and a State for Lebanon*. Beirut: Riad El-Rayyes Books, 2020.
Nassif, Nqoula. *Jumhuriyat Fuad Shihab*. Beirut: Dar al-Nahar, 2008.
Obeid, Michelle. "Searching for the 'Ideal Face of the State' in a Lebanese Border Town." *Journal of the Royal Anthropological Institute* 16, no. 2 (2010): 330–46.
Przeworski, Adam. *Capitalism and Social Democracy*. Cambridge: Cambridge University Press, 1985.
Przeworski, Adam. "What Have I Learned from Marx and What Still Stands?" *Politics and Society* 49, no. 4 (September 2020): 433–50.
Salem, Sara. "Gramsci in the Postcolony: Hegemony and Anticolonialism in Nasserist Egypt." *Theory, Culture and Society* (2020): 1–21.
Salibi, Kamal S. *A House of Many Mansions: The History of Lebanon Reconsidered*. Berkeley: University of California Press, 1988.
Salloukh, Bassel F. "The Art of the Impossible: The Foreign Policy of Lebanon." In *The Foreign Policies of Arab States: The Challenge of Globalization*, new rev. ed., edited by Bahgat Korany and Ali E. Hillal Dessouki, 283–317. Cairo: American University in Cairo Press, 2009.
Salloukh, Bassel F. "The State of Consociationalism in Lebanon." *Nationalism and Ethnic Politics* (2023). https://doi.org/10.1080/13537113.2023.2187970
Salloukh, Bassel F. "Taif and the Lebanese State: The Political Economy of a Very Sectarian Public Sector." *Nationalism and Ethnic Politics* 25, no. 1 (2019): 43–60.
Salloukh, Bassel F. "War Memory, Confessional Imaginaries, and Political Contestation in Postwar Lebanon." *Middle East Critique* 28, no. 3 (2019): 341–59.
Salloukh, Bassel F., Rabie Barakat, Jinan S. Al-Habbal, Lara W. Khattab, and Shoghig Mikaelian. *The Politics of Sectarianism in Postwar Lebanon*. London: Pluto Press, 2015.

Samaha, Petra, and Amer Mohtar. "Decoding an Urban Myth: An Inquiry into the Van Line 4 System in Beirut, Lebanon." *Journal of Transport Geography* 85 (2020): 1–9.

Santini, Ruth, and Simone Tholens. "Security Assistance in a Post-interventionist Era: The Impact on Limited Statehood in Lebanon and Tunisia." *Small Wars and Insurgencies* 29, no. 3 (2018): 491–514.

Schellen, Thomas. "We Could Have Built a Second Singapore: Q&A with Economist Freddie Baz." *Executive Magazine* (July–August 2020): 32–38.

Shaery-Eisenlohr, Roschanack. *Shi'ite Lebanon: Transnational Religion and the Making of National Identities*. New York: Columbia University Press, 2008.

Sharara, Waddah. *Dawlat Hizballah: Lubnan Mujtama'an Islamiyan*. Beirut: Dar al-Nahar, 2007.

Stel, Nora. "Mediated Stateness as a Continuum: Exploring the Changing Governance Relations between the PLO and the Lebanese State." *Civil Wars* 19, no. 3 (2017): 348–76.

Thomas, Peter. *The Gramscian Moment: Philosophy, Hegemony, and Marxism*. Leiden: Brill, 2009.

Traboulsi, Fawwaz. *Al-Tabaqat al-Ijtima'iya fi Lubnan: Ithbat Wujood*. Beirut: Heinrich Böll Stiftung, 2014.

Traboulsi, Fawwaz. *Silat Bila Wasel: Michel Chiha wal-Idiologia al-Lubnaniya*. Beirut: Riad El-Rayyes lil-Kutub wal-Nashr, 1999.

Tripp, Charles. "The State as an Always-Unfinished Performance: Improvisation and Performativity in the Face of Crisis." *International Journal of Middle East Studies* 50, no. 2 (2018): 337–42.

Weiss, Max. *In the Shadow of Sectarianism: Law, Shi'ism, and the Making of Modern Lebanon*. Cambridge, MA: Harvard University Press, 2010.

Wittgenstein, Ludwig. *Philosophical Investigations*. Translated by G. E. M. Anscombe. Oxford: Basil Blackwell Ltd, 1958.

Zamir, Meir. *Lebanon's Quest: The Road to Statehood, 1926–1939*. London: I. B. Tauris, 1997.

Zbeeb, Mohammad. "Ayna Dhahabat Kul Hadhihi al-Rasamil?" *Al-Akhbar*, October 29, 2018.

Zbeeb, Mohammad. "Bil-Asma' wal-Arqam." *Al-Akhbar*, January 13, 2017.

SIX

The "Business of Government"

The State and Changing Patterns of Politics in the Arab World

Lisa Anderson

Regional politics in the Arab world are often characterized as an endless game of rivalries, struggles, and competition for influence: the players may vary but the rules do not change.[1] In fact, today's rivals are fighting battles over very different stakes and deploying very different arsenals than their predecessors in the 1950s or even the 1990s. Just as the early post-independence battles about the configuration of states gave way to Cold War struggles to sustain the stability of regimes, today's competition reflects new divides over the instruments and beneficiaries of government policy. To understand the patterns of contemporary Arab politics, we must examine not just the new players but their new purposes and new powers.

To that end, we must be prepared to go beyond the conventional analytical categories of contemporary political science. Just as we have been urged to abandon the constraints of "methodological nationalism"—the assumption that the state is the fundamental unit and arena of politics—we must expand our examinations of political authority beyond the conventions of both state and regime.[2] Particularly in nondemocratic settings, in which the vast majority of humankind—including almost everyone in the Middle East—resides, the realms of power and authority often extend far

---

1. Parts of this chapter appeared in Anderson, "Shifting Patterns of Arab Politics," *Cairo Review of Global Affairs*, no. 44 (Winter 2022).
2. Hanieh, *Lineages of Revolt*, 10.

beyond the limits of what we think of as political institutions. Indeed, the intent of this contribution is to suggest that the very premise of the volume in which it is included—that the "state" in its many manifestations is the best framework by which to make sense of politics in general and in the Arab world in particular—may be mistaken.[3]

It is well to remember that the modern state is but one way politics can be organized and understood, and its appearance in human history is relatively recent. Before the mid-seventeenth century there were no states as we know them now—empires, churches, dynasties, tribes, feudal estates, guilds, trade networks, yes; geographically delimited states claiming exclusive sovereignty, no.[4] This device for organizing political authority was exported from Europe to the rest of the world in fits and starts over the next several centuries through imperialism. It reached its apogee in the United Nations' patently fictitious but politically powerful "principle of sovereignty of all its Members," whose criteria for membership are moreover that the applicant be "a peace-loving State . . . able and willing to carry out the obligations contained in the Charter."[5] Obviously, many United Nations members are not peace loving or able or willing to, for example, promote "universal respect for, and observance of, human rights and fundamental freedoms for all without distinction as to race, sex, language, or religion."[6] Yet social scientists persist in deploying the conceptual framework of the state to examine politics, regularly acknowledging that the states they study vary in strength, capacity, success, legitimacy, fierceness, and many other dimensions, while failing to consider that at some point differences in degree may signal a difference in kind.

This chapter represents an effort to challenge the primacy of the state and to historicize the exercise of political authority through examination of three eras of contestation about, over, and beyond the polity in the Arab world. In the first decades after independence, the principal focus of contention in the Arab world was definition and control of the states bequeathed to the region by imperialism. In the latter quarter of the twentieth century, the emphasis shifted from addressing the legacy of the past to preserving the present, that is, to stability, represented by regime longevity. Steven Heydemann's contribution to this volume details much of

---

3. Hence, a special word of thanks to the editors for in fact including it!
4. Or, as Max Weber famously put it: "A human community that successfully claims the monopoly of the legitimate use of physical force within a given territory." Weber, "Politics as a Vocation."
5. United Nations Charter, Articles 2 and 4.
6. United Nations Charter, Article 55.

that development. By the time of the US invasion of Iraq in 2003, however, international investment in stability was being abandoned in favor of regime change—often framed as "democracy promotion." The uprisings of the Arab Spring less than a decade later sealed the fate of many regimes that had based their rule on longevity and familiarity.

What followed the demise of regimes as the locus of authority represented the culmination of decades of neoliberal enthusiasm for the market and its putative promise of a prosperous future; the business enterprise now supplements and increasingly supplants both state and regime as the unit of political authority and the standard of political aspiration. This turn to the market, which was encouraged internationally and embraced by governments across the region, reflected a dramatic reformulation of the principles and norms of human rights and citizenship—never widely embraced in the region even when the ideologies of states and regimes prevailed—as it redefined the relationship of rulers and ruled.

Obviously, the shift from one site of authority to another—from state to regime to enterprise—is not reflected in clean breaks, nor is it simultaneous in all polities of the region. Indeed, one of the signal features of regional politics is the power of the past—virtually no ruler over the last seventy-five years does not have followers somewhere: the last kings of Egypt and Libya are remembered wistfully in some (albeit dwindling) circles, while enthusiasts for state builders Habib Bourguiba and Gamal Abdel Nasser or regime stalwarts Muammar Qaddafi and Hafez al-Asad continue to argue their cases. Nonetheless, the trends are clear—and they cannot be reassuring for partisans of the universalist values of the United Nations Charter.

Securing Independent States: Debating the Past

> There is an Arab circle surrounding us and . . . this circle is as much a part of us as we are a part of it.
> —Gamal Abdel Nasser, 1959[7]

In the early postimperial years, when memories of European control were still fresh, political debates within the Arab world centered on the shape of the postcolonial order: how much of the legacy of European rule would survive? Sovereignty and statehood were prized as the symbols of autonomy, authority, and agency in a world structured, at least in part, by a global

---

7. Nasser, *Philosophy of the Revolution*, 59.

order reflected in the new United Nations. But who would exercise that sovereignty, and what states would be recognized as exercising it?

From the 1950s through the 1970s, these questions were debated in many forms, and for a time the relationships between nations, states, and governments were all contested. At that time, as Picard has succinctly put it, "state sovereignty was still based on Westphalian criteria (the world was organized into independent and equal state units) and Weberian criteria (the state was meant to be the only legitimate holder of physical force)."[8] Thanks to its demographic weight, cultural influence, and charismatic President Nasser, Egypt played a major role in the region, and Nasser's embrace of pan-Arab nationalism reflected and sustained the tension between revolutionary nationalism and state sovereignty that characterized the era. From the toppling of European-imposed monarchs in Egypt, Iraq, and Libya and the wresting of Algeria from France to the creation (and dissolution) of the United Arab Republic to the repeated (and failed) efforts to liberate Palestine from what was widely seen as an illegitimate foreign occupation, the region was convulsed in existential argument and dispute about the shape and authority of states. Boundaries were porous and identities fluid as pan-Arab aspirations justified intervention in states across the region, and republics and monarchies alike pursued proxy wars in civil conflicts in Yemen, Lebanon, Jordan, and elsewhere.

With the Arab military defeat and loss of territory to Israel in 1967, the heady ambitions to redraw the European map of the region gave way to more modest efforts simply to secure its borders. The withdrawal of the British from their last possessions east of Suez and the independence of the small Gulf states in 1971 marked the end of formal European control. By the end of the decade, the Egyptian-Israeli peace treaty signaled the triumph of state interests over nationalist ambitions. Efforts to remake the past were finished.

Continuing ambiguity in the rationales and sources of political authority was reflected in periodic reflections on the existential, if not empirical, fragility of the region's states. As Alexander Wendt argued more generally, the state was an artifact of international interpretation: as he put it, "sovereignty norms are now so taken for granted, so natural, that it is easy to overlook the extent to which they are both presupposed by and an ongoing artifact of practice."[9] This, as Timothy Mitchell contended, was also reflected in what he described as an "effect" of "detailed processes of spatial

---

8. Picard, "The Virtual Sovereignty of the Lebanese State," 259.
9. Wendt, "Anarchy Is What States Make of It," 414.

organization, temporal arrangement, functional specification, and supervision and surveillance," which, he argued, "create the appearance of a world fundamentally divided into state and society."[10]

The durability of the state as both artifact and appearance was substantial. The centenary of the 1916 agreement between Britain and France outlining an eventual partition of the Ottoman Empire after World War I occasioned a spate of commentary noting, and sometimes decrying, the remarkable permeability and "artificiality" of the states that had been created in the European imperial era. Yet despite efforts in the second decade of the twenty-first century to revive nationalist claims against existing states by Kurds in Iraq, Cyrenaicans in Libya, and heirs of the post–World War I Rif Republic in Morocco, among others, state borders proved enduring.[11] Continuing commitment to the scaffolding of the international state system on the part of great powers secured boundaries. As Laura Guazzone and Daniela Pioppi put it, the state "remains the main internationally recognized framework for political action and the main mediation structure between the global and the local." But this did not mean that these states were necessarily Weberian administrations, preserving public order and serving the public interest. Often, as they pointed out, "local ruling elites derive their power and their patronage networks precisely from their control of a globally recognized state."[12]

Safeguarding Stable Regimes: Prolonging the Present

> Here there is no state; here people live in a state other than the state.
> —Cairo resident, 2005[13]

In the post-independence struggles over the shape, and even existence, of newly independent countries, statehood and sovereignty had been the prize. Over the succeeding decades, however, as control of territory was secured and international recognition assured, regime stability came to take precedence over state building as the principal political priority in the region. The global superpowers settled into a Cold War détente and, prizing predictability over uncertainty, supplied client regimes with the foreign

---

10. Mitchell, "The Limits of the State," 90, 95.
11. Saouli, *The Arab State*; Ahram, *Break All the Borders*; Young, "A New Rif Revolt?"; Aidi, "Is Morocco Headed Toward Insurrection?"
12. Guazzone and Pioppi, "Interpreting Change in the Arab World," 6–7.
13. Quoted in Ismail, *Political Life in Cairo's New Quarters*, 165.

and military aid that ensured policy continuity and, not unrelatedly, regime stability. So, too, the availability of increased oil revenues, among both the oil producers and their regional allies, supported stability; after decades of military coups, there was no regime change in the Arab world in the thirty years between the oil price increases of 1973 and the US invasion of Iraq in 2003. Orderly succession upon the death of the ruler in Egypt, Saudi Arabia, Jordan, Morocco, and Syria illustrated the investment in regime continuity across the region.

Yet this stability obscured important changes in the dynamic of politics in the region; it represented not only the surrender of earlier nationalist aspirations but the abandonment of more conventional state building. Regimes began to supersede states as the focus of political loyalties. As Heydemann and Salloukh show in this volume, the autocratic rulers relied not on the popular support of citizens so much as on financial subsidies from external patrons that they used to create and sustain clienteles at home, shifting from appeals to citizens—appeals that might have produced demands for greater freedom and participation, not to say more government services, more equitably distributed—to claims for allegiance based on ethnic and religious solidarities. This deliberate and often cynical tactic to evade accountability to a broad-based citizenry quickly escaped the control of the regimes, however, as such identities proved at least as effective in mobilizing opposition as support. By the 1980s, the state-based order was challenged by Islamist and sectarian mobilization as groups based on networks of religious affiliation and ethnic kinship proliferated, providing aid and solace in communities where the state itself was weakening.

Indeed, although state boundaries were largely immoveable and regimes seemed similarly secure, ordinary people were increasingly vulnerable. Conflict raged across the region, taking a major toll in human life, without discernable impact on political regimes. The Lebanese civil war of 1975–90 cost an estimated 150,000 lives, and almost one million people fled the country, but it produced no change in the regime that governed the state: indeed, shortly after the war ended, the parliament declared amnesty for all political and wartime crimes, promoting an outcome in which there was "no victor, no vanquished." Similarly, after more than eight years and as many as one million casualties, the Iran-Iraq War of the 1980s produced a stalemate and, again, no change in regime: in 1990 the war was settled with an exchange of prisoners and a return to the status quo ante. The global investment in stability was confirmed in the decisive rejection of the Iraqi claims on Kuwait in 1991 and, less decisively, in the continuing failure to address Palestinian aspirations to statehood.

The Oslo Accords' creation of a Palestinian "Authority" with limited self-governance in parts of the West Bank and Gaza in 1994 illustrated and exacerbated the ambiguity of statehood in the region. The protracted absence of sovereignty undermined efforts to build administrative capacity, which in turn served to justify continued denial of sovereignty. Despite the apparent growing indifference to the status of Palestine among other Arab countries, however, the preemption of state formation in the Occupied Territories was not solely a Palestinian dilemma. The obligation to administer substantial refugee populations that were both formally and effectively stateless hindered state-building efforts and reinforced the salience of non-state identities throughout the region.[14]

With the end of the Cold War, the decades-old bargain of international aid for domestic stability seemed in jeopardy. Many of the regimes of the region, particularly but not exclusively those led by military officers, turned to "securitization" of once civilian functions.[15] In part this was a response to declining non–military aid budgets in the United States and Europe; in part it reflected regime priorities, notably the growing emphasis on loyalty. Security establishments originally designed for state purposes—national defense—were turned inward as borders proved resilient and regimes looked for domestic safeguards. The authoritarian contract was increasingly based on security rather than widespread distribution or even ethnic or sectarian solidarity; as William Reno put it about Africa, such "regimes exercise power more exclusively for the interests of individuals who make up these regimes and refrain from providing non-exclusive benefits such as order, security, or economic opportunity to populations."[16] By the early years of the twenty-first century, many of the regimes had become beholden to their erstwhile international guarantors. The resulting competing networks of interests were often reflected in the proliferation of multiple internal security agencies with overlapping jurisdictions as the "security sector" grew ever larger and more complex. In Libya, Saudi Arabia, Iraq, Egypt, Algeria, Tunisia, and elsewhere, the military and police forces, intelligence, and security agencies—and the associated prisons—grew dramatically.[17]

---

14. Khalidi, *The Iron Cage*; Tessler, *A History of the Israeli-Palestinian Conflict*; Kamrava, *The Impossibility of Palestine*; Anziska, *Preventing Palestine*.

15. Korany and Brynen, eds, *The Many Faces of National Security in the Arab World*; Ammar, *The Security Archipelago*.

16. Reno, "The Privatization of Sovereignty and the Survival of Weak States," 229; see also Droz-Vincent, "The Security Sector in Egypt"; Springborg, "Economic Involvements of Militaries."

17. Quinlivan, "Coup-Proofing," 133; Khalili and Schwedler, eds., *Policing and Prisons in the Middle East*.

After the United States launched what was to be called the "Global War on Terror" in the aftermath of the 9/11 attacks of 2001, the incentive to construe virtually all political opposition as a security threat was further enhanced, as regimes secured external support to confront domestic opponents, especially if they could be portrayed as Islamist.[18] Unlike earlier foreign and military aid, however, the international patrons—in this instance, the United States and its "coalition allies"—were much more intimately involved in the distribution and utilization of the aid. Indeed, in many countries—Iraq after 2003 being the most obvious case but elsewhere too, including Tunisia, Jordan, and Saudi Arabia—local security forces, including the military, were confined to internal policing while the United States and its allies managed regional security and military operations.[19] Money and materiel continued to pour into the region—since 1990 the Middle East and North Africa saw the highest military expenditures in the world, both in total and as a proportion of GDP—but the regimes had less and less control over how it was used.[20]

The human costs of regime stability were reflected not only in war casualties and refugee counts. By the 1990s, population growth and economic stagnation had conspired to erode gains in health, education, and employment of the preceding decades across the region, and the post–Cold War era saw little improvement as neoliberal policy prescriptions discouraged large-scale government investment in social welfare provision. By the turn of the century the Arab world had among the lowest adult literacy rates in the world; only 62 percent of the region's adults could read, well below the world average of 84 percent and the developing country average of 76 percent.[21] The region's economies had stagnated: its share of global exports fell from 2.3 percent in 1990 to 1.8 percent in 2008, most of which was accounted for by oil and gas. This reliance on oil and neglect of labor-intensive sectors amplified scandalously high unemployment, especially among the young.[22]

In fact, as the twenty-first century opened, the Middle East was becoming what Thomas Piketty and his colleagues called "a pioneer region in terms of extreme inequality."[23] Between 1990 and 2016 almost all income

---

18. Anderson, "Shock and Awe."
19. Picard, "The Virtual Sovereignty of the Lebanese State"; Lawson, "Armed Forces, Internal Security Services, and Popular Contention in the Middle East and North Africa."
20. Del Sarto, "Contentious Borders in the Middle East and North Africa."
21. Hammoud, "Illiteracy in the Arab World."
22. McKee et al., "Demographic and Economic Material Factors in the MENA Region."
23. Facundo, Assouad, Piketty, "Measuring Inequality in the Middle East 1990–2016."

growth in the Arab world was absorbed by population increases. Although the wealthy got wealthier—excluding the Gulf countries, the top 10 percent of the region's population received more than 50 percent of total income—by 2018, two-thirds of the population was living precariously: 40 percent of the population was classified as poor and an additional 25 percent vulnerable to poverty. As Rami Khouri observed, "This trend seems to be directly associated with the steady recent decline in the quality of state managed basic social services, mainly outside the Gulf region, including health care, education, water, electricity, transport, and social safety nets."[24]

The gap was filled by private sources: family networks and charitable associations. As urban slums proliferated, charitable associations assumed welfare responsibilities, corruption ate away at the public bureaucracy, and regimes saw their control—even their understanding—of their citizenry slip away.[25] As Salloukh shows of Lebanon, the neglect was sometimes deliberate; everywhere it was debilitating to state and regime alike. In the slums of Cairo, residents reported that "here there is no state; here people live in a state other than the state."[26]

From Hamas to Hezbollah to the Muslim Brotherhood, region-wide networks secured support from private benefactors, rallied supporters among followers across state boundaries, and opposed regimes whose stability had been built largely on external rents, from oil money to foreign and military aid. And there were plenty of prospective recruits. Many governments complained about the inroads made by Islamist movements and other sectarian organizations in providing social services: as the interior minister put it when the Egyptian government grew concerned about the relief operations of the Muslim Brotherhood after a 1992 earthquake in Cairo: "If anyone wants to do anything they should do it through the Government. What is this becoming, a state within a state?"[27]

In fact, of course, neither the government nor the Brotherhood presided over robust states, nor were they particularly attentive to those citizens who were not members of their clientele. Indeed, as Anthony Cordesman observed, it does not matter whether "the regime is ruled by a King, Sheikh, President, or some [product of] a coup d'état"; it was apparent

---

24. Khouri, "Poverty, Inequality and the Structural Threat to the Arab Region."
25. Singerman, *Avenues of Participation*; Bayat, *Life as Politics*; Nucho, *Everyday Sectarianism in Urban Lebanon*; Wickham, *Mobilizing Islam*; Cammett and McLean, *The Politics of Non-State Social Welfare*; Cammett, *Compassionate Communalism*; Hibou, *The Force of Obedience*; Imam and Jacobs, "Effect of Corruption on Tax Revenues in the Middle East"; Anderson, "The State and Its Competitors."
26. Ismail, *Political Life in Cairo's New Quarters*, 165.
27. Hedges, "Cairo Journal, after the Earthquake, a Rumbling of Discontent."

that "many Middle Eastern states have no enemy greater than their own governments."[28]

It was in this context that the uprisings of 2010–13 broke out. The governments were taken by surprise, itself an indication of how detached they had become from the preoccupations of their putative charges, and the initial response to the popular disturbances was confused. Many governments—and some of their opponents—resorted to what was by then tired reliance on sectarianism to frame expressions of popular discontent despite its irrelevance to the calls for bread, freedom, dignity, and social justice. Civil disobedience and protest in Bahrain was characterized as Shi'i rather than popular; the post-uprising presidential elections in Egypt eventually turned on a contest between the military and the Muslim Brotherhood; the Syrian regime quickly rallied Alawi allies to battle protestors; and Yemen slid into civil war characterized by claims of Iranian support for Shi'i rebels.[29]

Within a few years, however, many of the efforts to capture popular support by reference to early nationalist commitments or the religious and sectarian loyalties of the succeeding decades had been abandoned. As governments struggled to regain the upper hand in battles with their own people, a new emphasis appeared, the product of the previous decades of both neoliberal hostility to the state and growing disenchantment with profligate regimes: the polity as business enterprise. Power would no longer be measured by chanting crowds or soldiers under arms; the revolutionary nationalist and the patronage-dispensing coreligionist were giving way to the business leader promising customer service and shareholder value. As Muhammad bin Rashid Al Maktoum, the ruler of Dubai, wrote: "Today's leaders are not the same as yesterday's. Today's leaders are the silent giants who possess money, not the politicians who make the noise.... The babble of politics and its messy entanglements [are] of little benefit to us in the Arab world."[30]

As the decade after the Arab uprisings wore on, the "messy entanglements" of regional politics were sorted out. The triumph of the Muslim Brotherhood in Egypt was quickly reversed as the United Arab Emirates (UAE) and Saudi Arabia supported the installation of a new military regime. The temptations to prolong sectarian mobilization within the region, represented principally by Qatari and Turkish support of groups affiliated with the Muslim Brotherhood in Tunisia, Libya, and elsewhere,

---

28. Cordesman, "Transitions in the Middle East."
29. See Salloukh, "The Sectarianization of Geopolitics in the Middle East."
30. Al Maktoum, *My Story*, 46.

were firmly and decisively resisted. Indeed, in 2020, in a spectacular indication that neither nationalist pride nor religious allegiance would define the new political landscape, the UAE and Israel signed what were known as the Abraham Accords, a move that opened the door to Israel's normalization of relations not only with the UAE but also with Bahrain, Sudan, and Morocco. Economic cooperation, tourism, and foreign investment, especially in technology industries (including artificial intelligence and defense production), soon followed.

Ensuring Private Interests: Promising the Future

> Never underestimate your role . . . for you are in the business of shaping lives, planning futures and building nations.
> —Mohammed bin Rashid Al Maktoum, on leadership, 2019[31]

What was the logic of the newly emerging regional dynamic? The neoliberal foundations of globalization were presented as a new opportunity to reframe political authority, bypassing both states and regimes—the "babble of politics"—for an entirely new notion of governance modeled on the modern multinational corporation. As the ruler of Dubai, himself a prominent advocate of this new approach, argued, "Maybe the time has come for [the Gulf Cooperation Council or the Arab League] to be overseen by leaders, managers, businessmen, heads of industry and entrepreneurs instead of foreign ministers."[32]

The ruling families of the Gulf were among the most eager proponents of the retreat of the state and the restructuring of regimes as they adopted the watchwords of the global private sector, positioning their countries as nimble, entrepreneurial, and innovative. They characterized themselves less as stewards of states or members of political regimes than as the management committees of family-owned businesses. The mobilization of cross-border networks of alliance and competition often worked at cross-purposes with state imperatives while cementing economic networks. The "resilience of monarchy" in the aftermath of the uprisings of 2011 was less a function of intrinsic features of this type of regime than a result of wealthy autocrats shoring up their counterparts elsewhere.[33] Just as migrant laborers spun networks of kin and coreligionists across the region, so too the

---

31. Al Maktoum, *My Story*, 216.
32. Al Maktoum, *My Story*, 143.
33. That is, the sort of elective affinity between absolutism and state building I once pro-

rulers themselves made alliances across national boundaries, promoting loyalty to transnational dynasties or, at least, to the idea of transnational dynasties. Soon after Saudi troops helped put down popular protests in Bahrain in 2011, a son of the Bahraini king was engaged to marry a daughter of the Saudi king. Another of his sons had already married a daughter of the ruler of Dubai, who had himself married a sister of the king of Jordan.[34]

These families were not merely dynasties, however, but business empires, with vast multinational holdings. Indeed, soon after assuming his responsibilities as crown prince, Mohammed Bin Salman of Saudi Arabia was described as the "CEO of al Saud Inc." for taking control of Aramco, the national oil company, and quickly becoming "deeply entwined with the fabric of the global financial system" as the major investor in the $100 billion Vision Fund as well as in other international funds.[35] It was a role the rulers embraced publicly: Muhammad bin Rashid Al Maktoum proudly styled himself the "CEO of Dubai."[36]

The Gulf rulers were hardly alone in accenting finance, entrepreneurship, and investment. Many regional governments seized the initiative to drive economic investment that they had once left to dependent crony capitalist allies, including a number of what are conventionally understood as military regimes. In fact, militaries across the region were increasingly embracing more assertive roles in the economy while they outsourced actual combat. In the many countries wracked by civil war, from Iraq to Syria, Libya, and Yemen, the armed forces and security agencies worked with local private militias, many of whom had an economic incentive in prolonging the violence, even at the expense of the interests, and ultimately the capabilities, of the state.[37] Even where sovereignty was not technically contested, state actors often engaged private providers for law and order, as the proliferation of foreign military contractors suggested.[38]

The military establishments of many countries in the Arab world had been slowly but perceptibly relieved of the duties associated with the armed forces of states or praetorian guards of regimes. Those responsibilities were increasing outsourced to other countries, the United States in many

---

posed; for example, see Anderson, "Absolutism and the Resilience of Monarchy in the Middle East"; Gause and Yom, "Resilient Royals."

34. Al-Qassemi, "Tribalism in the Arabian Peninsula"; Al-Khalidi, "Jordan Keeps Silent in Case Pitting Princess Against Sheikh."

35. Sabga, "MBS."

36. Kanna, *Dubai*, 139.

37. Wehry, "A Minister, a General, and the Militias"; Khatib, "Syria's Transactional State."

38. Mazzetti and Hager, "Secret Desert Force Set Up by Blackwater's Founder"; Ghiles, "Growing Reliance on Mercenaries Spells More Chaos in the Region."

instances, and to private security contractors, both foreign—American Blackwater Security Consulting and Russian Wagner Group being notorious examples—and domestic, such as Egypt's Falcon Group.[39] Partly as a result of the erosion of their traditional roles, partly because of the lure of enterprise as the locus of political authority (not to say wealth), the military establishments grew increasingly involved in the economies of their countries, and officers increasingly constituted a "military party" concerned with protecting their privileges.[40] As Shana Marshall put it, in Egypt, for example, "by protecting the strategic assets of its major investment partners during periods of unrest and taking control of the bidding process for major government procurement," the armed forces became "the primary gatekeeper for the Egyptian economy."[41]

That Arab governments were increasingly relying on private sources of investment rather than the tax revenues associated with states, or the sectarian tributes and clientelist extortion characteristic of regimes, was suggested by the Egyptian government's announcement in 2020 that the country's sovereign wealth fund would move to privatize two subsidiaries of the military's National Service Products Organization—gas station operator Wataniya and water company Safi. The fund said at the time that the state would first market the firms to private investors, before selling additional shares on the stock exchange.[42] In 2020 Algeria's military government followed suit, announcing that foreign investors could buy majority stakes in projects in nonstrategic sectors, and took additional steps to seek new financing sources, including developing the Algiers Stock Exchange.[43]

This putative privatization was encouraged by the international community, despite the fact that the decades-long "structural adjustment" programs advocated by the International Monetary Fund (IMF) had widely recognized negative effects on inequality. After the uprisings of 2011, Managing Director Christine Lagarde claimed that "the IMF had learned some important lessons from the Arab Spring. . . . Let me be frank, we were not

---

39. Singer, "The Dark Truth about Blackwater"; Kim, "What Is the Wagner Group?" Falcon's website states that "Falcon are experts in the field of security services. The company introduces armored and unarmored security services for private and governmental premises and institutions in Egypt, offering highly trained, handpicked security personnel that are selected based on meticulous standards and after passing numerous tests and a full inspection."
40. Picard, "The Virtual Sovereignty of the Lebanese State," 254–55.
41. Marshall, "The Egyptian Armed Forces and the Remaking of an Economic Empire"; Abul-Magd, *Militarizing the Nation*.
42. *Reuters*, "Egypt to List Army Companies Wataniya and Safi"; "Cabinet Approves Military IPOs."
43. *Reuters*, "Algeria Prepares New Investment Law, Aims for Non-Energy Funding Sources."

paying enough attention to how the fruits of economic growth were being shared."[44] There was little evidence, however, that the IMF policies after 2013 changed appreciably; IMF staff were said to still have "a difficult time assessing the impact of IMF policies [on] poverty, equity concerns, unemployment, and provision of social services like health and education."[45] In fact, the IMF continued to be concerned with fostering cross-border trade and investment, even if it exacerbated inequality or contributed to the erosion of state capacity.

Domestic, politically connected, and economically dependent capitalists were soon joined to regional and international networks.[46] By the turn of the century, increasing regional "permeability" reflected not only labor mobility and IMF-sponsored trade and investment initiatives but also new information and communication technologies. In 2018, the Middle East and North Africa was one of the most digitally connected regions in the world: an average of 88 percent of the population was online daily, and 94 percent of the population owned a smart phone.[47] Even where there was little formal government transparency, there was increasing cross-border visibility, as Marc Lynch shows in his contribution to this volume.[48]

The growth of foreign direct investment originating in Gulf countries created transregional webs of connection between governments and private entrepreneurs, particularly as the business community in the Middle East moved into finance. According to the American management consulting firm McKinsey and Company, itself a major player in shaping the intersection of public and private sectors in the Middle East, the number of private investors in the region increased by 30 percent between 2015 and 2017 and total funding more than doubled.[49] The World Bank deliberately encouraged investment across state boundaries, arguing that growth had been slowed by a lack of economic integration among regional states and pledged to make the deepening of economic ties within the Middle East and North Africa a strategic priority. Sixty percent of this expansion

---

44. Lagarde, "The Arab Spring, One Year On."
45. Mossalem, "The IMF in the Arab World," 4. See also Hanieh, "Shifting Priorities or Business as Usual?"
46. Hanieh, *Lineages of Revolt*.
47. El Hamamsy et al., "How Investors Can Support Entrepreneurship in the Middle East and North Africa."
48. Salloukh, "From State-Building to State-Fraying Permeability"; Heydemann, "After the Earthquake."
49. Jones, "Adviser to The King"; Forsythe et al., "Consulting Firms Keep Lucrative Saudi Alliance, Shaping Crown Prince's Vision"; El Hamamsy et al., "How Investors Can Support Entrepreneurship in the Middle East and North Africa."

originated in the Gulf Cooperation Council (GCC), and much of it went to small and medium businesses and technology start-ups as short-term equity investments.

The importance of Gulf investment projected Gulf domestic economic and political practices onto the larger canvas of the region. In most of the Gulf oil-producing companies, members of the ruling families routinely sit on the boards of major financial and commercial enterprises, ensuring alignment of the interests of the economic and political elite. When political intervention became a priority of the rulers, as after the 2011 Arab uprisings, such links permitted "economic statecraft." In the case of Egypt, for example, Saudi and Emirati aid to the government of President Abdelfattah El-Sisi included not only direct government budget support but large-scale private investment in real estate development projects that contributed to job creation in construction, partnerships with military-owned companies, and increased activity for the local banking sector.[50]

In many ways, the 2017–21 dispute between the UAE and Qatar was a contest for regional market share, as they each developed competing franchises across the region—and beyond—through grants, loans, and investments for friendly political movements, parties, and leaders. By investing in Sisi in Egypt, Khalifa Haftar in Libya, Rached Ghannouchi in Tunisia, and many others, the Gulf governments jockeyed for position. For both donor and recipient, the intertwining of public and private purposes often eclipsed what might ordinarily be construed as state interests in favor of private preoccupations. As Young suggested of post-2013 Emirati investments in Egypt, "It remains to be seen whether the profit motive or the state power motive will dominate. There are early indications that the state is willing to scale back investment promises and commitments via commercial engagement when the profit motive is disappointing."[51]

In part as a hedge against commodity market volatility—and as a response to the expected "energy transition" in countries dependent on hydrocarbon revenues—many of the countries of the region managed sovereign wealth funds; of the world's top fifty sovereign wealth funds, twelve were in the Middle East, including Egypt's, which ranked forty-sixth.[52] These funds often partnered with international private funds that typically made investments in relatively risky ventures such as technology firms,

---

50. Young, "The New Politics of Gulf Arab State Foreign Aid and Investment."
51. Young, "The New Politics of Gulf Arab State Foreign Aid and Investment," quote in penultimate paragraph: https://blogs.lse.ac.uk/mec/2015/11/25/the-new-politics-of-gulf-arab-state-foreign-aid-and-investment.
52. SWFI, "Top 100 Largest Sovereign Wealth Fund Rankings by Total Assets."

entertainment companies, and real estate projects, as befit funds responsible not to citizens but to shareholders.[53]

In fact, the accent on business and the adoption of the role of investor on the part of governments created claims on them based less on citizenship or even clientelism and more on "the idea of getting a fair return on one's share."[54] How such "shares" were determined and how "fair" returns should be calculated were increasingly complicating and even superseding rights-based claims on governments. In Egypt, for example, one of the most important public investments was said to be in housing, but, as Yezid Sayigh points out, "although social housing for low-income groups is often cited, the bulk of investment is directed primarily at so-called smart cities aimed at upper middle class and expatriate Egyptians, and secondarily at non-Egyptian customers such as the Syrian and Yemeni business diasporas."[55]

In the Gulf, as Calvert Jones put it, the governments had a "vision of a citizen as a loyal, entrepreneurial bourgeois" while a different legal or normative regime governed the proletariat.[56] As Zahra Babar observed, "Labor rights have been cast in a nonessential basket and divorced from citizenship. . . . Labor rights are presented in Gulf states as a replacement for citizens' rights."[57] In fact, Mohammed Bin Salman made a revealing observation when he described the legal framework of Neom, a new Saudi development on the Red Sea that was to be the centerpiece of his visionary future for the country.

> He said that in a place like New York, there's an inconvenient need for laws to serve citizens as well as the private sector. "But Neom, you have no one there," he said, omitting mention of the tens of thousands of Saudis then living in the area. As a result, regulations could be based on the desires of investors alone. "Imagine if you are the governor of New York without having any public demands," MBS said. "How much would you be able to create for the companies and the private sector?"[58]

An "ambiguous 'tiered system' of economic, political and social rights" that permitted creating value for investors without attending to "public

---

53. Young, "What's Yours Is Mine."
54. Beaugrand, "Oil Metonym, Citizens' Entitlement, and Rent Maximizing," 59.
55. Sayigh, "Retain, Restructure, or Divest?"
56. Jones, *Bedouins into Bourgeois*, 2.
57. Babar, "The Vagaries of the In-Between," 768–69.
58. Nereim, "MBS's $500 Billion Desert Dream Just Keeps Getting Weirder."

demand" was taking root across the region, even in countries far less reliant on migrant labor than the Saudi Kingdom.[59] Various kinds of exceptional jurisdictions and privatized enclaves operating under special legal regimes, profiting and protecting their investors, were appearing from Morocco to Iraq. From special economic zones, self-contained "techno-cities" and science parks, gated residential communities, and offshore cruise ships to labor compounds and private islands, such enclaves provide a regional and even global class of wealthy entrepreneurs with bespoke legal regimes—including not only tax exemptions but also dispute arbitration rather than the jurisdiction of national courts and private security in lieu of the local police. Wherever there was foreign investment, there were local partners, agents, and representatives looking for shares of the wealth—and governments prepared to accommodate them. When protests broke out against a law granting amnesty to corrupt civil servants in Tunisia in 2017, in what Nadia Marzouki called a shift from transitional to transactional justice, President Caid Essebsi argued that the law was necessary to restore the confidence required to bring back investors after the upheavals of the uprisings earlier in the decade.[60]

Even citizenship itself was being commercialized. In 2018, the UAE government purchased forty thousand Comoran passports for stateless UAE residents—*bidoun*—at an estimated cost of more than $200 million, or about a third of the Comoros annual gross domestic product.[61] These newly minted "Comorans" were now able to travel out of the UAE, but they enjoyed few other rights, in either the Comoros Islands—it was not clear that they could take up residence there if they wanted—or the UAE itself, where they were now classified as foreign nationals.[62] In 2019, the Saudi government announced the launch of a new "golden visa" program that targeted wealthy foreigners. At the same time, it extended citizenship to fifty thousand refugees and provided identification papers to another eight hundred thousand.[63]

The appeal of arbitrary and capricious, or merely commercial, deployment of citizenship to relatively poor countries was obvious: by 2020, the Egyptian government was considering a proposal to grant Egyptian citi-

---

59. Jamel, "The 'Tiering' of Citizenship and Residency and the 'Hierarchization' of Migrant Communities," 602.
60. Marzouki, "Whatever Happened to Dignity?"
61. Lori, "Time and Its Miscounting."
62. Abrahamian, "Who Loses When a Country Puts Citizenship Up for Sale?" Also see Beaugrand, "Torn Citizenship in Kuwait."
63. Bsheer, "The Limits of Belonging in Saudi Arabia," 753.

zenship to foreigners who will pay for it ("deposit a non-refundable USD 250k into a local bank account that goes directly to the government") or will invest in local projects or property.[64] And the value of people as tradeable goods extended beyond citizenship as such: people were useful even for rent-seeking regimes. For example, Jordan's recognition as "a world leader in refugee hosting" positioned it to access substantial international aid, while Tunisian workers working abroad to send home remittances were said to feel like "a commodity that can be bought and sold."[65] As Natalie Delia Deckard and Alison Heslin, summed it up: "Economic viability trumps moral equality."[66]

Resort to rules as tools, as opposed to norms or principles, seemed to be widespread.[67] The scaffolding of international legal arrangements that supported cross-border finance and trade also shaped criminal and humanitarian law: the tribunal that investigated the assassination of Lebanese prime minister Rafiq Hariri was commissioned under Chapter 7 of the United Nations Charter and, as Picard pointed out, represented "the externalization of one more attribute of the sovereign state—administering justice."[68] This disregard for local law permitted the growth of what has been called an archipelago of enclaves stretching across the region that knit together transnational networks of special financing, exclusive investment opportunities, commercial security firms, isolated airports, cloistered villas, and private meetings.

Saudi Arabia had ambitious plans for Neom and also for the country's capital, Riyadh, but dramatic efforts to create investment-ready enclaves were widespread.[69] In Jordan, for example, Jose Ciro Martinez argues that "an archipelago of specialized economic enclaves" developed across the country, of which "the Aqaba governorate's conversion into a decentralized hub for direct foreign investment and luxury tourism is a key example." With little support from Jordan's elected representatives but enthusiastic backing by the United States, the European Union, and the World Bank, Martinez tells us, "Aqaba was to become an

---

64. "Gov't Mulls Granting Citizenship in Exchange for Increasing Working Capital."
65. Arar, "Leveraging Sovereignty"; Yaghi, "Neoliberal Reforms, Protests, and Enforced Patron-Client Relations in Tunisia and Egypt," 128.
66. Deckard and Heslin, "After Postnational Citizenship." See also Anderson, "Is Citizenship Dead?"
67. Leenders, "Prosecuting Political Dissent."
68. Picard, "The Virtual Sovereignty of the Lebanese State," 267.
69. Nerien, "Saudi Arabia Wants Its Capital to Be Somewhere You'd Want to Live."

"extra-territorial city," a shining "symbol of a forward looking country that wants to play a role in the new global economy."[70] Multinational security companies guarded gated residential communities and high-end development projects. Real estate investors, largely from the Gulf, called upon allies in Amman to cut through red tape and fast-track their business ventures.

Egypt's new administrative capital is similarly marketed as business friendly. As part of Egypt's Vision 2030, the new capital is being built halfway between Cairo and Suez, with all of the national ministries in a dedicated campus, 21 residential districts, several thousand schools, a technology and innovation park, nearly 700 hospitals and clinics, 1,250 mosques and churches, a 90,000-seat football stadium, 40,000 hotel rooms, a theme park four times the size of Disneyland, and a new international airport.[71] The population is expected to be 6.5 million; part of the avowed purpose is to decant the overcrowded downtown of Cairo with its overburdened and decaying infrastructure. The military-controlled Administrative Capital Urban Development Company inherited the prime real estate vacated by government ministries and agencies relocated from downtown Cairo to the new capital, itself constructed on military land.[72]

From the vantage point of the denizens of these "symbols of forward-looking countries"—gated communities with private security and special economic zones with exclusive jurisdiction—the purpose of government had shifted from securing independence or safeguarding stability to ensuring the ease of doing business. The purpose of government was to facilitate the ability of captains of industry and finance to fly from enclave to enclave, making deals, securing licenses, and visiting theme parks easily and conveniently. In this context, the Abraham Accords, which established diplomatic relations between the UAE and Bahrain, and eventually Morocco and Sudan, and Israel were merely a smart business arrangement; the Jewish state was understood as neither a nationalist settler colony nor a sectarian regime but just another business-friendly enclave of technology transfer, investment financing, and technological innovation.

---

70. Martinez, *States of Subsistence*, 143–44.
71. Kingsley, "A New New Cairo."
72. Sayigh, "Retain, Restructure, or Divest?"

The Business of Government: "Re-Imagining What the Middle East Looks Like"

> What will happen to the rest of us?
> —Khaled Fahmy, 2015[73]

The appeal of this new approach to governance in the Arab world—the promise of socially tolerant, economically prosperous illiberal autocracy—was considerable, at least for those who expected to benefit. It shared the "techno-optimism" of Silicon Valley, where companies from Facebook to Amazon transformed social life by making communication and commerce easier and more convenient, all the while creating vast invisible stores of surveillance data and fast-growing disparities in wealth. Still reeling from the Arab Spring, many governments were, as Jon Alterman put it, "converging on a model that combines authoritarianism with a . . . more liberalized social space, and an invigorated private sector. It might be called the 'GCC consensus,' but its practice reaches from Tunisia to Jordan and beyond."[74]

The visionaries understood both sides of the coin they were tendering. The ruler of Dubai's first rule of leadership, for example, was that "processes, laws and systems" are to "serve the people, make their lives easier and more comfortable"—hardly a clarion call for freedom or social justice. In a context of decades of frustration and disappointment, however, convenience had its appeal, and to further that end the ruler reminded his audience that such processes and laws "can be changed at any time."[75] These rulers are not subject to the rule of law or accountable to citizens; they prefer consultants to voters, marketing to campaigning, and customers to citizens. Indeed, this model, in which business intelligence is proprietary, also justified the lack of transparency in the use and abuse of digital media documented in this volume by Lynch.

The designers, promoters, and beneficiaries of this new pattern of Arab politics were optimists. As Yousef Al Otaiba, the UAE's long-serving ambassador to Washington, put it, "What I've watched over the last several years is a shift in mindset, a shift in attitude; younger people are tired of conflict, they're tired of ideology. They want solutions. They want jobs. They want what every young person around the world wants. . . . We're trying to approach longstanding issues with a completely different lens . . . essen-

---

73. Fahmy, "Chasing Mirages in the Desert."
74. Alterman, "The End of History in the Middle East."
75. Al Maktoum, *My Story*, 214.

tially going from analog to digital. . . . We are in the very, very early stages of re-imagining what the Middle East looks like and how it operates."[76]

Yet in these very early stages, there were already disquieting signs about what the Middle East might look like and how it might operate. Certainly, the legacy of unfinished business from the eras of state building and regime stability continued to haunt the region; the "temporary" had become enduring. Israel had been in a "state of emergency" since its establishment more than seventy years earlier; the United Nations Relief and Works Agency for Palestine Refugees, which began operations in 1950, saw its mandate extended to 2023; and the Israel-Palestine "peace process" was proving interminable.[77] The referendum on the status of the Western Sahara, scheduled for 1992, had yet to take place a quarter of a century later, although as a condition for signing the Abraham Accords, Morocco secured US recognition of its sovereignty over the disputed region. Longtime residents of the Gulf states awaited regularization of their citizenship applications for decades, even generations, in what Noora Lori called "permanent temporary status." If "postponement" was the preferred way of nation-states and international organizations "to deal with displaced populations," it also served to suspend ordinary politics: in Egypt, a decades-long state of emergency was lifted in 2021 and many of its provisions were written into law. As Human Rights Watch put it, the "emergency provisions were made permanent."[78] Indeed, many of the governments grew adept at what Bishara called "the politics of ignoring," and the Abraham Accords seemed to be a region-wide example.[79] As a one-time Palestine Liberation Organization lawyer observed, "Israel has long tried to get the world to ignore its occupation and its apartheid regime, and now it seems these other states are going along with it."[80]

But change was nonetheless easily discernable. In the first two years of the COVID-19 pandemic, wealth inequality in the Arab region grew dramatically, with the richest 10 percent of the population controlling more than 80 percent of total regional wealth by early 2022. The region had many more millionaires, and their average wealth had increased by 20 percent since 2019, while the bottom half of the population saw its wealth diminished by one-third. As a result, six Arab countries (Bahrain, the UAE, Yemen, Saudi Arabia, Oman, and Kuwait) were among the top

---

76. Tällberg Foundation, "Reimagining the Middle East."
77. Margalit, "State of Emergency in Israel."
78. Human Rights Watch, "Egypt."
79. Lori, *Offshore Citizens*, 240; Bishara, "The Politics of Ignoring."
80. "Israel, U.S. and 4 Arab Nations Focus on Security at Summit."

twenty most unequal countries worldwide. By comparison, in 2019, only two Arab countries were on that list.[81] As the pandemic seemed to recede, there was little evidence that the pace was slowing. In the summer of 2022, the Sovereign Fund of Egypt signed a draft agreement with Saudi Arabia's Public Investment Fund to launch a new company in Egypt—the Saudi Egyptian Investment Company—to attract investments worth $10 billion in potential investments in "promising" sectors such as infrastructure, real estate, health care, financial services, food and agriculture, manufacturing, and pharma, with particularly large investments to be channeled to Sharm el-Sheikh to complement the Saudi development of Neom.[82]

Similarly, the first two years of the Abraham Accords saw significant economic activity. As the United States Institute of Peace opined, "The bilateral hope and promise" had born fruit, including in a Free Trade Agreement (FTA) signed between Israel and the UAE in May 2022. The agreement, which was to lift tariffs on almost all trade between the two countries, served "as a reminder that . . . these agreements are about far more than . . . a shared Iranian threat. . . . The cooperative economic, social and technological dividends already yielded by the accords tell us that for all concerned, normalization is as much a matter of creating opportunities as it is of warding off challenges."[83]

One of the "opportunities" that went unseized, however, was the promise in Ambassador al-Otaiba's declaration at the time of the signing that the "most immediate and significant outcome" of the deal was Israel's pledge to suspend its planned annexation of Palestinian land and pursue a negotiated peace deal.[84] As such, it is perhaps more remarkable that the FTA was signed in the immediate wake of a flare-up of tensions following a parade of Jewish nationalists through a Palestinian neighborhood of Jerusalem and a month of rising violence in response to incursions into the courtyard of Al-Aqsa Mosque. Although the UAE Foreign Ministry condemned the attacks on the day the FTA was signed, the message was clear: unless it can be monetized, the Palestinian cause is not a significant part of the business of government.[85]

The challenge to this model of governance was the question of what

---

81. ESCWA, "Historic Rise in Wealth Concentration in the Arab Region."
82. "New Saudi Egyptian Investment Company to Attract $10 Billion Investments"; "Saudi Wealth Fund Sets Up Company to Invest in Egypt."
83. Kurtzer-Ellenbogen, "Historic UAE-Israel Trade Deal Proves Abraham Accords' Resilience."
84. Hassan and Muasher, "Why the Abraham Accords Fall Short."
85. Kurtzer-Ellenbogen, "Historic UAE-Israel Trade Deal Proves Abraham Accords' Resilience."

will happen to those in the interstices, outside the enclaves, and how long they can be ignored. There were millions of people in southern Tunisia, across Libya, in Palestine, Yemen, Syria, Lebanon, and, as Schwedler and Yom both show in their contributions to this volume, Jordan who—absent the resources to be investors or shareholders, customers, or even employees—seemed to be little more than inconveniences to these governments. And those who saw themselves left behind were growing uneasy. As Fahmy wrote of the Egyptian capital: "Assuming that the aim of building a new administrative capital is to alleviate the pressure from downtown Cairo where the majority of government offices are located, and assuming, for argument's sake, that the 5 million inhabitants will actually be moved from the overcrowded city, what will happen to the rest of us?"[86]

In fact, across the region, government neglect was already taking its toll in areas outside the favored enclaves. Even within such developments, the inconvenient existence of people who were neither employees nor shareholders was addressed by outsourcing services. In Jordan's Aqaba, as Martinez shows,

> NGOs with royal patronage take charge of educational tasks, real-estate developers contract private companies to secure certain neighborhoods, and foreign agencies care for "community development." All these tasks were once the responsibility of the central government or the elected municipalities; today they are carried out by a diverse group of actors. For all intents and purposes, an unelected regional body linked to local markets, Gulf capital, USAID, and various NGOs now governs the citizenry.[87]

Charity is, of course, not a right, and it can be extended and withdrawn for reasons entirely divorced from the interests or needs of the recipients. Jordanian citizens were keenly aware of the disparities: As one resident of a provincial town protested, "Ma'an is poor and ignored. The rich can't make money there so the state doesn't give a shit about it, except when it revolts. Otherwise, they are happy to let Ma'an rot."[88]

With growing investments in security and "urban renewal," governments—from Bahrain's destruction of Manama's Pearl Roundabout, to Egypt's renovation of Tahrir Square in Cairo, to Jordan's fencing of Amman's Fourth Circle—are attempting to make protest more diffi-

---
86. Fahmy, "Chasing Mirages in the Desert."
87. Martinez, *States of Subsistence*, 155.
88. Quoting a Jordanian colleague, Martinez, *States of Subsistence*, 145, 137.

cult.[89] This suggests that even episodic and occasional efforts to draw the attention of governments to the concerns of citizens are going to be more difficult. Martinez quotes a baker: "The state takes and no longer gives back. It's just there to keep the powerful well-fed. But one day there will be nothing for the poor to eat—except for the rich. We will see what the state does then."[90]

That gruesome vision was not limited to Jordan. In 2008, a novel was published in Egypt called *Utopia*, set in the distant future of 2023. The United States has developed a new fuel source, making oil obsolete, and the government has collapsed. The young protagonists live in Utopia, a gated US Marine–protected colony on the Egyptian north coast to which the wealthy retreated; outside the colony live the Others, mired in hunger, disease, and violence. Looking for a thrill, several of Utopia's youth escape the gated compound to hunt Others, knowing that a parent can always send a Marine helicopter to rescue them from the savages living in an abandoned Cairo, where drug addicts feed on stray dogs in the empty metro tunnels. Almost unimaginably bleak, the book was an instant bestseller.

BIBLIOGRAPHY

Abdel Nasser, Gamal. *Philosophy of the Revolution*. Economica Books, 1959.
Abrahamian, Atossa Araxia. "Who Loses When a Country Puts Citizenship Up for Sale?" *New York Times*, January 5, 2018. https://www.nytimes.com/2018/01/05/opinion/sunday/united-arab-emirates-comorans-citizenship.html
Abul-Magd, Zeinab. *Militarizing the Nation: The Army, Business and Revolution in Egypt*. New York: Columbia University Press, 2017.
Ahram, Ariel I. *Break All the Borders: Separatism and the Reshaping of the Middle East*. Oxford: Oxford University Press, 2019.
Aidi, Hisham. "Is Morocco Headed Toward Insurrection?" *The Nation*, July 13, 2017.
Al-Khalidi, Suleiman. "Jordan Keeps Silent in Case Pitting Princess against Sheikh." *Reuters*, July 31, 2019.
Al Maktoum, Mohammed bin Rashid. *My Story: Fifty Memories of Fifty Years of Service*. Dubai: Explorer Publishing and Distribution, 2019.
Al-Qassemi, Sultan. "Tribalism in the Arabian Peninsula: It Is a Family Affair." *Jadaliyya*, February 1, 2012.
Alterman, Jon. "The End of History in the Middle East." Center for Strategic and International Studies, November 22, 2021. https://www.csis.org/analysis/end-history-middle-east
Ammar, Paul. *The Security Archipelago: Human-Security States, Sexuality Politics and the End of Neoliberalism*. Durham, NC: Duke University Press, 2013.

---

89. Schwedler, *Protesting Jordan*.
90. Martinez, *States of Subsistence*, 230.

Anderson, Lisa. "Absolutism and the Resilience of Monarchy in the Middle East." *Political Science Quarterly* 106, no. 1 (1991).
Anderson, Lisa. "Antiquated before They Ossify: States That Fail before They Form." *Journal of International Affairs* 58, no. 1 (Fall 2004).
Anderson, Lisa. "Is Citizenship Dead?" *Global Perspectives* 1, no. 1 (2020).
Anderson, Lisa. "Shifting Patterns of Arab Politics." *Cairo Review of Global Affairs* 44 (2022).
Anderson, Lisa. "Shock and Awe: Interpretations of the Events of September 11." *World Politics* 56, no. 2 (2004).
Anderson, Lisa. "The State and Its Competitors." *International Journal of Middle East Studies* 50, no. 2 (2018).
Anziska, Seth. *Preventing Palestine: A Political History from Camp David to Oslo*. Princeton, NJ: Princeton University Press, 2018.
Arar, Rawan. "Leveraging Sovereignty: The Case of Jordan and the International Refugee Regime." *Refugees and Migration Movements in the Middle East*. POMEPS Studies 25 (2017).
Babar, Zahra R. "The Vagaries of the In-Between: Labor Citizenship in the Persian Gulf." *International Journal of Middle East Studies* 52, no. 4 (2020).
Bayat, Asef. *Life as Politics: How Ordinary People Change the Middle East*. Stanford: Stanford University Press, 2010.
Beaugrand, Claire. "Oil Metonym, Citizens' Entitlement, and Rent Maximizing: Reflections on the Specificity of Kuwait." *Politics of the Rentier State in the Gulf*. POMEPS Studies 33 (January 2019).
Beaugrand, Claire. "Torn Citizenship in Kuwait: Commodification versus Rights-Based Approaches." In *Challenges to Citizenship in the Middle East and North Africa Region*, LSE Middle East Centre Collected Papers, Volume 2, April 2015. http://eprints.lse.ac.uk/61773/1/Challenges%20to%20citizenship%20in%20the%20Middle%20East%20and%20North%20Africa%20region.pdf
Bishara, Dina. "The Politics of Ignoring: Protest Dynamics in Late Mubarak Egypt." *Perspectives on Politics* 13, no. 4 (2015).
Bsheer, Rosie. "The Limits of Belonging in Saudi Arabia." *International Journal of Middle East Studies* 52, no. 4 (2020).
Cammett, Melani. *Compassionate Communalism: Welfare and Sectarianism in Lebanon*. Ithaca, NY: Cornell University Press, 2014.
Cammett, Melani, and Lauren M. McLean. *The Politics of Non-State Social Welfare*. Ithaca, NY: Cornell University Press, 2014.
Cordesman, Anthony. "Transitions in the Middle East." Address to the Eighth US-Mideast Policymakers Conference, September 9, 1999.
Deckard, Natalie Delia, and Alison Heslin. "After Postnational Citizenship: Constructing the Boundaries of Inclusion in Neoliberal Contexts." *Sociology Compass* 10, no. 4 (April 2016).
Del Sarto, Raffaella A. "Contentious Borders in the Middle East and North Africa: Context and Concepts." *International Affairs* 93, no. 4 (2017).
Droz-Vincent, Philippe. "The Security Sector in Egypt." In *The Arab State and Neo-Liberal Globalization*, edited by Laura Guazzone and Daniela Pioppi. Berkshire, UK: Ithaca Press, 2012.
El Hamamsy, Omar, Ahmad Alkasmi, Luay Khoury, and Abdur-Rahim Syed, "How

Investors Can Support Entrepreneurship in the Middle East and North Africa." McKinsey and Company, May 2018. https://www.mckinsey.com/featured-ins ights/middle-east-and-africa/how-investors-can-support-entrepreneurship-in -the-middle-east-and-north-africa#

ESCWA. "Historic Rise in Wealth Concentration in the Arab Region: Richest 10 Percent Control More Than 80 Percent of Wealth." ESCWA, March 10, 2022. https://www.unescwa.org/news/escwa-historic-rise-wealth-concentration-arab -region-richest-10-control-more-80-wealth

Facundo, Alvaredo, Lydia Assouad, and Thomas Piketty. "Measuring Inequality in the Middle East 1990–2016." CEPR Discussion Paper No. DP12405, 2017.

Fahmy, Khaled. "Chasing Mirages in the Desert." *Cairo Observer*, March 14, 2015. https://cairobserver.com/post/113543612414/chasing-mirages-in-the-desert #.YbzSLH3MLnU

Forsythe, Michael, Mark Mazzetti, Ben Hubbard, and Walt Bogdanich. "Consulting Firms Keep Lucrative Saudi Alliance, Shaping Crown Prince's Vision." *New York Times*, November 4, 2018.

Gause, F. Gregory, and Sean Yom. "Resilient Royals: How Arab Monarchies Hang On." Brookings Institution, October 15, 2012.

Ghiles, Francis. "Growing Reliance on Mercenaries Spells More Chaos in the Region." *Arab Weekly*, November 17, 2020. https://thearabweekly.com/growing -reliance-mercenaries-spells-more-chaos-region

"Gov't Mulls Granting Citizenship in Exchange for Increasing Working Capital." *Enterprise*, August 12, 2020. https://enterprise.press/stories/2020/08/12/govt -mulls-granting-citizenship-in-exchange-for-increasing-working-capital-20 241/

Guazzone, Laura, and Daniela Pioppi. "Interpreting Change in the Arab World." In *The Arab State and Neo-Liberal Globalization*, edited by Laura Guazzone and Daniela Pioppi. Berkshire, UK: Ithaca Press, 2012.

Hammoud, Hassan R. "Illiteracy in the Arab World." DVV International. https:// www.dvv-international.de/en/adult-education-and-development/editions/aed -662006/education-for-all-and-literacy/illiteracy-in-the-arab-world

Hanieh, Adam. *Lineages of Revolt: Issues of Contemporary Capitalism in the Middle East*. Chicago: Haymarket Books, 2013.

Hanieh, Adam. "Shifting Priorities or Business as Usual? Continuity and Change in the Post-2011 IMF and World Bank Engagement with Tunisia, Morocco and Egypt." *British Journal of Middle Eastern Studies* 42, no. 1 (2015).

Hassan, Zaha, and Marwan Muasher. "Why the Abraham Accords Fall Short: Sidelining the Palestinians Is a Recipe for Violence, Not Peace." *Foreign Affairs*, June 7, 2022. https://www.foreignaffairs.com/middle-east/why-abraham-accor ds-fall-short

Hedges, Chris. "Cairo Journal, after the Earthquake, a Rumbling of Discontent." *New York Times*, October 21, 1992.

Heydemann, Steven. "After the Earthquake: Economic Governance and Mass Politics in the Middle East." *Critique International* 61 (2013/2014).

Hibou, Béatrice. *The Force of Obedience: The Political Economy of Repression in Tunisia*. 1st edition. Cambridge, UK: Polity, 2011.

Human Rights Watch. "Egypt: Emergency Provisions Made Permanent." November 5, 2021. https://www.hrw.org/news/2021/11/05/egypt-emergency-provisi

ons-made-permanent?gad_source=1&gclid=Cj0KCQiAyKurBhD5ARIsALam
XaEqa5Fpmjd7qr7UHw-tdmZTCA7W1xo3rZJfLnpdCI7XNzEaDqXXYvsa
AmdnEALw_wcB
Imam, Patrick A., and Davina F. Jacobs. "Effect of Corruption on Tax Revenues in the Middle East." IMF Working Papers, 2007.
Ismail, Salwa. *Political Life in Cairo's New Quarters: Encountering the Everyday State.* Minneapolis: University of Minnesota Press, 2006.
"Israel, U.S. and 4 Arab Nations Focus on Security at Summit." *New York Times*, March 28, 2022.
Jamel, Manal. "The 'Tiering' of Citizenship and Residency and the 'Hierarchization' of Migrant Communities: The United Arab Emirates in Historical Context." *International Migration Review* 49, no. 3 (2015).
Jones, Calvert. "Adviser to The King: Experts, Rationalization, and Legitimacy." *World Politics* 71, no. 1 (2019).
Jones, Calvert. *Bedouins into Bourgeois: Remaking Citizens for Globalization.* Cambridge: Cambridge University Press, 2017.
Kamrava, Mehran. *The Impossibility of Palestine: History, Geography, and the Road Ahead.* New Haven, CT: Yale University Press, 2016.
Kanna, Ahmed. *Dubai: The City as Corporation.* Minneapolis: University of Minnesota Press, 2011.
Khalidi, Rashid. *The Iron Cage: The Story of the Palestinian Struggle for Statehood.* Boston: Beacon Press, 2007.
Khalili, Laleh, and Jillian Schwedler, eds. *Policing and Prisons in the Middle East.* London: Hurst and Company, 2010.
Khatib, Lina. "Syria's Transactional State: How the Conflict Changed the Syrian State's Exercise of Power." Chatham House, October 2018. https://www.chathamhouse.org/sites/default/files/publications/research/2018-10-10-syrias-transactional-state-khatib-sinjab.pdf
Khouri, Rami. "Poverty, Inequality and the Structural Threat to the Arab Region." *Shifting Global Politics and the Middle East.* POMEPS Studies 34 (2019).
Kim, Victoria. "What Is the Wagner Group?" *New York Times*, March 31, 2022.
Kingsley, Patrick. "A New New Cairo: Egypt Plans £30bn Purpose-Built Capital in Desert." *The Guardian*, March 16, 2015.
Korany, B., P. Noble, and R. Brynen, eds. *The Many Faces of National Security in the Arab World.* London: Palgrave Macmillan, 1993.
Kurtzer-Ellenbogen, Lucy. "Historic UAE-Israel Trade Deal Proves Abraham Accords' Resilience." USIP, June 2, 2022. https://www.usip.org/publications/2022/06/historic-uae-israel-trade-deal-proves-abraham-accords-resilience
Lagarde, Christine. "The Arab Spring, One Year On." International Monetary Fund (blog), December 2011.
Lawson, Fred. "Armed Forces, Internal Security Services, and Popular Contention in the Middle East and North Africa." In *Armies and Insurgencies in the Arab Spring*, edited by Holger Albrecht, Aurel Croissant, and Fred H. Lawson. Philadelphia: University of Pennsylvania Press, 2016.
Leenders, Reinoud. "Prosecuting Political Dissent: Courts and the Resilience of Authoritarianism in Syria." In *Middle Eastern Authoritarianisms*, edited by Steven Heydemann and Reinoud Leenders. Stanford: Stanford University Press, 2013.

Lori, Noora. *Offshore Citizens: Permanent Temporary Status in the Gulf.* Cambridge: Cambridge University Press 2019.
Lori, Noora. "Time and Its Miscounting: Methodological Challenges in the Study of Citizenship Boundaries." *International Journal of Middle East Studies* 52 (2002): 721–25.
Margalit, Lila. "State of Emergency in Israel: Is It Really Necessary?" Israel Democracy Institute, June 2019.
Marshall, Shana. "The Egyptian Armed Forces and the Remaking of an Economic Empire." Carnegie Middle East Center, 2015.
Martinez, Jose Ciro. *States of Subsistence: The Politics of Bread in Contemporary Jordan.* Stanford: Stanford University Press, 2022.
Marzouki, Nadia. "Whatever Happened to Dignity? The Politics of Citizenship in Post-Revolution Tunisia." *Middle East Report* 301 (Winter 2021). https://merip.org/2021/12/whatever-happened-to-dignity-the-politics-of-citizenship-in-post-revolution-tunisia-2/
Mazzetti, Mark, and Emily B. Hager. "Secret Desert Force Set Up by Blackwater's Founder." *New York Times*, May 14, 2011.
McKee, Musa, Martin Keulertz, Negar Habibi, Mark Mulligan, and Eckart Woertz. "Demographic and Economic Material Factors in the MENA Region." *Middle East and North Africa Regional Architecture: Mapping Geopolitical Shifts, Regional Order and Domestic Transformation*, Working Paper No. 3, October 2017. http://www.iai.it/sites/default/files/menara_wp_3.pdf
Mitchell, Timothy. "The Limits of the State: Beyond Statist Approaches and Their Critics." *American Political Science Review* 85 (1991).
Mossalem, Mohammed. "The IMF in the Arab World: Lessons Unlearned." Bretton Woods Project, December 18, 2015. https://www.brettonwoodsproject.org/2015/12/imf-policy-in-the-mena-region-lessons-unlearnt/
Nereim, Vivian. "MBS's $500 Billion Desert Dream Just Keeps Getting Weirder." Bloomberg, July 14, 2022.
Nerien, Vivian. "Saudi Arabia Wants Its Capital to Be Somewhere You'd Want to Live." Bloomberg, December 16, 2021.
"New Saudi Egyptian Investment Company to Attract $10 Billion Investments." Egyptian Streets, August 6, 2022. https://egyptianstreets.com/2022/08/06/new-saudi-egyptian-investment-company-to-attract-10-billion-investments/
Nucho, Joanne Randa. *Everyday Sectarianism in Urban Lebanon.* Princeton, NJ: Princeton University Press, 2016.
Picard, Elizabeth. "The Virtual Sovereignty of the Lebanese State: From Deviant Case to Ideal-Type." In *The Arab State and Neo-Liberal Globalization*, edited by Laura Guazzone and Daniela Pioppi. Berkshire, UK: Ithaca Press, 2012.
Quinlivan, James. "Coup-Proofing: Its Practice and Consequences in the Middle East." *International Security* 24, no. 2 (1999).
Reno, William. "The Privatization of Sovereignty and the Survival of Weak States." In *Privatizing the State*, edited by Béatrice Hibou. New York: Columbia University Press, 2004.
Rosefsky Wickham, Carrie. *Mobilizing Islam.* New York: Columbia University Press, 2002.
Rouis, Mustapha, and Tabor, Steven R. *Regional Economic Integration in the Middle East and North Africa: Beyond Trade Reform (English).* Directions in Develop-

ment: Trade Washington, D.C.: World Bank Group. http://documents.worldbank.org/curated/en/813531468052157933/Regional-economic-integration-in-the-Middle-East-and-North-Africa-beyond-trade-reform
Sabga, Patricia. "MBS: Why the World May Be Stuck with the 'CEO of Saudi Inc.'" Al-Jazeera, October 2, 2020.
Salloukh, Bassel. "From State-Building to State-Fraying Permeability: NSAs in the Post-Popular Uprisings Arab World." *Shifting Global Politics and the Middle East.* POMEPS Studies 34 (2019).
Salloukh, Bassel. "The Sectarianization of Geopolitics in the Middle East." In *Sectarianization: Mapping the New Politics of the Middle East*, edited by Nader Hashemi and Danny Postel. Oxford: Oxford University Press, 2017.
Saouli, Adham. *The Arab State: Dilemmas of Late Formation*. London: Routledge, 2012.
"Saudi Wealth Fund Sets Up Company to Invest in Egypt." *Enterprise*, August 7, 2022. https://enterprise.press/am-edition/#tldr-story-02
Sayigh, Yezid. "Retain, Restructure, or Divest? Policy Options for Egypt's Military Economy." Carnegie Middle East Center, January 31, 2022. https://carnegie-mec.org/2022/01/31/retain-restructure-or-divest-policy-options-for-egypt-s-military-economy-pub-86232
Schwedler, Jillian. *Protesting Jordan: Geographies of Power and Dissent*. Stanford: Stanford University Press, 2022.
Singerman, Diane. *Avenues of Participation: Family, Politics, and Networks in Urban Quarters of Cairo*. Princeton, NJ: Princeton University Press, 1995.
Springborg, Robert. "Economic Involvements of Militaries." *International Journal of Middle East Studies* 43, no. 3 (2011).
Tällberg Foundation. "Reimagining the Middle East." June 17, 2021. https://tallbergfoundation.org/articles/reimagining-the-middle-east/
Tessler, Mark. *A History of the Israeli-Palestinian Conflict*. Bloomington: Indiana University Press, 2009.
Weber, Max. *Weber's Rationalism and Modern Society*. Translated and edited by Tony Waters and Dagmar Waters. New York: Palgrave Books, 2015.
Wehry, Fredric. "A Minister, a General, and the Militias: Libya's Shifting Balance of Power." *New York Review of Books*, March 19, 2019.
Wendt, Alexander. "Anarchy Is What States Make of It: The Social Construction of Power Politics." *International Organization* 46, no. 2 (1992).
Yaghi, Mohammad. "Neoliberal Reforms, Protests, and Enforced Patron-Client Relations in Tunisia and Egypt." In *Clientelism and Patronage in the Middle East and North Africa*, edited by Laura Ruiz Elvira, Christoph Schwarz, and Irene Wepert-Fenner. Milton Park, UK: Routledge, 2019.
Young, Karen E. "The New Politics of Gulf Arab State Foreign Aid and Investment." LSE Middle East Centre, Collected Papers Vol. 1, April 2015. https://blogs.lse.ac.uk/mec/2015/11/25/the-new-politics-of-gulf-arab-state-foreign-aid-and-investment/
Young, Karen E. "What's Yours Is Mine: Gulf SWFs as a Barometer of State-Society Relations." *The Politics of the Rentier State in the Gulf*. POMEPS Studies 33 (January 2019).
Young, Michael. "A New Rif Revolt?" Carnegie Middle East Center, June 2017.

SEVEN

Palace Politics as "Precarious" Rule

Weak Statehood in Afghanistan

Dipali Mukhopadhyay

In her book on the production of knowledge (and the perpetuation of ignorance) about Afghanistan, Nivi Manchanda explains how "a vocabulary of state fragility, failure, collapse, and corruption" became synonymous with the country after 2001. This vernacular proved so ubiquitous that it seemed to reflect "almost inherent and a priori conditions of Afghanistan as a political (and territorial) entity."[1] When leveled by foreign governments and militaries, the characterization of ungovernability represented, at least in part, an attempt to absolve interveners of their own sins, Manchanda argues. And, quite usefully, it fit neatly within a longer discursive history that conceived of the Afghan state as "a morally, socially and politically bankrupt space of contestation," where great powers and their great ambitions came to die.[2]

As Steven Heydemann contends in this volume, "Taking state failure as a starting point for research" has been a theoretical and empirical choice made by many scholars of the Middle East; and "it has come at a cost," namely, that it elides the often extraordinary persistence of various forms of political order.[3] In the scholarly and policymaking imaginaries,

---

1. Manchanda, *Imagining Afghanistan*, 70.
2. Manchanda, *Imagining Afghanistan*, 72.
3. Heydemann, "Seeing the State or Why Arab States Look the Way They Do," chap. 1, this volume.

few states evoke the notion of "failure" more than Afghanistan. And, yet, despite relentless foreign interference, occupation, and war, the Afghan state has persisted. Radical swings in regime type (from monarchical to republican to communist to Islamist to democratic and back) notwithstanding, a collection of diverse ethnic, sectarian, and territorial communities have remained tied to this delimited geography for close to 150 years.[4] Manchanda contends that the absence of an established colonial presence in the territory precluded the institutionalized consolidation of prosaic everyday social processes we recognize and name as the state."[5] But the absence of colonial rule in Afghanistan—a largely anomalous condition in the region—did not mean the absence of state making.

On the contrary, the relationship into which the late nineteenth-century king Abdur Rahman Khan entered with the British Crown laid the groundwork for a generations-long rentier state-building project in Afghanistan. The so-called Iron Amir settled on terms with the British that foreclosed his control over foreign affairs in exchange for a steady source of international income and recognition.[6] So commenced Afghanistan's status as a "buffer state," situated in a kind of international in-between, filling the space between rival powers and extracting a form of strategic rent for its geographic utility. Abdur Rahman received British funds and weapons that positioned him to commence the work of regime consolidation. He conscripted troops and raised revenue through taxation. And the new king pursued an ambitious series of campaigns to lay claim to the lands and peoples beyond his initial writ in Kabul.[7]

Abdur Rahman Khan undertook state making on much the same terms that Charles Tilly described in early Europe, "a mixed strategy: eliminating, subjugating, dividing, conquering, cajoling, buying as the occasions presented themselves."[8] This new king's approach to state building, a kind of "internal imperialism," involved torture, rape, forcible displacement, and even enslavement.[9] So brutal was this campaign that Hasan Kakar likened it to the kind of warfare that an Islamic ruler might have deployed "in a non-Muslim land (*dar al-harb*)."[10] This ferocious brand of consolidation

---

4. As Omar Sharifi has argued, "Afghanistan is the only country in the region that has never witnessed a secessionist or separatist movement." Sharifi, "The Nauroz Festival as a Social Site," x.
5. Manchanda, *Imagining Afghanistan*, 74.
6. Rubin, *The Fragmentation of Afghanistan*, 48.
7. Rubin, *The Fragmentation of Afghanistan*, 48–49.
8. Tilly, "War-Making and State-Making as Organized Crime," 175.
9. Dupree as quoted in Barfield, *Afghanistan*, 147.
10. Kakar, *Political and Diplomatic History of Afghanistan*, 138. All told, the Amir's heavy-

was not only permitted but, in fact, enabled by British patronage. But his regime's methodology involved more than naked aggression. Abdur Rahman's rule combined brute force, an appeal to divine legitimation, patronage politics, tribal maneuvering, and a novel subnational administration that parceled the periphery into provinces, districts, and subdistricts with centrally appointed governors in each.[11] He co-opted a range of defeated and potential rivals, drawing those with the capacity to threaten him into the fold.[12]

A little more than a century after the Iron Amir's rule, Afghanistan's new president, Hamid Karzai, found himself in the midst of a novel exchange with a foreign patron of his own, the United States. This time, the country's ruler would not have the freedom and flexibility to take on his sundry competitors on the same terms as his predecessor. This new configuration of rentiership, conceived in 2001, predicated Western military, diplomatic, and material support on the host regime's sustained provision of access to the country's territory for the pursuit of violent extremist actors. The perceived link between ungoverned (or ill-governed) space and terrorism justified regime change, foreign-led reconstruction, and ongoing kinetic military activity on the part of US and coalition forces.[13] It also meant that Karzai was expected to embrace an ethos of "good governance" anchored in constitutional checks and balances, electoral politics, and a respect for the rights of Afghanistan's citizenry.

The exceptionally tight strictures within which the new Afghan government was forced to rule produced a "precarious" kind of sovereignty that kept the Afghan state in an impossible political limbo.[14] It is only in con-

---

handed model provoked "forty disturbances, including ten major rebellions, four of which he called civil wars" across what is now modern-day Afghanistan. Rubin, *The Fragmentation of Afghanistan*, 50.

11. Rubin, *The Fragmentation of Afghanistan*, 50–51.

12. As Barfield noted, "One of the amir's political strengths was that he aimed his attacks at specific targets and thereby kept conflict from spreading too widely against him at any time. He also took on hostile tribes and regions in sequence, often rewarding victims of earlier repressions with opportunities to gain wealth and political influence by allying with him in later attacks on others." Barfield, *Afghanistan*, 147.

13. Fukuyama, "The Imperative of State-Building"; Woodward, *The Ideology of Failed States*.

14. In her writing on migration and statelessness, Noora Lori coined the concept of "precarious citizenship," into which governments deposit populations, extracting their labor while withholding final status. Analogously, powerful states deposit weak states into geopolitical "in-between" spaces marked by a kind of "structured uncertainty." Lori, "Statelessness, 'In-between' Statuses, and Precarious Citizenship" 745–66. Audra Simpson, in her book on Mohawk politics also writes of the "precariousness" of sovereignty, in her case with respect to the American colonial settler state. Simpson, *Mohawk Interruptus*. On Afghanistan, as Rubin put it: "The intervention in Afghanistan was a counter-terrorist intervention. That, not ana-

fronting the hypocritical logic underpinning this American enterprise—
one that simultaneously demanded and precluded the creation of an independent Afghan state—that its ultimate failure can be understood. And, yet, even in this profoundly restrictive space, the Karzai regime found the means by which to rule. Dismissive characterizations like "the mayor of Kabul" betrayed the influence the president exerted beyond the palace walls.[15] He did not have the freedom to wield violence or capital on the terms the Iron Amir did more than a century earlier, but he had the authority to choose who would represent his regime and its interests subnationally on account of the state's exceptionally centralized architecture.

Karzai employed that architecture to construct a politics of accommodation that reflected a much longer lineage of rule and offered him significant influence and governing authority beyond Kabul. His successor, President Ashraf Ghani, took a different approach, employing institutional centralization to authoritarian ends and transforming a palace politics of accommodation into one of exclusion and imposition. There are many reasons why the Ghani regime collapsed in 2021, a number of which lay beyond the president's control. But the authoritarianism of the president's governing style was redolent with echoes of previous regimes that aggressively overstepped their writ, and the outcome was the same: insurgent victory.

Afghanistan and the Arab State

In this volume, scholars of Middle Eastern politics look across the region and revisit concepts of state strength and weakness in critical terms. We move beyond the simplistic strong-weak binary to offer new means of articulating the many relationships we have observed between ruler and ruled and the countless institutions and practices that mediate them. In broad terms, a number of us seek to unravel what Raymond Hinnebusch calls the "weakness-resilience paradox" at play within the region. States appear enfeebled but persist just the same, their endurance the result of some "historic interaction of structure and agency" that often goes overlooked.[16] Upon closer inspection, their apparent weakness gives way to a

---

lytical errors or bureaucratic politics, is why some U.S. policies proved to be obstacles to peace and stability." Rubin, "What I Saw in Afghanistan," https://www.newyorker.com/news/news-desk/what-have-we-been-doing-in-afghanistan

15. Robinson, "Karzai's Kabul"; Bergen, "Hamid Karzai."
16. Hinnebusch, "Understanding State Weakness in the Middle East and North Africa," chap. 2, this volume.

kind of push-and-pull that need not be interpreted as fragility but, rather, as a series of dialogues, even contentious interactions, that shape rather than threaten state order.

As Heydemann and Marc Lynch put it, these states are "expressions of specific social actors," and those expressions reflect all kinds of struggle and collaboration that cannot and ought not to be simplified, let alone ignored.[17] Jillian Schwedler reminds us that state formation, in this sense, is not an achievement but rather "the ongoing maneuvering of state actors to dodge challengers, woo supporters, deflate resistance, respond to demands from allies and so on."[18] In considering Iraq, Toby Dodge describes the state itself as "better understood as a series of competitive arenas or fields," while Bassel Salloukh characterizes the Lebanese state as "the armature around which all kinds of activities configure themselves."[19]

Even moments of confrontation like the one Sean Yom explores in Jordan between the monarchy and surrounding tribal elites need not be read as rebellion but rather, as he puts it, "a grand refusal to relinquish [the tribal] demands about the most appropriate ordering of space and resources within social life."[20] There is a temptation among those who observe the politics of the Middle East through the dichotomy of success versus failure to interpret every little rumble as portending the state's undoing. A more fluid, dialogical understanding that accounts for contention, even competition, *as part of* rather than *at odds with* state making affords us the possibility to notice the conversational qualities by which states shape and are shaped by what surrounds them. It is that competition and how the post-2001 presidential palace in Kabul managed it that I will consider as part of the latest chapter of Afghan state building.[21]

Before I proceed, it bears noting that Afghanistan is nearly always excluded from the region of study known as "the Middle East" even as it remains bound up in the historical imaginings and contemporary geopolitics of this corner of the world in numerous ways. With gratitude to the

---

17. Heydemann and Lynch, "Introduction: Making Sense of the Arab State," this volume.
18. Schwedler, "State Capacity and Contention: A View from Jordan," chap. 8, this volume.
19. Dodge, "Rethinking the Post-Colonial State in the Middle East," chap. 3, this volume; Salloukh, "What We Talk about When We Talk about the State in Postwar Lebanon," chap. 5, this volume.
20. Yom, "Water, Stateness, and Tribalism in Jordan," chap. 9, this volume.
21. With heartfelt thanks to my remarkable research assistant Malyar Sadeq Azad, who collected all the data on gubernatorial appointments. Much of his work was supported generously by the U.S. Institute of Peace. I also received invaluable support from my brilliant research assistant Priyanka Sethy, whose quantitative skills and sharp insights enabled a good deal of this analysis.

editors for including the case here, my own analysis of Afghan state formation and "building" resonates with insights offered up by several colleagues in this volume, as noted above. Afghanistan is often cased, to borrow Joe Soss's phrasing, as exemplary, exotic, even singular in terms that obscure the many commonalities it shares with states across the developing world.[22] Its inclusion in this volume affords readers the opportunity to learn more about the particulars of contemporary Afghan governance in conversation with and through the lens of the Arab state while also considering whether the Arab state should, itself, be hived off from others with which it might actually share quite a bit.

Attention to what Heydemann and Lynch call "regime-ness" is an especially fruitful site for comparison and contrast. The notion that, in Heydemann's words, particular "institutional configurations—combinations of state and non-state modes of governance"—represent "regime preferences about how best to ensure their stability and survival" is central to my analysis of the Afghan case.[23] Like in Salloukh's Lebanon, Afghan regimes have repeatedly enacted deliberate forms of absence in strategic terms; as Heydemann put it, "Under certain conditions rulers prefer limited statehood to its more expansive alternative."[24] Only in taking those preferences seriously can we begin to understand how regimes persist even under the most trying of conditions.

Having outlined these points of convergence, it bears noting that the Afghan experience with state formation is distinct, or at least an exemplar, in certain ways that inform my analysis below but may also have reverberations for Arab (and other) states. My argument centers on the notion that twenty-first-century palace politics represented an instrument of Afghan regime survival and state building under the exceptionally restrictive conditions imposed by foreign intervention. The latest chapter of Afghan state formation unfolded as part of the neo-imperial "Global War on Terror," underscoring the interaction between domestic governance and international relations in exemplary terms, some of which will have resonance in Arab states marked by different sorts of foreign interference and engagement.

The contemporary Afghan case also unearths the relationship between regime survivalism and fledgling democracy. While many of the Arab

---

22. Soss, "On Casing a Study versus Studying a Case." With thanks to Haroun Rahimi for sharing this formulation about Afghanistan as a case with me.
23. Heydemann, "Seeing the State or Why Arab States Look the Way They Do," chap. 1, this volume.
24. Salloukh, "What We Talk about When We Talk about the State in Postwar Lebanon," chap. 5, this volume.

regimes considered in this volume have employed ruling strategies in the service of authoritarian resilience, Karzai and Ghani helmed one of the world's youngest, albeit imperfect democracies. And because the United States and its allies insisted on the ostensibly democratic nature of this state-building project, neither regime could avail itself of the kinds of "fierce" instruments of rule Heydemann identifies across the Middle East. And yet they privileged "regime-ness" as much as their dictatorial counterparts. Ultimately, like their fierce counterparts, success depended on, in Heydemann's words, "the very institutions, norms, and practices that fragility-based models treat as causes of poor governance and symptoms of institutional weakness."[25] In that sense, the effective management of competition can be understood as a modality of rule common to authoritarian and democratic regimes alike.

State Making as Competition Management

In the seventeenth century, the Ottoman sultanate struck a deal with the notorious bandit Canboladoglu Ali Pashi. As a major powerholder in the challenging and strategically valuable region of northern Syria, Canboladoglu was prepared to offer the empire the support of his sixteen thousand men in exchange for the benefits and trappings of state power. In 1606, he was named governor-general of Aleppo. As Karen Barkey explained it, the rationale behind his appointment reflected a brand of palace politics oriented around the effective, often unsavory, management of competition. As she wrote, "The existence of contending forces in society does not necessarily mean state breakdown; and it does not necessarily mean total loss of control on the part of government."[26]

Those concerned with the political economy of state formation have long argued that the promise of profit and prestige has consistently motivated strongmen to lay down their arms in favor of joining new forms of order that became the basis for statehood.[27] Scholars have also drawn our attention to contemporary innovations by which politicians have leveraged their access to state institutions to patronize their clientele and find profit for

---

25. Heydemann, "Seeing the State or Why Arab States Look the Way They Do," chap. 1, this volume.
26. Barkey, *Bandits and Bureaucrats*, 19. For the story of Canboladoglu Ali Pasha, 189-228.
27. Tilly, "War Making and State Making as Organized Crime"; Olson, "Dictatorship, Democracy, and Development"; North, Wallis, and Weingast, *Violence and Social Orders*.

themselves.[28] Even Max Weber, whose work is most closely associated with a rational, bureaucratic ideal, meditated on government in terms that did not leave power to the side. On the contrary, in his renowned essay "Politics as Vocation," he described politics as "striving to share power or striving to influence the distribution of power . . . among groups within a state."[29]

This dimension of Weber's argument gets lost in the language of regulation and law and the derivative focus on service delivery, accountability, and democratization. That focus features frequently in the "good governance" discourse and does the work of obscuring or even maligning the role of politics and power in the governing project.[30] But Weber was clear, through his chronicling of the European historical experience, about the extent to which political offices were often prized material commodities, "pure institutions for the provision of spoilsmen."[31]

Recent scholarship on modern state building and counterinsurgency has begun to unravel those narratives that espouse the import and effectiveness of a softer, gentler model of rule, deconstructing some of the lore around historical successes in cases from Malaya and Oman to El Salvador and Northern Ireland. This work alerts us to the reality that intervening states and indigenous governments have both employed a range of what Joel Migdal called "dirty tricks" to assert dominance in the face of rebellion.[32] Many states that survived insurgency did so not by building strong and capable formal institutions or by improving access to public goods for ordinary citizens. On the contrary, their methods involved various combinations of brute force and patronage politics—in the words of Christopher Day and William Reno, "strategies aim[ed] to co-opt rebels through amnesty and settlements, or to defeat them through the use of armed proxies such as local militias and rebels from neighboring countries."[33]

Empirically grounded portraits of state making lend insight into the dark underbelly of state formation but also reveal the possibility of important dividends arising from the kinds of shadowy dealings that often go ignored in twenty-first-century parlance about the work of governing. They point to one means by which the Gordian knot of endemic (often

---

28. Reno, "Reinvention of an African Patrimonial State"; Ganev, *Preying on the State*; de Waal, "Mission without End"; Lake, "Building the Rule of War."
29. Weber, "Politics as Vocation," 78.
30. Kaufmann and Kraay, "Governance Indicators"; Fukuyama, "What Is Governance?"
31. Weber, "Politics as Vocation," 87.
32. Migdal, *State in Society*, 80; Hazelton, "The 'Hearts and Minds' Fallacy: Violence, Coercion, and Success in Counterinsurgency Warfare"; Dixon, "'Hearts and Minds'?"; and Migdal, *Strong Societies and Weak States*.
33. Day and Reno, "In Harm's Way," 107.

violent) competition can be cut: the apportionment of spoils—literal and metaphorical. Politicians are trafficking in financial privilege and territorial gain but also in influence, prestige, and honor.[34] As Barkey explained of the Ottoman approach, "Even those once labeled the worst enemies of the state could later be treated to the best of Ottoman panache," and, indeed, that temptation proved salient in the sultanate's political work.[35] It is this less tangible impulse—to be recognized and empowered—that offers the sovereign additional leverage in his management of competition.

This accommodationist approach was best exemplified in Afghanistan by the mid-twentieth-century kings of the Musahiban dynasty, who oversaw decades of stable rule.[36] The first, Nadir Shah, rose to power on the back of a tribal military campaign with a twelve-thousand-strong militia that captured Kabul on his family's behalf. As Amin Saikal described it, Nadir Shah and his brothers (and then his son, King Zahir Shah) embraced "a concept of sober nationalism ... a gradual process of change and development, based on peaceful coexistence with conservative forces."[37] The Musahibans constructed a state premised on the insulation of their regime from the strife of contentious politics. They relied on key elite intermediaries as social brokers and shielded these local notables from the heavier burdens of conscription, taxation, and reformist policies that might have otherwise provoked center-periphery conflict. They compensated for the loss of domestic revenue by deepening their ties with the outside world through exports and foreign aid, forming what Rubin called an "enclave" state.[38]

Centralized governance, enshrined in the 1931 and 1964 constitutions, meant neither transformational politics nor policies that would interfere acutely in the lives of ordinary people. Instead, informal actors and institutions—both tribal and religious—were shown deference consistently. As Asta Olesen observed, Nadir Shah's constitution was "a showpiece of appeasement of the various power groups in society."[39] And even Zahir Shah's constitution, which promised more liberal institution building, did not prompt the kind of aggressive attempts at reforms it might have otherwise suggested. The Musahiban approach, marked by conservative forms of state engagement with the greater society, brought

---

34. Weber, "Politics as Vocation."
35. Barkey, *Bandits and Bureaucrats*, 192.
36. For my more extensive consideration of the history of accommodationist rule in Afghanistan from which I base this discussion, see Mukhopadhyay, "Ambition and Retreat: State-Building in Afghanistan"; see also Mukhopadhyay, *Warlords, Strongman Governors, and the State in Afghanistan*.
37. Saikal, *Modern Afghanistan*, 97.
38. Rubin, "Lineages of the State in Afghanistan."
39. Olesen, *Islam and Politics in Afghanistan*, 179.

four decades of peace to Afghan politics. It would find its next exponent in Hamid Karzai after 2001.

Before diving into the particularities of Karzai's (and then Ghani's) approach, it is worth pausing to reflect on one more insight that leaps out from the pages of this volume. Many of my colleagues contend that one of the reasons so many observers—scholars and policymakers—fixate on the imperative for "strength" and the perils of "weakness" derives from the inherently normative gaze they adopt. "Expressions of disappointment," as Schwedler notes, point us in the direction of "deficits" or "failures" that often have little to do with "an inability to govern so much as the failure of state institutions and practices to meet the needs and expectations of foreign entities seeking to advance their own interests and agendas."[40] Dodge similarly describes the relentless imposition of "a European ideal" as the benchmark against which all political outcomes are judged, rendering alternate outcomes as "supposed pathologies, absences or failures."[41]

The Afghan case affords us a key opportunity to understand what lies beneath these "expressions of disappointment." The Afghan state-building project was, after all, ostensibly driven by a Western interest in promoting democracy, liberal politics, and market economics through military intervention. Such an intervention would theoretically address the pathological nexus between state weakness and terrorism. But the Afghan experience does more than expose the systematic biases that mark so many interventions of this kind. It also exposes the hypocrisy that lies beneath that supposed disappointment. The United States and its allies undermined both the development and the capacity of the very state they claimed to be emboldening, often encouraging undemocratic, illiberal, and corrupt people and practices along the way. I will argue that the feeble aspects of contemporary Afghan statehood must be understood as a function of, rather than despite, the neo-imperial undertaking that brought that version of the state into being. Afghanistan offers, in that sense, an opportunity to consider the dialectic between indigenous power politics and Western adventurism in the region that yields a distinct kind of "precarious" statehood.

President Karzai's Palace Politics

In his writings on weak states in strong societies, Migdal cataloged a series of strategies that rulers have long employed to ensure their own perse-

---

40. Schwedler, "State Capacity and Contention," chap. 8, this volume.
41. Dodge, "Rethinking the Post-Colonial State in the Middle East," chap. 3, this volume.

verance in the face of competing social forces. At the helm of a shattered state, Hamid Karzai faced "vast, but fragmented social control embedded in the nonstate organizations of society."[42] From 2001 to 2014, his regime pursued its own version of a Migdalian "politics of survival" but within an exceptionally confined margin for maneuver.[43] The young government's Western benefactors complicated the country's already crowded warscape through a series of strategic decisions—to collaborate with the warlord commanders of the Northern Alliance in 2001; to exclude the decimated Taliban from politics; and to employ the kinetic use of force on their own terms—that disadvantaged the palace in Kabul in meaningful, lasting ways. At the same time, the normative scaffolding of twenty-first-century state building imposed a set of "good" governing requirements and restrictions on the Afghan state that further limited its room for maneuver.

Karzai employed his own version of palace politics to curb the power of many strongmen empowered by the counterterror campaign. He transformed them into a bulwark against an insurgency that emerged, at least in part, because that same counterterror effort precluded his administration from making a serious attempt at peaceful, political engagement with the defeated Taliban. In the process, Karzai created a tableau of power politics that reflected the geographic, ethnic, sectarian, and ideological diversity of the Afghan elite and the larger citizenry.[44] That tableau, a "limited access order" of sorts, did a kind of political work that had little to do with service delivery, bureaucratic efficiency, transparency, or accountability. Instead, it reflected the utilization of accommodation as a means of preempting, exploiting, and curbing rivalries to bring about a modicum of security and development in the midst of an ongoing war. It also enabled forms of representation and popular participation that might otherwise have triggered even greater unrest in such a young democracy.

Starting from "the Zero Point"

On arrival, Karzai had limited influence beyond Kabul. In the words of one Afghan observer, "Karzai came in a U.S. helicopter and got his power."[45]

---

42. Migdal, *Strong Societies and Weak States*, 207.
43. Migdal, *Strong Societies and Weak States*, 213.
44. I first made this argument, some of the points and language of which I use in this chapter, for a policy audience in Mukhopadhyay, "Provincial Governors in Afghan Politics."
45. AFG 14 Interview 1. I conducted interviews in 2014 in Afghanistan with the financial support of the United States Institute of Peace. I have refrained from including details about my key informants in this chapter to preserve their confidentiality, particularly in light of the

As another put it, "Karzai, with his friends, started from the zero point."[46] But, as a result of the highly centralized formal architecture that has long marked the Afghan state, his regime's ability to appoint, promote, rotate, and remove officials in the provinces proved a very valuable asset in this particular brand of survival politics.[47] The 2004 constitution afforded the executive tremendous formal control over subnational institutions; its design produced one of the most centralized states in the world.

Critiques of this acutely centralized architecture abounded. Institutional devolution, some suggested, would have wrested political power from the historically dominant Pashtun elite and redistributed resources and decision making more equitably and effectively across the regionalized ethnic blocs of the periphery.[48] Concerned observers also argued that the exceptional powers of the presidency resembled those of earlier Afghan monarchs whose own constitutions (in particular, King Zahir Shah's in 1964) had served as the template for this one.[49] The president's grip on appointments, administration, and budgeting, they worried, came "at the expense of broader democratization goals" and encouraged the kinds of cronyism and corruption at odds with transparent, representative, accountable governance."[50]

The gap between the Weberian ideal and the reality of weak state politics was nowhere more apparent than in the arena of political appointments. Efforts at governance promotion aim, after all, to produce "professional politicians" who answer to impersonal institutions rather than the sovereign as an individual.[51] Instead, subnational appointments served, in Martine van Bijlert's words, as "a vehicle for relationship building and the distribution of privileges to leaders and communities that [were] considered loyal," a means for the Karzai regime "to re-assert its authority and to strengthen its network."[52]

---

cataclysmic events of August 2021. A number of these interviews were quoted and cited in the 2016 USIP Special Report.

46. AFG 14 Interview 7.

47. The palace's capacity to dole out gubernatorial appointments formed the heart of a "politics of relationships." Van Bijlert, "Between Discipline and Discretion," 8.

48. Shahrani, "Afghanistan's Alternatives for Peace, Governance and Development"; Barfield, *Afghanistan*.

49. Shahrani, "Afghanistan's Alternatives for Peace, Governance and Development."

50. Nixon and Ponzio, "Building Democracy in Afghanistan," 35; Shurkin, "Subnational Government in Afghanistan." Also, "the original sin of this intervention was to resurrect old institutions that had their roots in the country's authoritarian past rather than giving Afghans the opportunity to build something new that embodied the norms of self-governance which characterized most parts of the country." Murtazashvili, "The Collapse of Afghanistan," 42.

51. Weber, "Politics as Vocation."

52. Van Bijlert, "Between Discipline and Discretion," 2–3, 8.

Given the range of rivals, potential rivals, and otherwise influential armed actors in its midst, one might argue that only a highly centralized architecture could offer the regime any hope of corralling the centrifugal forces at work to maintain some influence beyond Kabul.[53] Some attributed the popular appetite for a strong central government to this hope, "a widespread desire for the authority of the central government to be extended to the provinces, replacing the illegitimate de facto states controlled by warlords and druglords."[54] They cautioned that this impulse did not translate into a popular wish for the president's office to control everything from Kabul. But, as one Afghan interlocutor mused, the performance of those subnational officials may not have facilitated the nation building that Afghans had imagined, but "it helped Karzai to be in power."[55] Another explained: "He is extremely good at defeating possible and potential alliances against him or political formations that will undermine his control."[56]

"The Big Shuffle"

Observers of Afghan politics expressed consternation with "an ongoing confusion" that permeated the business of gubernatorial appointments after 2001. The central government unfurled new rules, standards, and institutions over the years, many of which were subsequently ignored or circumvented by the very officials in whose custody they resided.[57] When one conceives of gubernatorial appointments as a patrimonial means of reengineering rivalries, it becomes clear why strategic opacity and dynamism on the palace's part were of great value. Karzai had a host of patrons, foreign and Afghan, to please, and their agendas were often not in harmony with one another. At the same time, he had a host of clients and potential clients, in Kabul and the countryside, who sought his patronage. He also faced formidable factions, strongmen, and tribal elites whose interests could not be ignored.

It was in this space of competing agendas and interests where Karzai

---

53. "Many serious Afghans argue that centralization is needed now to help overcome the obstacle posed by extralegal local powerholders." Rubin, "Crafting a Constitution for Afghanistan," 16.
54. Wilder and Lister, "State-Building at the Subnational Level in Afghanistan," 97.
55. AFG 14 Interview 1.
56. AFG 14 Interview 2.
57. World Bank, "Service Delivery and Governance at the Sub-National Level in Afghanistan"; Nixon, "Subnational State-Building in Afghanistan"; van Bijlert, "Between Discipline and Discretion," 10; see also AFG Interview 1.

operated by balancing different camps, playing one against another, and ensuring that they took on each other rather than him. To effectively stay above the fray, ambiguity and agility were key. A rational, rule-based system that was predictable and formalized would have undermined his advantage as the principal in this turbulent political environment.[58] Here, Karzai's method comported quite neatly with what Patrick Chabal and Jean-Pascal Daloz called "the political instrumentalization of disorder."[59]

From 2002 onward, Karzai commenced Migdal's "big shuffle," appointing close to two hundred governors to represent the government in the country's thirty-four provinces. And so began a "dizzying game of musical chairs," whereby governors were appointed, dismissed, and reappointed at a swift and unpredictable tempo.[60] Out of the country's thirty-four provinces, twenty-six (more than 75 percent) had five or more governors during Karzai's time in office. Several of these provinces had upwards of seven, eight, or nine appointments. The shuffle not only involved a significant amount of appointing and dismissing. It also involved a high degree of rotation and recycling.[61]

The Karzai regime utilized a mix of local and imported governors, all of which it kept on the move at a steady clip. In the majority of cases (59 percent), the palace followed the lead of previous rulers by sending individuals to provinces other than their own, severing them from their homegrown networks and diminishing the likelihood that they would sink deep roots.[62] On average, governors were fired or moved elsewhere after less than two and a half years in office. Thirty-nine gubernatorial terms did not last a full year. As of September 2014, only eleven terms (6 percent) lasted for five years or more. Meanwhile, the longest-serving governor managed to hold onto his seat for over a decade. And so went the unpredictable, "irrational," big shuffle.

58. Nixon, "Subnational State-Building in Afghanistan," 57–58; van Bijlert, "Between Discipline and Discretion," 17.
59. Chabal and Daloz, *Africa Works*, 13.
60. "The big shuffle is a set of preemptive actions taken by state leaders, using these powers, to prevent loyalties in potentially strong agencies from developing in the first place." Migdal, *Strong Societies and Weak States*, 214.
61. At least thirty-six individuals (more than 25 percent of those appointed) served in more than one province. At least ten received three or more appointments. In one case, the president made a clean swap, appointing the former governor of Faryab to become the governor of Samangan and transferring the governor of Samangan to become the governor of Faryab. In another, one governor of Takhar left office in 2010 only to return in 2013.
62. Barfield described a similar phenomenon with respect to mid-twentieth-century appointments in the northern province of Kunduz. Barfield, "Weak Links on a Rusty Chain."

Disguised Warlordism

The most striking feature of Karzai's pantheon of governors was the ubiquity of mujahideen commanders who had made their names fighting the Soviets, the Taliban, and one another in the two decades before he came to office. As mentioned above, their prominence in the political landscape was not an accident; it was the result of a military campaign with their involvement at the heart of its design. Former commanders occupied 131 (68 percent) of the country's governorships during Karzai's tenure. In 29 of the 34 (85 percent) Afghan provinces, at least half of the governors appointed were strongmen; and, in seven (21 percent) provinces, only commanders ruled.

Meanwhile, a major, if not primary, aim of the foreign-led state-building effort that followed the Taliban's toppling was the disarmament, demobilization, and reintegration (DDR) of militia commanders and combatants and the creation of a reformed security sector in their stead. Instead, the incorporation of dozens upon dozens of commanders into government was read by many as imposing yet another era of warlordism on the Afghan people.[63] But the aspiration to banish this population of powerholders did not acknowledge their role in Afghan political, social, and economic life and their potential to contribute to the new order.[64]

From the Karzai regime's perspective, commander inclusion on this scale could be read precisely as a kind of informal, indigenous DDR program. Here, the Afghan state was hardly alone in its approach. Ken Menkhaus described Somaliland's experience with proto-state formation as advancing security, economic recovery, revenue generation, and even formal institutional growth. He justified government expenditures of approximately 50 percent on ex-combatant salaries in the formal security sector as follows: "A case can be made, in fact, that the Somaliland government's principal role has been as a large demobilization project." He concluded that "since 2000, Somaliland has consolidated its state-building accomplishments in an impressive manner."[65]

Afghanistan had long been a country marked by what Tilly called high accumulation and low concentration of coercion.[66] As one Afghan interlocutor explained, "You had a lot of military capital, skills, and mobilization

---

63. Wilder and Lister, "State-Building at the Subnational Level in Afghanistan"; Marten, "Warlordism in Comparative Perspective."
64. Bhatia, "The Future of the Mujahideen"; Giustozzi, *Empires of Mud*; Mukhopadhyay, *Warlords, Strongman Governors, and the State in Afghanistan*; Malejacq, *Warlord Survival*.
65. Menkhaus, "Governance without Government in Somalia," 91.
66. Charles Tilly, "Armed Force, Regimes, and Contention in Europe since 1650," 37–81.

Palace Politics as "Precarious" Rule 213

but also mobilization capacity. . . . The mindset, the ideology of resistance was there."[67] Commanders previously consumed by warfare, but also by plunder and other forms of illicit activity, could be otherwise occupied, at least partially. Governorships created access to untapped business opportunities; they engendered grander political aspirations that required broader, more inclusive platforms and strategies; and they incentivized "good" behavior for foreign donor audiences. Governors now had opportunities to take care of their own substantial clienteles and to grow invested, politically and financially, in the success of this regime and, by extension, the Afghan state.[68]

"Disguised" commanders could, moreover, leverage their informal sources of strength to innervate governors' offices and, by extension, police stations, district governorates, mayorships, and ministerial directorates.[69] The inclusion of warlords as governors proved doubly valuable to the fledgling government in this sense. Not only did these appointments divert substantial energy previously reserved for a militarized brand of politics to other ends, but they amplified the state's coercive power in the face of more elusive rivals. This version of reintegration enabled the regime in Kabul to exercise its own forms of influence and control over the use (and users) of force. In the begrudging words of the above interviewee: "You see there is a big change and, if you call this monopoly over the use of violence in that sense, then you can see that, yes, Karzai's strategy at least on that side has been effective."[70]

"Balancing Acts"

In this matrix of disguised warlordism, the substantial presence of governors associated with the Jamiat-i-Islami and Hezb-i-Islami parties bears

---

67. AFG 14 Interview 2.
68. On this, see Giustozzi, *Empires of Mud*; Mukhopadhyay, *Warlords, Strongman Governors, and the State in Afghanistan*; and Malejacq, *Warlord Survival*.
69. I first used the term "disguised combatanthood" to describe disarmament efforts in Balkh province in Mukhopadhyay, "Disguised Warlordism & Combatanthood in Balkh." A quantitative analysis assessed the performances of Afghan governors as a function of their relative "professionalism." It found that two of the telling traits with respect to a governor's capacity to secure a province from insurgency involved links to "patronage networks" and access to "militias of their own." The credential of a higher education abroad, on the other hand, was "associated with more attacks," albeit to a degree that was not statistically significant. The authors concluded that a governor most capable of countering insurgents aligned in profile most closely with the canonical strongman. Englehart and Grant, "Governors, Governance, and Insurgency in Karzai's Afghanistan," 312, 319, 320.
70. AFG 14 Interview 2.

note. They represented the two most formidable camps among the mujahideen, with a famed animosity for one another that nearly tore the country asunder. Inspired by the Egyptian Muslim Brotherhood and Pakistan's Jamaat-i-Islami, the Jamiat organization was the first prominent manifestation of Islamist politics in 1960s Afghanistan. Gulbuddin Hekmatyar eventually parted ways with Jamiat in the 1970s, forming his own party, Hezb-i-Islami.[71] Both factions would go on to form the vanguard of the fight against Soviet occupation, only to turn on one another in the bloody civil war that followed Soviet withdrawal.

After September 11, 2001, Jamiat found itself, once again, in a prominent position. Ahmed Shah Massoud, the group's famed leader, had been assassinated just two days before, but the party's political elites and fighting commanders remained a force to be reckoned with as key members of the Northern Alliance. Northern Alliance commanders joined forces with the US military that fall, and from that moment on, Jamiat would reclaim its place as one of the country's dominant political forces. Hezb-i-Islami occupied a more complicated position. Hekmatyar remained outside the political process, opting to assert his opposition to the new government. That did not preclude, however, the majority of former Hezb figures from engaging with the Karzai administration.[72] This wing of the movement took its place in state-based politics and lent a stable of provincial governors to the president in the years to come.

During Karzai's time in office, of the more than 190 governorships across the country's thirty-four provinces, more than 50 were Jamiat affiliated and more than 30 were Hezb-i-Islami affiliated. The palace's decision to populate nearly half of the country's governorships with representatives from these two factions can be interpreted as a form of what Migdal called "balancing acts," political moves that do the work of "balancing large and threatening power centers against one another."[73] The Jamiat leadership, and its rank and file, required appeasement. And, while Hekmatyar remained a spoiler, the entire Hezb-i-Islami faction was not averse to engagement with the government. On the contrary, Michael Semple interpreted the inclusion of many within the party as "the most successful example of a reconciliation strategy so far pursued since [2001]," in part because it undercut the influence of Hezb-i-Islami's militant faction and Hekmatyar himself.[74] Both Jamiat and Hezb-i-Islami were kept inside the

---

71. Rubin, "Political Elites in Afghanistan," 81, 83.
72. Semple, *Reconciliation in Afghanistan*, 61–62.
73. Migdal, *Strong Societies and Weak States*, 211, 212.
74. Semple, *Reconciliation in Afghanistan*, 63.

same tent. Unable to accommodate one another in a single government after the Soviet withdrawal, they had found room for themselves and one another in this new era, now led by a third party, their new patron, Karzai.

The president's impulse to balance power was not limited to Jamiat and Hezb-i-Islami. The country's political landscape was a mosaic of armed political factions with contentious histories and competing claims. Attention paid to the balance of power meant elaborate calculations with respect to who would be governor in a particular province. Under Karzai, one could identify the provincial and regional spheres of influence dominated by key figures as a function of the governors sent to rule in their territories of concern.[75] The balance of power mattered not only among factions operating across the country but also within a given region. In fact, many of the country's provinces had a mélange of factional and ethnic affiliations represented in their governorships.

The president's efforts to incorporate various factions—many of which were organized along ethnopolitical lines—were mirrored by his approach to ethnopolitics more generally. Some provinces were governed by individuals from a single ethnic group, suggesting a vocal constituency that had made its preferences known to the palace over the years or a belief on the palace's part that certain provinces would be better off in the hands of one ethnic bloc.[76] This was not, in other words, a case of Karzai simply flinging his cronies about the country. The patterns revealed by his appointments reflected a logic that a wide range of factions and constituencies had to be accommodated. Karzai's approach differed, in this sense, from many of his predecessors, who had sent a largely singular brand of exponent—the Pashtun official—to represent their interests outside of Kabul.[77]

---

75. In a handful of provinces (Balkh, Panjshir, and Parwan), only Jamiat-affiliated governors were appointed, a nod to the faction's longtime de facto grip on the politics of these places. The president seemed similarly inclined to accommodate other powerful factions. Uzbek strongman (and later vice president) Abdur Rashid Dostum's party Junbish had a number of governors clustered in the northern provinces (Faryab, Jowizjan, Sar-i-Pul, and Samangan) historically associated with his sphere of influence. Vice President Khalili's wing of the Hazara party Hezb-i-Wahdat had governors clustered in the central provinces of the Hazarajat region.

76. Bamyan and Daikundi provinces in the Hazarajat region were governed exclusively by Hazara governors. Only Tajiks governed Balkh, Panjshir, and Parwan provinces, while Nuristan province was governed exclusively by Nuristanis. Many provinces in the southeastern Pashtun belt—Ghazni, Kandahar, Khost, Nangarhar, Paktika, Paktiya, Urozgan, Wardak, and Zabul—were governed exclusively by Pashtuns.

77. Barfield, writing of local politics in 1970s northern Afghanistan, detailed the wide psychological distance between officials and the rural population this monoethnic approach yielded: "The most striking aspect of provincial administration was its domination by Pashtuns. . . . They had little knowledge of the areas under their jurisdiction, and they had little

The twenty-first-century presidential palace limited any inclination to construct a subnational political architecture that simply reflected its own composition. Instead, Karzai, a Popalzai Kandahari Pashtun, and his team often found themselves in the position of deferring to key elites and provincial demographics to weave and reweave this piece of subnational political life. This did not mean, of course, that provincial governors were engaged with or beloved by their constituents; it did, however, mean that governorships served as a tool to reflect and balance power in both the center and the periphery. Given the factional diversity that marked Karzai's gubernatorial pantheon, the absence of many Taliban affiliates is striking. Had Karzai been given the leeway to pursue his own modes of accommodation, there may have been few Talibs interested in serving him. Still, one must consider the possibility that appointments of more former Taliban members might have at least blunted the insurgency's virulence.

From Traditionalism to Technocracy . . . to Authoritarianism?

One could imagine no more different a successor to Hamid Karzai than Dr. Ashraf Ghani. A *New Yorker* profile described him as "the technocratic alternative to the politics of warlordism and corruption."[78] Ghani, an anthropologist by training, built his scholarly and political career on the philosophy that a so-called failed state can be "fixed" through the construction of an independent and law-bound bureaucratic architecture.[79] But his ability to translate his theories of state building into the practice of governance proved profoundly limited, and his tenure came to an ignominious end in August 2021 when, with Taliban forces at the gates of Kabul, he fled the presidential palace.

From the start of his tenure in 2015, Ghani found himself surrounded by acute forms of competition that threatened the viability of his regime and, over time, the viability of the Afghan republic. Having failed to secure a decisive lead in the 2014 election, Ghani was accused of wide-scale fraud and entered a months long standoff with Abdullah Abdullah, a longtime leader of the Northern Alliance. US secretary of state John Kerry flew to Kabul and brokered a power-sharing deal between the two, resulting

---

interest in creating close ties with local leaders." Barfield, "Weak Links on a Rusty Chain," 172.
78. Packer, "Ashraf Ghani Takes on Karzai."
79. Ghani and Lockhart, *Fixing Failed States*.

in a so-called National Unity Government. Abdullah's allies—the same array of strongmen who had stalked the periphery for decades—once again laid claim to the political pie. But Ghani opted to set aside much of Karzai's accommodationist ethos and double down on an ostensibly reformist agenda that became an exercise in concentrating the palace's power at the expense of the state it helmed.

Provincial Governors 2.0

A comparison of Ghani's first-term (2015–19) gubernatorial appointees with Karzai's governors reveals differences of the kind one would expect given their purported proclivities for "technocracy" versus "tradition." Ghani's governors were better educated than Karzai's: 26 percent versus 11 percent had a postgraduate degree, and 88 percent versus 65 percent had a college education. Moreover, he appointed, on average, a much lower proportion of commanders to governorships than his predecessor: while 68 percent of Karzai's governors had warlord backgrounds, only 36 percent of Ghani's did. The presidential palace seemed to be forging ahead with a progressive governing agenda. Early on, Christine Roehers and Qayoom Suroush described this new generation of governors as follows:

> The youngest, Nasratullah Arsala for Paktia (hailing from Nangarhar's powerful Arsala clan), is only 33 years old (breaking the criteria the president himself had set for suitable candidates). With all this, the government has indeed initiated a generational change. This is particularly visible in President Ghani's candidates, many of whom are not only younger than previous governors but also lack one of the main credentials of the past: fighting experience. . . . Conspicuously many seem to have experience in working with the international donor organizations, NGOs, or civil society bodies. Experience in working with the government is rare, though.[80]

In a telling opening move, just weeks after taking office, Ghani set about turning the key northern province of Kunduz into "the pilot test in local governance for the rest of the nation." He not only sent a first-time appointee with no political experience, Mohammad Omar Safi, into this complex and turbulent environment but then emboldened the new gov-

---

80. Roehrs and Suroush, "Young Technocrats Taking Over."

ernor to antagonize those who already occupied positions of influence in the province. The results proved disastrous, as the governor's own deputy vowed to take up arms on behalf of threatened militia leaders while the provincial police chief defied the governor's orders.[81] Within months, Taliban forces were able to capture the provincial capital, Kunduz City, for the first time.

The new president privileged those who looked like good Weberian bureaucrats—educated, young, and without colorful pasts. Many of them had pursued careers, as Roehers and Suroush noted, with the so-called international community and had no anchor in indigenous politics. Their relative political inexperience meant they had not been caught up in the country's messy past. It also meant that they could not leverage the kinds of political capital available to their more locally grounded predecessors in the service of establishing social control. Governor Safi's experience in Kunduz was telling in this regard.[82]

Weaker governors were disadvantaged on the ground in key ways, making them exceptionally beholden to their political patron, Ghani. Tellingly, the president left governorships across the country in the hands of anemic caretakers or interim appointees for months at a stretch, depriving subnational authorities of the already limited powers they had to manage politics. For all the president's intellectual commitments to institution building, Roehers and Suroush reported no discernible system with respect to appointments. As one of their interlocutors, a government official, put it, "It is still the president who decides."[83]

Ultimately, Ghani maintained his predecessor's tempo with respect to gubernatorial appointments: both leaders appointed, on average, between fourteen and fifteen governors per year. And both kept them in office, on average, for between one and a half to two and a half years. Ghani departed from Karzai, however, with respect to the ethnopolitics of provincial appointments. While 56 percent of provinces under Karzai had governors who hailed from more than one ethnic group, only 35 percent did under Ghani. Ghani was inclined, in other words, to engage with provinces on more rigidly monoethnic terms, hardly a mark of rationalized bureaucracy but, rather, one that reflected a larger parochialism vis-à-vis the country's identity politics.

---

81. Matta, "The Failed Pilot Test."
82. "His background in security management looks fairly useful; one could not discredit him for being wholly unfit for a governance position in Afghanistan—the governor's post in volatile Kunduz province seems a stretch, though." Matta, "The Failed Pilot Test."
83. As quoted in Roehrs and Suroush, "Young Technocrats Taking Over."

Exclusion as Ethnochauvinism?

The president's disinclination to share power made itself clear within his first year in office. As Roehers and Suroush observed, in the fall of 2015 more than one-quarter of the country's provinces remained without governors. They called it "conspicuous" that the unfilled positions were largely those "to be appointed by CEO Abdullah's camp (or, being his immediate spheres of influence, would need his blessing), according to an internal agreement between President and CEO."[84]

The president's unwillingness to make room for those beyond his immediate circle contributed to growing tension with Abdullah, who had been promised substantial say over governorships, as well as seats in the cabinet and other national institutions, including those associated with the peace process. Ghani stalled on those appointments and on the institutional changes he had promised, namely, "elections, electoral reform, a Loya Jirga [tribal assembly] and amendments to the constitution that could allow the establishment of the post of executive prime minister."[85] In so doing, he effectively secured total de facto power for his camp indefinitely.

This exclusionary brand of governing was read by many as a new kind of ethnochauvinism, one that stood in contrast with the more inclusive tenor of Karzai's rule. Even efforts by the president that were otherwise accommodationist were interpreted by observers through the lens of a pernicious brand of identity politics. One of the landmark decisions of his first term in office, Ghani's reconciliation deal with Hezb-i-Islami's Hekmatyar—known as "the butcher of Kabul" for his leading role in the 1990s civil war—represented a remarkable overture, one with echoes of the Ottoman sultan's outreach to the Aleppine warlord Canboladoglu.[86] Indeed, the once-US-designated "global terrorist" was removed some months later from the UN sanctions list, after which the insurgent leader and the Afghan government moved forward in their rapprochement. Hekmatyar returned to Kabul in 2017.

But concerns about the deal abounded, as did explanations for the president's motives. As Borhan Osman noted, Hekmatyar's jihadi back-

---

84. Roehrs and Suroush, "Young Technocrats Taking Over."
85. Van Bijlert, "Afghanistan's National Unity Government Rift (2)."
86. In anticipation of the agreement, Ruttig and van Bijlert described its likely implications in 2016: "The agreement, if indeed signed and implemented as drafted, will result in a display of prestige for Hezb leader Hekmatyar, providing him a red-carpet return to the country, as well as honours, support and special treatment for him and his followers." Ruttig and van Bijlert, "Almost Signed?"

ground could not be separated from the fact that "the backbone of his base has always been Pashtun." This fact did not escape those increasingly concerned with the Ghani administration's approach to ethnopolitics more generally.[87] Van Bijlert explained, of this deal and similar outreach toward the Pashtun-dominated Taliban, that "some see efforts to bring Hezb-i-Islami and the Taleban into the government fold as an attempt to strengthen the Pashtun hand in a political field that is in many ways increasingly organized along ethnic lines (Pashtun/non-Pashtun)."[88] Meanwhile, other social movements that would otherwise have little by way of shared interest with Abdullah's strongman cabal found common ground as they began to read their own economic, political, and security grievances with Kabul through the prism of ethnic exclusion.

The Enlightenment (Roshnawi) Movement, for example, rose out of a 2016 government decision to reroute a major energy project, depriving the central highlands' Hazara Shi'a population of this major investment. The perception that this minority community, historically marginalized by the country's ruling Pashtun Sunni elite, was being pushed aside yet again led to unprecedented and sustained protest. Subsequent Islamic State attacks, which targeted the Hazara neighborhoods of Kabul in deliberately sectarian terms, further alienated this population from a government that could not (or would not) protect them.[89] As van Bijlert put it:

> Although the Enlightenment Movement is not related to the Abdullah campaign—several of its prominent members are former Ghani supporters—there is potential for common cause. Among Hazaras, but also other non-Pashtun groups, there is a latent suspicion that Ghani's unilateralism, rather than representing a personal leadership style, in reality stems from an un-willingness to share power based on a Pashtun nationalist outlook.[90]

Even the country's vice president, Abdur Rashid Dostum, took aim at his boss's tendencies. In late 2016, he jibed, "For the president, whoever speaks Pashto is a good person, but if they speak Pashto and are from Logar [the president's home province], it is even better."[91] This comment reflected Ghani's inability to translate yet another major accommodation-

---

87. Osman, "Charismatic, Absolutist, Divisive."
88. Van Bijlert, "Afghanistan's National Unity Government Rift (2)."
89. Crisis Group, "Afghanistan," 16.
90. Van Bijlert, "Afghanistan's National Unity Government Rift," 2.
91. As quoted in Adili and Thomas Ruttig, "The 'Ankara Coalition.'"

ist move into a lasting political alliance. Having garnered only 3 percent in his first attempt at the presidency, Ghani had traded in his 2009 campaign adviser, American political strategist James Carville, for running mate and notorious strongman General Dostum in 2014. Dostum's position on the ticket offered Ghani access to Afghanistan's Uzbek voting bloc, and thus one of the country's fiercest critics of warlordism came to share a ticket with the country's fiercest warlord. This election strategy, an effort to, in analyst Kate Clark's words, "present himself as someone who looks, sounds, and acts" like one of the masses, made his candidacy a viable one.[92]

But, two years later, Dostum had moved on and, in a remarkable turn of events, found common cause with the very rivals with whom he had been (often violently) competing for decades. In 2017, a new alliance emerged, the Coalition for the Salvation of Afghanistan (Etelaf baray Nejat-e-Afghanistan), a front that opposed Ghani "from within the government," as Ali Adili and Thomas Ruttig described it. Karzai had managed to divide and rule with (or around) these key strongmen of northern Afghanistan. Now they had joined forces to oppose Ghani, setting aside their differences in the service of highlighting their grievances with the current administration, including:

> criticism of the centralization of power by the president's circle; accusations of the government's involvement in some of the high profile attacks, which they felt were targeted; and the general deterioration of security in the north . . . sometimes explicitly blamed on leading Pashtun politicians close to the president in what the coalition deems to be an attempt to destabilize the northern leaders' local power bases.[93]

The "Republic of Three"

These rumblings of domestic opposition came at a time when the Taliban insurgency was breathing down the neck of the Afghan state, gaining territory just as the United States and its allies were making clear their wish to bring their part in this long war to an end. The republican form of rule in Afghanistan was as vulnerable as ever, so one might have expected the president to court those leaders with serious coercive heft, capital endowments, and social ties to shore up the state's defenses against this existential

---

92. As quoted in Frud Bezhan, "Ghani Hopes Makeover Leads to Election Victory."
93. Adili and Ruttig, "The 'Ankara Coalition.'"

threat. Instead, Ghani's competitors of all stripes, including his predecessor Karzai, came together in the service of exposing the illegitimacy of his presidency and undermining the fundamental credibility of the constitutional order as a result.[94]

In the 2019 election season, few Afghans turned out to vote their president back into office, and, once again, Ghani faced a legitimacy crisis. Ali Adili estimated that around 12 percent of those eligible to vote did so. Accusations of fraud resounded as the ballots were counted, and months of contentious back-and-forth threatened, once again, to break the republic's back. Even high-level intervention from US envoy Zalmay Khalilzad could not prevent parallel presidential inauguration events from moving forward in March 2020. With the tepid blessing of Western governments, Ghani assumed office with a winning margin of less than twelve thousand votes even as Abdullah "had already started appointing his own provincial governors" in defiance of the outcome.[95]

A year into his second term, Ghani's National Unity Government remained skeletal in form, missing key figures on account of disagreement with his still number two, Abdullah, as well as a growing tendency to create alternate decision-making structures over which he could exercise unbridled control.[96] In the fall of 2020, Adili described a cabinet with several unled ministries and a provincial map with sixteen out of thirty-four governorships still vacant. Parliamentary-, provincial-, and district-level elections, long delayed, had yet to be held. Meanwhile, the High Council for National Reconciliation, meant to lead the government in efforts at making peace with the Taliban, remained nonfunctional.[97] The president's concentration of decision-making authority in the palace earned his government the moniker of a "republic of three," an allusion to Ghani and his two aides, Hamdullah Mohib and Fazel Fazly.[98]

Of course, the context of the Ghani government's unraveling cannot be divorced from the looming American retreat. What little momentum Afghanistan's democratic politics still had was largely stymied by the US government's effectively unconditional effort to court the Taliban at the government's expense.[99] The February 2020 pact between the United

---

94. Rubin and Gagnon, "The U.S. Presence and Afghanistan's National Unity Government."
95. Adili, "Afghanistan's 2019 Elections (31)."
96. On this point, see Murtazashvili, "The Collapse of Afghanistan."
97. Adili, "Afghanistan's 2019 Elections (31)."
98. Murtazashvili, "The Collapse of Afghanistan."
99. Adili, "Afghanistan's 2019 Elections (31)."

States and the Taliban, known as the Doha Agreement, unambiguously privileged an expedient rapprochement between the Americans and their erstwhile enemy over any commitments the insurgents might make to acknowledge, let alone come to an accommodation with, the government in Kabul. As Carter Malkasian put it: "Better to complete a US-Taliban agreement and be on the road toward an Afghan political settlement. . . . How the government's democracy could be reconciled with the Taliban's emirate was unexplored territory."[100]

The United States and its allies had long served as a collective backstop for Afghan politics, a kind of guarantor that kept together an otherwise unwieldy cabal of elite rivals. The prospect of Western defection from the state-building game provoked a sense of collective uncertainty and, ultimately, disinvestment on the part of those who increasingly saw the political writing on the wall. If the Afghan state lost its foreign backers, its value would plummet and those with other options would rationally look elsewhere.[101] Under these increasingly precarious circumstances, Ghani had to convince his rivals (and constituents) that the palace could step into a role of greater sovereignty so as to preserve, let alone advance, the republic's cause.

Conclusion

The latest republican experiment in Afghanistan imploded in August 2021. Many were tempted to interpret the state's collapse as confirmation that the country was, after all, ungovernable. A closer look at the tenures of Afghanistan's two twenty-first-century presidents reveals the profound, externally imposed constraints within which these two rulers were expected to establish dominion over their country's politics. It also suggests that accommodationist brands of palace politics served, to use Judith Butler's phrase, as "improvisation within a scene of constraint."[102] They opened up possibilities for the Afghan president to check, and even turn, competitors, thereby translating informal forms of power into assets for the regime that might otherwise threaten its already tenuous grip.

The acutely centralized design of the Afghan state meant that the presidential palace had outsized influence over political appointments in par-

---

100. Malkasian, *The American War in Afghanistan*, 437–38.
101. Mukhopadhyay, "The Afghan Stag Hunt."
102. With thanks to Helen Kinsella for pointing me to this apt framing by Butler in *Undoing Gender*, 1.

ticular; those appointments could be used in the service of accommodation or as part of an authoritarian turn. Karzai's approach privileged the former, while his successor, Ghani, opted for the latter. As Jennifer Murtazashvili put it after the government's fall:

> In these later years, Ghani focused far more time and attention on subduing the *mujahideen* commanders who opposed him than he did either on governing or on fighting the Taliban. Ghani did eventually succeed in defanging his foes. And this, ironically, was his undoing, as the commanders and warlord commanders were his strongest source of protection against the Taliban offensive. . . . By early 2021, the government had uncontested control of just 30 percent of Afghan territory.[103]

While Karzai adopted a methodology of rule resonant with the gradualist Musahiban kings of the mid-twentieth century, Ghani embraced a more aggressive posture reminiscent of those Afghan rulers whose reigns ended in revolt. Like the modernizing King Amanullah of the 1920s and the communist People's Democratic Party of Afghanistan in the 1970s, the Ghani government overreached at the expense and exclusion of too many key social stakeholders, whose collective energies coalesced to violently undo their governments.[104] Perhaps more than any other case in this volume, twenty-first-century Afghanistan's politics involved a violent rough-and-tumble that challenged the viability not only of the regimes in power but also of the state itself.[105] Those challenges came from a virulent insurgency and its foreign sponsors, as well as a host of militant actors—Afghan and Western—ostensibly invested in the republic's success but capable of turning on it at any time.

Under such precarious conditions, the skillful use of palace political maneuvering was essential to any chance at survival for the ruling elite in Kabul. In Ghani's case, his bungling of politics, paired with his inept micromanagement of the security sector, meant that those with the capacity and incentive to defend the state in its moment of greatest need had no reason to do so and, instead, defected.[106] The Migdalian palace politics of survival

---

103. Murtazashvili, "The Collapse of Afghanistan."
104. On these historical precedents, see Rubin, "Lineages of the State in Afghanistan"; Olesen, *Islam and Politics in Afghanistan*; Nawid, *Religious Response to Social Change in Afghanistan*; Suhrke, "Reconstruction as Modernisation"; and Mukhopadhyay, "Ambition and Retreat."
105. With thanks to Sean Yom for underscoring this point.
106. The impulse to concentrate power translated into a failure to appoint and embolden capable leadership and to motivate and manage the rank and file in the Afghan National Defense and Security Forces and the Ministry of Defense. Far from a Weberian merit-based

had transformed into centralization-as-exclusion on Ghani's watch. As the last American soldiers made their way home, instead of "closing the sovereignty gap," to borrow his own phrase, the chasm between Afghan state and society opened up and swallowed his regime whole.[107]

BIBLIOGRAPHY

Adili, Ali Yawar. "Afghanistan's 2019 Elections (31): A Review of the Disputed Presidential Election and Its Aftermath." Kabul: Afghanistan Analysts Network, September 2020. https://www.afghanistan-analysts.org/en/reports/political-la ndscape/afghanistans-2019-elections-31-an-overview-of-the-disputed-preside ntial-election-and-its-aftermath/

Adili, Ali Yawar, and Thomas Ruttig. "The 'Ankara Coalition': Opposition from Within the Government." Kabul: Afghanistan Analysts Network, July 2017. https://www.afghanistan-analysts.org/en/reports/political-landscape/the-anka ra-coalition-opposition-from-within-the-government/

Barfield, Thomas J. *Afghanistan: A Cultural and Political History*. Princeton, NJ: Princeton University Press, 2010.

Barfield, Thomas J. "Weak Links on a Rusty Chain: Structural Weaknesses in Afghanistan's Provincial Government Administration." In *Revolutions and Rebellions in Afghanistan*, edited by M. N. Shahrani and Robert L. Canfield, 170–83. Berkeley: University of California Berkeley Press, 1984.

Barkey, Karen. *Bandits and Bureaucrats: The Ottoman Route to State Centralization*. Ithaca, NY: Cornell University Press, 1994.

Bergen, Peter. "Hamid Karzai: Afghanistan's Bridge-Building President or Just a Corrupt Pol?" *Washington Post*, September 15, 2016. https://www.washingtonp ost.com/opinions/hamid-karzai-afghanistans-bridge-building-president-or-ju st-a-corrupt-pol/2016/09/15/6d6a47a6-5804-11e6-9aee-8075993d73a2_story .html

Bezhan, Frud. "Ghani Hopes Makeover Leads to Election Victory." *Radio Free Europe/Radio Liberty*, March 10, 2014.

Bhatia, Michael. "The Future of the Mujahideen: Legitimacy, Legacies, and Demobilization in Post-Bonn Afghanistan." *International Peacekeeping* 14, no. 1 (2007): 90–107.

Chabal, Patrick, and Jean-Pascal Daloz. *Africa Works: Disorder as Political Instrument*. Bloomington: Indiana University Press, 1999.

Crisis Group, "Afghanistan: The Future of the National Unity Government." Asia Report No. 285. Brussels: Crisis Group, 2017.

Day, Christopher, and William Reno. "In Harm's Way: African Counter-Insurgency and Patronage Politics." *Civil Wars* 16, no. 2 (2014): 105–26.

de Waal, Alex. "Mission without End: Peacekeeping in the African Political Marketplace." *International Affairs* 85, no. 1 (2009): 99–113.

Dixon, Paul. "'Hearts and Minds'? British Counter-Insurgency from Malaya to Iraq." *Journal of Strategic Studies* 32, no. 3 (June 2009): 253–81.

---

bureaucracy, corruption and inefficiency haunted the security sector, including the police, which were described by the Crisis Group as "ridden with nepotism." In Crisis Group, "Afghanistan," 15.

107. Ghani, Lockhart, and Carnahan, "Closing the Sovereignty Gap."

Englehart, Neil, and Patrick Grant. "Governors, Governance, and Insurgency in Karzai's Afghanistan: The Limits of Professionalism." *Asian Survey* 55, no. 2 (2015): 299–324.

Fukuyama, Francis. "The Imperative of State-Building." *Journal of Democracy* 15, no. 2 (April 2004): 17–31.

Fukuyama, Francis. "What Is Governance?" Working Paper 314. Washington, DC: Center for Global Development, 2013.

Ganev, Venelin I. *Preying on the State: The Transformation of Bulgaria after 1989.* Ithaca, NY: Cornell University Press, 2007.

Ghani, Ashraf, and Clare Lockhart. *Fixing Failed States: A Framework for Rebuilding a Fractured World.* Oxford: Oxford University Press, 2008.

Giustozzi, Antonio. *Empires of Mud: Wars and Warlords in Afghanistan.* New York: Columbia University Press, 2009.

Hazelton, Jacqueline. "The 'Hearts and Minds' Fallacy: Violence, Coercion, and Success in Counterinsurgency Warfare." *International Security* 42, no. 1 (Summer 2017): 80–113.

Kakar, Mohammad Hassan. *Political and Diplomatic History of Afghanistan, 1863–1901.* Leiden: Brill Academic Publishers, 2006.

Kaufmann, Daniel, and Aart Kraay. "Governance Indicators: Where Are We, Where Should We Be Going?" *The World Bank Research Observer* 23, no. 1 (2008).

Lake, Milli. "Building the Rule of War: Postconflict Institutions and the Micro-Dynamics of Conflict in Eastern DR Congo." *International Organization* 71 (Spring 2017): 281–315.

Lori, Noora. "Statelessness, 'In-between' Statuses, and Precarious Citizenship." In *The Oxford Handbook of Citizenship*, edited by Ayelet Shachar, Rainer Baubock, Irene Bloemraad, and Maarten Vink. Oxford: Oxford University Press, 2017.

Malejacq, Romain. *Warlord Survival: The Delusion of State-Building in Afghanistan.* Ithaca, NY: Cornell University Press, 2020.

Malkasian, Carter. *The American War in Afghanistan: A History.* New York: Oxford University Press, 2021.

Manchanda, Nivi. *Imagining Afghanistan: The History and Politics of Imperial Knowledge.* Cambridge: Cambridge University Press, 2020.

Marten, Kimberly. "Warlordism in Comparative Perspective." *International Security* 31, no. 3 (Winter 2006/2007): 41–73.

Matta, Bethany. "The Failed Pilot Test: Kunduz's Local Governance Crisis." Kabul: Afghanistan Analysts Network, 2015. https://www.afghanistan-analysts.org/en/reports/war-and-peace/the-failed-pilot-test-kunduz-local-governance-crisis/

Menkhaus, Ken. "Governance without Government in Somalia: Spoilers, State Building, and the Politics of Coping." *International Security* 31, no. 3 (Winter 2006/2007): 74–106.

Migdal, Joel. *State in Society: Studying How States and Societies Transform and Constitute One Another.* Cambridge: Cambridge University Press, 2001.

Migdal, Joel. *Strong Societies and Weak States: State-Society Relations and State Capabilities in the Third World.* Princeton, NJ: Princeton University Press, 1988.

Mukhopadhyay, Dipali. "The Afghan Stag Hunt." *Lawfare*, February 25, 2019. https://www.lawfareblog.com/afghan-stag-hunt

Mukhopadhyay, Dipali. "Ambition and Retreat: State-Building in Afghanistan." In *Contested Sovereignties: Government and Democracy in Middle Eastern and Euro-*

pean Perspectives, edited by Elisabeth Ozdalga and Sune Persson, 69–100. London: I. B. Tauris, 2010.

Mukhopadhyay, Dipali. "Disguised Warlordism & Combatanthood in Balkh: The Persistence of Informal Power in the Formal Afghan State." *Conflict, Security, and Development* 9, no. 4 (2009): 535–64.

Mukhopadhyay, Dipali. "Provincial Governors in Afghan Politics." Special Report No 385. Washington, DC: U.S. Institute of Peace, January 2016. https://www.usip.org/sites/default/files/SR-385-Provincial-Governors-in-Afghan-Politics.pdf

Mukhopadhyay, Dipali. *Warlords, Strongman Governors, and the State in Afghanistan*. New York: Cambridge University Press, 2014.

Murtazashvili, Jennifer Brick. "The Collapse of Afghanistan." *Journal of Democracy* 33, no. 1 (January 2022): 40–54.

Nixon, Hamish. "Subnational State-Building in Afghanistan." Kabul: Afghanistan Research and Evaluation Unit, 2008. https://www.refworld.org/pdfid/481043672.pdf

Nixon, Hamish, and Richard Ponzio. "Building Democracy in Afghanistan: The Statebuilding Agenda and International Engagement." *International Peacekeeping* 14, no. 1 (2007): 26–40.

North, Douglass, John Wallis, and Barry Weingast. *Violence and Social Orders: A Conceptual Framework for Interpreting Recorded Human History*. Cambridge: Cambridge University Press, 2009.

Olesen, Asta. *Islam and Politics in Afghanistan*. Richmond: Curzon Press, 1995.

Olson, Mancur. "Dictatorship, Democracy, and Development." *American Political Science Review* 87, no. 3 (1993): 567–76.

Osman, Borhan. "Charismatic, Absolutist, Divisive: Hekmatyar and the Impact of His Return." Kabul: Afghanistan Analysts Network, May 2017. https://www.afghanistan-analysts.org/en/reports/political-landscape/charismatic-absolutist-divisive-hekmatyar-and-the-impact-of-his-return/

Packer, George. "Ashraf Ghani Takes on Karzai." *New Yorker*, April 30, 2009.

Reno, William. "Reinvention of an African Patrimonial State: Charles Taylor's Liberia." *Third World Quarterly* 16, no. 1 (1995): 109–20.

Robinson, Simon. "Karzai's Kabul: Fit for a King?" *Time*, April 18, 2002. http://content.time.com/time/world/article/0,8599,231457,00.html

Roehrs, Christine, and Qayoom Suroush. "Young Technocrats Taking Over: Who Are the New Afghan Governors and What Can They Achieve?" Kabul: Afghanistan Analysts Network, September 2015. https://www.afghanistan-analysts.org/en/reports/political-landscape/young-technocrats-taking-over-who-are-the-new-afghan-governors-and-what-can-they-achieve/

Rubin, Barnett R. "Crafting a Constitution for Afghanistan." *Journal of Democracy* 15, no. 3 (July 2004): 5–19.

Rubin, Barnett R. *The Fragmentation of Afghanistan: State Formation and Collapse*. New Haven, CT: Yale University Press, 1995.

Rubin, Barnett R. "Lineages of the State in Afghanistan." *Asian Survey* 28, no. 11 (1988): 1188–209.

Rubin, Barnett R. "Political Elites in Afghanistan: Rentier State Building, Rentier State Wrecking." *International Journal of Middle East Studies* 24, no. 1 (1992): 77–99.

Rubin, Barnett R. "What I Saw in Afghanistan." *New Yorker*, July 1, 2015. https://www.newyorker.com/news/news-desk/what-have-we-been-doing-in-afghanistan

Rubin, Barnett R., and Georgette Gagnon. "The U.S. Presence and Afghanistan's National Unity Government: Preserving and Broadening the Political Settlement." New York: Center on International Cooperation, 2016.

Ruttig, Thomas, and Martine van Bijlert. "Almost Signed? The Peace Agreement with Hezb-i-Islami." Kabul: Afghanistan Analysts Network, 2016. https://www.afghanistan-analysts.org/en/reports/war-and-peace/almost-signed-the-peace-agreement-with-hezb-e-islami/

Saikal, Amin. *Modern Afghanistan: A History of Struggle and Survival*. London: I. B. Tauris, 2004.

Semple, Michael. *Reconciliation in Afghanistan*. Washington, DC: U.S. Institute of Peace, 2009.

Shahrani, M. Nazif. "Afghanistan's Alternatives for Peace, Governance and Development: Transforming Subjects to Citizens and Rulers to Civil Servants." Waterloo, ON: Centre for International Governance Innovation, 2009.

Sharifi, Omar. "The Nauroz Festival as a Social Site: Understanding Faith, Ethnicity, and Nation-ness in Afghanistan." PhD diss., Boston University, 2019.

Simpson, Audra. *Mohawk Interruptus: Political Life Across the Borders of Settler States*. Durham and London: Duke University Press, 2014.

Shurkin, Michael. "Subnational Government in Afghanistan." Santa Monica, CA: RAND Corporation, 2011.

Tilly, Charles. "Armed Force, Regimes, and Contention in Europe since 1650." In *Irregular Armed Forces and Their Roles in Politics and State Formation*, edited by Diane E. Davis and Anthony W. Pereira, 37–81. Cambridge: Cambridge University Press, 2003.

Tilly, Charles. "War-Making and State-Making as Organized Crime." In *Bringing the State Back In*, edited by Peter Evans, Dietrich Rueschemeyer, and Theda Skocpol, 169–91. Cambridge: Cambridge University Press, 1985.

van Bijlert, Martine. "Afghanistan's National Unity Government Rift (2)." Kabul: Afghanistan Analysts Network, September 2016. https://www.afghanistan-analysts.org/en/reports/political-landscape/afghanistans-national-unity-government-rift-2-the-problems-that-will-not-go-away/

van Bijlert, Martine. "Between Discipline and Discretion: Policies Surrounding Senior Subnational Appointments." Kabul: Afghanistan Research and Evaluation Unit, 2009.

Weber, Max. "Politics as Vocation." In *From Max Weber: Essays in Sociology*, edited by H. H. Gerth and C. Wright Mills. New York: Oxford University Press, 1946.

Wilder, Andrew, and Sarah Lister. "State-Building at the Subnational Level in Afghanistan: A Missed Opportunity." In *Building State and Security in Afghanistan*, edited by Wolfgang Danspeckgruber with Robert P. Finn, 85–101. Princeton, NJ: Woodrow Wilson School of Public and International Affairs, 2007.

Woodward, Susan. *The Ideology of Failed States: Why Intervention Fails*. New York: Cambridge University Press, 2017.

World Bank. "Service Delivery and Governance at the Sub-National Level in Afghanistan." Washington, DC: World Bank, 2007.

SECTION 3

Contesting Stateness
Society and Sites of Resistance

EIGHT

State Capacity and Contention
A View from Jordan

Jillian Schwedler

States remain central to the organization of coercion and domination despite the growth of transnational networks, intra- and cross-regional security and financial alliances, and diverse methods for challenging and weakening state power. Despite the range of approaches to the state, from Max Weber and neo-Weberian approaches to Karl Marx, Antonio Gramsci, Michel Foucault, Timothy Mitchell, and others, a central question in diverse literatures concerns state power (and thus state weakness)—the state's ability (or not) to assert the agenda and priorities of the leadership on a national scale. Many scholars have, of course, pushed back against the strong versus weak state analytic framework. In this volume, those critiques are well reflected in Steven Heydemann and Marc Lynch's introduction and in the chapters by Heydemann, Bassel Salloukh, and others. State power is better portrayed, as those chapters show, as entailing multiple dimensions that are not necessarily (if ever) in symmetry. Still, however, questions of state capacity remain.

But what does it mean to talk about state development and state capacity? In their most straightforward meanings, *state development* refers to the establishment of government institutions aimed toward implementing some agenda advanced by those in power, and *state capacity* means the ability of those in power (let us call them "the government") to utilize those institutions to accomplish what they aim to do, whether in terms of enacting specific policies, bringing dissent under control, overseeing the welfare (or neglect) of the population, or simply managing regime survival. As noted by Lynch in this volume, both concepts often appear in debates about strong versus weak states, but strong or weak in reference to what?

Here it bears noting that a significant portion of the state capacity literature is policy oriented, and as such the very definitions of analysis are structured by certain assumptions about what it means to provide useful or actionable policy proposals. To wit, "strong" equates to "good" because "weak" means an unreliable or unstable unit with which "strong" states find interactions difficult or unpredictable. "Strong" thus often entails a vision by some (often Global North) states about how state institutions *should* be organized to achieve such outcomes as "good" governance and "sound" economic policies. These evaluations or judgments about development and capacity are often pronounced by external agencies, financial institutions, or foreign governments that desire for the state in question to take a particular institutional form and adopt the forms or policies that facilitate certain kinds of reforms or to enact certain policies. That is, advice for how states can become "strong" is often about how they can be structured in ways that facilitate engagement with foreign institutions and states. The irony here is that when "weaker" states follow such advice and reform their institutions to better interact with other foreign states, they often in practice become more "penetrable" by foreign actors, thus effectively weakening their control over their own institutions, policy priorities, and financial practices.[1]

I note this connection with foreign interests because normative judgments about where state capacity is lacking are often expressions of disappointment: "deficits" or "failures" may not signal an inability to govern so much as the failure of state institutions and practices to meet the needs and expectations of foreign entities seeking to advance their own interests and agendas. Indeed, in "failed states" debates, the language of "state" capacity as opposed to "government" capacity neatly fits into debates within international relations about the interaction and relations *among* states. Weak states cannot engage fully with strong states because they do not have the same institutional capacity or even institutions as their counterparts in other states.

But does this measure of state capacity provide analytic traction in understanding how states function in practice, how governments seek to advance their agendas, or how regimes or even states survive? These questions return us to the matter of the capacity of whom and to do what?

---

1. See Bustani, *(Dys)functional Polities*.

Do we have room in our theories to think about how ostensibly weak states might "survive" for long periods despite not conforming to Weberian notions of what states can and should look like? This issue is examined by Lisa Wedeen in her discussion of pre-uprising Yemen. In her aptly titled article "Don't Call Yemen a Failed State," she argues that describing Yemen's "weak" institutions as indicative of a potentially failed state misunderstands how politics has worked for decades in Yemen. The rule of President Ali Abdullah Salih from 1978 until his death in 2017 was not sustained by the kind of institutional or infrastructural development or capacity envisioned in the academic and policy literatures. Yet his regime remained in power for more than thirty years. Indeed, Wedeen shows that Salih's survival was not in spite of weak state capacity but at least in part *because* he did not attempt to create the kinds of institutions that would seek to obtain a monopoly on the use of violence or even assert absolute control over all of Yemen's territory.[2] I experienced such imbricating spheres of sovereignty in Yemen on one visit when a UN convoy with which I was traveling was stopped by armed tribesmen outside of Ma'rib. Despite having an escort of government officials, the convoy was held for several hours by the armed tribesmen until they could ascertain that their sheikh had given permission for us to pass.

If we put aside these normative framings that shape judgments about what form(s) state development *should* take and what level and, more importantly, type of state capacity *should* be achieved, we can reconceptualize state development and capacity in ways that bring other aspects of political power and its challengers into view—such as how states come into being, how diverse actors "inside" and "outside" of state circles shape those processes, and how states obtain and maintain power and where they do not.

In this chapter, I aim to make three interventions into debates about state development and capacity from the standpoint of a focus on contentious politics. I do not reject those concepts so much as unpack what they mean through the lens of challengers to those who hold state power. These interventions engage the arguments of some of the other chapters in this volume, drawing attention to areas of agreement and in several aspects going beyond them. The first intervention is that state making is an ongoing process. While this insight is not new, it bears on how one thinks about state institutions, development, and perceptions of state capacity and its

---

2. Wedeen, "Don't Call Yemen a Failed State." For an extended discussion of why the concept of failed states "makes no sense," see Woodward, *The Ideology of Failed States*.

unevenness both spatially and experientially. The second intervention is that resistance to state policies or to those in power can at times strain state capacity while simultaneously working to reproduce state power. States respond to where and how challengers engage in claim making, including by directing resources to certain projects or practices while neglecting others. And finally, the third intervention explores how the built environment both produces and provides a material basis to state capacity while also revealing where it is strong and where it is lacking. I illustrate these interventions with two empirical examples from Jordan.

State Making Is an Ongoing Process

A first intervention into debates about state development and capacity is to emphasize that state making and state maintaining are ongoing processes, and thus state capacity across diverse areas or sectors must also be continuously reproduced. A state does not establish a standing army, for example, never to think much about the army again. This insight, of course, is not new. Anthropologists of the state have long attended to the ongoing character of state making and the uneven reach of stateness (that is, state capacity), and recent political science debates have also taken up this position.[3] Many classic works, several of which are engaged by others in this volume, also conceptualize state making or stateness as partial, limited, or always incomplete. In Michael Mann's oft-cited work, for example, the state is seen as evolving in response to various challenges, even if the focus of the work is how state institutions and infrastructures develop relative stability and social power. The state can dominate, he notes, without "final unity or even consistency."[4] In this vein, Heydemann in 2007 coined a new term for state adaptation, *authoritarian upgrading*, to capture the ongoing efforts of the Middle East's authoritarian regimes to maintain authority in the face of challenges—an idea he further develops in his contribution to this volume.[5] Lisa Anderson's chapter here likewise stresses that state maintaining is always "unfinished business," as Charles Tripp put it succinctly.[6] Sean Yom argues similarly "the state not as a unified act of vertical power but rather as a field of contested practices, some of which will instigate more

---

3. For one recent collection, see Morgan and Orloff, eds., *The Many Hands of the State*.
4. Mann, *The Sources of Social Power*, 56–57.
5. Heydemann, "Upgrading Authoritarianism in the Arab World"; see also Stacher, *Adaptable Autocrats*.
6. Tripp, "The State as an Always-Unfinished Performance," 337.

resistance from society than others given the inherently limited nature of statehood."[7] And as I argue alongside Lawrence Cox and Alf Gunvald Nilsen, crises of state power and authority are more the norm than many analyses imply.[8]

As a starting point for an analysis of state development and state capacity, the recognition of state making as an ongoing process shifts attention away from measurement of particular "outputs"—such as the ability to provide adequate infrastructure, education, and other issues of social welfare, as well as more nefarious capacities for regime survival like the ability to repress, coerce, and silence dissent. Instead, the focus is on the struggles between and among diverse actors both "inside" and "outside" of the state. By putting these concepts in scare quotes, I join others who have called into question the neat dichotomy of state and non-state actors. Mitchell, for example, showed more than three decades ago how the boundary between state and society (or non-state actors) was elusive because, in part, state power worked more efficiently by rendering the distinction blurry.[9] I would add that the elusiveness also worked to allow those in power considerable room to maneuver and adapt to challengers. Inevitably, how political leaders, as well as would-be political leaders, "contend with resistance to and claims about their efforts to establish authority shapes the institutions and practices of governance," and not only during the initial state-making period.[10] Institutions, practices, and capacities emerge to contend with dissent, as well as to placate allies or would-be allies, and as forms of dissent and resistance evolve, reform, and move into new locations, so must the state constantly remake itself to meet the task at hand. And, indeed, state capacity is uneven spatially, as well as experientially. People perceive of state capacity in a variety of ways, depending on their expectations based on past experiences and their normative views of what states *should* be doing.

The theoretical stakes of viewing state capacity in terms of largely stable and resilient institutions, as opposed to ongoing maneuvering, are whether a better explanation of the forms and functioning of political power can be found in attention to the formal institutions and practices of the state or whether we might gain more insights from attending to the multiple forms of contention and struggle that emerge between and among supposed state and non-state actors. I argue that the latter is both theoretically more nuanced and empirically more accurate.

---

7. Yom, "Water, Stateness, and Tribalism in Jordan," chap. 9, this volume.
8. Schwedler, *Protesting Jordan*; Cox and Nilsen, *We Make Our Own History*.
9. T. Mitchell, "The Limits of the State."
10. Schwedler, *Protesting Jordan*, 4.

The next two sections examine the dialectal relationship between and among those who hold power (whether as a component of controlling state institutions and practices or as concerning other power holders and local social and economic elites) and those who seek to challenge the status quo. I first examine resistance and protest as a window into understanding state development and state capacity reconceptualized in terms of the ability of the state to respond to challenges rather than in terms of the "well functioning" of particular institutions of governance. The later section then locates those struggles not abstractly at the national level—for example, in the Weberian monopoly on the use of violence or provision of services like education or electricity—but locally in the built environment.

Resistance Is Central to Understanding State Development and Capacity

In *Protesting Jordan: Geographies of Power and Resistance*, I show how diverse forms of protests ranging from armed rebellions to peaceful sit-ins have been key methods of claim making in the Hashemite Kingdom of Jordan from the Ottoman period to the present.[11] More than moments of rupture within "normal time" politics, protests have been central to challenging state power, as well as reproducing it. In bringing this argument to bear on debates about state development and state capacity, the focus shifts from the top-down creation of state institutions and the Weberian monopolization of the use of violence in a given territory to the ongoing maneuvering of state actors to dodge challengers, woo supporters, deflate resistance, respond to demands from allies, and so on. As Heydemann puts it, rulers use "their power to extend or withhold the development of stateness and state capacity—in particular functional, spatial, or social domain—as a potent bargaining chip in their interactions with allies and adversaries alike."[12] This approach also rejects the temporality of a foundational or transitional period after which state institutions are basically established and developed, even as they might evolve gradually over time. Rather than periods of stability punctuated by moments of crisis, "routine" politics can entail both simultaneously, as I will show with examples below. This approach brings into view all sorts of politics usually rendered invisible or irrelevant by conventional temporalities of

---

11. Schwedler, *Protesting Jordan*.
12. Heydemann, "Seeing the State or Why Arab States Look the Way They Do," chap. 1, this volume.

state making, state development, and state capacity. Let us turn now to Jordan to see how this is so.

The conventional story of the modern state-making project in Jordan is a story of a British colonial state. The newly established League of Nations granted Britain a "mandate" to oversee the creation of a modern nation-state in the Transjordanian area east of the Jordan River and south of Damascus. To head this would-be state, Britain did not choose someone from the greater Transjordanian area but rather the Hijazi emir Abdullah, son of Sharif Hussein of Mecca (of the Great Arab Revolt of World War I). Strictly speaking, Abdullah was an outsider to the Transjordanian area, although the southern portion of what would become the state of Jordan was broadly recognized as the northernmost portion of the Hashemite-dominated Hijaz. Because Abdullah was from a prominent Arab family that descended from the family of the Prophet Muhammad, some of the people in the Transjordanian area welcomed him, particularly following the period of foreign Ottoman rule and its brutal suppression of rebellion. In this conventional narrative, the early institutions of the Jordanian state—notably the bureaucracy, rule of law, and a standing army—were created with substantial assistance from Britain beginning in 1921. Through a combination of British military force, cash payments, and the granting of land to local tribal authorities to buy their allegiance (what Jordanians still refer to as the social contract), Hashemite authority was gradually established over the lands that would become the state of Jordan. By the late 1940s, the basic state institutions were in place, even if many of them (besides the military) lacked much capacity. Jordan gained formal independence in 1946, and the last British officers departed a decade later. In sum, a tumultuous two decades of state making gave way to a relative period of stability that saw a single monarch, King Hussein, both reign and rule over Jordan from 1953 until his death in 1999, when the crown passed to his eldest son, Abdullah II. At the time of his death, King Hussein was the second-longest-reigning monarch alive.

But what of the decades of resistance to that colonial project, the outrage at Abdullah's audacity of establishing a Hashemite monarchy, the peaceful and violent rebellions over jobs, resources, and the weakening of local authorities? As I write in *Protesting Jordan*,

> Transjordanians' articulations of their desires, and their reactive demands to British and Hashemite efforts to establish centralized authority, contributed to form the new state as much as, or perhaps even more than, the colonial authorities that dominated Jordanian

society. Bedouin revolts in the 1920s and 1930s created so many problems for the would-be centralized authority that the colonial powers could stop them only by providing the Bedouin with permanent employment and benefits. Settled tribal leaders during the same period—frustrated with both favoritism toward rival tribes and government employment of people hailing from elsewhere in Greater Syria (*Bilad al- Sham*)—frequently revolted and sometimes marched to Amman to express their grievances and make demands on the new regime.[13]

The British and Hashemites eventually gained the backing of many powerful tribal leaders, but the latter never stopped making demands and asserting their grievances, and not only around issues like the massive influx of Palestinian refugees during and after the 1948 and 1967 wars.

An example from the mid-1950s is illustrative. When the young King Hussein came to power in 1952, Jordan's institutions remained weak as the nation was absorbing hundreds of thousands of Palestinians forced from their homes in the wake of the 1948 war. Arab nationalism was strong and ascendant, along with desires for independence from Western rule in both its colonial and postcolonial forms. The king sought to navigate this context by opening up the political system and allowing a range of groups across the political spectrum to operate. Leftists were particularly ascendant, and as the king publicly signaled his desire for Jordan to join the Baghdad Pact, Jordanians took to the street in massive protests. The king ultimately relented and withdrew plans to join the regional security alliance, much to the disappointment of both Britain and the United States. Not only did the protests directly shape Jordan's role in regional security arrangements, but subsequent protests likewise pressured the regime not to renew its expiring agreement with Britain in 1956—despite British cash being critical to the functioning of the state. In the aftermath, the regime turned to the United States for support, again shaping Jordan's place globally.[14] Key here is not that protesters always get what they want—although they did so in a surprising number of instances in Jordan—but that the government and regime also evolve and restructure institutions and relations with its constituents in direct response to protests.

Following the disruption of an alleged military coup in 1957, for example, the king imposed martial law and outlawed political parties and free

13. Schwedler, *Protesting Jordan*, 10.
14. Yom, *From Resilience to Revolution*.

press. Yet leftist activism continued in the 1960s, and local support for Palestinian fedayeen guerrillas (both before and during the violent Black September clashes in 1970) led to the CIA-assisted creation of the General Intelligence Directorate, or *mukhabarat* (secret police). During that same period, the regime launched a "Jordanization" program that, in part, led to the rapid expansion of the welfare state as a means of placating East Bank communities. The regime even created the Ministry of Supply in 1974 to provide subsidies for basic goods in direct response to protests by military officers and their troops in Zarqa over their salaries and the growing cost of living. Here again protests and resistance shaped Jordan's state institutions, the course of their development, and their capacity at every turn. What is also critical in this example is that the pressure from protests on the regime and government comes not always from opposition quarters but also from supposed loyalists as well. The East Bank communities that provide the regime with support, as noted above, also feel entitled to jobs and other services, a kind of moral economy of welfare state. The protests and claim making from East Bank quarters have been—as we have seen and will see again below—among the most powerful forces in the regime's ongoing state-maintaining efforts.

Yet, precisely because Jordan has confronted so many challenges, many scholars (and policymakers, too) have characterized Jordan as at risk of collapse, as indexed by the trope "forever on the brink."[15] Jordan and, indeed, the Hashemite regime have survived repeated existential challenges—several wars, economic crises, violent conflicts on its borders, at least one military coup plot, both successful and foiled bombings by Islamist extremists, and multiple waves of refugees that have rendered Jordanians of East Bank descent the minority. Do these crises suggest that Jordan's state institutions are weak or that they are resilient? Does the state lack capacity—to provide water, electricity, and economic opportunities? Or are its institutions instead nimble and adaptable?

As these examples illustrate, state capacity is not something that can be easily empirically measured, in part because people hold diverse expectations about state capacity based on past experiences and their normative views of what states *should* be doing. In Jordan, one might describe state capacity in the 1950s and 1960s as weak, especially given the existential challenges it faced, but the very ability to pivot, adapt, create new institutions, and respond to dissent from both inside and outside of the regime's broader support base itself illustrates a kind of state capacity, even as par-

---

15. Abu-Rish, "Getting Past the Brink"; Lynch, ed., *Jordan*.

ticular institutions remain "weak" by conventional definitions. As we will see, the ability to repress, direct capital flows, deliver services, and even just set policies reflects different kinds of state capacities that are not readily brought to the fore in many conceptions of state capacity and state development.

Furthermore, I suggest that the strong-to-weak continuum, even when particular institutions are disaggregated (for example, a strong military but weak infrastructure), is the wrong way to approach the question. Rather, where does such a narrative of strength or weakness come from? Perhaps surprisingly, the Hashemite regime advances both the "stability" and "looming instability" narratives simultaneously. It advances narratives of stability to attract foreign investment by projecting the guarantee of that stability into the future. Gulf billionaires, for example, would not build multibillion-dollar megaprojects in Amman and Aqaba if they were concerned about the regime's stability into the future. Why, then, would the state also traffic in narratives of potential instability? Because those narratives—of being located in a "bad neighborhood" of war and conflict (Israel/Palestine, Syria, and Iraq all border Jordan), the seemingly endless waves of refugees and what it takes to manage and care for them, and the looming Shi'i Crescent and threat of Islamic extremism—each provide compelling reasons for foreign states to hand over more economic and military aid to the kingdom. The regime also references potential instability to slow the pace of economic reforms to forefend against the real potential that massive, nationwide protests may (again) bring the country to a standstill in response to International Monetary Fund–mandated structural adjustment reforms. To be sure, these crises are real, and the state has had to maneuver continually to deflate challenges, absorb critics, and defeat enemies (like Islamic militants). But a part of state capacity is not about the strength of specific institutions but rather about the regime's ability to wield seemingly contradictory narratives of crisis and stability to serve its needs.

And it bears repeating that the state has had to be nimble not only in response to challengers but also in response to the grievances of its supposed traditional East Bank tribal support base. In addition to the creation of the Ministry of Supply, as noted above, the regime has responded to protest and dissent by lifting martial law, holding nationwide elections, repeatedly sacking prime ministers, redrawing electoral districts, gerrymandering to prevent certain segments of the population from gaining voice in parliament, relocating development projects, and so on. And as Yom discusses in this volume, the Jordanian state is not always able to assert control even when it tries.[16]

Having shown how protest and resistance have been central to institutional development in Jordan, I now turn to how these contests play out both geographically and spatially in the built environment. We also see the unevenness of state capacity across space.

State Development and Capacity in the Built Environment

Given conventional attention to formal institutions, most studies of state development and capacity forego any serious attention to geography and space beyond noting that the location of investment and development projects and decisions about investment and development often create or exacerbate inequalities. Mann's notion of infrastructural power is an important exception, as he addresses the uneven ability of the state to penetrate society, control territory, mobilize support, and carry out policy. The literature on neoliberal investments, in democracies and autocracies alike, offers even more nuanced examination of these spatial issues as they occur "on the ground" and vary across space. Here I want to connect the preceding discussion about the centrality of protest and resistance with spatial and geographic dimensions to bring into view new insights that might contribute to debates about state development and state capacity.

There is nothing new about the idea that state power is unevenly distributed across space, just as investments, developments, and capacities are unevenly distributed. But instead of broad claims, how can specific empirical examples illustrate that unevenness? The first has to do with the location of Jordan's capital city, Amman. Let us return to the early colonial state-making period, when the emir Abdullah arrived in the southern part of the Transjordanian area in 1921 and set up camp in the town of Ma'an. Although Ma'an is part of the larger Transjordanian area, the town is located at the northernmost part of the Hashemite-ruled Hijaz region, and thus Abdullah was welcomed upon his arrival, as many already viewed it as Hijaz domain. He set up tents in the southern part of the town, known as Ma'an Hijaziyya (Hijazi Ma'an). A smaller neighborhood to the north was (and still is) known as Ma'an Shamiyya (Shami Ma'an), thus registering the local understanding of Ma'an as divided between Hijazi and Shami (Greater Syria, Bilad

---

16. See also Schwedler, *Protesting Jordan*.

al-Sham) neighborhoods. This distinction shows how Abdullah understood that his political ambitions and claims of authority were going to have to contend with local authorities and their own understandings of the boundaries of the domains. These local authorities, and particularly their willingness (or not) to accept British-backed Hashemite authority, quite literally shaped how the emergent state was spatially located.

A new state needs a capital, and the Transjordanian area had several contenders. Ma'an was not centrally located, so a location to the north would be preferable. Karak, Madaba, and Salt were possibilities, but each had local authorities who did not welcome Abdullah to form his seat of power in their traditional domains of authority. Locals in Salt even protested in the streets when Abdullah arrived to discuss establishing his capital there. Others, however, saw an opportunity to elevate their status without challenge to their traditional authority. The paramount sheikh of the Bani Sakhr tribal confederation—one of the larger Bedouin confederations and one with rivals—had the foresight to invite Abdullah to establish the capital in Amman, which was located on Bani Sakhr land but was not where the tribal authorities made their seasonal home. Rather, Amman was, in 1921, a small town of some three thousand—mostly traders, along with Circassian and Chechen refugees who had been settled there by the Ottomans following conflicts with Russia in the 1880s. What the town lacked—strong local Transjordanian authority structures—was an asset to the new monarchy, and Amman's size, status, and built environment ballooned.

As Amman grew over the next decades, the choice proved consequential for Jordan's larger political geography. Whereas the established towns located along the north-south trade corridor were for centuries the site of local settled authority, the growth of the capital gradually pushed them to the periphery. Major political institutions were located in the capital, of course, but as a result the city became a place where people migrated for jobs, as well as social, political, and economic opportunities. With the massive influx of Palestinian refugees into the greater Amman area as a result of the 1948 war, the demographic shift was sealed, and from then until today the majority of Jordan's citizens have been based in the greater Amman area.

This inversion, however, created a major political problem, as the regime's East Bank support base—those who had bought into the social contract of the 1920s—was now firmly part of the periphery. Jordanians of East Bank descent continued to dominate the military, police, security, and other public sectors, but it was the capital that was economically booming. For decades, the regime addressed this imbalance with public sector jobs, expanding the welfare state dramatically during the economic boom of the 1970s and early 1980s. This period also saw the aforementioned "Jordanization" project following the Black September violence between the Palestinian fedayeen guerrillas and the Jordanian Army. Although spatially peripheral from the capital, the East Bank communities enjoyed the flush times while most Palestinians in the capital struggled to build business opportunities in the private sector.

The late 1980s saw economic collapse, however, and the state turned to the International Monetary Fund, which mandated structural adjustments, including currency devaluation and the lifting of subsidies. When subsidies on fuel were lifted in April 1989, the reaction was immediate and extreme: protests broke out nationwide, but they started first in Ma'an and spread to the other East Bank towns before they reached the capital. Protests were also more violent among members of the East Bank communities, who blocked roads, burned down government offices and vehicles, and even chased, stoned, and beat government officials. King Hussein responded by temporarily restoring some of the subsidies and arresting hundreds, but as most were from East Bank areas they were eventually released without charge. The next move was institutional: the king restored the national parliament with new elections that fall and lifted martial law the following year. When the 1989 parliament was dominated by urban-based Islamists and leftists, the regime restructured the electoral system and districting prior to the 1993 elections in a manner that all but guaranteed an East Bank–dominated assembly—the spatial (and economic) periphery was thus returned to the political center. These maneuvers—from the acts of protest to the state's responses to them—illustrate how deeply resistance has shaped the institutions of the Hashemite state in ways that have key spatial and geographic dimensions.

To turn to another example of the interconnections between protest, state capacity, and the built environment, consider the vastly different state responses to protests depending on not only the subject of the protest but also who is protesting and where. It turns out that not all large protests are threatening to the regime. Why might massive protests in the capital, for example, be less threatening than small gatherings in out-of-the-way places? The answer comes into view when we recognize that protests in certain locations tend to develop their own spatial repertoire. In downtown Amman, for example, protesters have for decades assembled at the Grand Husseini Mosque and marched west to end at the Municipal Complex before disbanding. Although police turn up to these protests, they seldom interfere; even shop owners and pedestrians are unconcerned and go about their business. In this and other locations, protests that adhere to known spatial routines are hardly contentious at all. In this way, routine protests in certain spaces—even when thousands of people turn out—do more to reproduce state power (by adhering to the acceptable routine) than to challenge it. The state has little need to intervene, save for distributing water bottles to protesters on particularly hot days (for real).

Other spaces, however, are more contentious because the regime wants to prevent people from protesting there—the Interior Circle and the Fourth Circle interchanges in Amman are two such places. Preventing protest in those locations has entailed the obvious use of security services to block protesters' ability to assemble, but the state has also exercised its power over the built environment in ways that render certain locations inaccessible through a variety of techniques: putting up walls and fences, landscaping open plazas, closing off routes for accessing protest sites, and even removing a planned plaza from a major megaproject in the capital out of fear that people would protest there. The ability of the state to reshape the built environment as a means of exercising control is underappreciated, even in the literature on protest and space. It can render spaces inaccessible to whom, or what kinds of people, it chooses, as well as police them differently. In this sense, state capacity can be both expanded and limited by the structure of the built environment. Furthermore, state capacity to control or repress political dissent can be spatially situated. As I explain elsewhere, "Protests can also expose as well as shape how social, economic, and political powers are organized, distributed, and located spatially and geographically."[17]

Geographer Don Mitchell sums up well the connection between resistance, space, and state development and capacity in his study of four hundred years of riots and rebellions in New York City. Protests do not merely disrupt "normal time" politics—to return to the first theme of this chapter. Rather, resistance is at the heart of the development of how state institutions and capacity develop over time.

> Violent upheaval influences investment decisions—how capital circulates in or flees from the urban landscape—and thus where and how New Yorkers can live, work, and play. Urban violence, whether organized or disorganized, shapes laws, leads to new strategies of policing, and influences the development of institutions (like the police department itself).[18]

---

17. Schwedler, *Protesting Jordan*, 5.
18. D. Mitchell, "The Lightning Flash of Revolt," 3.

In similar ways, one cannot understand the institutional shape of the Jordanian state, or how it is situated geographically and spatially in the built environment, without examining the extensive and ongoing ways in which protest and dissent have shaped it, its trajectory of development, and its capacities to rule, if not govern.

Conclusion

This chapter seeks to show that diverse forms of resistance shape state institutions and capacity in ways that conventional approaches to strong or weak institutions cannot capture. It argues that one cannot understand the Jordanian state—how it is organized as well as how it exists materially and spatially—without careful attention to the multiple forces that challenge state authority and make demands from and against the regime. As Heydemann puts it in his chapter in this volume, governance is not only a matter of who gets what, when, and how, but "who does not get, why they do not get, and what they do about not getting."[19] What they do about not getting what they want is, in many ways, to affect ongoing state-maintaining processes, forcing regimes to adapt, adjust, and restructure the very institutions of governance. A careful examination of state capacity to respond to protests and other challenges to regime power shifts the focus of attention from state institutions and development toward a more dialectical understanding of state power that highlights ongoing and changing challenges.

BIBLIOGRAPHY

Abu-Rish, Ziad, "Getting Past the Brink: Protests and the Possibilities of Change in Jordan." *Jadaliyya*, November 15, 2012.

Bustani, Hisham. *(Dis)functional Polities: The Limits of Politics in the Postcolonial Arab Region* (two volumes in Arabic). Beirut: Arab Institute for Studies and Publication, 2021.

Cox, Lawrence, and Alf Gunwald Nilsen. *We Make Our Own History: Marxism and Social Movements in the Twilight of Neoliberalism*. London: Pluto Press, 2014.

Heydemann, Steven. "Upgrading Authoritarianism in the Arab World." Washington, DC: Brookings Institution, October 15, 2007.

Lynch, Marc, ed. *Jordan: Forever on the Brink*. POMEPS Briefings 11, May 9, 2012.

Mann, Michael. *The Sources of Social Power*. Vol. II. New York: Cambridge University Press, 2012.

Mitchell, Don. "The Lightning Flash of Revolt." In *Revolting New York: How 400*

---

19. Heydemann, "Seeing the State or Why Arab States Look the Way They Do," chap. 1, this volume.

Years of Riot, Rebellion, Uprising, and Revolution Shaped a City, edited by Neil Smith and Don Mitchell, 1–9. Athens: University of Georgia Press, 2018.

Mitchell, Timothy. "The Limits of the State: Beyond Statist Approaches and Their Critics." *American Political Science Review* 85, no. 1 (March 1991): 77–96.

Morgan, Kimberly J., and Ann Shola Orloff, eds. *The Many Hands of the State: Theorizing Political Authority and Social Control*. New York: Cambridge University Press, 2017.

Schwedler, Jillian. *Protesting Jordan: Geographies of Power and Resistance*. Stanford: Stanford University Press, 2022.

Stacher, Joshua. *Adaptable Autocrats: Regime Power in Egypt and Syria*. Stanford: Stanford University Press, 2012.

Tripp, Charles. "The State as an Always-Unfinished Performance: Improvisation and Performativity in the Face of Crisis." *International Journal of Middle East Studies* 50, no. 2 (2018).

Wedeen, Lisa. "Don't Call Yemen a Failed State." *Foreign Policy*, Middle East Channel, March 30, 2010. https://foreignpolicy.com/2010/03/30/dont-call-yemen-a-failed-state/

Woodward, Susan. *The Ideology of Failed States: Why Intervention Fails*. New York: Cambridge University Press, 2017.

Yom, Sean. *From Resilience to Revolution: How Foreign Interventions Destabilize the Middle East*. New York: Columbia University Press, 2016.

NINE

Water, Stateness, and Tribalism in Jordan
The Case of the Disi Water Conveyance Project

Sean Yom

A cash-strapped, water-poor autocracy in the Middle East inks a lucrative contract with a foreign company backed by Western donors to dramatically improve its water supply infrastructure. In one swoop, the power holders of the state have achieved the elusive win-win scenario of Global South governance, upgrading their meager capacity to deliver a life-sustaining public good at little domestic cost thanks to foreign aid and private capital. What could go wrong?

In the Hashemite Kingdom of Jordan, plenty. Yet the debacle surrounding its Disi Water Conveyance system (DWC) surprised even longtime observers of the country. At first glance, this is a curious conundrum. Unlike many other megaprojects in neoliberalizing states beholden to crony capitalism, the DWC actually worked. Criss-crossing Jordan's parched desert highlands, the DWC's scheme of wells, pumps, and pipelines began drawing from the southern Disi-Mudawarra aquifer in late 2013 to help quench the kingdom's residential water needs. Unlike many other capital-intensive investments within the public sector, the billion-dollar DWC was not riddled with corruption and graft. The aqueduct system was also not sullied with political repression; the project was built during the protest-laden Arab Spring years, but it never figured into the anti-regime demonstrations mounted by organized opposition movements.

The fiasco of the DWC instead emerged only after it came online and exposed an enigma at the heart of the Jordanian state regarding how much control it brandished over its citizenry—and, more broadly, how statehood and governance manifest for those who live under them. In 2014, the Turkish subsidiary contracted to build and operate the DWC, Gama Energy, filed a staggering $460 million arbitration case against the Jordanian government. Gama alleged that the system's 2010–13 construction was plagued by rampant criminal violence committed by local tribal groups, resulting in massive costs and delays. At the Europe-based Permanent Court of Arbitration, Gama argued that in rural areas that hosted DWC worksites, assailants injured employees, extorted engineers, hijacked vehicles, burglarized wellfields, sabotaged pumps, pillaged food reserves, destroyed pipelines, and occupied camps—essentially, primeval lawlessness.

In their defense, Jordanian officials denied responsibility over these acts committed by private citizens. Their state was not failing like Syria, and their governance was hardly powerless like in Lebanon. They had monitored the events, arrested some perpetrators, mediated many disputes, and beseeched tribal communities to leave DWC facilities alone. They did not succeed, but they reminded the arbitration court that even strong, well-governed Western states could suffer from crime. In any case, the government could not be held liable for local problems that it did not cause by its own hand.

In the end, the arbitration court ruled in favor of Jordan, largely for technical reasons relating to the procedural stipulations of the DWC contract. However, the outcome of the arbitration remains less important than the events revealed through its proceedings. The most expensive water-related project in Jordan's history was followed by its most titanic sovereign legal battle, one that exposed the frayed edges of a social contract between an authoritarian state and the societal forces it putatively controlled. A conventional interpretation would see the DWC violence as a straightforward question of state strength: Jordan is weak, and its autocratic rule makers lacked the capacity to enforce their laws.

Yet this explanation does not suffice. No Weberian institution collapsed during 2010–13, and at no point did the Jordanians attacking the DWC challenge the Hashemite monarchy's juridical sovereignty. Indeed, those years coincided with the Arab Spring, and authorities ably arrested protesters and controlled thousands of demonstrations demanding democracy that occurred elsewhere in the kingdom. Those Arab Spring protests ended without political change and with Jordan's autocratic regime entirely intact. A decade later, not much has changed. Today, there remains no uncertainty about the fate that awaits dissenters who call for radical political change—including even members of the ruling family, as Prince Hamzah discovered during the April 2021 royal crackdown on his alleged coup conspiracy against his half-brother, King Abdullah.

Rather than interpreting the DWC crisis as evidence that Jordan has a weak or failing state, this chapter presents an alternative viewpoint. It reinforces theoretical precepts from this volume's introductory chapter by Steven Heydemann and Marc Lynch, particularly how the absence of a Western-style "strong" state can reveal more about social forces and historical peculiarities than it does about the measurable institutional capabilities of that state. In that vein, in investigating the DWC controversy, I discard conventional verbiage about strong versus weak states, or good versus bad governance, in favor of more nuanced conceptualizations of *uneven* stateness. The state is not a unified act of vertical power but rather a field of contested practices. A repressive autocracy within an established, stable, and sovereign state can cohabit the same space as social resistance that disrupts public order and that commands political significance despite not targeting the locus of state power or calling for revolution. Resistance or lawbreaking in one field—say, disobeying edicts and attacking a water pipeline project—does not mean the state is failing or that its coercive and political institutions can no longer control media, punish dissidents, or police borders. It does mean, however, that resistance against specific practices of state power becomes scrutable only when unpacking their moral and historical contexts. Such resistance from society is limited and deep: it is limited because it does not aim to overthrow the state, but it is deep because it critiques the legitimate basis upon which that state exercises authority.

These theoretical imperatives drive this chapter. I argue that during 2010–13, some tribal communities in Jordan's rural south adjacent to the DWC refused to obey the law not because they opposed who governed the kingdom or sought revolution during this period of the Arab Spring but rather because they pursued a different moral economy of rulemaking. That moral economy stemmed from deep attachment to land and water. For generations, their rural claims of informal ownership over these natural resources operated as a crucial element of the tribal-state coalition that underlay Jordan's political order. For nearly a century, this social contract rendered these East Bank or Transjordanian communities—unlike the Palestinian majority of Jordan—as pillars of Hashemite rule.

All that changed with the 2000s, when neoliberal economic reforms under King Abdullah radically altered this topography. The DWC, a public-private partnership reflecting new confidence in the marketed provision of public goods, meant that tribal groups in the rural south lost customary access to water, which now flowed northbound to water the homes of Amman. By privileging private actors like Gama, which not only built the DWC megaproject but was licensed to operate it with a subsidiary called the Disi Water Private Shareholding Company, Jordanian authorities exposed their core social constituencies to market-driven dislocations whose logic was incompatible with local tribal understandings about the monarchical state's obligations to honor their livelihoods. Thus, some tribal Jordanians saw their predations upon the DWC not only as legal transgressions but also as expressions of corrective justice. The companies and workers on their land were intruders; and anything they had, such as vehicles, food, tools, jobs, and money, became *theirs* as a matter of right.

In essence, the controversy over the DWC encapsulates the innate contradictions of uneven stateness. Here, the Jordanian government and state achieved a laudable goal in improving public goods provision in a parched country; but tribal communities also contravened authority in quotidian ways that conveyed the gaping disconnect between autocratic authority and its rural periphery. This chapter unravels this puzzle in five sections, relying upon both historical analysis and intensive fieldwork conducted during the summer of 2016 in both Amman and two rural governorates (Aqaba and Karak). First, it critiques notions of state strength and weakness, and good versus bad governance, as applied to Jordan from Western analyses. Second, it presents more useful perspectives about limited statehood, which emphasize why practices of rulemaking can vary so remarkably within states where authoritarian rule appears stable and secure. The third section sketches out the DWC controversy, highlighting the insecurity and attacks that prolonged its construction. The fourth segment dives into the historical context of tribal-state relations in Jordan, laying out the underlying resentments of many tribal communities by the time the Disi project began. The final section connects insights gleaned from fieldwork in tribal communities to the theoretical argument, showing why local perpetrators carried out their raids—and, in the end, how such disobedience carried resonant meaning despite not serving as a political revolt against the state itself.

Strong State, Weak State, Poor State, Jordan

In Jordan, comparative political science has fertile ground to explore classical conceptions of state strength and state capacity. There are two perspectives to deconstruct: the global systemic view, or how Jordan looks from the international system, and the domestic governance view, or how its rulership represents an institutional structure of authority that fulfills the needs of society. Both make Jordan look *weak*; but both notions of weakness also neglect to capture the rhythms of governance today.

First, from a systemic Westphalian standpoint, Western observers have long accentuated the Hashemite Kingdom's profile as a diminutive state within the modern international system. Neorealists see Jordan as a territorial runt defined by what it is *not*—not big, not rich, and not militarily threatening to any other state. The ruling monarchy, implanted by the same British imperials who drew Jordan's absurdly illogical borders, relies upon external alliances to compensate for its structural deficiencies. Since the 1950s, the United States as a global power and occasionally regional patrons like Saudi Arabia have provided the diplomatic cover, economic funding, and military assistance needed for Jordan to defend its borders and finance its budget.[1] Moreover, its own sovereignty remains incomplete: while the majority of the populace is of Palestinian origin (most of whom have Jordanian nationality), hundreds of thousands of Palestinian refugees still reside in ten camps where the United Nations Relief and Works Agency for Palestine Refugees provides for their rights and protections as a "phantom sovereign."[2] In all, then, Jordan represents an enigma from a systemic approach—a fragile colonial artifice whose very existence still depends upon external largesse and that seems just one crisis away from state "failure" or breakdown.[3]

The domestic governance perspective tackles a different question, namely, how Jordan's ruling institutions can wield power despite lacking resources and doing few things well. Its authoritarian monarchy has periodically suppressed popular uprisings and democratic threats from opposition groups dating back to its colonial inception in the 1920s. Yet having a "fierce" coercive apparatus, as Nazih Ayubi memorably argued decades ago, hardly translates into good governance.[4] For instance, Jordan is not financially self-sufficient. It lives off foreign aid and meets tenacious pushback whenever it seeks to ramp up its paltry capacity to extract more taxes from the populace, as witnessed in the May-June 2018 anti-tax protests.[5] Encaged by the legacies of a postcolonial political economy defined by

---

1. Brand, *Jordan's Inter-Arab Relations*; Ryan, *Inter-Arab Alliances*.
2. Hanafi, Hilal, and Takkenberg, *UNRWA and Palestinian Refugee*.
3. Rotberg, ed., *When States Fail*.
4. Ayubi, *Over-stating the Arab State*.
5. Moore, "The Fiscal Politics of Rebellious Jordan."

neopatrimonial logic and state-led development, governance today is hobbled by rent-seeking pathologies endowed generations ago. Corruption is endemic, education and other social services are of low quality, patronage and clientelism saturate the public sector, and most citizens exhibit low trust in the government.[6]

These perspectives portray Jordan as a fragile state, stunted by internal weakness and exposed to external aggression.[7] They are not completely wrong, but they also give rise to fruitless analytical exercises. The most pernicious is the tendency of Western observers to fixate upon Jordan's vulnerabilities and prophecy its collapse when a major crisis erupts, such as a neighboring war, refugee influx, or popular protests. "Look at a map to hear the clock ticking on the monarchy," Stephen Glain advised when seeing Jordan squeezed between two conflicts after 2003—the Al-Aqsa Intifada in Palestine to the west and US-occupied Iraq to the east.[8] The same rhetoric accompanied the 2011–12 Arab Spring and the 2018 anti-tax protests. That Jordan has been relatively free from the border-breaking turmoil wracking nearby states like Iraq, Syria, and Lebanon since the late twentieth century hence serves as the backdrop to popular writing, which zooms in on the same trope: why Jordan still exists and its Hashemite monarchy still reigns, when common sense predicts otherwise.

Understanding the DWC puzzle requires recalibrating these stagnant theoretical presumptions. Undoubtedly, Jordan has both external fragility and domestic troubles; its tumultuous regional neighborhood hardly helps, and neither does its scrawny economy. Yet such vocabulary suffers severe limitations. For one, it gives little traction to explain counterintuitive outcomes, such as why some citizens would sabotage a massive infrastructural project like the DWC, when its very creation for Jordan signals better domestic governance and more viability as a sovereign water-providing state—something they should rationally *want*. For another, such imagery itself is often exploited by Jordan's authoritarian power holders, who often emphasize these failings to angle for more foreign aid and external support so that the kingdom can become a stable, secure, and well-governed country—and not, instead, a fractured state unable to uphold its peace treaty with Israel or host Western military forces in accordance with its geopolitical alignment.

Above all, none of these weaknesses make Jordan exceptional, which

---

6. Jreisat, "Public Administration Reform in Jordan."
7. See, for instance, Susser, *Jordan*; George, *Jordan*; and Kumaraswamy, ed., *The Palgrave Handbook of the Hashemite Kingdom of Jordan.*
8. Glain, *Mullahs, Merchants, and Militants*, 135.

simple comparisons can show.[9] First, most Middle East and North Africa (MENA) states, by virtue of their late development through colonialism and war, feature what scholars call "hybrid" sovereignty marked by highly "permeable" boundaries.[10] Outside pressures constantly disrupt domestic governance. Cross-border conflicts, inflows of refugees and Western military interventions, external capital in the form of energy rents or foreign aid, and great power sponsorship have all distorted the formation of these states as Westphalian entities. These make Jordan, for all its external liabilities, not an extraordinary case but rather the regional norm.

Second, the same historical factors that drive weak or bad governance in Jordan also vex other Arab autocracies. The Hashemite regime is hardly the only dictatorship in the MENA region that struggles to furnish public goods or cultivate economic growth. Some, like Tunisia and Egypt, experienced regime-changing insurrections during the Arab Spring; others, like Algeria and Sudan, followed suit at the end of the 2010s. And yet others, like Morocco and to a lesser degree Kuwait, trudge onward despite that most citizens are convinced that their governments are incompetent, tone-deaf, and unable to satisfy popular demands. Again, Jordan hardly looks unique in this regard.

Finally, Jordan is no different from other Global South states in that marked variation exists in terms of how much its rulemaking authorities can regulate social forces. For instance, Jordanians know that to call their state an efficacious one in many spheres of action, from urban planning to welfare distribution, is comedy; the inefficiency of public bureaucracy, even when greased by petty corruption, is one of the few constants of popular chatter. But in some areas, the government can achieve its goals quite efficiently, even to the point of suggesting it is effective and capable. In matters of regime security, for instance, the coercive apparatus has little difficulty penetrating local communities and eliminating threats to autocratic order, from political opposition to Salafi-jihadist militants. Jordan undertook one of the world's most draconian COVID-19-related lockdowns throughout 2020 partly because its military and security forces functioned like well-oiled machines. And, arguably, the gargantuan DWC project itself represented a marked improvement in governance, one that many cynics doubted the Jordanian state could spearhead given its notorious reputation for bungling the provision of public goods like water through corruption and ineptitude.

---

9. Tell, "The Resilience of Hashemite Rule."
10. Bacik, *Hybrid Sovereignty in the Arab Middle East*; Salloukh and Brynen, eds., *Persistent Permeability?*

These critiques unveil a more innate point. Explaining why certain social groups contravene legal or political diktats in specific contexts, such as competing claims over water and land, requires abandoning Western norms that project what capable, well-governed, and democratic countries *should* look like. Yahya Sadowski warned of such conceptual trickery nearly three decades ago.[11] Then, Orientalist explanations for why democracy seemed so scarce in the Muslim world meant lambasting authoritarian states as too strong in terms of their repressive intolerance and their societies as too weak in terms of their desire for liberal freedoms. However, when the same observers saw Islamist movements flex their muscle in the shadow of the Iranian Revolution, their tune changed: now Muslim societies were too strong and rowdy in mobilizing for change, and their pro-Western autocratic leaders too weak and fickle in suppressing the Islamizing masses.

The limitations of all these prevailing frameworks in charting out Jordanian politics underscore the need for alternative approaches. As this section has shown, Jordan is not a case of state failure, for all its structural shortcomings as a Westphalian enterprise. Likewise, its internal dysfunctions explain neither the areas of effective governance nor the limitations of domestic authority. Needed instead is a more flexible rubric, one that explores how specific practices of power shape the relationship between rule makers and social forces.

Contested Practices, Limited Statehood, and Infrastructural Power

The fundamental question with the Disi Water Conveyance project's construction more than a decade ago is why some Jordanians, who need public goods like water and have little desire to overthrow Hashemite rule, would ignore state mandates and disrupt the construction process, thereby subjecting the DWC and its workers to conditions of violence. Moving beyond static conceptions of strong versus weak states, or good versus bad governance, requires carefully disentangling practices of state power. Here, theoretical debates about how states radiate authority and regulate social life run across the arc of comparative politics. This section plucks out a few of those strands to shed light into the quotidian dynamics of compliance, resistance, and lawfulness at play in Jordan.

The first building block comes from Joel Migdal's state-in-society approach, which underscores the conceptual chasm between the Weberian

---

11. Sadowski, "The New Orientalism and the Democracy Debate."

ideal type that portrays states as powerful political actors able to vertically dominate societies and achieve their goals with little fuss and the lived reality of these political orders.[12] In the postcolonial world, Migdal discarded this state-society binary in favor of refracting the state as a horizontal field of power, whereby the dictates of those with authority to make rules are frequently contested by local and regional communities. Thus, laws governing economic transactions, social codes shaping public action, statutes over political discourse, and other practices of rulemaking fall under continual renegotiation by those expected to follow the rules. Governance is best conceptualized as a "heap of loosely connected parts or fragments," not the heroic outgrowth of unitary, Leviathan-esque behemoth states.[13]

That statehood can be imagined as a field of practices under continual negotiation with society comports with a second idea, that of "limited statehood."[14] Scholars of limited statehood discard highly functionalist definitions that render states little more than service transactors whose governance is simply gauged by whether they monopolize violence. Instead, they concede innumerable circumstances in which rulers cannot implement their policies and decisions perfectly. Sometimes, as Stephen Krasner argues, this results from a conscious decision to specialize in some practices more than others—such as developmental states that cultivate "islands of excellence" in financial budgeting or educational programming, while leaving other issues such as decentralization or welfarism to wither.[15] In other cases, rulers can outsource governance over citizens itself to third parties. In Jordan, for example, the United States Agency for International Development (USAID) historically has created "parallel institutions," such as the Jordan Valley Authority and the Aqaba Special Economic Zone, which administer public goods and services independent of the local authority.[16] Thus, unevenness within domestic governance is quite common.

Such sensitivity to variations of compliance and resistance implicates a final source of inspiration, namely, contemporary work drawing upon Michael Mann's theory of infrastructural power.[17] Early applications of this idea held that strong states were those that enjoyed the physical capacity and organizational reach—say, the probing tax agency or meticulous cen-

---

12. Migdal, *Strong Societies and Weak States*; Migdal, *State in Society*.
13. Migdal, *State in Society*, 22.
14. Risse and Stollenwerk, "Legitimacy in Areas of Limited Statehood"; Börzel, Risse, and Draude, "Governance in Areas of Limited Statehood."
15. Krasner, "Theories of Development and Areas of Limited Statehood."
16. Zimmermann, *US Assistance, Development, and Hierarchy in the Middle East*.
17. Mann, *The Sources of Social Power*.

sus bureau—to regulate its populace. Purveyors of this concept today have diversified their understanding of infrastructural reach. One finding is that social factors, such as group identities, historical memory, and geographic depth, can influence how potent or legitimate that state authority appears to local communities.[18] For instance, a repressed ethnic minority in a peripheral region might see the collection of taxes or military conscription very differently than elite families living in the urban capital, even if the bureaucratic institution enforcing them is the same. Efforts to make society more "legible," such as cadastral surveys or periodic censuses, might fail not because authorities lack administrative knowledge or financial resources to pierce their territorial space but because local actors distrust the government so much that they shrug off demands for compliance.[19]

These snippets of work on stateness are useful starting points. The state-in-society strategy suggests paying close attention to how practices of power instigate varied forms of resistance, suspicion, and alteration by society. Theories of limited statehood concede that this process of governance, and the degree to which citizens obey and behave in desired ways, will be inherently uneven, even if the formal locus of state authority is never challenged by revolution. Finally, newer studies of infrastructural power advise focusing not on the capabilities and resources of the institutions acting upon a populace but rather on the social relationship between ordinary people with their rule makers—and, equally important, the factors that influence whether they *perceive* an expectation or demand as appropriate.

Collectively, these lineaments converge upon what the DWC project represented throughout its 2010–13 construction: an episode of tense confrontation between rule makers and rule followers. It should be analyzed not as an overarching assessment of the Jordanian state's strength or weakness or the robustness of national governance but rather as a contextual moment in which the horizon of legal authority and the imprimatur of officialdom clashed with localized perceptions of what constituted justifiable behavior. What resulted was not the epic breakdown of autocratic order or a triumphalist narrative of criminality against law but instead a piquant demonstration of how disruptive violence fit into the social routines of marginalized citizens seeking to restore a sense of justice into their moral economy.

---

18. Soifer, "State Infrastructural Power."
19. Lee and Zhang, "Legibility and the Informational Foundations of State Capacity."

Violence and Predation upon the DWC

Jordan ranks as one of the most water-stressed countries in the world. Drought and freshwater shortages, the latter caused by both groundwater depletion and resource mismanagement, have long stalked the residents of the East Bank. Today, only about a dozen other countries receive less annual rain than the Hashemite Kingdom. While agriculture has always claimed significant freshwater supplies, rising household consumption most piquantly exposes Jordan's hydrological paucity.[20] In 1987, the state began strictly rationing water distribution at a national scale, and created a Water Ministry to manage this process. In most areas, residents saw their free-flowing water supply shrivel to just a few days per week and often less in the summertime. Given their usually dry municipal taps, many areas became dependent upon a parallel economy of private tankers and middlemen, who filled up the storage and rooftop tanks of homes at considerable prices.[21]

In the 2000s, authorities recognized one of Jordan's last untapped water reserves as the Disi-Mudawarra aquifer, which straddles the southern Jordanian-Saudi border. Under King Abdullah, the Water Ministry in collaboration with Western consultants began planning an ambitious overland conveyance scheme to abstract water from this transboundary basin. By the late 2000s, the $1.1 billion venture had received enough foreign aid funding to move forward. Jordan would front $400 million of the project cost, with most of the remainder coming from the European Investment Bank, France, and USAID. Critically, Disi water would be pumped not for the entire country or even for the southern rural governorates close to the aquifer; it instead was designated primarily for Amman, several hundred kilometers away, with secondary allotments for nearby Zarqa and the southern port city of Aqaba.

The contract to build the DWC system—at 325 kilometers long, the largest water conveyance project in Jordanian history—went to Gama Energy, a Turkish firm (at the time partly owned by General Electric), under a build-operate-transfer agreement. The tendering process was remarkably free from favoritism and corruption, due to close monitoring by Western donors. Within the cloistered sector of Middle East utilities, the DWC was a groundbreaking endeavor roundly championed by development specialists. The aqueduct required a colossal scheme of wellfield pumps, power generators, supply stations, collection tanks, repair depots,

---

20. Whitman, "A Land without Water."
21. Mustafa and Talozi, "Tankers, Wells, Pipes and Pumps."

and pipelines beginning from the southernmost governorates of Aqaba and Ma'an (where the aquifer was located and raw abstraction took place) and meandering northward throughout Ma'an, Karak, and Tafileh governorates until most of the water reached Amman's distributional grid. While these poorer southern areas did not receive Disi water, they did receive temporary jobs by virtue of the Water Ministry's project agreement. At least 60 percent of the total project workforce was Jordanian, and in total Gama utilized thirty-three contractors to build the project, of which twenty-seven were Jordanian firms.[22]

The project became fully operational by January 2014. Pumping one hundred million cubic meters annually, the DWC began supplying Amman with more than half of the capital's drinking water needs. In the capital—which holds nearly half the national populace, including refugees—most residents saw their municipal taps work from one day to three or four days per week. To be sure, the DWC is not a permanent national fix. Most other areas outside Amman still receive municipal water just once a week or less.[23] Moreover, Jordan will deplete its share of the Disi aquifer, based on its 2015 transboundary agreement with Saudi Arabia, in a few decades. The exigencies of climate change mean that Jordan will inevitably run out of groundwater, either leaving large-scale desalination from the Red Sea or else bartering with Israel (with which it shares riparian stewardship over the Jordan River) as its last options. Nonetheless, for the intermediate term, the DWC seemed like a chiliastic success for the Jordanian state. It delivered a precious public good to millions in desperate need—and through one of the most ambitious and complicated infrastructural projects ever completed in national history, to boot.

Gama's international arbitration case against the Jordanian government cast a pall over this triumph. Once the legal proceedings began in summer 2015, Gama divulged that the DWC had suffered extensive construction delays resulting in massive cost overruns. The main reason was conditions of violence and danger that befell the small army of engineers, contractors, and workers employed to build the DWC in rural southern areas. In all, over seven hundred documented "security events" took place from 2010 to 2013, creating work stoppages and productivity losses that prolonged construction by 264 days.[24] The European legal teams representing Gama and the Jordanian Water Ministry battled in court over the technicalities of this claim, such as whether such events constituted force majeure that

---

22. "Wazir al-miyaah."
23. "Nearly Empty Dams Foretell a Worrying Year for Jordan's Water Sector."
24. "Hay'at al-tahkeem al-duwwaliyyah."

breached the project agreement. The Jordanian government was understandably relieved when, in February 2018, the Permanent Court of Arbitration rejected Gama's $460 million claim for compensation.[25]

Yet this ruling in favor of Jordan did not dispute the fact that the DWC did suffer frequent predation by tribal communities adjacent to worksites during its 2010–13 construction. Insecurity, indeed, transpired in ways seemingly incompatible with Jordan's image as a stable country girded by rule of law. The most violent example occurred in January 2011, when two Gama-contracted employees were killed by members of a nearby tribe over a work-related dispute; this resulted in three days of reciprocal rioting and tit-for-tat escalation by the DWC workers' own tribe.[26] Some months later, another local faction sought to wrest away from a rival tribe its DWC contract to transport supplies by truck, sparking a veritable all-out battle waged with axes and clubs to capture the vehicles themselves.

Fortunately, such bloodshed was rare. Most of the hundreds of other documented transgressions involved targeted types of destruction, such as assaults, thefts, and vandalism against DWC facilities and workers. In Aqaba governorate, for instance, the Disi wellfields were plundered by individuals from the nearby Zawayda tribal community. One Amman-based subcontractor reported that Zawayda representatives repeatedly occupied its worker camps with armed guards, only departing when they obtained various goods—such as enough food from the cafeterias to feed their village, as well as dozens of trucks that were never returned.[27] Expensive supplies such as drills, computers, and wiring were regularly looted from supply warehouses. When the subcontractor was perceived as noncooperative, tribespersons conducted drive-by shootings at the worksite. Physical attacks and armed intimidation were commonplace. The offer of job contracts to local men, sometimes given under gunpoint, did not mitigate what the subcontractor described as outright banditry; some tribal recipients never showed up to work but still demanded salaries. When the subcontractor chose to pull out due to the deteriorating situation, the buses evacuating the workforce needed to take a roundabout way to escape armed men attempting to intercept them.

The pipeline infrastructure, which connected the Aqaba wellfields and ran northbound through the Ma'an and Karak governorates, also fell under spells of insecurity. For instance, another Amman-based subcontractor

---

25. "Water Ministry Wins Disi-Related Arbitration Case."
26. "Haditha al-shidiyyah thulathah qutla."
27. Personal interview with Gama subcontractor 1, Amman, Jordan, July 25, 2016.

reported a consistent pattern of offenses against its conveyance facilities.[28] Project supplies, such as instruments and gauges, were frequently in short supply due to burglaries from private and government depots. Carjacking incidents regularly occurred around remote worksites, with informal checkpoints used to wrest vehicles or else extract "safe passage" fees from delivery caravans. Neither foreign engineers nor Jordanian managers were able to reach local sheikhs to identify the perpetrators; when they proposed to hire private security, masked gunmen retaliated by shooting at pipeline structures—and then offered their own services to guard the pipelines from future attacks. Over time, local groups also developed ever more creative tactics to secure bribes, such as blocking the entrances of worker dormitories. As with the Aqaba wellfields, much of the aqueduct workforce either could not complete their tasks or else preemptively pulled out; the subcontractor interviewed here reported a 70 percent worker desertion rate. By fall 2011, construction stoppages had become so dire, and pipeline structures so dilapidated due to the impossibility of safe repair, that even the national media began commenting on the situation.[29]

Over time, tribal antagonisms against the DWC evolved in creative ways. Sometimes they resembled more contentious politics rather than criminal acts. For example, one June 2012 incident in Karak featured a group of one hundred local shopkeepers who organized a sit-in around the main worksite to protest disruptions of local commerce caused by construction.[30] They blocked project personnel from carrying out trenching and other tasks for a two-month period and halted only after being promised financial compensation from the responsible contractor to recompense their claimed losses. In other cases, violence seemed random and inscrutable. Gama managers, for example, frequently reported gunfire against exposed pipeline and overnight sabotage of relief valves. Such incidents required expensive repairs, but often no assailants claimed these attacks, which seemed to have no financial motive.

This record of disruptive insecurity left Gama managers with an acerbic view. Indeed, some made a startling comparison during our conversations. They were used to working in conditions of rural precarity; some had just finished similar projects in Afghanistan or Iraq. Indeed, one of Gama's major subcontractors was HESCO, a Syrian firm that was simultaneously completing infrastructural projects in new conflict zones in Syria. Yet, interviewees from this firm claimed, nothing approximated the unbri-

---

28. Personal interview with Gama subcontractor 2, Amman, Jordan, July 29, 2016.
29. *Al-Dustour*, "Gama wa-hesco."
30. "Tujjaar al-qatranah yuqifun mashru' al-disi."

dled lawlessness they saw in Jordan's rural south, where it seemed there was neither government nor state—just criminality.[31]

For its part, the Jordanian government refuted such imagery throughout the arbitration. It conceded that the DWC had endured delays and damages. Yet Jordan was no broken state like Yemen or Libya, and unforeseen violence was hardly a signal of bad governance. After all, criminal aggression could afflict even the most vaunted well-ordered countries, from democracies like the United States to dictatorships like China. Moreover, Jordanian authorities claimed they were hardly negligent in the face of the reported incidents. As their own evidence at the court showed, various officials launched multiple and repeated interventions into the attacks.

At the local level, the Desert Police had cataloged the violence and even arrested a small number of perpetrators; but it could not thwart every anticipated crime, without blanketing each worksite with a massive security presence. At the regional level, officials from governorate offices—including, in Aqaba, the governor himself—held numerous summits with tribal communities and their sheikhs accused of preying upon the DWC, beseeching them to stop. Delegations from the Interior Ministry and Water Ministry in Amman used every tool in their clientelistic arsenal to palliate the problem, from threatening punitive sanctions to providing positive incentives, such as job offers, to tribes. On more than a few occasions, Interior Ministry officials also warned tribal liaisons that they would deploy heavily armed gendarmerie (*darak*, paramilitaries that specialized in close-quarter security and crowd control) if the violence did not stop.

The final trump card flaunted by Jordanian authorities played on Western discomfit over regional stability. The government reminded the court that the 2010–13 construction period coincided with the Arab Spring, when the kingdom saw thousands of unrelated protests and demonstrations for political reform erupt in other parts of the country. Yet unlike Tunisia, Egypt, Yemen, Libya, Bahrain, or Syria, the Hashemite regime proved more than capable of controlling these tides of public dissent. Jordan did not see any civil conflict or bloodshed during these protest-laden years, which proved that Jordanian authorities could act responsively and capably. However, short of a military-style occupation of the sprawling DWC work areas, it could not convince some Transjordanians to obey the most basic of rules—to let an infrastructural project proceed so that it could pump water. The resigned sighs were palpable: criminals were crimi-

---

31. Various personal interviews with Gama and Disi Water Private Shareholding Company staff, Amman, Jordan, July 19–21, 2016.

nals, and it was unreasonable to expect even a well-functioning state to halt every violation of its laws.

In retrospect, the DWC disputation was a nexus of overlapping truths. At play was not the physical capabilities of Jordan's state or governance but rather the relationship between political order and some tribal communities across Jordan's southern expanses. As the state-in-society, limited statehood, and infrastructural power approaches raised earlier suggest, conceptualizing the state as a horizontal field of contested practices allows for the possibility of social resistance that is both *limited* and *deep*. It is limited because it does not seek to overthrow the legal supremacy of the incumbent regime or the juridical statehood of Jordan itself; but it is also deep, because it questions the moral fabric of political order through subversive ways that even a proficient authoritarian system found difficult to prevent.

The Tribal-State Compact

Insights into this dilemma come from the social terrain of tribalism because that is the context that imbricates the DWC attacks. In Jordan, Transjordanian communities that identify as tribal—that is, organized around social kinship defined by patrilineal descent and connected through imagined and real ties of belonging that provide purposeful identity—are extremely diverse.[32] Those that resided in the East Bank prior to the Hashemite arrival and creation of the British Mandate in 1921 hailed from variegated backgrounds; some were Bedouin (fully nomadic), while others were semi-nomadic or settled cultivators. Most, however, exerted customary claims over local lands and thus also water resources that sustained their agrarian livelihoods.[33] Unlike other late Ottoman holdings in the region, the aridity and geography of Jordan foreclosed the emergence of feudal agricultural production. There were no landowning elites because there was not much arable land to own. Instead, most lands fell under communal ownership, and not until the late 1920s did British officials and the nascent Hashemite monarchy begin systematically registering and recognizing land titles in an effort to make the tribal populace more legible to centralized rule.[34]

The 1920s also commenced the state-building process, albeit under colonial guidance. As Tariq Tell and other observers have noted, decades before Jordan gained its Palestinian majority through the Arab-Israeli

---

32. For an overview of the tribes, see al-Rawabdeh, *Mu'jam al-'asha'ir al-urduniyyah*.
33. Allinson, *The Struggle for the State in Jordan*; Abujaber, *Pioneers over Jordan*.
34. Fischbach, *State, Society, and Land in Jordan*.

wars, the Hashemite monarchy and Transjordanian tribes crafted a "tribal-state compact," meaning coalitional arrangements that linked the social and economic well-being of these communities to the political survival of monarchical rule.[35] Forged in conditions of mutual hardship, particularly amid the devastating droughts and famines of the late 1920s, the tribal-state alliance manifested through a conditionalized pact whereby Transjordanian groups would support Hashemite rule in return for various forms of privilege and patronage.

This compact endured in succeeding decades, even as other new constituencies entered the ruling coalition underpinning Hashemite rule—merchant families, elite retainers, and Palestinian factotums. It embodied what Steven Heydemann notes in his chapter in this volume as the predominant theme in state development across the Arab world in the postcolonial period, namely, the reconfiguration of economic and political institutions to ensure regime survival. Hence in Jordan, foreign aid from the United States and other donors from the late 1950s onwards provided the financial and military means for the government to distribute goods and services to tribal constituencies at the center of its social base, such as public employment, welfarist benefits, and cultural favoritism.[36] The transactional reasoning was austere but effective, tailoring the nature of governance to match the preferences of a favored minority.

As Palestinians came to predominate as the demographic majority, this political economy transmogrified into ethnocracy. After the 1970 Black September civil war, fought between the tribal-staffed army and Palestinian commando organizations, Palestinian Jordanians found themselves frozen out of political institutions and targeted by state discrimination. Meanwhile, the protectionist economy ramped up tribal patronage. Many rural areas became reliant upon public sector provisions, particularly work in the civil service, state-owned enterprises, and the military. Influential tribal sheikhs also enjoyed close proximity to royal circles. The social views and class identity of many tribes came to revolve around this reciprocal arrangement, which anointed Transjordanians as the true stewards of the East Bank, whose lives became interwoven with the perceived inclusiveness of Hashemite rule.

The tribal-state compact was not solely predicated upon welfarist dependency, although such redistributive commitments laid the backbone of this alliance. It also meant that Jordanian authorities, at both the local

---

35. Tell, *The Social and Economic Origins of Monarchy in Jordan*.
36. Yom, *From Resilience to Revolution*.

and the national levels, would accommodate tribal interests at the communal level, even when doing so contravened official laws. It "enmeshed" them within a particular modality of *pliable* governance, which tribal voices came to see as the normalized routine of social life.[37] Governance became selective and uneven not because the monarchical regime could not apply its laws evenly but rather because it refused to do so. Stateness was limited by choice. In rural areas, for instance, tribal customary laws were institutionalized in tribal courts that operated in parallel with the civil and criminal legal systems. Even after the formal abolishment of those specialized courts in 1976, tribal norms—particularly mechanisms for resolving disputes and adjudicating blood crimes—remained operative in many areas, with the full knowledge (and often participation) of local police.[38]

Those accommodations also extended into water and land policy. In many rural areas, Transjordanian tribes could develop lands that they historically claimed, despite the official status of those tracts as public property. For instance, in the central highlands outside Amman, where prominent tribes like the Bani Hassan and 'Abbadi resided, the government allowed tribal leaders to divide and sell lands that legally belonged to the state.[39] Water usage also fell into this pattern. In the southern expanses where the DWC would later be built, tribal communities illegally but regularly drilled for wells that tapped underground basins. Independent from municipal grids and the national utilities infrastructure, such informal practices allowed small-scale cultivators to irrigate their plots while giving small villages and towns access to drinking water.[40] When the Water Ministry was created in 1988 to tighten administrative control over Jordan's patchwork system of water distribution and supply networks, it did little to rein in these practices. As one official rationalized, "This is the price we always paid with those communities. Punishing them for criticizing the government was easy, because that is politics. But this is different. Who wants instability just because some village needs water?"[41]

During the 2000s, the neoliberal reforms enacted by King Abdullah began dramatically overhauling this statist political economy and the tribal-state alliance it incubated. Under pressure since the late 1980s finan-

---

37. The idea of coercive "enmeshment" uniquely departs from the standard rational-institutionalist models of authoritarian rule, and its emphasis on social perceptions linking power holders to subjects informs this reflection. See Albertus, Fenner, and Slater, *Coercive Distribution*.
38. Watkins, *Creating Consent in an Illiberal Order*.
39. Razzaz, "Contested Space."
40. Al-Naber and Molle, "The Politics of Accessing Desert Land in Jordan."
41. Personal interview with Water Ministry official, Amman, Jordan, July 27, 2016.

cial crisis, the Jordanian state began implementing new development policies that prioritized market-based capitalist development. This neoliberal turn—endorsed heartily by the United States, as well as multilateral organizations like the World Bank and World Trade Organization—cut into many tribal communities. Fiscal austerity meant slashing food and fuel subsidies, while privatization meant spinning off the largest state-owned enterprises, including industries like phosphate mining that had previously offered employment sinecures to tribal labor.[42] As impoverishment rose in rural areas, the Hashemite regime sought new partners in its drive to redevelop Jordan. A new stream of technocratic elites—Western educated, young, and sometimes Palestinian—replaced the old guard of Transjordanian politicians and tribal figures who held sway in royal decision-making circles. Commercially, authorities also began aggressively partnering with private sector actors to build new commercial and infrastructural megaprojects, which government ministries—bloated after decades of neopatrimonial inefficiency—could not possibly attempt alone. Among those new endeavors was the DWC.

Crucially, these neoliberal transformations began seeding Transjordanian dissent in the mid-2000s, as a succession of tribal sheikhs, military veterans, and East Bank intellectuals publicly demanded a return to the previous statist political economy. Years later, the Arab Spring protests unleashed a torrent of rural demonstrations from grassroots (or *hirak*) movements, which enabled younger tribal voices to criticize the perceived corruption, mismanagement, and cronyist abuses that they saw as saturating the rule of King Abdullah.[43] The rural south, hardest hit by the post-1990s austerity shift and suffering the country's worst poverty and food insecurity, became a hotbed for *hirak* mobilization. Tribal Jordanians saw the gradual rollback of universal welfarism and public sector employment as an existential violation of their social contract and a betrayal of sorts by a monarchical state for which they had sacrificed much for generations.[44]

This backdrop of political dissonance within an authoritarian regime coalition creates a deceptively easy explanation for the violence outlined in the previous section. Tribal communities, long the benefactors of autocratic governance, revolted against Hashemite rule by attacking a prized water delivery project. However, the facts cast doubt on this facile answer, one that conflates social resistance with anti-regime upheaval. The DWC-related violence did not emanate from *hirak* movements or other known

---

42. See, for instance, Knowles, *Jordan Since 1989*; Baylouny, "Militarizing Welfare."
43. Yom, "Tribal Politics in Contemporary Jordan."
44. Martínez, *States of Subsistence*; Lacouture, "Privatizing the Commons."

opposition groups. The tribal groups that perpetuated the attacks were not connected with the Arab Spring protests unraveling elsewhere in the kingdom, including in the same governorates across the south. The relatively few assailants detained by police were not identified as political activists; they were criminals by the letter of the law, but they were not revolutionaries or rebels demanding the end of Hashemite rule.

This should not be surprising when juxtaposed against how social enmeshment operates in authoritarian settings. Undoubtedly, the frequency and intensity of tribal critiques against the Jordanian state have risen since the 2000s, given the shifting economic and political landscape. However, as Jillian Schwedler argues in her chapter in this volume and elsewhere, Transjordanian communities have always mobilized to advance their interests—and that is to be expected, because even apparently stable relationships of power between rule makers and rule followers gestate hidden tensions that play out through acts of critique.[45] And as I have argued elsewhere, projections of revolutionary uprisings in Jordan predicated upon the tattered remnants of the tribal-state compact are too deterministic. Complaining *how* a regime governs is not equivalent to condemning *that* this regime exists. Most tribal voices, hence, have little desire to capture the Jordanian state or topple the Hashemite monarchy, not least because they fear the demographic uncertainties heralded by the reality of living within a Palestinian-majority country.[46]

Despite these caveats, the eroding vessel of the tribal-state concord does serve as a guide to understanding the DWC debacle. Like a compass, it points in the general direction of why rural communities would predate upon the Disi water project so intently, given their general sense of marginalization and discontent; but it does not clarify their intentions. The next section does so.

"This Is Our Soil": A Moral Economy of Contestation

When speaking with several of the tribal communities alleged by Gama to have orchestrated the worst attacks against the DWC, it was striking that nobody sought to hide the extent of the violence.[47] My interlocutors

---

45. Schwedler, *Protesting Jordan*.
46. Yom, "Bread, Fear, and Coalitional Politics in Jordan."
47. I am particularly indebted to my interlocutors from the Qatranah clan, of the Hajaya confederation in Karak governorate, as well as the Zawayda of Aqaba governorate, a semi-settled tribe with some lineal ties with the larger Huwaytat confederation.

understood these actions were criminal in nature by virtue of violating the law, but they also did not see them as *illicit*—because, in their view, everyone in their communities knew who the responsible parties were.

What accounts for such solidary standing? One common theme emphasized the emotive affinities between tribe, land, and water and the sense of ownership that local communities held over the areas where the DWC was constructed. In their view, Gama and its contractors were interlopers. Particularly in Aqaba—where Zawayda tribal communities had long drawn upon underground water sources for their villages and farms—local sheikhs argued that they had the informal prerogative to exact what we might call a "tribute" from the "outsiders" (including Jordanians from Amman), whose arrival as workers symbolized the guttural victory of neoliberal privatization over their customary endowment. As one interviewee recounted, "This is not about *who* was here. There were foreigners, but there were also Jordanians [working here]. . . . But they were all on our land. This is our soil, [which] our fathers upon fathers watered with their blood. What we wanted was compensation from those who lived and worked here without our permission."[48]

Cynics might dismiss such rationalization as exploitative rent seeking—glorified gangsterism from ne'er-do-wells who saw the DWC workforce as easy quarry. Yet a second, more resonant theme also abounded. When asked why they rebuffed official pressures to halt the raiding, tribal voices based their noncompliance on the reason that the government had lost its right to stipulate such demands because it had abandoned the tribes under King Abdullah. The issue was not whether the monarchy merited deposal; indeed, the interviewees took pains to identify themselves as loyal Jordanians, separate from the Arab Spring protesters elsewhere. Rather, for the Qatranah clan of Karak, the attacks represented a conscious act of resistance against what was described as the "path" (in Arabic, *nahj*) chosen by their political order. In the words of one sheikh, the violence did not entail revolution against the state because "*we* are the state. Every family here built this state. We are not like the [*hirak* movements] who are protesting on the street now. We are not opposition. But we think the ones who run this state now have turned their backs upon us. And we do not accept this."[49]

Such rationalizations suggest that noncompliance was locally understood as acts of corrective justice. They tug upon a shared sense of social

---

48. Personal interview with tribal representative, Aqaba, Jordan, July 21, 2016.
49. Personal interview with tribal sheikh, Karak, Jordan, July 17, 2016.

dislocation wrought by the kingdom's broader neoliberal transformation, which imposed particular constraints upon land and water usage. In the 2000s, in line with the stricter mandate of harnessing public resources for market-oriented development, the government began restricting the land and water privileges that many tribal communities had enjoyed for generations. In some cases, large parcels of land were privatized and sold off. For instance, invoking the notorious 2007 Casinogate scandal involving a failed bid to build casinos around the Dead Sea, Zawayda tribespersons in Aqaba recalled an equally specious 2008 effort by Gulf investors to erect touristic hotel complexes in the Disi-Mudawarra area in which they lived—without seeking any tribal input.[50] Fairly, such megaprojects do not seem exceptional given the luxury-oriented reconstruction of Amman also occurring in the same time period, such as Abdali District, Taj Mall, and Jordan Gate Towers. The difference was that, whereas Amman's redevelopment entailed transacting real estate in a dense urban setting, rural projects like the DWC required wholesale land allocations in peripheral regions where tribal groups had no recourse apart from public protest.[51]

Traditional water rights were also upended. Tribal interlocutors pointed out innumerable inequities in how the Water Ministry had reconfigured public water usage across the south starting in the 2000s. For instance, with the DWC project agreement, the Jordanian government outright banned unregulated well drilling, which devastated small farms and villages that long relied upon such informal accommodation. Authorities appealed to technocratic reason in such decrees: a parched country like Jordan could not possibly conserve water unless it tightly managed its usage.[52] Yet, a handful of large agribusinesses were not subject to these restrictions, by virtue of having inked contracts guaranteeing unfettered water access years earlier. Among them was Rum Farms, owned by business magnate Sabih Masri, which today still grows water-intensive produce like tomatoes and grapes primarily for export.[53] Beyond this imbalance was the revelation that the DWC was designed to flow northward to hydrate Amman. By contrast, southern areas, except for the port city of Aqaba, had no physical connection to its pipeline. Thus, not only would Transjordanian households and farmers across the south lose informal water access, but they also had no formal rights to Disi water, either.

Such understandings shaped the views of those rural communities that

---

50. "Al-disi."
51. "Hatha hisaad al-'aatham ya ashaab al-dawlah."
52. Yorke, "Jordan's Shadow State and Water Management."
53. Salameh, "Sharikaat al-junub al-ziraa'iyyah."

observed an armada of engineers and workers transmuting their lands. Many locals saw the DWC as not the Jordanian state itself, for they identified *with* the state, given the historical consanguinity between tribe and crown. Rather, they perceived the project as a specific state practice, one that originated in the neoliberal vision of King Abdullah's regime and to which they never consented. Invariably, those who deserved blame were the nefarious outsiders whose presence cemented the harsh reality that the old ways were gone. In this context, Gama and its contractors represented what other analysts have called "shadow actors" in official decision-making over water—parties that short-circuit the tribal-state compact by carrying out the hard work of privatization to the detriment of tribal forces but that do not hold the juridical power of the state despite acting on its behalf.[54]

In this milieu, for many of the tribal perpetrators, attacking the DWC and sometimes profiting from those raids exemplified not just an appropriate response but the *only* possible response. Even in the face of coercive reprisals and more policing from Jordanian authorities, it encased a grand refusal to relinquish long-standing preferences about the most appropriate ordering of space and resources within social life, but without dipping into the fiery cauldron of revolutionary politics. Anchored by reference to this moral economy, those transgressions never intended to threaten Hashemite rule. At stake, instead, was the restoration of what many saw as justice, however contingent and fleeting. Taking water away from these communities was "like a father abandoning his sons. For we are the true sons of Jordan, and what we deserve is an explanation for why everything is changing."[55]

Conclusion

The troubles with the DWC did not end after 2014. As soon as the project became operational, the Water Ministry began installing control and monitoring equipment to better regulate the flow of Disi water. Partly funded by USAID and other donors, this has become one of Jordan's most sophisticated remote surveillance efforts, one that has securitized water by allowing the police and intelligence directorate to oversee the entire infrastructure.[56] Ironically, such interventions were precisely what Gama

---

54. Hussein, "Tomatoes, Tribes, Bananas, and Businessmen."
55. Personal interview with tribal sheikh, Aqaba, Jordan, July 22, 2016.
56. Abdallat and Al-Zareer, "Security of Water Infrastructures against Sabotage and Damage in Jordan."

had desired during the 2010–13 construction period. Still, ongoing attacks against the DWC in the tribal south continue to the point of interrupting its operation, such as arson against wellfields, burglary of equipment, and theft by private tankers that extract Disi water from its pipeline and sell it to nearby households.[57] Rural denizens continue to disobey the writ of the state and contest its practice of power—but without challenging the parameters of statehood and the existence of government itself.

These ongoing agitations reiterate this chapter's key point about why stateness should be conceived as uneven. The conflict over the Disi Water Conveyance project shows that assessing social resistance through classically holistic concepts—such as whether states are strong or weak or have high or low capacity to govern—is not useful. Such dichotomies feed into unproductive debates about Jordan's survival or collapse at the macro-level, whereas at the micro-level, practices of power are contested in frequent and obstinate ways. As this chapter elucidated, the tribal raids against the DWC's construction occurred not because Jordan is a failing state or its government lacks the capacity to make laws. Rather, it expressed how members of tribal communities sought to restore a historical understanding of protected geography and customary rights, which economic changes under neoliberalism under King Abdullah had extinguished.

In moving forward, the Jordanian case deposits two important implications in pondering the future of states, statehood, and state strength in Global South regions like the Middle East. First, theoretical pronouncements about stateness should be continually tested during specific episodes of resistance. Typological frameworks and conceptual schemes are integral to making sense of how institutions of formal power function in macrostructural terms, but they should incorporate the lives and worldviews of communities that reject the rules placed upon them.

Second, acts of noncompliance inscribe social content—historical memory, communal preferences, group identities—that is not always plainly political and, hence, not easily categorized as anti-state or revolutionary. With the DWC, tribal Jordanians perpetrated criminal acts that violated the law, but they nonetheless did not aim to dislodge any power holders from their perch despite occurring in the context of the Arab Spring, when many similarly marginalized voices across Jordan and the region were seeking to do precisely that. The Jordanian state saw its decrees flaunted, but its future as an authoritarian entity was never in any danger. Yet this did not make the actions of the Transjordanians involved any less meaningful.

---

57. See, for instance, "Disi Resumes Pumping Water after Assault Damages Fixed."

BIBLIOGRAPHY

"Al-disi: tafwidh araadhin li-raful 'almal 'arabi" [Al-Disi: Allocating Lands to Arab Businessmen]. Khaberni.com, May 4, 2008.

Al-Naber, Majd and Francois Molle. "The Politics of Accessing Desert Land in Jordan." *Land Use Policy* 59 (2016): 492-503.

Ayubi, Nazih. *Over-stating the Arab State: Politics and Society in the Middle East*. London: I. B. Tauris, 1995.

Bacik, Gokhan. *Hybrid Sovereignty in the Arab Middle East: The Cases of Kuwait, Jordan, and Iraq*. London: Palgrave Macmillan, 2005.

Baylouny, Anne Marie. "Militarizing Welfare: Neo-liberalism and Jordanian Policy." *Middle East Journal* 62, no. 2 (2008): 277–303.

Börzel, Tanja A., Thomas Risse, and Anke Draude. "Governance in Areas of Limited Statehood." In *The Oxford Handbook of Governance and Limited Statehood*, edited by Anke Draude, Tanja A. Börzel, and Thomas Risse. Oxford: Oxford University Press, 2018.

Brand, Laurie. *Jordan's Inter-Arab Relations: The Political Economy of Alliance-Making*. New York: Columbia University Press, 1995.

"Disi Resumes Pumping Water after Assault Damages Fixed." *Jordan Times*, May 27, 2020.

Fischbach, Michael. *State, Society, and Land in Jordan*. Leiden: Brill, 2000.

"Gama wa-hesco al-amilitani fi-disi tatawaqqafani 'an al-aml li-'adm tawaffur al-zuruf al-amina" [GAMA and Hesco, Al-Disi Project Operators, Stop Work Due to Unsafe Conditions]. *Al-Dustour*, 29 September 2011.George, Alan. *Jordan: Living in the Crossfire*. London: Zed, 2005.

Glain, Stephen. *Mullahs, Merchants, and Militants: The Economic Collapse of the Arab World*. New York: Thomas Dunne, 2004.

"Haditha al-shidiyyah thulathah qutla: rafadha al-'utwah al-amniyyah wa-taw'id hukumi bi-ta'aqqub al-faa'ilin" [Eshidiya Incident Results in Three Deaths: Security Offering Rejected and Government Vows to Pursue the Perpetrators]. *AmmonNews*, January 3, 2011.

Hanafi, Sari, Leila Hilal, and Lex Takkenberg. *UNRWA and Palestinian Refugees: From Relief and Works to Human Development*. London: Routledge, 2014.

"Hatha hisaad al-'aatham ya ashaab al-dawlah" [To Those Who Own the State: These Are the Fruits of Your Sins]. *AmmonNews*, January 5, 2011.

"Hay'at al-tahkeem al-duwwaliyyah tarudd mutaalabaat DIWACO wal-baalighah 460 milyun dulaar" [International Arbitration Tribunal Rejects DIWACO's Demands Reaching 460 Million Dollars]. Petra News Agency, February 22, 2018.

Hussein, Hussam. "Tomatoes, Tribes, Bananas, and Businessmen: An Analysis of the Shadow State and of the Politics of Water in Jordan." *Environmental Science and Policy* 84 (2018): 170–76.

Jreisat, Jamil. "Public Administration Reform in Jordan: Concepts and Practices." *International Journal of Public Administration* 41 (2018): 781–91.

Knowles, Warwick. *Jordan since 1989: A Study in Political Economy*. London: I. B. Tauris, 2005.

Krasner, Stephen D. "Theories of Development and Areas of Limited Statehood."

In *The Oxford Handbook of Governance and Limited Statehood*, edited by Anke Draude, Tanja A. Börzel, and Thomas Risse. Oxford: Oxford University Press, 2018.

Kumaraswamy, PR, ed. *The Palgrave Handbook of the Hashemite Kingdom of Jordan*. London: Palgrave Macmillan, 2019.

Lacouture, Matthew. "Privatizing the Commons: Protest and the Moral Economy of National Resources in Jordan." *International Review of Social History* 66 (2021): 113–37.

Lee, Melissa, and Nan Zhang. "Legibility and the Informational Foundations of State Capacity." *Journal of Politics* 79 (2016): 118–32.

Mann, Michael. *The Sources of Social Power*. Vol. 2. Cambridge: Cambridge University Press, 1993.

Martínez, José Ciro. *States of Subsistence: The Politics of Bread in Contemporary Jordan*. Stanford: Stanford University Press, 2022.

Migdal, Joel. *State in Society: Studying How States and Societies Transform and Constitute One Another*. Cambridge: Cambridge University Press, 2001.

Migdal, Joel. *Strong Societies and Weak States: State-Society Relations and State Capabilities in the Third World*. Princeton, NJ: Princeton University Press, 1988.

Moore, Pete. "The Fiscal Politics of Rebellious Jordan." *Middle East Report Online*, June 21, 2018.

Mustafa, Daanish, and Samer Talozi. "Tankers, Wells, Pipes and Pumps: Agents and Mediators of Water Geographies in Amman, Jordan." *Water Alternatives* 11 (2018): 916–32.

"Nearly Empty Dams Foretell a Worrying Year for Jordan's Water Sector." *Jordan Times*, July 17, 2022.

Razzaz, Omar. "Contested Space: Urban Settlement Around Amman." *Middle East Report* 181 (1993): 10–14.

Risse, Thomas, and Eric Stollenwerk. "Legitimacy in Areas of Limited Statehood." *Annual Review of Political Science* 21 (2018): 403–18.

Rotberg, Robert, ed. *When States Fail: Causes and Consequences*. Princeton, NJ: Princeton University Press, 2004.

Ryan, Curtis. *Inter-Arab Alliances: Regime Security and Jordanian Foreign Policy*. Gainesville: University Press of Florida, 2009.

Sadowski, Yahya. "The New Orientalism and the Democracy Debate." *Middle East Report* 18 (1993): 14–21, 40.

Salameh, Dalal. "Sharikaat al-junub al-ziraa'iyyah: qissat arba'in 'aaman min 'ihdaar miyahuna al-shahihah" [Southern Agricultural Companies: A Story of Forty Years of Wasting Our Scarce Water]. 7iber.com, March 16, 2022.

Salloukh, Bassel F., and Rex Brynen, eds. *Persistent Permeability? Regionalism, Localism, and Globalization in the Middle East*. London: Routledge, 2004.

Schwedler, Jillian. *Protesting Jordan: Geographies of Power and Dissent*. Stanford: Stanford University Press, 2022.

Soifer, Hillel. "State Infrastructural Power: Approaches to Conceptualization and Measurement." *Studies in Comparative International Development* 43 (2008): 231–51.

Susser, Asher. *Jordan: Case Study of a Pivotal State*. Washington, DC: Washington Institute for Near East Policy, 2000.

Tell, Tariq. "The Resilience of Hashemite Rule: Studies in the History of Jordan, 1946–67." In *The Resilience of Hashemite Rule: Politics and the State in Jordan, 1946–67*, edited by Tariq Tell, 89–114. Beirut: CERMOC, 2001.
Tell, Tariq. *The Social and Economic Origins of Monarchy in Jordan.* New York: Palgrave Macmillan, 2013.
"Tujjaar al-qatranah yuqifun mashruʻ al-disi . . ." [Qatraneh Merchants Halt Al-Disi Project]. FactJO.com, June 4, 2012.
"Water Ministry Wins Disi-Related Arbitration Case Worth $460m." *Jordan Times*, February 23, 2018.
Watkins, Jessica. "Seeking Justice: Tribal Dispute Resolution and Societal Transformation in Jordan." *International Journal of Middle East Studies* 46 (2014): 31–49.
"Wazir al-miyaah: 60 fil-mi'ah min al-quwwa al-ʻamila fi mashruʻ miyaah al-disi' urduniyun" [Water Minister: 60 percent of the Disi Workforce is Jordanian]. KhabarJo.net, January 21, 2012.
Whitman, Elizabeth. "A Land without Water." *Nature* 573 (2019): 20–23.
Yom, Sean. "Bread, Fear, and Coalitional Politics in Jordan: From Tribal Origins to Neoliberal Narrowing." In *Economic Shocks and Authoritarian Stability: Duration, Financial Control, and Institutions*, edited by Victor Shih, 210–35. Ann Arbor: University of Michigan Press, 2020.
Yom, Sean. *From Resilience to Revolution: How Foreign Interventions Destabilize the Middle East.* New York: Columbia University Press, 2016.
Yom, Sean. "Tribal Politics in Contemporary Jordan: The Case of the Hirak Movement." *Middle East Journal* 68 (2014): 229–47.
Yorke, Valerie. "Jordan's Shadow State and Water Management: Prospects for Water Security Will Depend on Politics and Regional Cooperation." In *Society, Water, Technology: A Critical Appraisal of Major Water Engineering Projects*, edited by Reinhard F. Hüttl, Oliver Bens, Christine Bismuth, and Sebastian Hoechstetter, 227–51. Cham: SpringerOpen, 2016.
Zimmermann, Anne Mariel. *US Assistance, Development, and Hierarchy in the Middle East: Aid for Allies.* New York: Palgrave Macmillan, 2017.

CONCLUSION

The Specter of the Spectrum

Escaping the Residual Category of Weak States

Dan Slater

Comparative political science is the science of political spectrums. When we comparativists try to explain any of the outcomes we care about most, we tend to array those outcomes on a spectrum from one extreme to another. When studying political regimes, for example, that spectrum runs from the most open democracies to the most closed dictatorships: from Sweden to Syria, shall we say. When the outcome of interest is economic development, it varies from the "developed" world of high-income industrialized countries to the "developing" world of low-income countries: from Britain (before Brexit, anyway) to Burundi. When our attentions turn to the relative weight of states and markets in governing a political economy, the spectrum runs from state-led to market-led economies: from North Korea to the Netherlands. And when examining the state apparatus itself, a spectrum imposes itself yet again on our thinking: from the "strong" states of Western Europe, North America, and East Asia to the "weak" states of sub-Saharan Africa, Latin America, and the Middle East. At the far end of this latter extreme, states are said to be not just weak but "failed."

All of these spectrums have serious limitations. The spectrum from democracy to dictatorship, typically divided sharply into a dichotomy between those that surpass and those that fall short of the "minimalist definition" of democracy, has received the greatest attention and critique, not least as a relic of Cold War–era thinking.[1] But in this concluding chapter I venture the argument that the spectrum from strong states to weak states is even more analytically unhelpful than the spectrums from democracy to dictatorship, from rich countries to poor countries, and from state-led to market-oriented economies.

This is because, when it comes to regimes, development, and marketization, the "negative" end of the spectrum actually contains valuable descriptive information. We know something very important and substantive about a country if we know that it is highly authoritarian, desperately poor, or economically dominated by state officialdom. But when we say a state is "weak," it tells us almost nothing about how politics actually operates in that setting. The negative end of the strong/weak state spectrum stands apart for how little content it conveys; this makes it effectively a residual category, standing apart in its analytical unhelpfulness.

This "specter of the spectrum" looms larger in some regions than others. In Southeast Asia, the region of greatest interest to me, the variation between strong states and weak states is both strikingly vast and legitimately puzzling. As a global paragon of state "strength," Singapore is impossible for any scholar of Southeast Asia to ignore. At the opposite end of the spectrum, the enduring "weakness" of the state in the Philippines, which, unlike neighboring American allies Taiwan, South Korea, and Japan, never leveraged massive American aid to construct powerful state institutions, is also too intriguing and normatively important to neglect. To study states in Southeast Asia is thus almost inexorably to study a spectrum—the spectrum from state strength to weakness.[2]

The Middle East, or "Arab world," is very different from Southeast Asia in this respect. Here, the problematique is not why some states are so strong while others are so weak. It is why all states in the region share a certain "weakness"—even while clearly differing dramatically from each other and even while collectively succeeding at many goals that political leaders hold dear, most notably the not-so-simple task of staying in power. There is no obvious Singapore crying out for explanation in the Middle East, although some oil-rich Gulf monarchies might come close.[3] The impera-

---

1. Wedeen, "Concepts and Commitments in the Study of Democracy," offers a particularly and characteristically trenchant critique.
2. There is self-reproach in this recognition. In *Ordering Power*, I offer an explanation for variation in both state strength and authoritarian durability that gives the riotous heterogeneity in both outcomes across Southeast Asia short shrift.
3. One might argue that Singapore's state strength is a natural byproduct of its small size

tive and impulse to explain variation on the spectrum from state strength to weakness thus loom larger in Southeast Asia than in the Middle East: the specter is so apparent it is practically solid rather than spectral.

From one perspective, this poses a problem for scholars of the Arab state. The Middle East simply lacks the striking variation in outcomes that lends itself to explanations for why some states are "strong" and others "weak." Scholars who wish to answer this question will find more variation to dig into in a region of pronounced variation like Southeast Asia. Additionally, and far more unfortunately, the problematique of shared state weakness also makes the Middle East prone to subtly Orientalist interpretations. The region's states are routinely depicted as deficient and dysfunctional, and not simply as different from Western Europe's bureaucratic states, to take the most obvious contrast.

But from an alternative perspective—the perspective I put forth here—this relative truncation of variation in state "strength" makes the Middle East an especially promising place to understand, far more fully, how states actually differ. We can easily set aside the typical question of how and why states vary on a strong-weak spectrum and consider how and why they exhibit heterogeneity in a multitude of other ways.

Politics obviously does not end wherever the state is "weak." Why some "weak" states experience such dramatically different politics than others is the kind of question ideally answered in a region like the Middle East. The preceding chapters in this volume are a testament to this promise.

In what follows, I distinguish *linear variation* from *multifaceted heterogeneity* as features of interest in comparative politics. My main point here is that to focus on variation in degree leads us to give short shrift to heterogeneity in kind. In basic statistical jargon, we need to think in terms of nominal variation and not just ordinal and continuous variation in comparative politics, especially when studying state power. I then move on to make the case that thinking in spectrums is especially problematic when thinking about the state, as opposed to other major outcomes in comparative politics. A major virtue of this volume is the way it pushes us to cast aside the specter of the spectrum as it relates to state strength versus weakness. It takes more seriously the heterogeneous ways in which state power shapes political life in the Arab world, even among countries similarly thought of as occupying the "weak" end of the scale.

---

and thus does not cry out for explanation at all—but that conclusion would be mistaken. State smallness is no monocausal predictor of state strength.

Variation versus Heterogeneity

When we look at the world as students of comparative politics, what should really strike us first is just how riotously heterogeneous it is.[4] Even when one approaches the world wearing the blinders of methodological nationalism and minimizes the complex ways that countries differ internally and affect each other externally, this heterogeneity remains riotous. Yet in our collective effort to make sense of this heterogeneity and to unearth patterns in this heterogeneity—and we should by all means be trying to make sense and find patterns—we tend to undertake a subtle but significant shift. The fact that countries are so different becomes flattened into the finding that countries vary on a specific set of dimensions. It is these linear variations that then become worthy of systematic exploration and explanation.

Pretty much every outcome of interest in comparative politics assumes this linear, variation-driven form: in short, a spectrum. In the study of the Middle East, to stick with this volume's region of interest, spectrums loom large.

Take the Arab Spring as an especially prominent example.[5] When apprehending the riotous heterogeneity of outcomes that arose from the upsurge in protest that rocked the Arab world in the early 2010s, scholars move quickly to explain sharp variations. Did the old regime survive or collapse? Here, Egypt, Tunisia, and Libya fall on the "collapse" end of the spectrum, while the rest get coded as "survive." Did protests give rise to civil war: yes or no? Here, Libya and Syria receive a "yes," while the rest receive a "no." Did a regime collapse give rise to a new democracy or an autocratic restoration? Here, Egypt suffered an autocratic restoration quite quickly, while Tunisia stood on the other end of the spectrum, as a surviving new democracy—at least until the referendum of July 25, 2022, seemingly put Tunisia alongside Egypt on the "autocratic restoration" side. In the future, one could imagine constructing yet another spectrum for depicting and comparing the outcomes of interest in Egypt and Tunisia—whether autocracy's return was "fast" or "slow" or was "immediate" or "gradual."

These variations are all very much worth explaining. Yet they all rest on an analytical assumption that wilts at least a bit, if not withering entirely, under scholarly scrutiny. Was it really plausible that Egypt and Tunisia would experience the same "outcome" after the Arab Spring? Does it really

---

4. I borrow the term, admiringly, from Scott's unforgettable depiction of the "riotous heterogeneity" of upland Southeast Asian societies in *The Art of Not Being Governed*.
5. Much of what I learned about the Arab Spring, I learned from Brownlee, Masoud, and Reynolds in *The Arab Spring*. Any faulty interpretations I offer are, of course, still mine alone.

make sense to say that Jordan and Morocco, two monarchies often portrayed as relatively comparable, experienced the same "outcome" too?

In reality, Egypt remains Egypt, Tunisia remains Tunisia, Jordan is still Jordan, and Morocco is still Morocco. A more democratic version of Tunisia was still Tunisia, with historically rooted and distinctive patterns of labor mobilization, women's rights, and civil-military relations that made Tunisia a dramatically different place from Egypt, even when both countries were experiencing their simultaneous democratic interregna in the early 2010s. To call Egypt and Tunisia "similar" just because their democracy scores were briefly similar would thus have been a heroic stretch. To appreciate Egypt's and Tunisia's many differences while trying to array those differences onto any single spectrum from strong to weak or high to low would be downright impossible.

Comparativists will always be drawn to puzzling variation in interesting outcomes, of course. But when countries are marked by so much underlying heterogeneity, variation in outcomes should perhaps become less puzzling. We should expect riotous heterogeneity across countries before they go through a colossally important historical process like the Arab Spring, and we should expect no less heterogeneity across countries after the process is through (if one can even say the waves of contention that emerged a decade ago are now "through").[6] Again, that heterogeneity becomes even more pronounced when we remove the blinders of methodological nationalism as well.

It might be too much to ask comparativists to explain such riotous heterogeneity; but it should certainly be our job to appreciate it, to explore it, and to describe it with as much justice as we can manage.

The Worst Spectrum of All

Thinking in spectrums comes up shorter with some spectrums than others. In the example just offered, arraying outcomes after the Arab Spring on spectrums from authoritarianism to democracy and from war to peace conveyed essential information about all the cases examined. We do not say of Egypt that it emerged from its brief pluralist interregnum from 2011 to 2013, after the decisive military coup of July 3, 2013, either as a "weak democracy" or with "low democracy." There is ample content at the other

---

6. In *Struggles for Political Change in the Arab World*, Blaydes, Hamzawy, and Sallam persuasively argue that the contentious shock of the Arab Spring continues to generate regional reverberations, more than a decade later.

end of the scale that we can use to describe what Egypt became. It became, once again, an authoritarian regime. It became, once again, a military-led regime. It became, once again, an anti-Islamist regime. It became, once again, an American client regime. We have no shortage of concepts to describe authoritarian regimes, especially after two decades of progress in shifting authoritarianism from a residual category (that is, the absence of democracy) to a definable category in its own right (for example, as a regime that actively and aggressively denies its opponents a level playing field on which to compete for government power).[7]

The same can be said of war and peace. We do not look at Libya and Syria and say they are cases of "low peace" or "weak peace." They both devolved, after President Muammar Gaddafi's regime collapsed but President Bashar al-Assad's regime did not, into outright, full-blown "civil war." Political science has an absolutely massive literature on civil wars: why they start, how they end, why combatants target or mobilize civilians, how rebels and the regimes they fight attract foreign support, and so on. To say that Libya and Syria failed to sustain even minimal levels of peace and stability after the Arab Spring is thus not to resign them to a residual category. Both ends of the war-peace spectrum contain positive information, which can be captured for purposes of rich description and leveraged for purposes of systematic comparison.

Something far more unfortunate happens when we array states on a spectrum from "strong" to "weak." At the positive end of the spectrum, arguably, tangible content is involved in depicting the existence of a "strong state." To say that a country has a strong state, like the paradigmatic example of Singapore, is also effectively to say that law and order prevail, that public goods are predictably provided, that the bureaucracy enjoys at least a modicum of autonomy from political interference and mass scrutiny, and much else besides.[8]

Strong states are by no means all identical, but they all share certain defining features. Tolstoy's aphorism about happy versus unhappy families thus at least loosely applies to strong versus weak states: strong states all exhibit their strength in relatively similar ways, but "weak states" all have a weakness—and perhaps in many cases a misery worthy of Tolstoy—that is entirely their own.

But we must look closely to know. Just because the state apparatus is not

---

7. We provide an operational definition of authoritarian regimes along these lines in Slater and Fenner, "Opposing Pluralism."
8. But for compelling evidence that bureaucrats are no longer so sealed off from public scrutiny in our unfolding information age, see Ding, *The Performative State*.

bureaucratically organized, or meritocratically recruited, or territorially encompassing, or hierarchically authoritative, or muscularly extractive, or generously redistributive, does not mean we know anything particular or specific about how politics works. Even more than "authoritarian regime," "weak state" is truly a residual category.

And it is one that is all too vulnerable to Orientalist assumptions and preconceptions. To dismiss Arab states as "weak states" is in many cases worse than not saying anything at all—in its worst guises, this epithet reinforces the notion that Middle Eastern states and societies are deficient in ways that their "Others," especially in Europe, presumably are not.

The point is not that Arab states have no maladies that differentiate them from states elsewhere. The point is that those maladies should be named for what they are and analyzed accordingly, just as we would examine states anywhere. And we must remain open to the possibility that what looks like a deficiency to an outsider might seem like a relatively reasonable and functional way for a state to work among observers and citizens on the ground.

Herein lies the greatest virtue of this volume, in my view. This conclusion cannot possibly do justice to all the riotous heterogeneity among Arab states that this volume captures. That is what the volume itself is for, after all. But it can urge the reader to appreciate the chapters with this distinction between linear variation and multifaceted heterogeneity in mind. If scholars of Arab states can transcend the hollow, residual category of "weak states" and offer us abundant new insights into the heterogeneous ways that Arab states work—making sense of Arab states as they are and not simply as what they are not—then the rest of us who study other parts of the world surely can as well. May this book lead the way.

BIBLIOGRAPHY

Blaydes, Lisa, Amr Hamzawy, and Hesham Sallam, eds. *Struggles for Political Change in the Arab World: Regimes, Oppositions, and External Actors after the Spring*. Ann Arbor: University of Michigan Press, 2023.

Brownlee, Jason, Tarek Masoud, and Andrew Reynolds. *The Arab Spring: Pathways of Repression and Reform*. New York: Oxford University Press, 2015.

Ding, Iza. *The Performative State: Public Scrutiny and Environmental Governance in China*. Ithaca: Cornell University Press, 2022.

Scott, James. *The Art of Not Being Governed: An Anarchist History of Upland Southeast Asia*. New Haven: Yale University Press, 2009.

Slater, Dan. *Ordering Power: Contentious Politics and Authoritarian Leviathans in Southeast Asia*. New York: Cambridge University Press, 2010.

Slater, Dan, and Sofia Fenner. "Opposing Pluralism: Authoritarian Regimes without Democratic Assumptions." *APSA-CD: Comparative Democratization* 15, no. 1 (February 2017): 6, 23–27.

Wedeen, Lisa. "Concepts and Commitments in the Study of Democracy." In *Problems and Methods in the Study of Politics*, edited by Ian Shapiro, Rogers M. Smith, and Tarek E. Masoud. New York: Cambridge University Press, 2004.

Contributors

Lisa Anderson is Special Lecturer and James T. Shotwell Professor Emerita of International Relations at the Columbia University School of International and Public Affairs. She is the former President of the American University in Cairo and Dean Emerita of the School of International and Public Affairs at Columbia.

Toby Dodge is Professor in the Department of International Relations at the London School of Economics (LSE). He is also Kuwait Professor and Director of the Kuwait Programme in the Middle East Centre of LSE.

Steven Heydemann is Ketcham Chair in Middle East Studies, Professor of Government, and Director of the Middle East Studies Program at Smith College; in addition, he is Senior Non-Resident Fellow of the Brookings Institution Center for Middle East Policy.

Raymond Hinnebusch is Professor of International Relations and Middle East Politics at the University of St. Andrews in Scotland; cofounder of the Institute for the Study of the Middle East, Central Asian, and the Caucasus; and Director of the Centre for Syrian Studies.

Marc Lynch is Professor of Political Science and International Affairs at George Washington University Elliott School of International Affairs; Director of the Project on Middle East Political Science (POMEPS); and Director of M.A. Middle East Studies.

Dipali Mukhopadhyay is Associate Professor at the Humphrey School of Public Affairs, University of Minnesota.

Bassel F. Salloukh is Associate Dean of the School of Social Sciences and Humanities, Professor of Political Science, and Head of the Politics and International Relations Program at the Doha Institute for Graduate Studies; in addition, he is Editor in Chief of *Middle East Law and Governance*.

Jillian Schwedler is Professor of Political Science at Hunter College and the Graduate Center, City University of New York.

Dan Slater is James Orin Murfin Professor of Political Science at the University of Michigan.

Sean Yom is Associate Professor of Political Science at Temple University and Senior Fellow in the Middle East Program at the Foreign Policy Research Institute.

Index

Abadi, Haider al-, 105
'Abbadi tribal community, 264
Abdullah Abdullah (leader of Northern Alliance), 216–17, 219–20, 222
Abdullah I, King of Jordan, 237, 241–42
Abdullah II, King of Jordan, 237, 249, 257, 264–65, 267, 269–70
Abdur Rahman Khan, 199–200
Abraham Accords, 179, 187, 189–90
Abrams, Philip, 89
accountability, 34, 37, 48, 205; lack of, 144, 148, 156, 162–63, 174, 188, 208–9; legibility and, 115
Adili, Ali, 221, 222
Afghanistan, 198–225; Arab state and, 9, 201–4; authoritarianism, 199–201, 216–23; central government, 210, 223; clientelistic patronage, 210–11; competition management, 204–7, 216–17, 223; corruption, 198, 207, 209, 216, 226n105; counterterrorism, 208; external constraints, 223; "good governance," 200, 208; infrastructural projects, 260; insurgency, 208, 224; local political orders, 6; National Unity Government, 217, 222; Northern Alliance, 208, 214, 216; patrimonialism, 210; political appointments, 209–18, 223–24; "precarious" statehood, 207, 224–25; regime survival and democracy, 7, 203–4, 207–23; regime types, 199; rentiership, 199–200; security sector, 212; sovereignty, 200; Soviet occupation of, 214; state building, 203; state failure, 198–201, 223–25; stateness, 17–18; taxation, 199; technocracy, 216–18; United States and, 17, 200–201, 207–9, 214, 216–17, 221–23; warlordism, 208, 212–13, 217, 221
African states, 5, 10, 175. See also *specific countries*
agency: of civil servants, 87, 90, 103; states system and, 56; state weakness and, 55–56, 66, 75–80
al-Bakr, Hassan, 94
Albertus, Michael, 14
Algeria: clientelism, 42; corporatist institutions, 38–39; economy, 9; foreign investors, 181; legibility, 117, 121, 129, 132; legitimacy, 74; military, 36; National Liberation Front, 42, 44n51; political factions, 33; regime survival, 27; security sector, 175; state building, 172; state strength, 68; surveillance, 116; uprisings in, 253
Algiers Stock Exchange, 181
Ali, Muhammed, 64

Al Maktoum, Mohammed bin Rashid, 178–80
al-Shadeedi, A. H., 42
Alterman, Jon, 188
Amanullah, King of Afghanistan, 224
anarchy, 57, 78–79
Anderson, Lisa, 4, 7, 9, 11, 13, 14, 17, 27, 120, 147, 151
anti-colonial nationalism, 39, 60, 66, 172, 237–38. *See also* independence
anti-imperialism, 74
anti-Zionism, 74
Aqaba Special Economic Zone, 255
Arab Mashreq, 62
Arab nationalism, 10, 11, 30, 64, 67–68, 71, 74–75, 122, 172, 238
Arab Spring uprisings, 12, 261; asymmetric stateness and, 48–49; causes of, 25–27; economic factors, 17, 76–77, 181–82; government responses to, 178, 188; internet and, 124–25; legibility and, 123–25, 133; outcomes, 78, 81–82, 171, 277–79. See also *specific countries*
Arab states, 1–8; compared with non-Arab states, 2–3, 9, 274–80; distinctiveness of, 8–14; isomorphism, 2, 12; regime-ness, dimensions of, 3–4, 14, 16–18; society as site of resistance to the state, 14, 18–19 (*see also* resistance to state policies); stateness, dimensions of, 1–3, 14–16. See also *specific countries*
Aramco, 180
arms sales, 64, 71, 105. *See also* military aid
Asaib Ahl al-Haq, 104–6
Aschar, Gilbert, 76
assabiyeh (tribal practice), 68, 73, 80
Assad, Bashar al-, 12, 35, 46, 79–80, 118–19, 279
asymmetric state capacity, 7, 13, 15, 29–31, 57; non-state governance, 43–49; parallel trajectories and segmented citizenship, 30, 37–43; regime survival and, 28–32, 34, 35–36, 44–46, 48–49; trajectories of stateness, 31–35, 48–50; transactional processes, 35–38, 40–42, 45–48
Ataturk, Mustafa Kemal, 61, 66, 74

authoritarianism: authoritarian bargains, 33, 34, 42, 47, 49; "authoritarian upgrading," 81, 123, 125, 128, 130, 234; coercive "enmeshment," 264n37; despotic power, 15 (*see also* despotic power); expansion of state capacity, 27; infrastructural power, 15; legibility and surveillance, 7–8, 117–18, 125–30 (*see also* surveillance); on political spectrum, 274, 278–80; social contracts and, 248–51. *See also* populist authoritarian republics
autonomy: of civil service, 87, 89, 90, 100, 103, 279; of regimes, 63; of social elites, 100; sovereignty and, 171; of the state, 2, 5, 13, 57–58, 81, 87, 90, 145–49, 171
Ayubi, Nazih, 8, 33n23, 73, 87–88, 114, 120, 251

Babar, Zahra, 184
Badr Brigades, 104–5
Baghdad Pact, 238
Bahrain, 178; clientelism, 40; inequality in, 189–91; Israel and, 179, 187; protests and uprisings in, 180, 261; regime survival, 35; surveillance, 129
Bani Hassan tribal community, 264
Bani Sakhr tribal community, 242
Banque du Liban (BDL), 148, 159–60
Barber, Benjamin, 75
Barfield, Thomas, 200n12, 211n62, 215n77
Barkey, Karen, 204, 206
Bates, Robert, 47n58
Ba'th Party, 36. *See also* Iraq; Syria
Bauman, Hannes, 148, 153
Bayat, Asef, 133
Bedouin confederations, 238, 242, 262
Belge, Ceren, 117
Bellin, Eva, 114
Ben Ali, Zine al-Abidine, 42
Binder, Leonard, 65
Bishara, Dina, 189
Blackwater Security Consulting, 181
Blaydes, Lisa, 116, 117, 119, 278n6
Bonapartist regimes, 63
Bourdieu, Pierre, 3, 15, 86, 88, 90–92, 94, 101, 103, 111, 120

Bourguiba, Habib, 171
Bremer, Paul, III, 100–101, 103
bribes, 119, 260
Britain: Afghanistan and, 199–200; colonialism, 10, 121, 132, 172; Jordan and, 70, 237, 262; protectorates, 66, 70
Brownlee, Jason, 277n5
built environment, 234, 241–45
bureaucratic field: defined, 91; in Iraq, 92–97, 99–103, 105–6
business enterprises, 178–92
Butler, Judith, 223

Cairo, Egypt, 187, 191
Canboladoglu Ali Pashi, 204, 219
Carville, James, 221
Cederman, Lars-Erik, 118
Chabal, Patrick, 211
charitable associations, 177, 191
Chiha, Michel, 155
China, 261; digital surveillance, 126, 128, 132
citizenship: commercialized, 185–86; in Gulf states, 189; neoliberalism and, 171; rights and limits of, 7–8, 18–19; segmented, 30, 37–43; transactional forms of, 15, 17, 30, 38
civil servants, 12, 87; agency of, 87, 90, 103; autonomy of, 87, 89, 90, 100, 103, 279; in Iraq, 93, 97, 102
civil society, 3, 123–24, 130, 143, 161–62
civil wars, 78, 180, 277, 279
Clapham, Christopher, 56
Clark, Ian, 75
Clark, Kate, 221
clientelism, 14, 31–49, 59, 68, 73, 80, 174; Jordan, 252, 261; Lebanon, 155–63; legibility and, 113–14, 122–24; revenue and, 181. *See also* neopatrimonialism; patronage
Coalition for the Salvation of Afghanistan, 221
Coalition Provisional Authority (CPA), 100–101
coercive capacity: hegemony and, 161n95; Jordan, 249, 253; Lebanon, 150, 161; regime resilience and, 27; repression and, 48, 123
coercive dependence, 14, 37, 42, 48–49

coercive distribution, 33, 36, 38, 47
coercive field: defined, 90–91; in Iraq, 92, 94–97, 99–101, 103–6
Cold War, 11–12, 30, 33, 72, 122, 173–75, 275
colonial regimes, 10; economies under, 62; legibility and ordering, 121, 132; public spending, 36. *See also* anticolonial nationalism; decolonization; imperialism
communism, 39n36, 67, 72, 75, 224
comparative politics, 2–3, 9, 19, 86, 274–80; deficit models, 2–3, 19, 26–28, 50, 207, 232, 276, 280; linear variation and heterogeneity in, 276–78
conscription, 69–70, 73, 114, 119
consociational regimes, 66–67; informal, 101–2, 106; integral state and, 144, 156
constituency clientelism, 34, 40, 47–48
contention and contestation: asymmetric stateness and, 32–33, 48–49; limited statehood and regime type, 32n17; state capacity and, 231–45; state development and, 18, 170–73. *See also* Arab Spring uprisings; Jordan; mobilized publics; protests; resistance to state policies
Cordesman, Anthony, 177
Corm, George, 155n72
corporatist institutions, 38–39, 41–42, 46, 68–69, 77
corruption, 25–26, 76, 119, 144, 177, 209, 252; Afghanistan, 198, 207, 209, 216, 226n105; Iraq, 92, 97; Jordan, 252, 253, 265; Lebanon, 157, 162–63, 177; Tunisia, 185
counterinsurgency, 17, 205
coups d'état, 13–14, 32, 39, 68, 70, 122, 174; Egypt, 36; Iraq, 94; Jordan, 238, 249
COVID-19 pandemic, 112, 117, 132, 189–90, 253
Cox, Lawrence, 235
Cox, Richard, 75
crony capitalism, 41, 63, 71, 76–77, 81, 123, 180, 209, 247, 265

Daloz, Jean-Pascal, 211
data collection. *See* informational capacity; legibility; surveillance

David, Steven, 13
Day, Christopher, 205
Deckard, Natalie Delia, 186
decolonization, 32–33, 35, 60–62. *See also* independence; postcolonial states
deficit approach. *See* comparative politics
democracy, 3, 274, 278; attitudes toward, 124–25; promotion of, 171, 207–23 (*see also* regime change)
despotic power, 15, 57–60, 63, 68–70, 73, 132; regime building and, 57–60
developmental capacity: asymmetric stateness and, 31, 48–50; failures in, 28–29, 48–50; increase in, 36–37; regime resilience and, 27–28, 34; telescoping developmental crises, 65, 67, 80; underinvestment in, 13. *See also* economic development; late development; social development; social welfare provision
developmentalist biases, 27–28, 50
developmental states, 2–4, 47, 72, 255
dictatorship, 274. *See also* authoritarianism
digital media, 16, 48, 111–12, 115, 125–33, 188
disaggregated state, 15–16, 88–106, 111, 240
Disi Water Conveyance system (DWC), 247–70
dissent, 128, 130–31, 133, 235, 244; repression of (*see* repression). *See also* Arab Spring uprisings; opposition groups; protests; resistance to state policies
divide and rule, 59, 81
Dodge, Toby, 3, 4, 7, 13, 15–16, 45, 156, 202, 207
Doha Agreement, 222–23
Dostum, Abdur Rashid, 215n75, 220–21
Dubai, 9, 178–80, 188
dysfunctional state model, 25–26, 50, 67, 97, 254, 276

economic dependency, 15, 80
economic development, 7, 65, 74, 111; global private sector and, 178–87; informational capacity and, 131; populist strategies of, 49; segmented market economies, 31; spectrum of, 274. *See also* neoliberal economic reforms
economic field: defined, 90–91; in Iraq, 92–100, 106
economic security, 25, 48
education, 7, 10, 26, 29, 36, 37, 41–43, 46, 69, 71, 100, 158, 176–77, 182, 217, 235–36, 252, 255
Egypt: authoritarian regime, 69, 279; citizenship, 185–86; clientelism, 41, 42; colonial bureaucracies, 121; corporatist institutions, 38–39; economy, 9; emergency provisions, 189; foreign investment, 183–84, 190; inequality, 191; Lebanon and, 146; legibility, 117–18, 122–24, 126, 127, 131–32; military, 36; National Democratic Party, 42, 117–18; National Service Products Organization, 181; political factions, 33; private sector, 181, 183–87, 190; regime collapse, 81; regime stability, 174; regime survival, 27, 47, 171, 173–74; regional influence, 12, 77, 80, 122, 172; repressive capacity, 112, 130; sectarianism, 177–78; security sector, 175, 181; state strength, 66, 68, 69; surveillance, 116; uprisings in, 78, 253, 261, 277–78; Western imperialism, 64
elections, 117–18, 123
elites: autonomy of, 100; competition, 92; economic interests of, 17; failures of governance, 25–26; monarchies based on, 70–71. *See also* Iraq; Lebanon
employment, 16, 37, 41–42, 74, 102, 125, 155, 176, 182, 238, 263, 265
enclaves, 185–87, 191
enclave states, 206
Enlightenment (Roshnawi) Movement, 220
entitlements, 7–8, 18, 37–38, 69, 71
Erikson, Stein Sundstol, 39
Essebsi, Caid, 185
ethnic identities, 76, 119, 174, 215, 218, 219, 256
Eurocentrism, 86–88, 207

Europe: aid to Arab states, 175, 186, 257 (*see also* foreign aid); early state building, 199. *See also* Britain; colonial regimes; France; global states system
exceptional jurisdictions, 185, 187
exclusion, 34, 36, 38, 41, 44, 59, 63, 75–76; Afghanistan, 201, 219–21, 224–25; Syria, 79
external dependency, 65, 67
extractive capacity, 30, 38, 73–74, 76, 111–13, 116, 118, 121, 146, 200n14, 251, 270, 280
Ezzedine, Nancy, 42

Facebook, 125, 128, 131
Fahmy, Khaled, 188, 191
failed states, 25–27, 57, 77, 81, 131, 233, 248, 261, 274; defined, 47n58. *See also* Afghanistan
Fakhoury, Tamirace, 148
Falcon Group, 181
Faust, Aaron, 94
Fearon, James, 118
Fenner, Sofia, 113–14
field theory, 90–92, 111. *See also* bureaucratic field; coercive field; economic field; political field
fierce states, 33–35, 47, 55, 73, 87–88, 114, 204, 251
foreign aid, 12, 65, 174–77, 186, 240, 251–53, 255, 257, 263, 269
foreign investment, 179–87
Foucault, Michel, 5, 89, 115, 231
fragile states, 28, 34–35, 172
France, 257; colonialism, 10, 121, 132
freedom, 115, 170, 188, 254
free trade agreements, 190
Fregonese, Sara, 150
Fromkin, David, 56

Gama Energy, 248, 250, 257–60, 266–67, 269–70
gated communities, 185, 187, 192
Gaza, 128–29
Gemayel, Amin, 148, 149
Ghani, Ashraf, 18, 201, 204, 207, 216–25
Ghannouchi, Rached, 183
Gill, Stephen, 75

Glain, Stephen, 252
globalization, 14–15, 28, 75, 179. *See also* neoliberal economic reforms
Global North, 5, 9, 232
Global South, 2, 9, 14, 31, 35, 86–88, 253
global states system, 56; Western core-periphery hierarchy, 5, 60, 62–66, 75, 80
Global War on Terror, 176, 203, 208
Gohdes, Anita, 127
"good governance," 34, 200, 205, 208, 232, 251
Gramsci, Antonio, 3, 63, 75, 142–44, 154, 156–57, 161, 161n95, 163, 231
Guazzone, Laura, 173
Gulf Cooperation Council (GCC), 179, 183, 188
Gulf states, 9, 183; asymmetric stateness, 36; as British protectorates, 10; bureaucracies, 12, 122; citizenship in, 17; emirates, 70; independence, 172; state strength, 82. *See also* oil states
Gunitsky, Seva, 127

Haftar, Khalifa, 183
Hage, Ghassan, 151–52
Hägerdal, Nils, 119
Hamas, 77, 177
Hammadi, Sadoun, 99n70
Hamzah, Prince of Jordan, 249
Hamzawy, Amr, 278n6
Hannoum, Abdelmajid, 121
Hanson, Jonathan, 116
Hariri, Rafiq, 149, 186
Harling, Peter, 97
Hashemite Kingdom of Jordan. *See* Jordan
Hassan II, King of Morocco, 33
Hazbun, Waleed, 150
health care, 7, 26, 37, 42, 43, 97, 176–77, 182, 190
Hegghammer, Thomas, 112
Hekmatyar, Gulbuddin, 214, 219
Hendrix, Cullen, 118
Hermez, Sami, 153
Hertog, Steffen, 31
Heslin, Alison, 186
heterarchy, 57, 78

Heydemann, Steven, 4, 6, 8, 13, 15, 77, 112, 114, 116, 123, 130, 144–45, 151, 170–71, 174, 198, 202–4, 231, 234, 236, 245, 249, 263
Heyderian, R. J., 76
Hezb-i-Islami, 213–15, 219, 220
Hezbollah, 77, 147, 149, 151, 177
High Council for National Reconciliation, 222
Hinnebusch, Raymond, 4, 11, 13–15, 17, 27, 38n35, 120, 122, 123, 201
Hourani, Albert, 153
Hourani, Najib, 149, 151, 155
Hudson, Michael, 8
Human Development Index, 80
humanitarian law, 186
human rights, 12, 127, 132, 170–71
Human Rights Watch, 189
Huntington, Samuel, 58–60, 70, 80
Hunziker, Philipp, 118
Hussein, King of Jordan, 237–38
Hussein, Saddam, 13–14, 55, 92–100, 106, 116, 117, 119
Hussein, Sharif, 237
Hussein, Uday, 97
hybrid states, 57, 59, 68, 86, 88, 253; Lebanon, 142, 150–51, 154

Ibn Khaldun, 58, 68, 73, 79–80
identities: Arab, 61 (*see also* Arab nationalism); ethnic, 76, 119, 174, 215, 218, 219, 256; national, 61–62, 65, 66, 69–70; social, 32; supra-state, 61–62, 65, 67–68, 73; trans- and substate, 61–62, 65, 73, 76, 79–80
identity-territory incongruence, 61–62, 65–66, 80
ideological power, 91
imperialism: resistance to, 66; statehood and, 172–73. *See also* colonial regimes
inclusion, 34, 36, 38, 41, 44, 59, 63, 75–76
independence, 67–68, 80, 122, 172, 237–38. *See also* anti-colonial nationalism; decolonization; postcolonial states
inequality, 176–77, 182, 188–92
informal consociationalism, 101–2, 106
informal governance, 36, 206. *See also* clientelism; non-state governance

informational capacity: defined, 111–12; public opinion survey research, 124–25. *See also* legibility; surveillance
infrastructural power, 15, 38, 68–69, 73, 80, 132, 241, 255–56, 262; legibility and, 113–14; state building and, 58–60
Institute of Peace (US), 190
insurgency, 62, 118, 131, 205
integral state, 16, 142–45, 151, 153–63
international dynamics, 12. *See also* Cold War; foreign aid
International Monetary Fund (IMF), 76, 181–82, 240, 243
internet, 48, 111, 124–31, 188
Iran: digital surveillance, 126; monarchy, 71; regional conflict, 77–79; state formation, 66; state strength, 71, 81
Iranian Revolution, 123, 254
Iran-Iraq War (1980–88), 69, 92, 95, 174
Iraq: asymmetric stateness, 45; Ba'th Party, 6, 36, 42, 45, 69, 86–87, 92–100, 102, 106, 126; bureaucratic field, 92–97, 99–103, 105–6; civil war, 180; clientelism, 40, 42; coercive field, 92, 94–97, 99–101, 103–6; corporatist institutions, 38–39; corruption, 92, 97; disaggregated state, 15–16, 92–106; economic field, 92–100, 106; elite competition, 7, 15–16, 98–102, 106, 156; enclaves, 185; informal consociationalism, 101–2, 106; infrastructure projects, 260; invasion of Kuwait, 86–87, 92, 96, 174; legibility and surveillance, 116, 126; legitimacy, 62, 92; National Alliance coalition, 104; neotribalism, 99; non-state governance, 36; oil revenue, 92–93; political factions, 33; political field, 93–98, 101–3, 106; Presidential Diwan, 94, 97; rationing system, 99; regime change, 55–56, 77–78, 92, 96, 100–106, 171; regime survival, 46–47, 99–100; sanctions on, 86–87, 96–99; security sector, 69–70, 92, 94–96, 99, 103–5, 175–76, 180; state building, 172; state failure, 77; state strength, 66, 68, 69; symbolic capital, 105; US invasion of (2003), 14, 45, 77, 92, 100–106, 252; US-Iraq

War (1990), 77; Western imperialism and, 64
Iraqi Communist Party, 94
Iraq Petroleum Company, 92, 94
irredentism, 61, 62, 67
Islamic State, 79–80, 104–5, 220
Islamic *umma*, 61
Islamist movements, 11, 46, 70, 76, 79, 123, 174, 176–77, 214, 240, 254
Israel: comparisons with, 9; conflicts with, 69, 74–75, 172; emergency provisions, 189; Jordan and, 67, 258; normalized relations with, 179, 187, 190, 252; regional conflict, 77; surveillance of West Bank, 113, 128–29

Jackson, Robert, 64
Jamaat-i-Islami, 214
Jamiat-i-Islami, 213–15
Japan, 275
Jessop, Bob, 15, 86, 88–91, 94
jihadist movements, 11, 75, 77–79, 219, 253
Jones, Calvert, 184
Jordan, 247–70; Amman, 157, 240, 241–44, 250; Aqaba, 186, 191, 240, 250, 255, 257–61, 266n47, 267–68; asymmetric stateness, 36, 45; British Mandate, 70, 237, 262; built environment, 234, 241–45; citizenship, 7–8, 18–19; civil war, 172; clientelism, 41, 261; coercive capacity, 249, 253; contested practices and disruptive violence, 7, 18, 248–50, 254–62, 265–70; corporatist institutions, 39; corruption, 252, 253, 265; Disi Water Conveyance system (DWC), 247–70; enclaves, 186; foreign aid, 240, 251, 252, 257, 263; General Intelligence Directorate, 239; grassroots *(hirak)* movements, 265, 267; Gulf states and, 12; Hashemite monarchy, 7, 9, 46n56, 237–45, 248–51, 262–66; independence, 237–38; inequality, 191–92; Interior Ministry, 261; Karak, 258–60, 267; legibility and surveillance, 115–16, 118, 122, 126, 129, 269–70; legitimacy, 62, 249; limited statehood, 46, 250, 264; Ma'an, 241–43, 258, 259; Ministry of Supply, 239, 240; moral economy of contestation, 249, 256, 266–69; neoliberal economic reforms, 247, 249–50, 265, 268–70; neopatrimonialism, 265; opposition groups, 247, 251; Palestinian majority, 249, 262–63, 266; patronage, 252, 263; political economy, 251–52; poverty, 265; refugees in, 45, 186, 238, 240, 242, 253, 258; regime stability, 174; regional conflict, 77; security sector, 176; sovereignty, 251; state capacity, 239–40; state strength/weakness, 67, 72, 248–54; Tafileh, 258; tribal communities, 18–19, 46, 46n56, 202, 238, 240–70; tribal-state compact, 262–66; uneven stateness, 249–50, 255, 256, 264, 270; uprisings in, 247–48, 252, 261, 265–67, 270, 278; Zarqa, 257
Jordan Valley Authority, 255

Kabyle, 116
Kakar, Hasan, 199
Kamal, Hussein, 97
Karzai, Hamid, 18, 200–201, 204, 207–16, 222, 224
Kataeb Party, 149
Kata'ib Hezbollah, 104–5
Kerry, John, 216
Khalaf, Sulayman, 37
Khalifa, Hamad bin Isa al-, 35
Khalizad, Zalmay, 222
Khatib, Lina, 151
Khouri, Rami, 177
King, Stephen, 77
Kingdom of Hejaz, 10
"King's Dilemma," 70–71
kinship networks, 117
Koehler, Kevin, 117
Kohli, Atul, 47
Krasner, Stephen, 255
Kurdish areas, 6, 45, 79, 116–17, 119, 173
Kurdistan Democratic Party, 96, 101n73, 102
Kuwait: inequality, 189–90; Iraqi invasion of, 86–87, 92, 96, 174; state strength, 72; uprisings in, 253

labor rights, 184–85
Lagarde, Christine, 181–82
Laitin, David, 118
LaPalombara, Joseph, 65
Lasswell, Harold, 44
late development, 5, 60–61, 65–67, 88, 253
League of Nations, 237
Lebanon, 141–63; asymmetric stateness, 33, 45; capital accumulation, 155–63; civil war, 150, 172, 174, 252; clientelist networks, 155–63; coercive capacities, 150, 161; colonialism in, 10; corruption, 157, 162–63, 177; criminal law, 186; fiscal and monetary policies, 157–60; gender and sexual differences, 142, 147–48; hybridity, 142, 150–51, 154; immaterial images of the state, 142, 145, 152–54; inequality, 191; integral state captured by elites, 142–45, 151, 153–63; justice system, 186; lawlessness in, 144, 151–52, 162–63, 248; legibility, 117, 122, 127, 132; legitimacy, 62; material interests, 142–45, 151, 154, 157–58, 161–63; opposition groups, 160–61; political economy, 142–45, 151, 155–63; protests and October 2019 collapse, 142–45, 148, 158, 163; refugees in, 45, 122, 148–49; regional conflict, 77; sectarianism, 142, 146, 151, 153–62; Shihabist strategy, 146–47; state absence, 6–7, 141–42, 144, 147, 162, 203; stateness/state capacity, 6, 16–17, 66, 142, 145–54; za'im elite, 146, 155
Lee, Melissa, 11, 112, 113
legibility, 6, 13, 16, 43, 111–33; clientelism and, 114, 122–24; compliance and, 256; defined, 112; dissent and, 131; infrastructural power and, 113–14; social transformation and, 132; state capacity and, 113–25, 129–33; state power and, 7–8. *See also* informational capacity; surveillance
legitimacy, 8; asymmetric stateness and, 49; citizenship and, 30; deficits, 71, 81, 92, 120; external rents and, 17, 66; national identities and, 62, 256; regime, 35; regional conflicts and, 74; struggles for, 32–33, 62, 249

legitimation, 8, 39
Levant: colonialism in, 10; legibility in, 122; state strength, 66–67. *See also specific countries*
LGBTQ communities, 119, 128, 132, 148
Libya: asymmetric stateness, 33, 45; civil war, 180, 277, 279; clientelism, 41, 42; colonialism in, 10; corporatist institutions, 39; Cyrenaicans in, 173; as failed state, 261; foreign investment in, 183; inequality, 191; loyalist tribes, 41, 42, 46; Muslim Brotherhood and, 178; regime change, 55–56; regime survival, 46–47, 171; security sector, 175, 180; state building, 172; state strength, 68; uprisings in, 78, 261, 277; Western intervention in, 78
limited statehood, 31, 32n17, 42–47, 57, 144, 156, 203, 250, 255–56, 262, 264
literacy, 37, 69, 176
local governance, 6, 44–47
Lori, Noora, 189, 200n14
Luna, Juan Pablo, 117
Lynch, Marc, 5–7, 13, 14, 16, 27, 32, 43, 144, 182, 188, 202–3, 231–32, 249

Maghreb, 121
Maliki, Nuri al-, 102–4
Malkasian, Carter, 223
Manchanda, Nivi, 198–99
Mann, Michael, 3, 4, 13, 15, 38, 57, 86, 88–91, 94, 99, 101, 111, 113, 114, 234, 241, 255–56
marginalized communities, 25, 30, 37, 48–49, 71, 94, 119, 132, 152–53, 220, 256, 266, 270
Marshall, Shana, 181
Martinez, Jose Ciro, 7, 186, 191–92
Marx, Karl, 231
Marxist perspective, 89
Marzouki, Nadia, 185
Masoud, Tarek, 277n5
Masri, Sabih, 268
Massoud, Ahmed Shah, 214
Mazur, Kevin, 118
Mbembe, Achille, 13
McKinsey and Company, 182
media: broadcast, 124; digital and social

media, 16, 48, 111–12, 115, 125–33, 188; integral state and, 144; satellite television, 124, 126
"mediated state" approach, 149
Menkhaus, Ken, 212
Meyer, John, 2
middle class, 48, 58–59, 68–71, 80, 98, 133, 148, 151, 184
Middle East and North Africa (MENA). *See* Arab states; *specific countries*
Migdal, Joel, 3, 5, 147, 154, 155, 205, 207–8, 211, 224–25, 254–55
Mikdashi, Maya, 121, 147
military aid, 174–77, 240. *See also* arms sales
military coups. *See* coups d'état
military regimes, 68, 178, 180–81
Mitchell, Don, 244
Mitchell, Timothy, 3, 5, 89, 115, 121, 153, 172–73, 231
mobilized publics, 71; asymmetric stateness and, 31. *See also* Arab Spring uprisings; contention and contestation; dissent; protests; resistance to state policies
modernization, 2, 26, 58–65, 69–72, 74, 80–81, 115, 132, 224
Mohtar, Amer, 156
monarchies, 4, 9, 12–13, 38–39, 68, 70–72, 74
Moore, Barrington, 63
Morocco, 9, 33; asymmetric stateness, 36, 45; clientelism, 41; enclaves, 185; Israel and, 179, 187, 189; legibility and surveillance, 115–16, 129; state strength, 66, 72, 173–74; uprisings in, 253, 278; Western protection, 70
Mossadeq, Muhammed, 71
Mouawad, Jamil, 148, 152–53
Mourad, Lama, 148
Mubarak, Hosni, 12, 131
Mufti, Malik, 69
mujahideen commanders, 212–14, 224
mukhabarat (intelligence services), 112, 114–16, 131, 239
Mukhopadhyay, Dipali, 4–7, 13, 14, 17–18, 33
Müller-Crepon, Carl, 118
Murtazashvili, Jennifer, 224

Musahiban dynasty, 206
Muslim Brotherhood, 46, 117, 122, 124, 177–78, 214

Nagle, John, 148
Nasser, Gamal Abdel, 36, 69, 146, 171–72
national identities, 61–62, 65, 66, 69–70
natural resources. *See* oil states; resource endowments
neoliberal economic reforms, 26, 63, 65, 75–76, 81, 123; austerity and, 265; built environment and, 241; governance and, 179–87; Iraq, 100; Jordan, 247, 249–50, 265, 268–70; legibility and, 122–23, 130; patronage networks and, 41; political authority and, 171; protests and, 178; social welfare provision and, 176–77. *See also* globalization
Neom (Saudi development), 184, 186, 190
neomedievalism, 80
neopatrimonialism, 33, 44–45, 59, 68, 73–74, 76, 80, 252; defined, 57. *See also* clientelism; patronage
Nettl, J. P., 3, 85
Nilsen, Alf Gunvald, 235
non-state governance, 13, 16, 28–31, 34–36, 39n35, 48; in Afghanistan, 208; asymmetric stateness and, 43–49; dichotomy between state and, 235; interdependency between state and, 149–51, 155–63
North, Douglass, 47
North Africa, 10. *See also specific countries*
Northern Alliance (Afghanistan), 208, 214, 216
NSO Group, 128

Obeid, Michelle, 153
oil states, 9–11, 66; bureaucracies, 122; revenues, 64, 70–71, 74, 174, 176, 177. *See also* Gulf states
Olesen, Asta, 206
oligarchies, 68–69
Oman, 41–42, 189–90, 205
opposition groups, 116, 120, 122, 123, 160–61, 176, 247, 251. *See also* dissent
Orientalism, 9, 12, 254, 276, 280

Oslo Accords, 175
Osman, Borhan, 219
Otaiba, Yousef Al, 188, 190
Ottoman Empire, 10, 60–62, 64, 66, 173, 204, 206, 219, 237, 242, 262

Palestine Liberation Organization, 149, 189
Palestinians: commando groups in Lebanon, 147; fedayeen guerrillas, 239, 243; Gulf states and, 12; national movement, 11, 172, 174–75, 190–91; refugee communities, 45, 122, 175, 189, 238, 242, 251; regional conflict and, 67, 77, 252; surveillance of, 128–29
pan-Arabism. *See* Arab nationalism
pan-Islamism, 30, 67
pan-Syrianism, 67
Pashtuns, 215–16, 220–21
patriarchy, 12, 73
patrimonial power-building, 59. *See also* neopatrimonialism
Patriotic Union of Kurdistan, 96, 101n73, 102
patronage, 40–42, 73; Afghanistan, 210–11; Iraq, 93, 99; Jordan, 252, 263. *See also* clientelism
Pegasus surveillance technology, 128–29
People's Democratic Party of Afghanistan, 224
peripheries: state control and, 44–45, 57, 59, 70, 72, 133, 200, 206, 209, 216, 242–43, 250, 256, 268; Western core-periphery hierarchy, 5, 60, 62–66, 75, 80
personalism, 31, 73, 80, 120
Philippines, 275
Picard, Elizabeth, 172, 186
Pierret, Thomas, 46
Piketty, Thomas, 176
Pioppi, Daniela, 173
political capital, 218
political economy, 11; core-periphery hierarchy, 5, 62–66, 75, 80; Jordan, 251–52; Lebanon, 142–45, 151, 155–63; of state formation, 204–7
political field: defined, 91; in Iraq, 93–98, 101–3, 106

political opposition. *See* opposition groups
political settlements, 32, 92, 105, 223
political spectrums, 274–80
Popular Mobilization Forces, 47
populist authoritarian republics, 37–39, 49, 59, 68–70, 73–75; post-populist republics, 59, 75–76, 81, 123
postcolonial states, 10, 49, 66, 68, 121–22, 171–74, 253. *See also* decolonization; independence
poverty, 79, 133, 177, 185, 191–92, 265, 275
power and political authority: creation of, 59–60; field of, 92; realms of, 169–71; struggles for, 32–33. *See also* despotic power; infrastructural power; legitimacy; legitimation; neopatrimonialism
privacy, 128. *See also* surveillance
private sector, global, 178–87
protests, 128–29; government responses to, 191–92; in Jordan, 236–41; in Lebanon, 145, 161, 163; regional dynamics and, 180; spatial and geographic dimensions, 241–45. *See also* Arab Spring uprisings; resistance to state policies
Przeworski, Adam, 161n95

Qaddafi, Muammar, 42, 45, 55, 78, 171, 279
Qatar, 42, 80, 178, 183
Qatranah clan, 267
quasi-states, 64, 80

Rabo, Annika, 37
Rahbani, Ziad, 162
rebellion, 55, 96, 118, 131, 200n10, 202, 205, 236–37, 244
redistributive social policies, 35–39, 48, 65, 79–80, 144, 145, 155, 209, 263, 280
regime change, 55–56, 77–78, 81, 92, 96, 100–106, 171, 174, 200
regime collapse, 81, 201, 277, 279
regime-ness, 3–5; Afghanistan, 203–4, 207–23; spectrum of, 274; state as society, 5, 16, 144; state development and, 29–30; stateness and, 19, 29–30

regime resilience, 14, 27, 71; weakness-resilience paradox, 55–56, 201–2
regime security, 13–14; asymmetric stateness and, 28–31, 34, 35–36, 44–50; effectiveness of, 253; hybridity and, 150–51; informational capacity and, 111; leaders and, 55–56; legibility and surveillance, 114–16, 119, 130. *See also* coercive capacity; regime survival
regime stability, 173–74, 176, 189
regime survival, 4, 13, 15–16, 76–78, 170–71, 277; asymmetric stateness and, 28–32, 34, 35–36, 44–46, 48–49; coercive capacity, 27; monarchic, 71; repression and, 235 (*see also* repression); Western alignment and, 70–72. See also *specific countries*
regional politics, 11–12, 30, 62, 169; conflicts, 63–64, 74–80, 183, 240, 261; economic networks, 178–87; security, 238
religious minorities, 119
Reno, William, 175, 205
rents and rentier states, 11, 17, 32, 65–66, 71–73, 76, 156, 177, 252–53
repression, 48, 73, 119–20, 122–23, 127, 130–31, 133, 235, 244, 254
republics, 72; corporatist institutions, 38–39. *See also* populist authoritarian republics
resistance to state policies, 14, 18–19, 234, 236–41; limited and deep, 249, 262. *See also* Arab Spring uprisings; contention and contestation; protests; rebellion
resource endowments, 11, 46, 62–63, 66. *See also* oil states
Revolutionary Command Council, 93
Reynolds, Andrew, 277n5
Risse, Thomas, 57
Rød, Espen, 126
Rodriguez-Muniz, Michael, 119
Roehers, Christine, 217–19
Rohde, Achim, 97
Rubin, Barnett, 200n14, 206, 210n53
Russia, 78, 79, 181
Ruttig, Thomas, 219n85, 221

Saba, Elias, 155n72
Sadowski, Yahya, 254
Safi, Mohammad Omar, 217–18
Saikal, Amin, 206
Saleh, Ali Abdallah, 40–41, 45
Salih, Ali Abdallah, 233
Sallam, Hesham, 278n6
Salloukh, Bassel, 4, 6, 13, 16, 33, 121, 174, 177, 202–3, 231
Salman, Mohammed bin, 115, 180, 184
Samaha, Petra, 156
Saouli, Adham, 88
Saudi Arabia, 12, 35n25, 70; asymmetric stateness, 45; citizenship, 185; Egypt and, 178, 183; inequality, 189–90; Jordan and, 251; legibility and surveillance, 129, 131; loyalist tribes, 42; military expansion, 10, 66; oil industry, 41; private sector, 184–86; regime stability, 174; regional conflict, 77–78, 180; security sector, 175–76; state strength, 70–71; suppression of political freedoms, 115; Western alignment, 70–71
Saudi Egyptian Investment Company, 190
Sayigh, Yezid, 184
Schlumberger, Oliver, 72
Schwedler, Jillian, 3, 4, 8, 13, 14, 18, 33, 191, 202, 207, 266
Scott, James C., 3, 7, 13, 43, 113–15, 121, 124, 132, 277n4
sectarianism, 26, 62, 73, 76, 79, 101, 174, 181; Egypt, 177–78; Lebanon, 142, 146, 151, 153–62
security sector, 175–76; private contractors, 180–81. *See also* coercive capacity; regime security; *specific countries*
Semple, Michael, 214
September 11, 2001 attacks, 176, 214. *See also* Global War on Terror
Shabiha, 47
Shah, Nadir, 206
Shah, Zahir, 206, 209
Shah of Iran, 71
Sharabi, Hisham, 12
Sharifi, Omar, 199n4
Shehab, Selma, 115
Sheikh, Sharm el-, 190
Shihab, Fuad, 146

Shi'a Muslims, 6, 45, 69, 78–79; in Afghanistan, 220; in Iraq, 102, 104–6, 116–17, 119; uprisings and, 178
Shi'i Crescent, 240
Simpson, Audra, 200n14
Singapore, 128, 275, 279
Sisi, Abdel-fattah El-, 183
Skocpol, Theda, 87
Slater, Dan, 3–4, 19, 113–14
Smith, Benjamin, 11
social capital, 90
social development, 15, 28–30, 49
social media. *See* media
social mobility, 25, 48
social pacts, 32
social welfare provision, 37, 46–47, 49, 69, 114–15, 123–24, 182, 235, 252; legibility and, 130–31; neoliberalism and, 176–77
Soifer, Hillel, 117
Somaliland, 212
Soss, Joe, 203
Southeast Asia, 19, 275–76
South Korea, 275
South Yemen, 44n51
sovereignty, 61; hybrid, 253; incomplete, 251; statehood and, 171–73
sovereign wealth funds, 181, 183–84, 190
Soviet Union, 12, 67, 72, 75, 214. *See also* Cold War
stability, 28–29, 40, 46, 90–91, 111, 125, 131, 169–71, 173–79, 187, 189, 203, 234, 236–40, 261, 279
state: capacity of (*see* state capacity; stateness); coherence of, 15, 43, 85–87, 90–91, 99–106, 146–47, 154; conceptual binaries, 143, 145, 149; normative views of, 207, 232, 235, 239–40, 254; polymorphous, 89, 91, 101; primacy of, 169–70, 173; sovereignty and, 171–73; "state as society," 5, 16, 144–45; "state effects," 5, 115, 153; "state in society," 5, 154–55, 254–56, 262. *See also* disaggregated state; global states system; Weberian and neo-Weberian statehood; Westphalian statehood
state capacity: absence of, 6–7, 141–42, 144, 147, 162, 203; built environment and, 234, 241–45; conceptual approaches to, 56–60; contention and (*see* contention and contestation); defined, 1–2, 231–32; enabling structural conditions of, 72–73; foreign interests and, 232; formation of, 67–82; increase in, 36–37; indicators of (*see* stateness); infrastructural power and, 58–60; intra-regional variations in, 65–67; legibility and, 113–25, 129–33; postcolonial state building, 122, 171–74; regime survival and, 4 (*see also* regime survival); strong-weak spectrum, 274–80; structural adjustment and, 182; temporalities of, 234–37. *See also* failed states; fierce states; fragile states; hybrid states; quasi-states; strong states; weak states
stateness: defined, 1–2 (*see also* state capacity); as dependent variable, 15–16, 85–87; in Global South, 9–10; performativity of, 19; trajectories in Arab Middle East, 31–35; uneven, 249–50, 255, 256; variation in presence, 6–7. *See also* non-state governance; transactional governance
Stel, Nora, 149
Stepan, Alfred, 85
strong states, 15, 231–32, 274–80. *See also* Weberian and neo-Weberian statehood
structural adjustment, 76–77, 181–82, 240, 243
Sudan, 179, 187, 253
Sunni Muslims, 6, 40, 77–79, 102, 116, 119, 123, 220
Suroush, Qayoom, 217–19
surveillance, 7–8, 16, 46, 81, 188; authoritarian regimes, 7–8, 117–18, 125–30; big-data analysis, 127; digital, 16, 48, 111–12, 115, 125–33, 188; expansion of, 32; mass collection of data, 16, 126–28, 131. *See also* regime security
Svolik, Milan, 29–30
Sykes-Picot Agreement, 62
symbolic capital, 90
symbolic power, 120
Syria, 12, 204, 260; asymmetric stateness, 45, 46; Ba'th Party, 36–38, 42, 44n51, 45, 69, 126; civil war, 118–19,

180, 277, 279; clientelism, 40–42; colonialism in, 10; competitive state remaking, 79–80; conflicts in, 252; corporatist institutions, 38–39; as failed state, 81, 248; inequality, 191; legibility, 118–19, 126, 131; military, 69–70; National Defense Forces, 47; non-state governance, 36; peasant unions, 37–38; political factions, 33; refugees in, 45; regime stability, 174; regime survival, 27, 35, 46–47; regional conflict, 77–78; security sector, 180; state strength, 66, 68, 69; territory, 62; uprisings in, 78–79, 178, 261

Taiwan, 275
Taliban, 18, 208, 218, 220–23
taxation, 73, 114, 116, 118, 119, 130, 181, 255–56
Tell, Tariq, 262
Tilly, Charles, 3, 17, 63, 199, 212
Topak, Özgün, 128
transactional governance, 30–31, 33, 35–38, 40–42, 45–48; citizenship and, 15, 17, 30, 38
Transjordan, 237, 241–42. *See also* Jordan
transparency, 34, 119, 131, 182, 188, 208–9
tribes and tribalism, 13, 46n56, 62; citizenship and, 18–19; clientelism and, 40–41; loyalist, 41–42; monarchies and, 70–71; rentier social contracts, 66. *See also* Jordan
Tripp, Charles, 153, 234
Tunisia: asymmetric stateness, 36; clientelism, 41, 42; corporatist institutions, 38–39; corruption, 185; Democratic Constitutional Rally, 42; foreign investment in, 183, 185; Muslim Brotherhood and, 178; regime collapse, 81; remittances, 186; security sector, 175–76; state strength, 68; uprisings in, 78, 253, 261, 277–78
Turkey: Kurdish areas, 6; legibility, 117; legitimacy, 74; regional conflict, 78–80, 178; state capacity, 60, 81; state formation, 66
Twitter, 125, 128

United Arab Emirates (UAE): citizenship, 185; inequality, 189–90; private sector, 188–89; regional dynamics, 12, 80, 178–79, 183, 187, 190; surveillance, 112, 122, 128–29
United Arab Republic, 172
United Nations: Relief and Works Agency for Palestine Refugees (UNRWA), 122, 189, 251; state sovereignty and, 170–72
United States: Afghanistan and, 17, 200–201, 207–9, 214, 216–17, 221–23; aid to Arab states, 12, 175, 186 (*see also* foreign aid); attitudes toward, 124; crime in, 261; democracy promotion, 207–8; global war on terror, 176, 203, 208; hegemony of, 75, 77–78; Iraq wars (*see* Iraq); Israel and, 75; Jordan and, 238–39, 251, 263, 265; security contractors, 180–81; surveillance, 127; Syria and, 79–80. *See also* Cold War
United States Agency for International Development (USAID), 255, 257, 269
urban renewal, 191–92

van Bijlert, Martine, 209, 219n85, 220
violence, 27; disruptive, in Jordan, 7, 18, 248–50, 254–62, 265–70. *See also* coercive capacity
Vision Fund, 180

Wagner Group, 181
Waldner, David, 11
war and war preparation, 69; constraints on expansion through, 63–65, 80. *See also* civil wars
weak states: agency and, 55–56, 66, 75–80; as cause of Arab uprisings, 25–27; contention and, 231–32; degrees of statehood, 56–57; development and, 28; external, 66; internal, 66–67; Lebanon and, 142, 145–54; legibility and, 130; monarchy and, 71–72; sources of, 73–75; spectrum of strong to weak states, 274–80; structural origins of, 60–65; weakness-resilience paradox, 55–56, 201–2

Weber, Max, 3, 205, 231
Weberian and neo-Weberian statehood, 13, 31, 68, 86–88, 90, 173, 233; defined, 170n4; historical sociology and, 56–61; ideal type, 19, 61, 87–88, 103, 142, 145–51.154, 205, 207, 209, 254–55; institutional forms, 87, 100, 103, 106, 115, 209, 218; monopoly on use of force, 35, 47n58, 57, 60, 78, 122, 147, 150, 170n4, 172, 213, 233, 236
Wedeen, Lisa, 6, 8, 120, 233
Weidman, Nils, 126
Wendt, Alexander, 172
West Bank, 113, 128–29
Western Sahara, 189
Westphalian statehood, 57, 60–61, 75, 81, 172, 251–54
WhatsApp, 128
Wittgenstein, Ludwig, 141
World Bank, 157, 161, 182, 186, 265
World Trade Organization, 265

Worldwide Governance Indicators, 29n13
Wyrtzen, Jonathan, 120, 121

Xu, Xu, 127

Yemen: asymmetric stateness, 33, 45; civil war, 172, 178, 180; clientelism, 42; corporatist institutions, 39; as failed state, 233, 261; General People's Congress, 42; inequality, 189–91; local political orders, 6; loyalist tribes, 40, 42; neopatrimonialism, 40–41; regime survival, 46–47; security sector, 180; state strength, 68; uprisings in, 78, 261
Yemeni Socialist Party, 44n51
Yom, Sean, 4, 7, 8, 13, 18, 33, 45, 46, 118, 191, 202, 234–35, 240–41
Young, Karen, 183

Zawayda tribal community, 259, 267, 268
Zhang, Nan, 112, 113